Guitar Logic

Patterns For Creative Expression

Fletcher Epperson

In gratitude to the Intelligence that provides
the consciousness, brain, senses and body for
communicating the knowledge of creative living.

iplayit@gmail.com

9th Edition / April 2018

8th Edition / January 2013 - The Guitar Game

Copyright © 1997 by Fletcher B. Epperson

Library Of Congress number available upon request

ISBN 9780692140178

All rights reserved

Table Of Contents

Table Of Contents i
Forward vii
Introduction viii
Five Essential Lessons ix
The Creative Person x
Overview xi

Section One - From The Beginning

1   Getting Acquainted

Guitar Parts 1-1
Holding The Guitar 1-2
Notes On The Fret Board 1-3
Notes On The Fret Board – Diagram 1-4
The Chromatic Scale, The Major Scale, The C Major Scale, Theory 1-5
Chromatic Scale - Diagram 1-6
How To Do It - Pressing Down The Strings 1-7
How To Do It - Strumming, Flat Picking And Chicken Pickin' The Strings 1-8
How To Do It - Finger Picking The Strings 1-9
Tuning The Guitar 1-10
The Five Basic Chords Lesson 1-11
Rhythm Practice 1-12

2   Introduction To Patterns For Improvisation

Patterns For Improvisation 2-1
How To Do It - Practice The Scale 2-2
How To Do It - Play The Chords 2-4
How To Do It - Practice The Mode 2-6
Guitar Expressions 2-8
E7 Blues Song – Licks And Expressions 2-9

Section Two - What Goes On

3   Notation

Instrument Ranges 3-1
Tones 3-2
Notation 3-3
Notation And The Guitar 3-4
Ledger Line Notation 3-5
Where's Middle C ? 3-6

Sheet Music Navigation 3-7
Form & Tempo 3-8
Dynamic Marks, Symbols, Repeats 3-9
Finger Picking - Picking The Strings, Picking Hand, Finger Picking Form 3-10
Arpeggio Study - Song 3-11

4 Time Signatures

Rhythm 4-1
Notes And Rest Values 4-2
Note Time Value Divisions - In Common Time 4-3
Note Time Value Divisions - Diagram 4-4
Time Signatures 4-5
Time Signatures - Diagram 4-6
Dotted Notes, Shuffle Notation 4-7
The Twelve Bar Blues, E7 Shuffle - Song 4-8
A7 Shuffle & D7 Shuffle - Songs 4-9
G7 Shuffle & C7 Shuffle - Songs 4-10
The Moveable E and A Forms 4-11
A7 Shuffle Barred & E7 Shuffle Barred - Songs 4-12

5 Technique

How To Do It - Finger Picking The Strings 5-1
Technique Builder 5-2
Chromatic Exercises 5-3

6 Key Signatures

Circle Of Fifths 6-1
Key Signatures 6-2
Key Of C 6-3
Key Signatures 6-4
Key Development Study – Diagram 6-5
Melody Study, Exercise 6-6
Melody Study - Key Of C - Song 6-7
Melody Study - Key Of G - Song 6-8
Melody Study - Key Of D - Song 6-9
Melody Study - Key Of A - Song 6-10
Melody Study - Key Of E - Song 6-11
Accidentals 6-12
Alternate Picking 6-14
Alternate Picking - Song 6-15

7 Chord Harmony

Scale Degrees, Intervals 7-1
Scale Degrees, Intervals - Diagrams 7-2

Chord Harmony	7-3
Chord Harmony - Diagram	7-4
The Major Chord	7-5
C Major Chord Scale - Open Position - Key Of C	7-6
Major And Minor Chords	7-7
Circle Of Fifths, Circle Of Fourths	7-8
Chord Development Study - Circle Of 5ths - Sharp Keys	7-9
Chord Development Study - Circle Of 4ths - Flat Keys	7-10
Chord Study, Exercise	7-11
Chord Study - Key Of C	7-12
Chord Inversions	7-14
Interval And Inversion Study	7-15
Delta Blues - Song	7-16

Section Three - Variations

8 Modes In The Open Position

Modes	8-1
Modes - A Half Step Study In The Open Position - Key Of C	8-2
The Seven Modes And The Five Basic Chord Forms - Open Position	8-3
The Seven Modes And The Five Basic Chord Forms - Open Position – Diagram	8-4
The Seven Modes And The Five Basic Chord Forms - Open Position – Practice	8-5

9 Chord Scales In The Open Position

Chord Scales - Open Position	9-1
Phrygian Mode - Open Position - Key Of C	9-2
C Major Chord Scale - Open Position	9-3
Aeolian Mode - Open Position - Key Of G	9-4
G Major Chord Scale - Open Position	9-5
Dorian Mode - Open Position - Key Of D	9-6
D Major Chord Scale - Open Position	9-7
Mixolydian Mode - Open Position - Key Of A	9-8
A Major Chord Scale - Open Position	9-9
Ionian Mode - Open Position - Key Of E	9-10
E Major Chord Scale - Open Position	9-11

10 Modes In The Moveable Position

Modes In The Moveable Positions - Key Of E	10-1
Modes In The Moveable Positions - Key Of E - Diagram	10-2
Modes In The Moveable Positions - Practice	10-3
Modes In The Moveable Positions - Practice - Diagram	10-4

11 Moveable Chords

Moveable Chords	11-1

Five Basic Chords, Open Position, Moveable	11-2
C - A - G - E - D	11-3
C - A - G - E - D - Diagram	11-4
C - A - G - E - D And The Modes	11-5
C - A - G - E - D And The Modes - Diagram	11-6

12 Chord Scales In The Moveable Position

Chord Scales - Moveable Positions	12-1
Improv 101	12-1
Phrygian Mode - C Form - Key Of C - 3rd Degree	12-3
C Major Chord Scale - C Form - Phrygian Mode	12-4
Scarborough Fair - Phrygian Mode - Open Position - Song	12-5
Lydian And Mixolydian Modes - A Form - Key Of C - 4th And 5th Degrees	12-6
C Major Chord Scale - A Form - Lydian And Mixolydian Modes	12-7
Scarborough Fair - Lydian Mode - Song	12-8
Scarborough Fair - Mixolydian Mode - Song	12-9
Aeolian Mode - G Form - Key Of C - 6th Degree	12-10
C Major Chord Scale - G Form - Aeolian Mode	12-11
Scarborough Fair - Aeolian Mode - Song	12-12
Locrian And Ionian Modes - E Form - Key Of C - 7th And 8th Degrees	12-13
C Major Chord Scale - E Form - Locrian And Ionian Modes	12-14
Scarborough Fair - Locrian Mode - Song	12-15
Scarborough Fair - Ionian Mode - Song	12-16
Dorian Mode - D Form - Key Of C - 2nd Degree	12-17
C Major Chord Scale - D Form - Dorian Mode	12-18
Scarborough Fair - Dorian Mode - Song	12-19
Phrygian Mode - C Form - Key Of C - 3rd Degree	12-20
C Major Chord Scale - C Form - Phrygian Mode	12-21
Scarborough Fair - Phrygian Mode - Octave - Song	12-22

13 The Conveyor Belt

The Conveyor Belt - Key Of E	13-1
The Conveyor Belt - Key Of G	13-2
Applying The Fretboard Map	13-3

Section Four - All Together Now

14 Patterns For Creative Expression

Patterns For Creative Expression - Jazz - The Relative Minor Key	14-1
Patterns For Creative Expression - Dominant Seven Blues - Rock And Country Music	14-2
Chord Scales For Jazz - Key Of G Major 7	14-5
Mode And Scale Patterns For Jazz - Key Of G Major 7	14-6
Chords And Scales For Minor Seven Blues - Key Of E minor 7	14-7
Chords And Scales For Dominant Seven Blues - Key Of E7	14-8
Chord Scales For Rock And Country - Key Of G	14-9

Scale Patterns For Rock And Country - Key Of G 14-10
E7 Blues Medley – Song 14-11

15 Integration Of Improvisation

Degrees And Notes - Symmetry 15-1
Chords 15-3
C Major Chord Scale 15-4
Chord Progressions – Chord Substitutions 15-6
The ii – V – I Chord Progression - The Blues Effect - As The Story Goes 15-8
What Is A Dominant Seven Chord? 15-10
The Integrated Blues - What Key Is The Song In? 15-11
Which Chords Are They Playing? 15-12
Which Modes And Scales Do I Play? - Summary 15-13

Section Five - The Finishing Touches

16 Chord Progressions

Chord Progressions 16-1
Key Modulations 16-3
The ii - V7 - I Chord Progression 16-4
Downstep Modulation 16-5
Chord Substitutions 16-6
Turnarounds 16-7
A Classic Blues Turnaround 16-8
A Standard Jazz Tune - Song 16-9
Analysis of A Standard Jazz Tune 16-10

17 Specialty Scales

Specialty Scales - Diminished Scale 17-1
Diminished Chords 17-2
Augmented Scale 17-3
Augmented Chords - Whole Tone Scale 17-4
Lydian Augmented Scale - Harmonic Minor Scale 17-5
E Minor 7 Blues Shuffle - Song 17-6

18 Linear Chord Scales

The Linear Chord Scale 18-1
C Linear Chord Scale 18-2
G Linear Chord Scale 18-3
D Linear Chord Scale 18-4
A Linear Chord Scale 18-5
E Linear Chord Scale 18-6
E Linear Chord Scale – Alternative 18-7

Section Six - Chords For Everyone

19　The Chord Guide

The Chord Guide 19-1
Variations Of The C Form - Open Position 19-2
Variations Of The C Form - Moveable Position 19-3
Variations Of The G Form - Open Position 19-4
Variations Of The G Form - Moveable Position 19-5
Variations Of The D Form - Open Position 19-6
Variations Of The D Form - Moveable Position 19-7
Variations Of The A Form - Open Position 19-8
Variations Of The A Form - Moveable Position 19-9
Variations Of The E Form - Open Position 19-10
Variations Of The E Form - Moveable Position 19-11
Standard Jazz Chords..19-12

Forward

Improvisation is a creative process that has been available to only a few that understand the theory and technique that is required to play it. The majority of improvisation today is merely guitarists borrowing phrases and technique already created by those few. Yes, it is necessary for the guitarist to learn phrases and technique from the masters to get ideas on the road to becoming a master. The problem is the guitarist today is satisfied with only copying someone else and not taking the time to learn the theory required for the creative process to come forth. The result is a society that has come to accept imitators as a standard. The majority of the music being recorded and played today are remakes of those great songs of the creative and exploratory periods of the 60's and 70's.

Jazz has become a music of the past. It is my personal opinion that jazz has faded into oblivion because it was an intellectual music that became a music for other jazz musicians. This occurred after the big band swing era. Horn players found they could play at blazing speeds by using the chromatic scale and so it became a contest between the players as to how fast they could play. The public lost interest because they wanted music with feeling to it. Classical, rock, country and blues are still popular because the music comes mostly from the heart.

With these two situations being presented to us today by the majority of our musical community this book has been written in hope of resolving the redundancy of today's music and encouraging an exciting new era of creative music to listen to, stimulate our lives with and most important, connect with nature.

To confront the issue of improvisation in jazz becoming intellectual and lacking in feeling, it has occurred to me that the traditional way of improvisational playing that requires thinking in terms of individual notes within a chromatic scale is limiting. These notes are played in relationship to the harmonic structure of intervals within the chords being played on the fly generally at fast tempos. This way of playing is limited to a few very gifted people. The rest of us are left either on the sidelines as imitators or listeners. Playing in patterns, on the other hand, is a way for the rest of us to improvise in jazz. If a student is willing to spend the short time it takes to memorize the seven patterns of the modes the guitar will open its vast possibilities for creative expression. The patterns of the modes are each a parameter from within which one can play the correct notes without the hesitation of the player who does not know where to put their fingers next in fear of playing a sour note. As a student of my own teaching, I now play by feel.

To address the other issue of musicians just wanting to imitate others and shrinking at the thought of music theory, I have found through the years of teaching that while playing others songs and improvisational phrases, it is a good idea to also intertwine the theoretical knowledge presented in this book. With this approach the student will understand that the successful musicians, they are learning from, also know the theory as well. The student will also be saved from the dry lecture. Creativity must have a way to be expressed. When listening to and learning from other peoples music, technique has been learned, theoretical analysis applied and the guitarist has the map of the guitar clearly laid out from the patterns learned, creativity will naturally come forth. It is a joy when a guitarist understands the theory of the instrument, has technique and a collection of great phrases. Freedom to explore the creative possibilities of the guitar are now unlimited.

Introduction

The purpose of this book is to present to you in a simplified, organized and efficient way with which the guitar can be approached and become understood. The guitar is a unique instrument that has infinite creative possibilities and with some concepts understood, the complete understanding of the guitar will begin to unfold its secrets.

Originally because of the many hours I spent doing exercises that were only good as technical builders, I began to put together the patterns contained in this book utilizing the chords and scales that are found in everyday guitar playing as the exercises used for technical development. I found this saved a great deal of time and is very effective. It is intentional that each practice session relates to the next, so as the student is practicing one exercise it will be found that the effort is being applied to the rest of the studies. It is all interactive and this is the foundation and efficiency of this book. Due to the technical ability required to complete this book it is important the correct approach is taken. Take the exercises one step at a time. The advanced player may take up to six months playing on a daily basis to accomplish this book, where a beginner might take up to two years. Realizing the technical level required to play the guitar, this is not a long time to become a quality guitar player. Each section presents a lecture with a practice routine. Although we are all unique and creative, everyone will find a routine that will work best for them and while this is encouraged, it will be to your advantage to start with the recommended routine first, then gradually adapt your own over time.

With the amount of information and technical requirements needed to play the guitar it is helpful to first understand how we learn. The conscious mind receives information from the senses, analyses it as it filters down to the subconscious mind. The subconscious mind is your memory bank where the information is stored. The process of storing and gaining access to memory is natural and is done automatically. The subconscious mind accepts whatever is presented to it from the conscious mind without question, acts upon it by integrating it with other stored memory and then projects it back into the conscious mind when called upon. The senses that allow us to experience the world around us transfer the information through the eyes, ears, fingertips and vibrations felt by our body from the instrument to the conscious mind. If the information is received in a slow and thoughtful manner and is repeated enough times correctly, the process of learning will take place easily. It can be seen here that what we practice is what we learn. If we practice our mistakes over and over again then the music with the mistakes is what we will learn and our performance will reflect those mistakes. If we take our time and practice the lessons properly focused, we learn to play correctly. "Perfect practice makes perfect performance". Each exercise should be practiced for about fifteen minutes then move on to another exercise. Fifteen minutes is average for a focused attention span. After fifteen minutes the mind begins to wander which will lead to mistakes. Practice overall should be for as long as the interest is stimulated.

Scales and chords are the two things we do when playing the guitar. Chords are harmonization of the scales. Practice the scales and chords and you will learn the guitar. Chords are used for rhythm and accompaniment. Scales are used for melodies, leads, improvisation and connecting chords together. Once again, when it all comes together, creativity will naturally come forth.

Have fun, enjoy and I thank you for supporting the Arts.

Five Essential Lessons

Notation

Being able to navigate and read sheet music.

Theory

Understand bass, rhythm, melody, harmony, improvisation and form as they apply to the guitar.

Skill

Develop the technical hand to mind coordination required to play any style of music.

Interval Association

Learn songs from recordings by hearing and knowing how to find the notes on the guitar.
Also utilizing interval association in improvisation.

Creativity

The presence of form is vibration manifesting from creation, which evolves for infinity.
As spirit in form, creativity is our nature. This is the magic of the universe.

When the student develops hearing by singing and playing and is able to learn songs from recordings with the aid of sheet music, the recorded media with all of its creativity becomes a powerful teacher. At our finger tips there are a vast amount of recordings that can be played whenever, wherever and for as long as needed until the songs are learned. Also, by understanding music theory as it relates to the guitar and to visualize the chord and scale patterns through technical exercises and memorization over the entire neck of the guitar, the student will easily be able to analyze and play any song.

Once this ability is reached the student will be able to play a song simply by knowing the melody. This is because the melody and the chords of a song intertwine with each other so intimately. To play a song exactly as it is recorded, it is necessary to learn it directly from the recording. Sometimes the song can be difficult to learn, that's when sheet music helps by notating the melody and chords, revealing a visual outline.

First, the student should learn the lessons of notation, theory, skill and interval association that are clearly and methodically presented in this book, then play by learning songs by ear with the aid of sheet music from recorded media and finally the ultimate - be creative and play your music whether it be your unique arrangements of others or your own originals.

The Creative Person

Excerpts from a lecture by Ira Progoff called Waking Dream and Living Myth

" Essentially, these are persons in whom the creative process of the psyche has been allowed to happen, and who have also been able to draw the dialectic of the psyche [to converse - more at dialogue] forward in their life experience. Their creativity consists essentially in their ability to move freely from the inner level to the outer level [subconscious to the conscious], and continues to go back and forth. The creative person is one who is able to draw upon the images within himself and then to embody them in outer works, moving inward again and again for the inspiration of new source material, and outward again and again to learn from his artwork ["listen"] what it wants to become while he is working on it."

"....it seems that if he remains committed to the dialectical process something new and unexpected emerges in his life. It is as though the core of a center forms within him. A new self forms, not from his directly seeking it, but as a side effect of the integrity with which he continues his inner-outer journey. With this new self there also comes a capacity of consciousness, a quality of realization that adds a major dimension to his life. This awareness could not be achieved by directly seeking it; but it comes about indirectly through the integrity of dialectical involvement."

The excerpt is from one of eleven lectures in a collection by different authors in the book, *Myths, Dreams And Religion* edited by Joseph Campbell. Spring Publications, Inc. Dallas, Texas (1988) P. 184-85

Overview

- Understand the guitar completely like never before.

- This innovative musical system easily and seamlessly integrates the improvisational theory of Blues, Rock, Country and Spanish music into the Western musical system.

- Written by a guitarist for the guitarist with step-by-step instruction from over 40 years of teaching.

- This guitar book of instruction provides a rich source of information that can be referenced or memorized for on the fly improvisation, solo development and songwriting.

- In your hands you are holding the definitive book of guitar instruction.

- "Pictures are worth a thousand words."

- Diagrams with detailed explanations are placed on facing pages for ease of learning the lessons.

- Easy notation, as a visual aid, is included with the lessons for those who want to learn to read.

- Everything that is played on the guitar will be played within seven modal patterns.

- Chords, melodies, harmonies, solo's and improvisations will all be played in these seven "playgrounds".

- There are five basic chords that all chords are derived from.

- Each of these five basic chords are presented with their variations in The Chord Guide.

- Now the guitarist has five chord form choices for every chord to play!

- Learn the rules of the guitar game first and then with this fascinating knowledge, play creatively from the intuitive.

Notes

Section One

From The Beginning

Notes

Chapter 1

Getting Acquainted

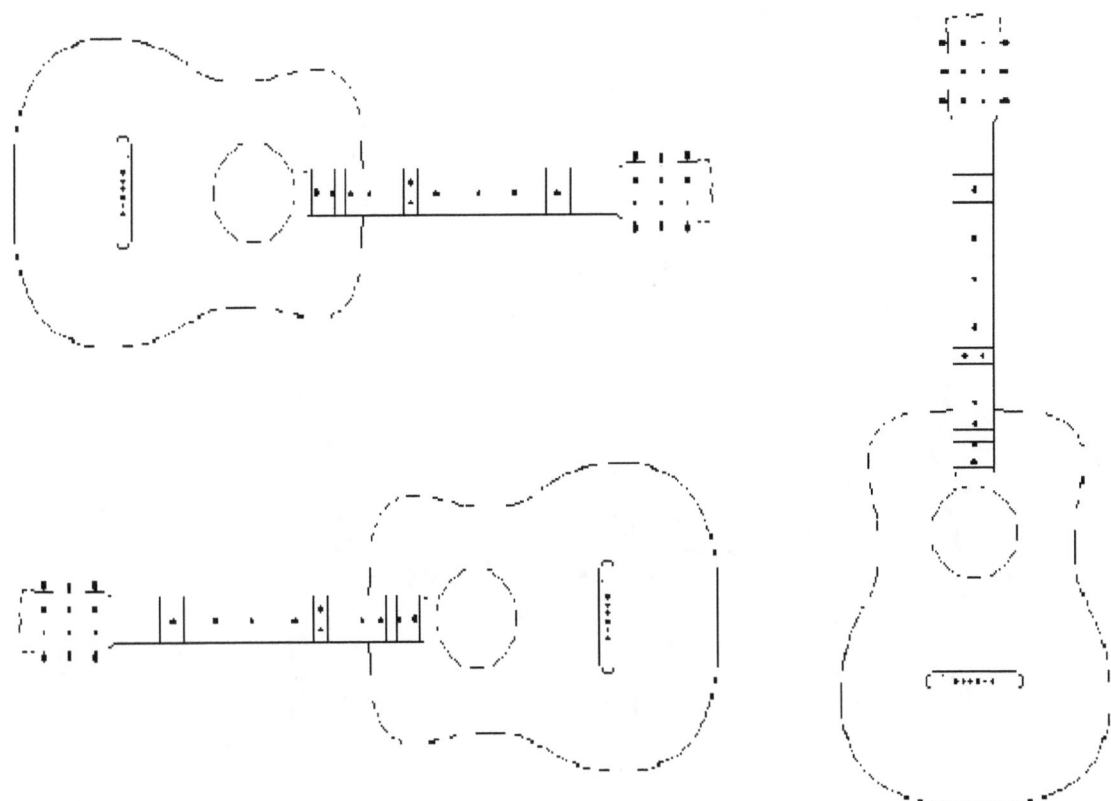

Guitar Parts

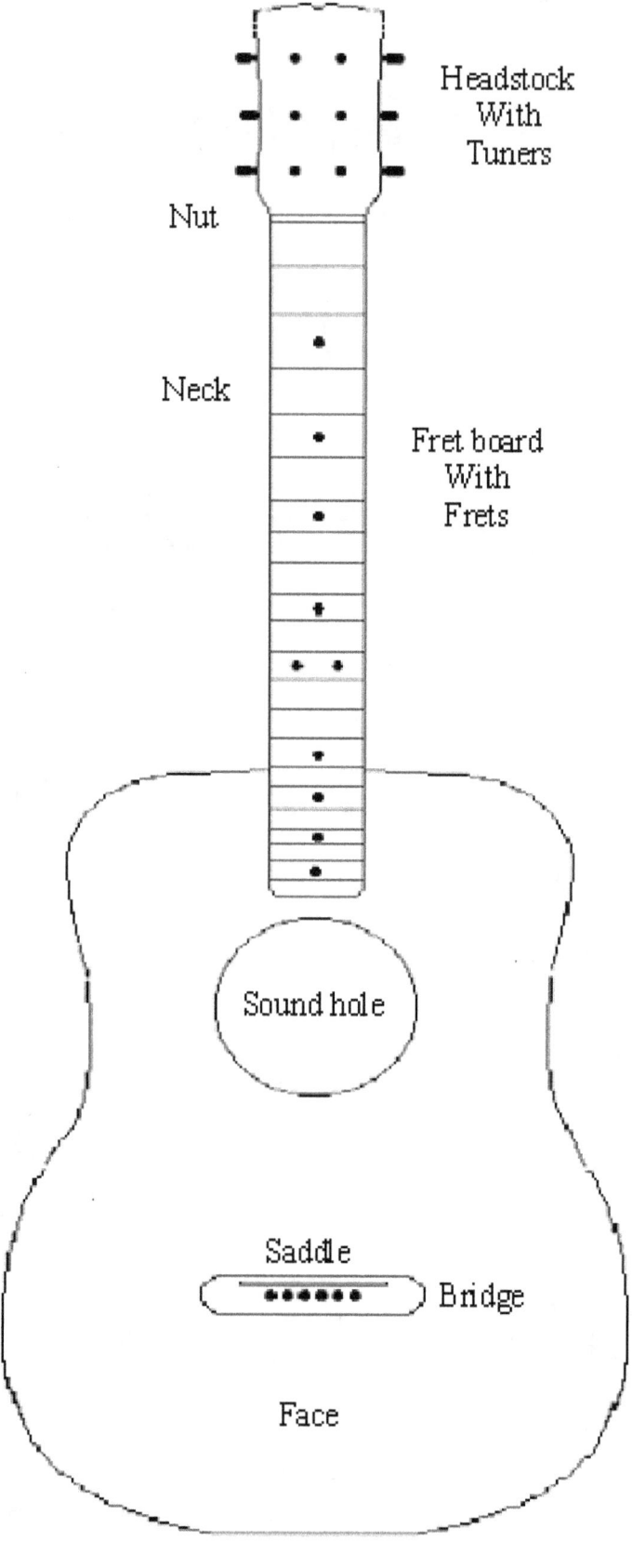

Holding The Guitar

There are several ways to hold the guitar. The two most popular while sitting are the Classical style and the Folk style. To stand, attach a guitar strap to the guitar then suspend the guitar by the strap over your shoulders. Adjust the strap until you are holding the guitar in the same position as the Classical style.

CLASSICAL STYLE

From the perspective of a right-handed person the Classical style places the guitar on the left leg, which is raised by a footstool. The headstock is pointing in the air approximately at a 45-degree angle (2:30). The right forearm rests on the top edge of the guitar near the elbow. The hand hangs down comfortably relaxed over the sound hole. The fret board hand places the thumb behind the neck between the first and second fingers. The hand should form a "C". The fingers should press down on the strings on their tips. The Classical style opens up the fret board hand, which in turn allows for longer reaches.

FOLK STYLE

Once again from the perspective of the right-handed person the folk style places the guitar on the right leg. The headstock is pointing at a 30 to 35 degree angle (3:00 to 3:30) horizontally. The left leg is not raised in the Folk style. The fret board hand follows the same instructions as taught in the Classical style above.

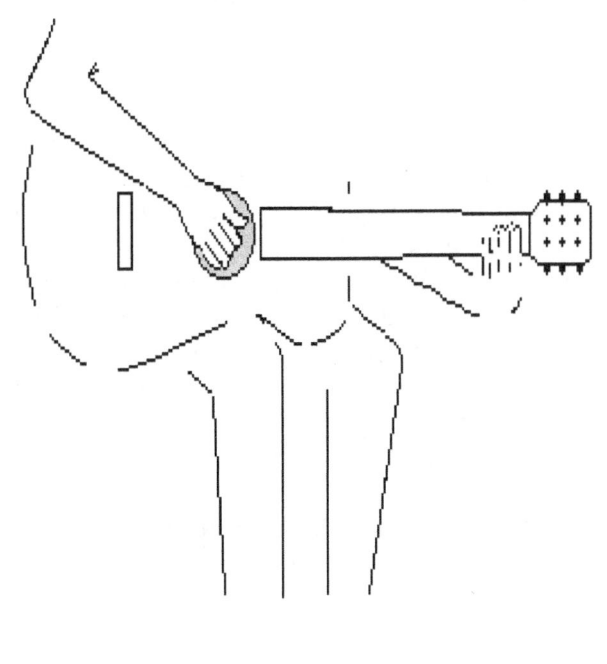

Notes On The Fret Board

The two diagrams in the Notes On The Fret Board diagram are drawings of the guitar fret board. The shaded area at the bottom of the fret board means that the rest of the neck is omitted.

Let's first take a look at the chromatic scale. The chromatic scale shows the enharmonic spellings of the half steps. Enharmonic spelling is the same note only with different names. Enharmonic spelling is used for the ease of reading. When the notes in the score (sheet music) ascend, the notes are sharped and when the notes descend, the notes are flatted.

Now let's look at the MAJOR SCALE diagram. It can be seen that the C major scale, which has no sharps (#) or flats (b), is derived from the chromatic scale. The 6th string is the heaviest gauge and closest string to you when playing and is the lowest in pitch. The 1st string is the lightest gauge and furthest away from you when playing and is the highest in pitch. The pitch (highness or lowness of sound) of each string becomes higher (treble) as we play the neck, that is, towards the body of the guitar and the pitch of each string becomes lower (bass) as we move the neck that is towards the nut at the tuning headstock. This may seem backwards at first, but when it is realized that the direction of the guitar is based on pitch, not the physical properties of the guitar, which can be up or down depending on how the instrument is held at any given time, it becomes clear. The letters E - A - D - G - B - E are the note names of the open strings on the guitar. It is easy to remember and will never be forgotten simply by pronouncing it as a word: EADG(a)BE. The note names in the diagram are shown for the convenience of learning. These notes are the same note names as the first seven letters of the alphabet A - B - C - D - E - F - G. Start with the open fifth string and count up the alphabet: A - B - C - D - E - F - G, ending with the octave A note on the twelfth fret. An octave is the distance of eight notes of the major scale. Chromatically speaking an octave traverses twelve half steps. A half step on the guitar is one fret, which is the wood between the metal bars of the neck.

It is essential to memorize the notes on the fret board. You'll need to know the note name on the string that corresponds to the root/bass note of the chord to play and to read the melody which is generally be played on the third, second and first strings. For more fun and creativity, knowing the notes on the fret board will enable you to build chords from the scales, know where you are and where you'll want to go next. Here's a few suggestions: 1) Memorize only the notes of the MAJOR SCALE diagram, the #'s (sharps) and (flats) are of the same letter name, they have only been raised (#) or lowered by a half step. 2) Start by learning the notes in the open position: E F G of the sixth string, A B C of the fifth string, D E F of the fourth string G A of the third string, B C D of the second string and last, E F G of the first string. 3) Understand the fret board by starting with each of the open string notes E A D G B E and go up each string saying the alphabet to the octave on the twelfth fret. Since the sixth string and the first string are the same note names only different octaves there's only five strings to learn.

Now that you see how the musical alphabet is presented on the whole fret board of the guitar in the C major scale learning and memorization will be easier and fun.

Notes On The Fret Board

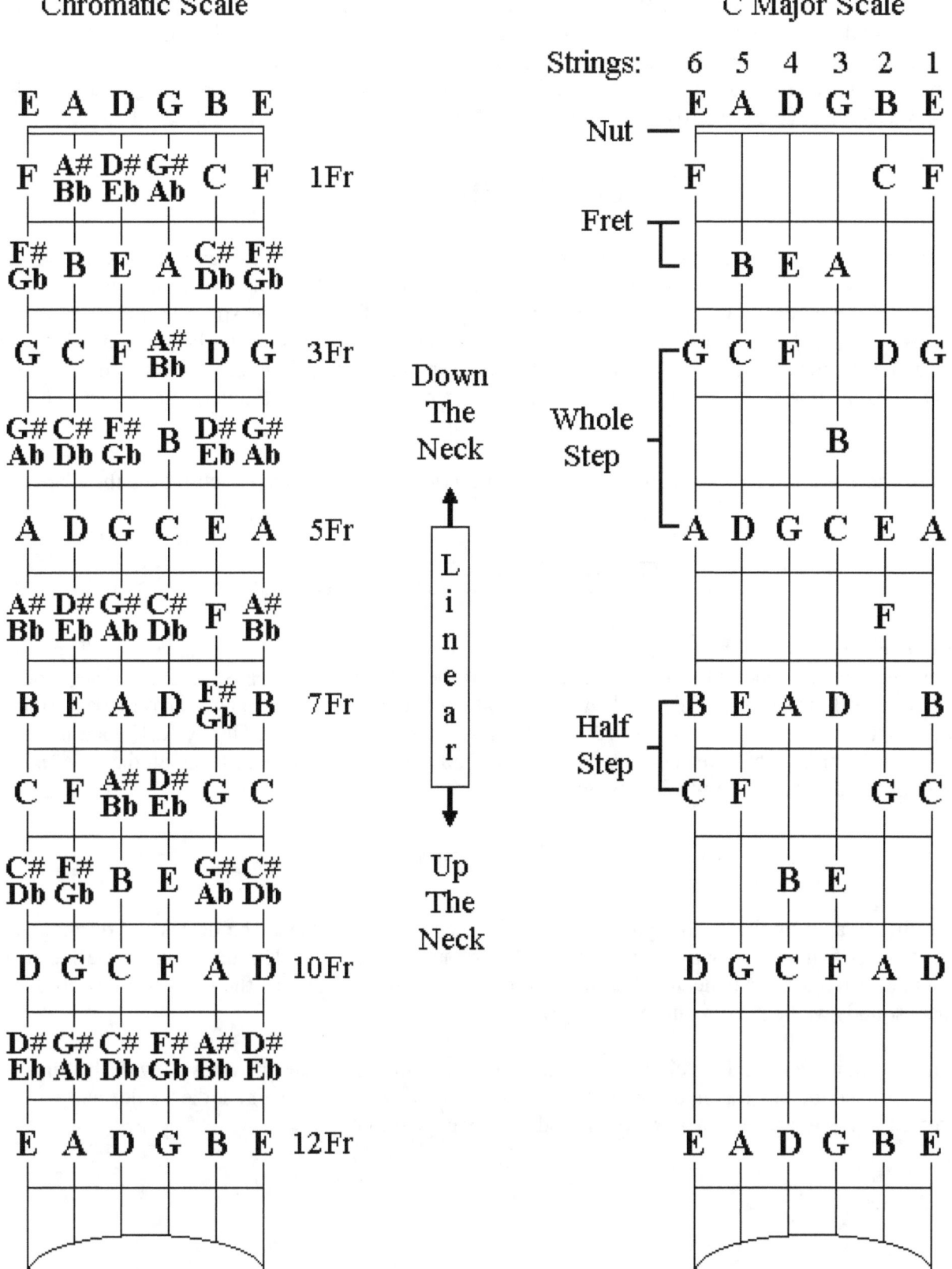

The Chromatic Scale

A scale is a succession of tones. What defines a scale is the distance or interval between its tones. The chromatic scale has twelve half steps: 1/2, 1/2, 1/2, 1/2, 1/2, 1/2, 1/2, 1/2, 1/2, 1/2, 1/2, 1/2. On the guitar that is each fret. There are twelve chromatic scales: A, A#, B, C, C#, D, D#, E, F, F#, G, G#. The A chromatic scale would start on A and proceed for twelve half steps, the A# chromatic scale would start on A#, the B chromatic scale would start on B, etc. The chromatic scale is the mother of all scales.

The Major Scale

The major scale, the heart of the musical system is derived directly from the chromatic scale. From the major scale we get the modes and scales to play melodies, solos, improvisation and chords. The structure of the major scale is a mixture of whole steps and half steps in the structured pattern of: 1 - 1 - 1/2 - 1 - 1 - 1 - 1/2. If the structure of the major scale is changed in any way it becomes another type of scale and therefore a different sound. Pythagoras, a philosopher of Greece, developed the Western musical system this way. We are born into it and accept its sound without question. The culture of Greece was notorious for its structural symmetry through mathematics.

Because there are twelve chromatic scales, there are twelve major scales, which means there are twelve keys.

The C Major Scale

The C major scale could be thought of as the template for the eleven other major scales. The C major scale is the natural scale in the Key of C. It is called the natural scale because it has half steps between the third, fourth and seventh, eighth degrees naturally without the need for any sharps or flats to force it into the structural pattern of: 1 - 1 - 1/2 - 1 - 1 - 1 - 1/2 steps. The C MAJOR SCALE diagram on page 1-4 shows the natural half steps occurring between the E, F and B, C notes. Notice all the other notes on the fret board diagram are a whole step apart.

Theory

Music theory as it applies to the guitar. This is the main focus point we'll be discussing throughout this book, as it is from these two scales that all of our music is derived. The diagram on the facing page presents a visual aid for understanding the relationships of these scales as the tools used to produce the musical sounds we hear from our instruments.

The major chord scale and the chords with their variations and inversions provides us with rhythm and harmony to accompany the modes with their variations of scales producing melodies, solos and improvisation that create endless rhythmic and harmonic possibilities.

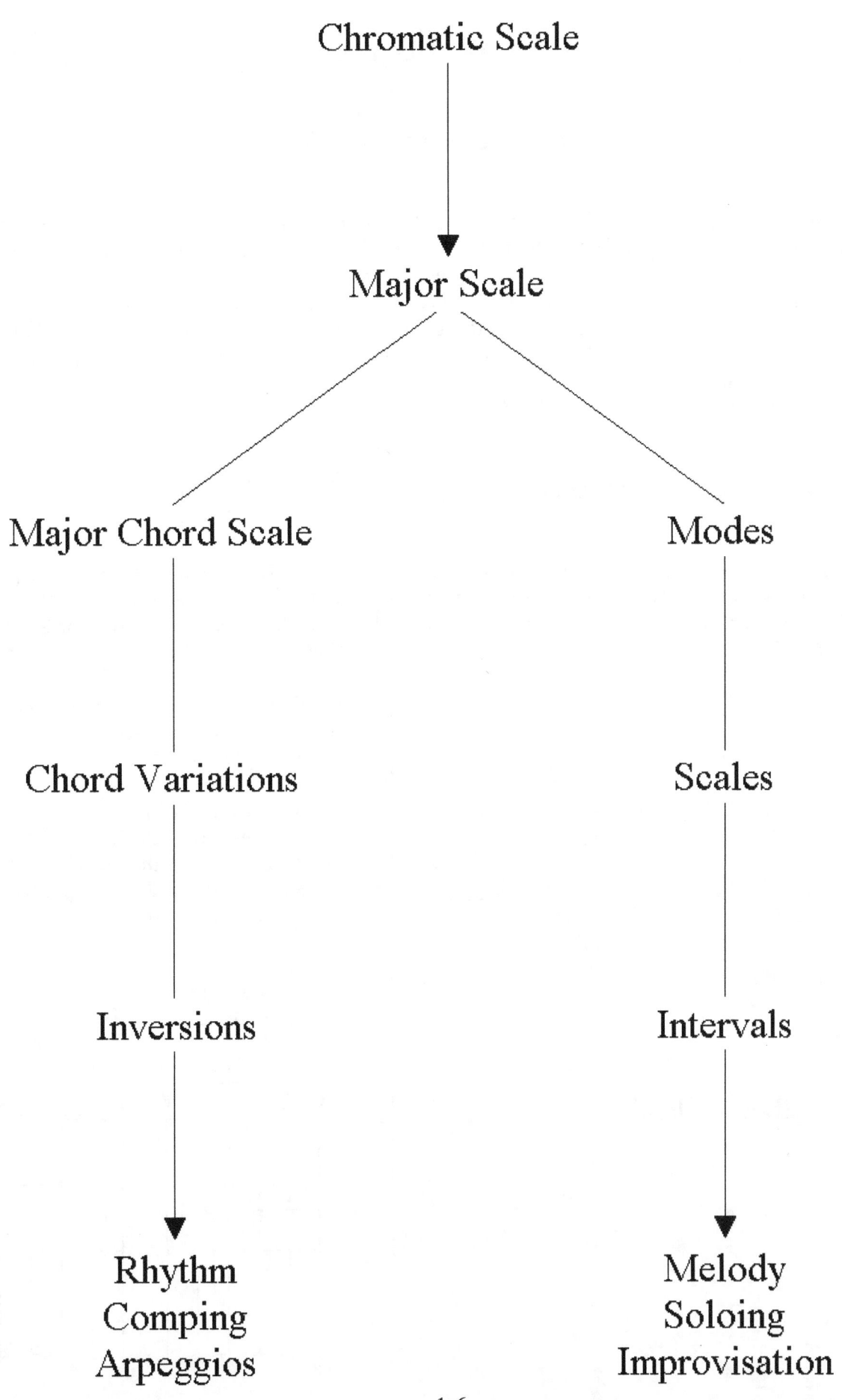

How To Do It

Pressing Down The Strings

In the Fret Board diagram below, the lettered fret board note names in the left diagram are shown to assist you with learning the notes on the fret board. Knowing the note names on the fret board is the similar to having street names on a map. The finger numbers in the right diagram show the musician which fingers are to play which notes on the fret board. Pressing our fingers down on the strings against the fret board is our direct interaction with the guitar. At first the fret board hand has a tendency to clamp the neck between the thumb and fingers hard, squeezing with lots of pressure. This is normal and is part of the learning experience. This will give way with practice and eventually the touch will become light and fast. Playing experience is the key.

Fret Board Hand Diagram

The fingernails of the fret board hand should be trimmed so the tips of the fingers will be able to press the string down on the fret to make it sound without buzzing.

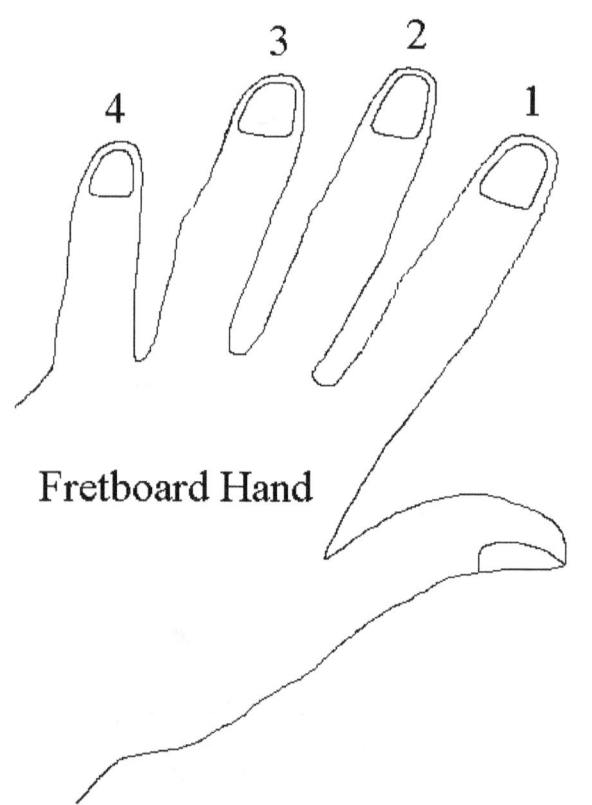

Fretboard Hand

Fret Board Diagram

The fret board Note Names will be presented so the student can learn the notes on the guitar fret board as the chords are being played.

The finger numbers are presented so the student will know which fingers are to be used when playing the chords.

0 = Play the open string.
1 = press down the first finger.
2 = press down the second finger.
3 = press down the third finger.
4 = press down the fourth finger.

How To Do It

Strumming, Flat-Picking And Chicken Pickin' The Strings

The Strumming And Chicken Pickin' Form diagram (below right) is a hand technique that utilizes the first finger for strumming and flat-picking. Traditionally a flat pick is used and is described below left. My preference is the direct hand to string contact without having to deal with the pick getting lost or flying out of my hand while playing. Most importantly there is the ease of shifting from strumming, to finger picking, to chicken pickin'. If you play a steel string acoustic guitar a pick would be a better choice, as the steel strings will wear down your fingernail.

Using A Pick

1) To flat-pick, bend the first finger at the first joint and place the pick between the thumb and the first finger. Keep your other fingers tucked gently in the palm of your hand. Rotate the hand and arm together in a back and forth circular motion as the pick lightly brushes across the top of a string. If your arm is moving up and down, your technique is not correct. 2) To strum, lightly brush your pick across the top of the strings using the same rotating motion as described in 1.

Using Your Finger

1) Gently yet firmly press your first finger and thumb together just below the first joint of the finger so the thumb gives it support. Keep your other fingers tucked gently in the palm of your hand. Your hand will resemble a chicken pecking at the ground as your finger bends at the second joint and your thumb bends at the first joint moving to and fro as if on a hinge.

NOTE: unlike the flat-picking technique your hand does not rotate.

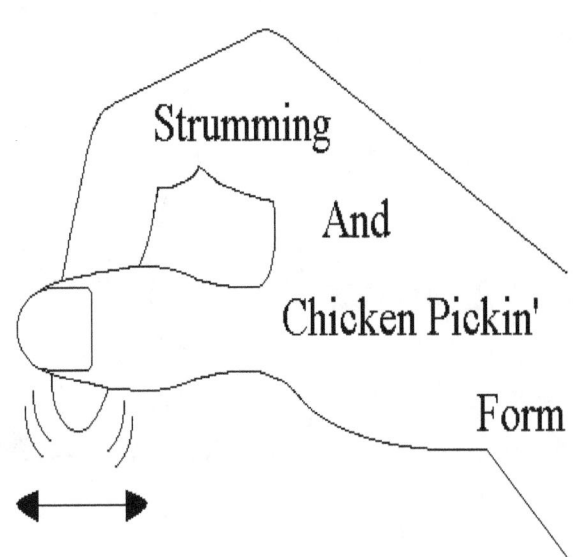

Strumming And Chicken Pickin' Form

How To Do It

Finger Picking The Strings

The Finger Picking Form diagram below is a hand technique that utilizes the thumb (p) on the 6th and 5th bass strings with the index finger (i) on the 4th string, the middle finger (m) on the 3rd string and the ring finger (a) on the 2nd and 1st strings.

With the crease of your elbow on the highest part of the guitar body your hand will naturally hang down at the wrist. The wrist will be slightly bent away from the guitar face. This angles the hand so the fingers will play the strings at an angle reducing the surface area, which in turn reduces the amount of friction.

Notice how the thumb (p) juts out in front of the fingers. This opens the hand causing the back of the hand to be parallel to the guitar face and allows the tips of the fingers flesh and nails to lightly brush the top of the strings. NOTE: If the thumb (p) goes in behind the fingers it will: 1) get in the way, 2) leave the bass string area it is intended to play in and 3) cause the hand to rotate downwards resulting in the fingers "clawing" the strings from underneath. All three of these actions will slow down your playing ability considerably.

The thumb (p) will use down strokes (away from you) over the tops of the strings while the fingers index (i), middle (m) and ring (a) will strike the strings upwards (towards you) over the tops of the strings.

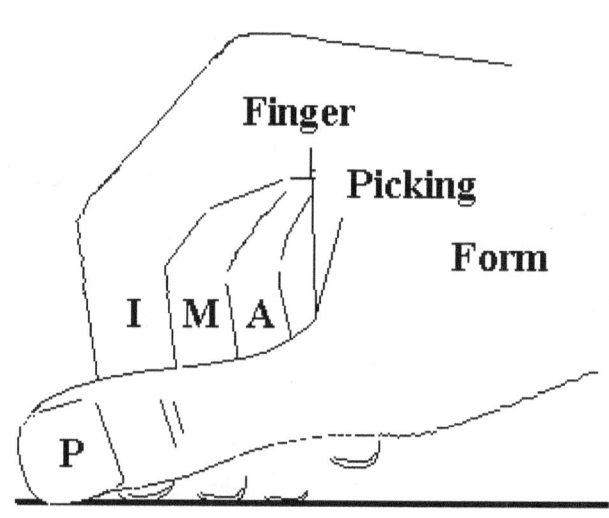

Tuning The Guitar

It is important that the guitar be tuned properly so the correct tone relationships will be heard while learning to play. Ear training is essential to the musician. Tuning requires a reference tone source and a tone that is to be tuned. There are two hearing factors involved: 1) If the two tones do not sound as "one" when played, you will hear a wah-wah like clashing vibration sound known as dissonance, which is caused by the two tones vibrating at different frequency rates. 2) Is the string being tuned, higher or lower in pitch then the reference tone?

Method 1

For the introductory guitarist, the best way to tune the guitar is with a digital tuner. There are several tuners with an LCD screen that are reasonably priced, very accurate and easy to use.

Method 2

A tuning fork is an accurate and inexpensive reference tone source to use for Method 2.

1) If you have an "A 440 tuning fork", strike the tuning fork first, then play the open 5th string without any fingers pressing it down and let it ring. Now tune the open 5th string "A" note to the tuning fork. If the pitch is low, turn the 5th string tuner away from you. If the pitch is high, turn the 5th string tuner towards you. To insure the strings will raise or lower in pitch correctly the classical guitar strings are strung over the tuning shaft while the acoustic and electric guitars strings are strung to the inside of the tuning shaft.

With the 5th string tuned, do not to adjust it again by mistake as it is now the reference tone.

2) Next tune the 6th string to the 5th string. Press and hold down the 6th string on the fifth fret, which is the "A" note, and simultaneously strike both the 6th string and 5th strings. Since the open 5th string is also an "A" note of the same octave the two strings should sound the same. If they do not vibrate as one, adjust the tuning peg for the 6th string until all dissonant vibrations cease and the two strings sound as though they are "one".

3) Then tune the 4th string to the 5th string by pressing down the 5th string on the fifth fret, which is the "D" note and simultaneously strike both the 5th string and 4th strings. Since the open 4th string is also a "D" note of the same octave, the two strings should sound the same. If not, adjust the 4th string until both strings sound as one. The same procedure will be used to tune 3rd string to the 4th, the 2nd string to the 3rd and the 1st string to the 2nd.

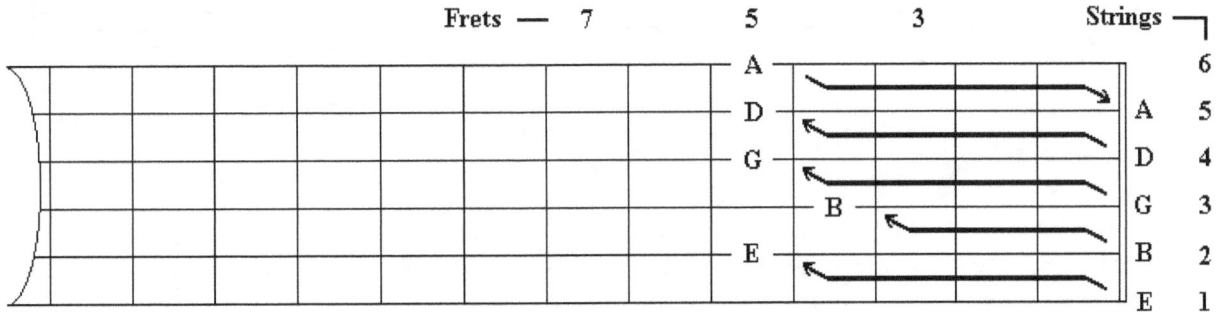

The Five Basic Chord Lesson

Open Position

These are the five basic chords. All the chords that you will ever play on the guitar will be these and a variation of these five chords.

Hold the C chord by putting your 3rd finger on the C bass note in the 3rd fret of the 5th string first, then place the rest of your fingers as shown below. Play each chord, using either the Strumming And Chicken Pickin' form or a flat pick, with down strokes starting with the bass note. Follow the same procedure for the G, D, A and E chords.

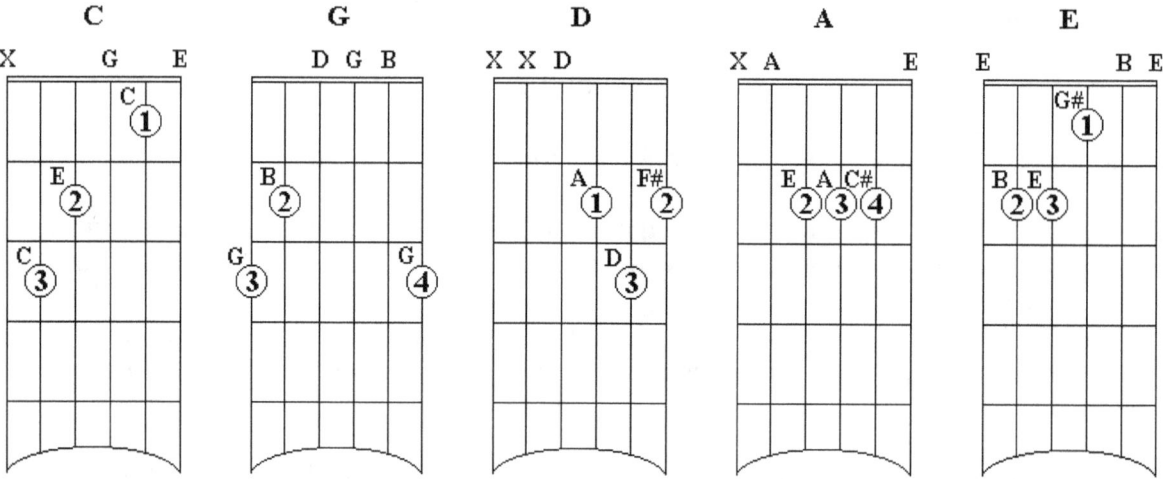

When you are comfortable playing each chord, play the song as shown in the staff diagram below changing from chord to chord. Play two down strokes across the strings, over the sound hole (acoustic) or between the pick-ups (electric) of the guitar for each chord with the exception of the E chord, which gets two measures of four beats. Each slash equals one beat, so the count would go as follows: **one** - two - three - four, **two** - two - three - four, **three** - two - three - four, **four** - two - three - four. It is important to keep the count even! Try that a few times to get the feel of it. The goal here is to make a smooth change, in time without any delay between each chord. Play only as fast as you can change from chord to chord!

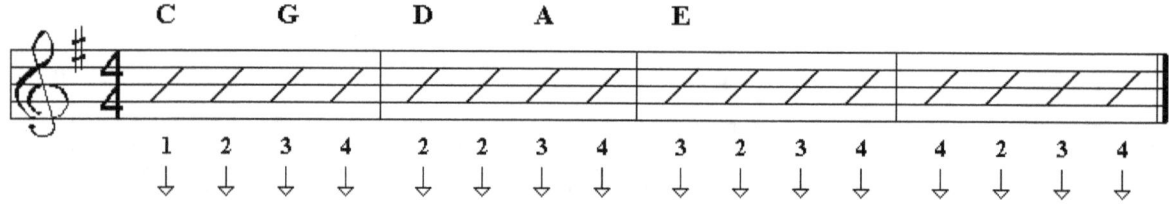

Notice that the lowest sounding or bass note played in each chord is the same letter name as the chord name. For example: the bass note of the C chord is "C". This is known as the root of the chord.

Rhythm Practice

Alternating Up And Down Strokes: Remember to rotate the strumming hand when using a pick or the Chicken Pickin' form. If your swinging your arm back and forth, your hand is leaving the string area and it will take that much more time to get your hand back over the strings for the next strum, resulting in an inefficient method that will slow your playing down considerably and wear your arm out quickly.

When strumming chords, the Chicken Pickin' form also requires you to rotate the hand over the strings. Because the up stroke has a tendency to pull your finger (i) away from your thumb (p), your thumb (p) must remain gently but securely attached to your first finger (i) otherwise your finger (i) will flap around resulting in lack of control.

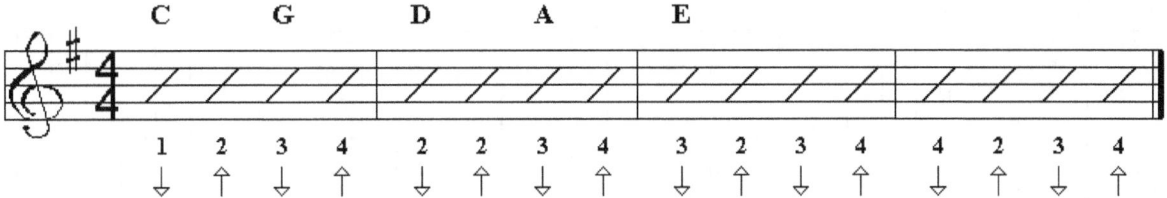

Double The Strums: Count the down-stroke as the "number" (1, 2, 3, 4) and count the up-stroke as the "and" (+). It helps to tap your foot to keep time. When the foot goes down, that's the down-stroke and the "number" (1, 2, 3, 4) is counted and when the foot goes up, that's the up-stroke and the "and" (+) is counted.

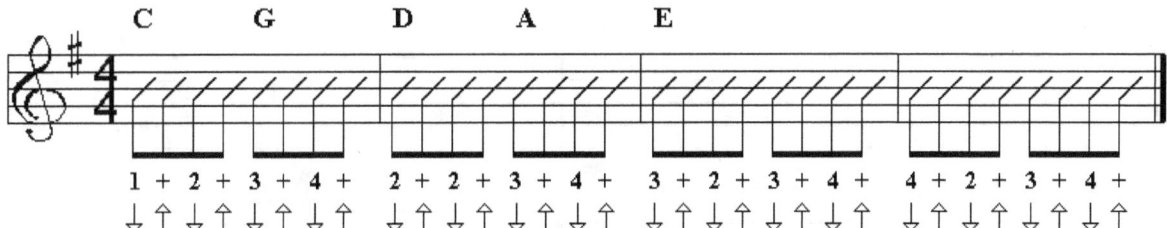

Syncopate The Feel: This is the strumming style that is used for most songs. It's lively and gives the feel that makes people want to get up and dance.

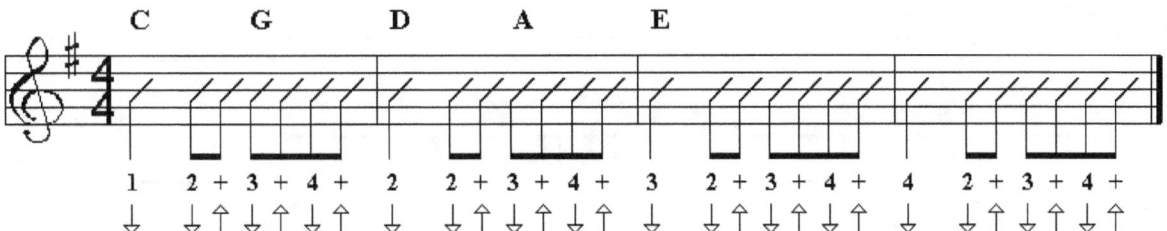

Notes

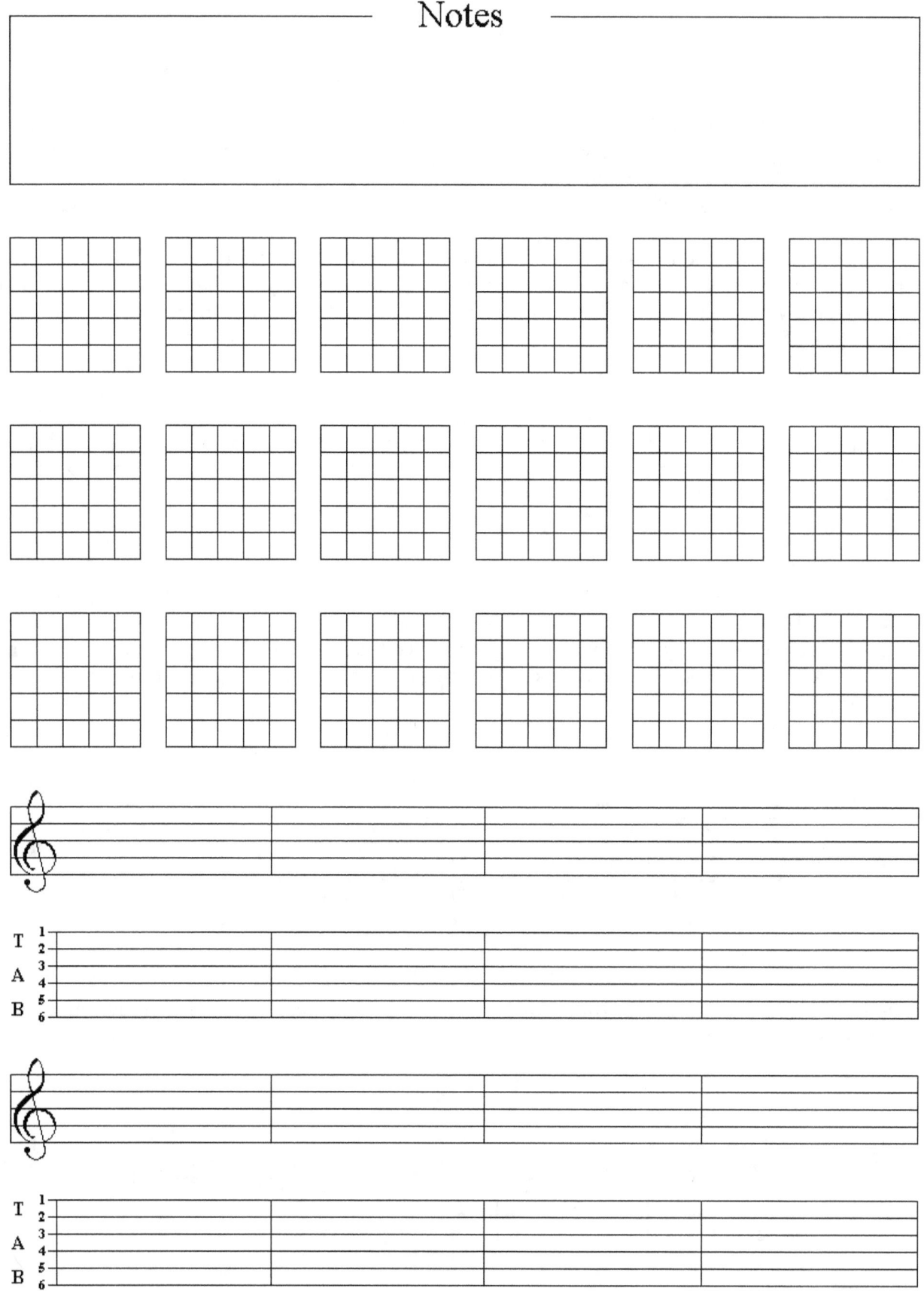

Reference

Key Of C

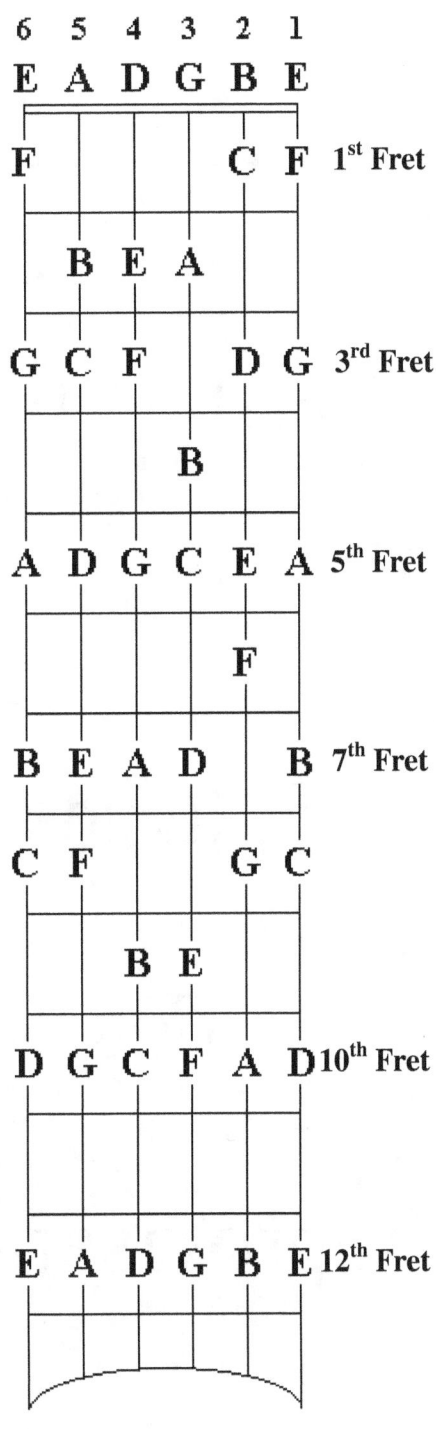

Chapter 2 Introduction To Patterns For Improvisation

Patterns For Improvisation

The Blues started the revolution of improvisation. Inventing the blues, the African/American under the adverse conditions of slavery found an outlet for their frustration and defined their culture. Educated by the English when Africa was overcome during England's expansion years, the African/American obviously had an understanding of the Western musical system. Every culture has unique art, dance and music that express their living philosophy. Through the Blues the African/American subculture was able to express its frustration of being held in slavery in the very culture that it wanted to be apart of. This created sadness of oppression while on the other hand created an excitement with the hope of being free and belonging. This combination of experience translated into the arts; particularly the guitar, voice and dance due to their ease of acquiring, led to the creation of the distinctive blues sound, which is explained in the working application taught in Chapter 14 – Patterns For Creative Expression.

Slavery was not allowed in the north so the free African/Americans created the famous underground railway, which was not a train at all, but an escape route from the south to the north. Free African/Americans infiltrated into the Southern plantations from the north informing the slaves of the way to escape. Once in the fields the singing began with the infiltrator singing about the landmarks to look for on the escape route. Each leg of the way was sung in a phrase, "Go down to the river and travel north for three days". The slaves would then respond in unison, "Go down to the river and travel north for three days". They did this in a song so they would remember the directions. This type of singing is done in a "call and response" format, which is so characteristic of the repetitive blues sound. Of course the words were sung in African so the plantation owners wouldn't know what was being said.

The African/Americans began acquiring guitars to accompany themselves at night, continuing to sing to remember the songs of freedom. Those who could not gain access to a guitar built them out of boxes and sticks with catgut for strings.

Prior to the creation of the Blues there was classical music that was reserved for the wealthy, usually in the kings court and folk music played by the common folk around campfires or in eateries as a means of story telling and reporting events that happened in another town. The wondering minstrel of past was in essence the equivalent of the news reporter in our present day. The king would send spies to report on what the common folk were up to. Neither classical nor folk music instrumentally improvised. Presently, classical music allows arrangement creativity and folk music evolved into country music, which uses the blues application in its lead work.

In a band setting, improvisation gives individuals a chance to express their experience instrumentally. For the soloist this means improvising while accompanying oneself. Playing notes in succession within the structure of a scale or across strings through a chord is the technical basis from which the guitarist improvises. The next two pages will introduce you to a scale with chords for the blues and a mode with chords for jazz that are the patterns or "playgrounds" within which you can learn to improvise. Scales and modes must be learned knowledgably and technically before the Creative Energy will flow through our being, finger tips and finally projected via the guitar expressing the unique experiences of our lives. The first step of improvisation is simply a matter of training our fingers through repetitive.

How To Do It

Practice The Scale

The first pattern we'll learn is the popular Aeolian pentatonic scale. Both the Guitar Grid diagram and the Notation And TAB Staff below show you how to do it:

1) On the Guitar Grid diagram, with the picking hand use the thumb (p) on strings 6 and 5, the index finger (i) on string 4, the middle finger (m) on string 3 and the ring finger (a) on strings 2 and 1. Start with the lowest open note "E" on the 6th string and play through the scale: each note is played in succession, one note at a time - one after the other, ascending up each string to the G note on the third fret of the first string. NOTE: The fretboard hand uses the third finger in the 3rd fret and the second finger in the 2nd fret. Keep your fingers in order in a position so they don't get tangled up and you won't have to think about them. Learn it the best way from the beginning so it won't slow down your playing later.

Aeolian Pentatonic Scale - Guitar Grid

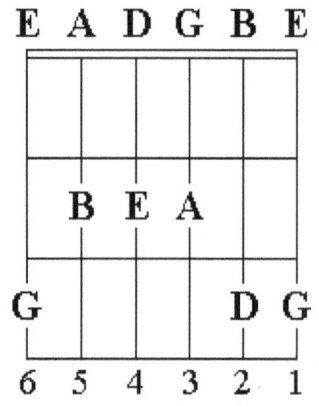 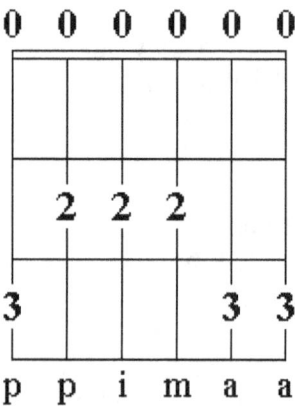

2) On the TAB staff (bottom), the six lines represent the six strings of the guitar with the 6th string being the bass string and the 1st string being the treble string. The numbers on the TAB staff strings are the fret numbers of the guitar. By playing the fret numbers from left to right you will be playing the same scale that you played in the Guitar Grid diagram above. The treble clef notation staff (top) will be explained in Chapter 3 – Notation.

Aeolian Pentatonic Scale - Notation And TAB Staff - Ascending

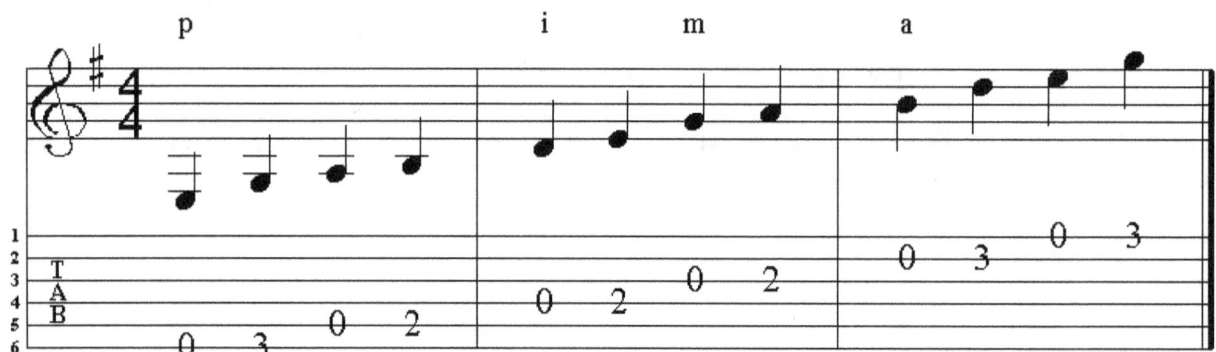

When the Aeolian pentatonic scale can be played smoothly ascending, play the scale descending, in reverse, starting with the G note on the 3rd fret of the first string and play down the scale to the low "E" note of the sixth string. NOTE: when descending, play the note in the fret first then play the open note on each string, which is now the opposite of the above ascending exercise.

Aeolian Pentatonic Scale - Notation And TAB Staff – Descending

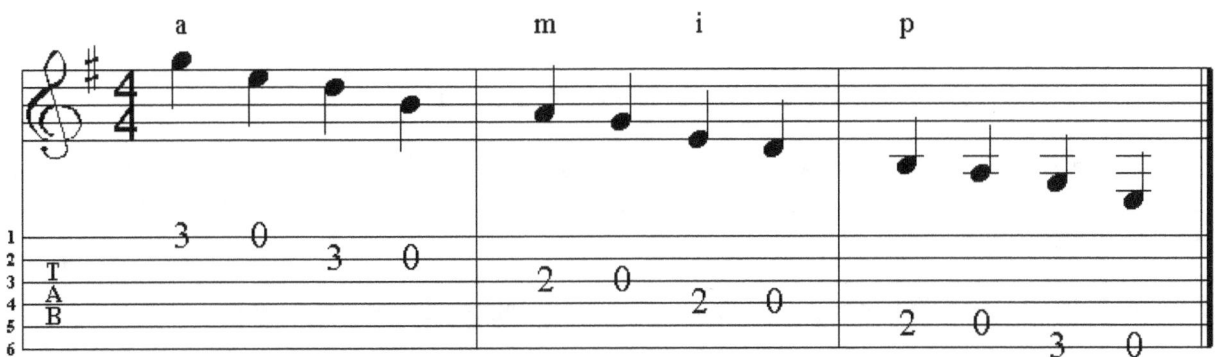

With that accomplished, play the Aeolian pentatonic scale ascending and descending without stopping.

Aeolian Pentatonic Scale - Notation And TAB Staff – Ascending & Descending

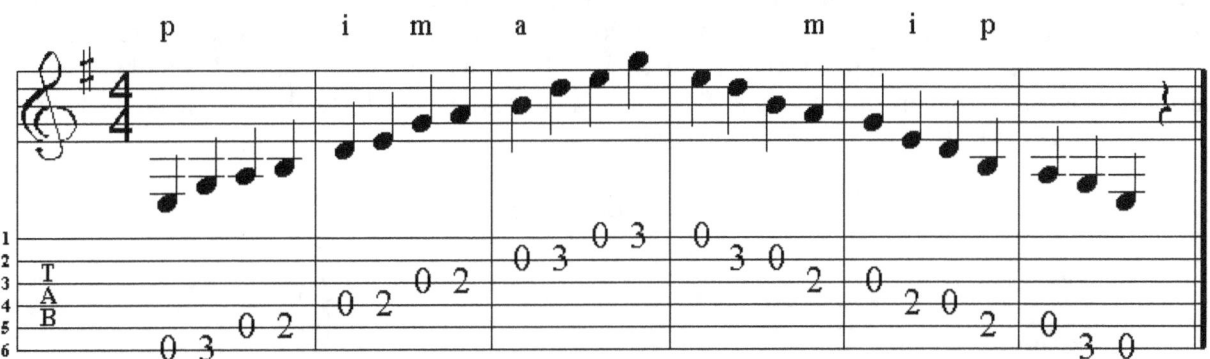

And finally, play the Aeolian pentatonic scale descending and ascending without stopping.

Aeolian Pentatonic Scale - Notation And TAB Staff – Descending & Ascending

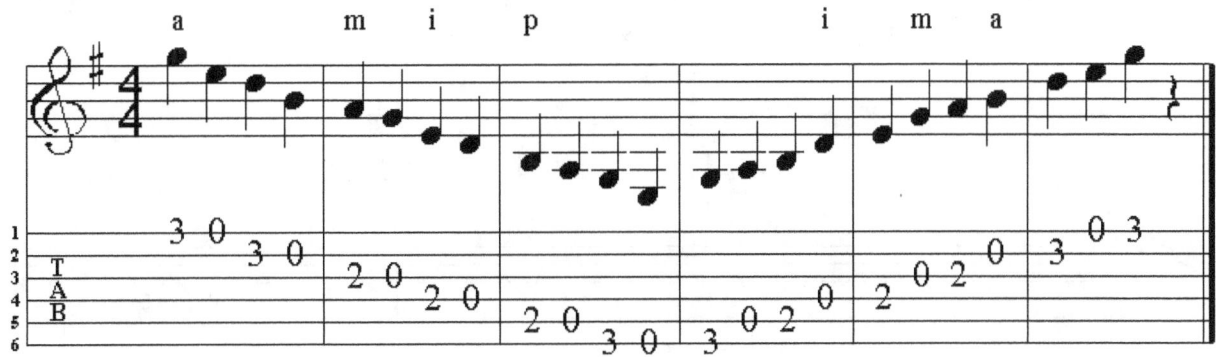

Practice

To become really good at playing the Aeolian pentatonic scale:

1) Play the scale ascending and descending three times in a row without stopping.

2) Play the scale descending and ascending three times in a row also without stopping.

To practice the Aeolian pentatonic scale using all of the picking hand techniques, repeat the above exercises with a flat pick or chicken pickin' style using the alternating down – up method.

On an ongoing basis: practice the Aeolian pentatonic scale ascending and descending then descending and ascending for fifteen minutes at least once a day for minimum exposure with three or more practice times a day being optimum.

After fifteen minutes the mind begins to wander and the mistakes will then be learned.

Play The Chords

Here we encounter our first variation of the five basic chords. The E7 Twelve Bar Blues song chords (below) are similar to the chords learned in Chapter 1 only now the E7 and A7 chords have one note missing. This missing note not only makes the chord easier to play but it creates the blues sound so familiar to us. These chords are called seventh or dominant seventh chords because the seventh tone of the chord is lowered a half step, making it minor which is unique to the Blues. It has been given the name dominant for communications sake. The dominant seven chord will be explained in Chapter 7. NOTE: pay attention to the chord grid finger numbers.

Strum the progression with down strokes using either a flat pick or chicken pickin' style.

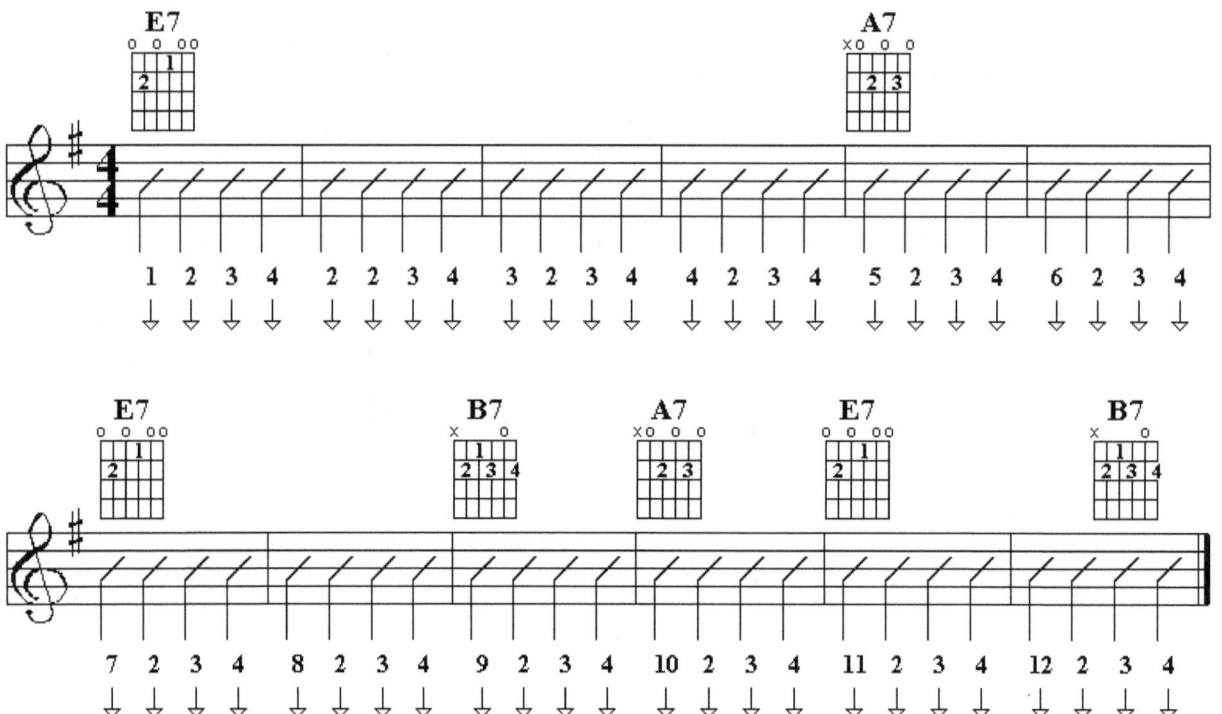

2-4

With a friend or a computer-generated band, play the Aeolian pentatonic scale over the E7 Twelve Bar Blues song. Take turns and learn both the chords and the scale. Find the perfect tempo that's not too slow or too fast. Both will cause you to make mistakes. Gradually speed up the tempo one notch at a time over days or perhaps weeks to 120 BPM (beats per minute) as your ability allows. The alternating picks ♡ instruct as to whether an up or down stroke will be used to pick the note. Practice both the Flat pick or chicken pickin' and finger picking techniques.

How To Do It

Practice The Mode

The Phrygian mode is a variation of the major scale. Mode is defined in the dictionary as "...a variety of something" and Phrygian is a Greek word used simply to give this variation a name.

Practice both the Guitar Grid and the Notation And TAB Staff below as previously learned with the Aeolian Pentatonic Scale on page 2-2. NOTE: The fretboard hand uses the first finger in the 1st fret, the second finger in the 2nd fret and the third finger in the 3rd fret.

Phrygian Mode – Guitar Grid

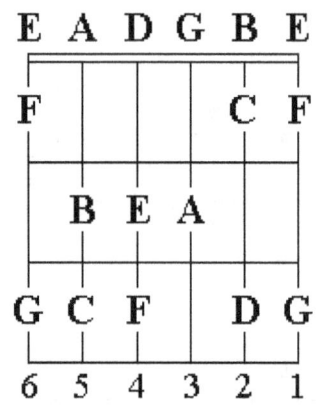
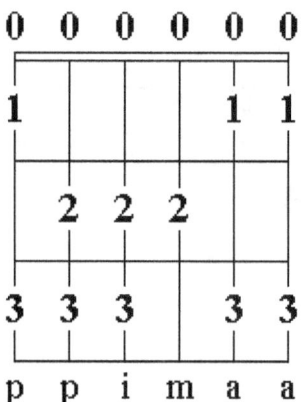

Phrygian Mode - Notation And TAB Staff – Ascending And Descending

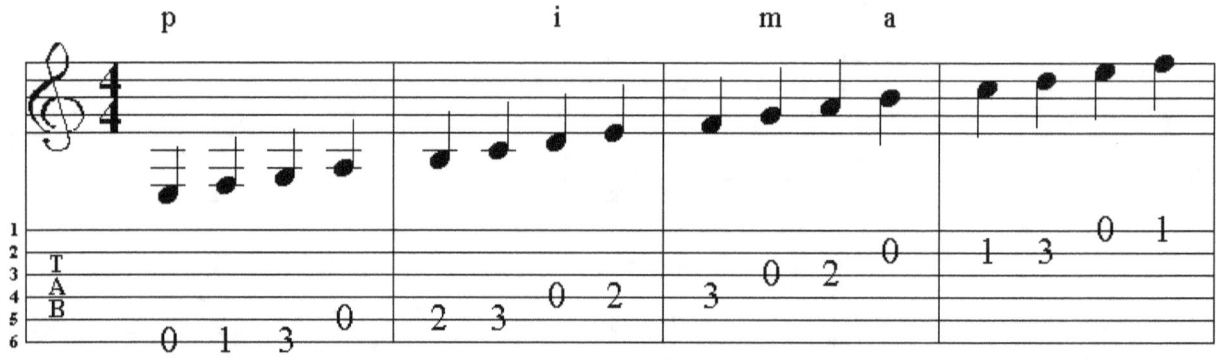
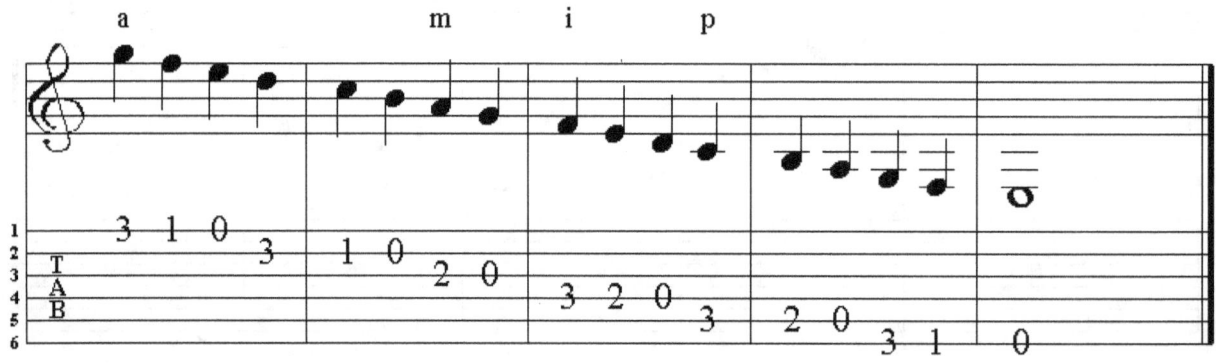

2-6

This time, with a friend or a computer-generated band, play the Phrygian mode over the C Major Seven Jazz song shown below. From the major scale they are derived from, the seventh tone in these chords are naturally major, (as opposed to the minor seventh tone in the dominant seven blues chords. This gives the sound of Jazz. Each song type has specific rules that give the song its sound. We have learned that the blues uses dominant seven chords and now we'll see that jazz uses major seven chords. The major seven chord will be explained in Chapter 7.

The Cmaj7, Fmaj7 and G7 chords have been chosen for this lesson due to their similar fingerings. Notice as you change from the Cmaj7 chord to the Fmaj7 chord that fingers 3 and 2 simply move from the 5th and 4th strings over to the 4th and 3rd strings in the same order. Also notice that the same fingers 3 and 2 of the Cmaj7 and Fmaj7 chords move to the 6th and 5th strings of the G7 chord in the same order. Fingers 3 and 2 remain in the 3rd and 2nd frets in all three chords. This will make it easier for you to learn how to change chords: by moving fingers 3 and 2 together as a unit and placing them down on the strings at the same time, as a unit, (as opposed to putting each finger down one at a time). You will now be able to change chords much faster. Strum the Cmaj7 Jazz song chords with four down strokes in each measure.

Pick the Phrygian mode ascending and descending using the alternating down - up ♡ method with a Flat pick or the chicken pickin' technique. Also practice the p-i-m-a finger picking style.

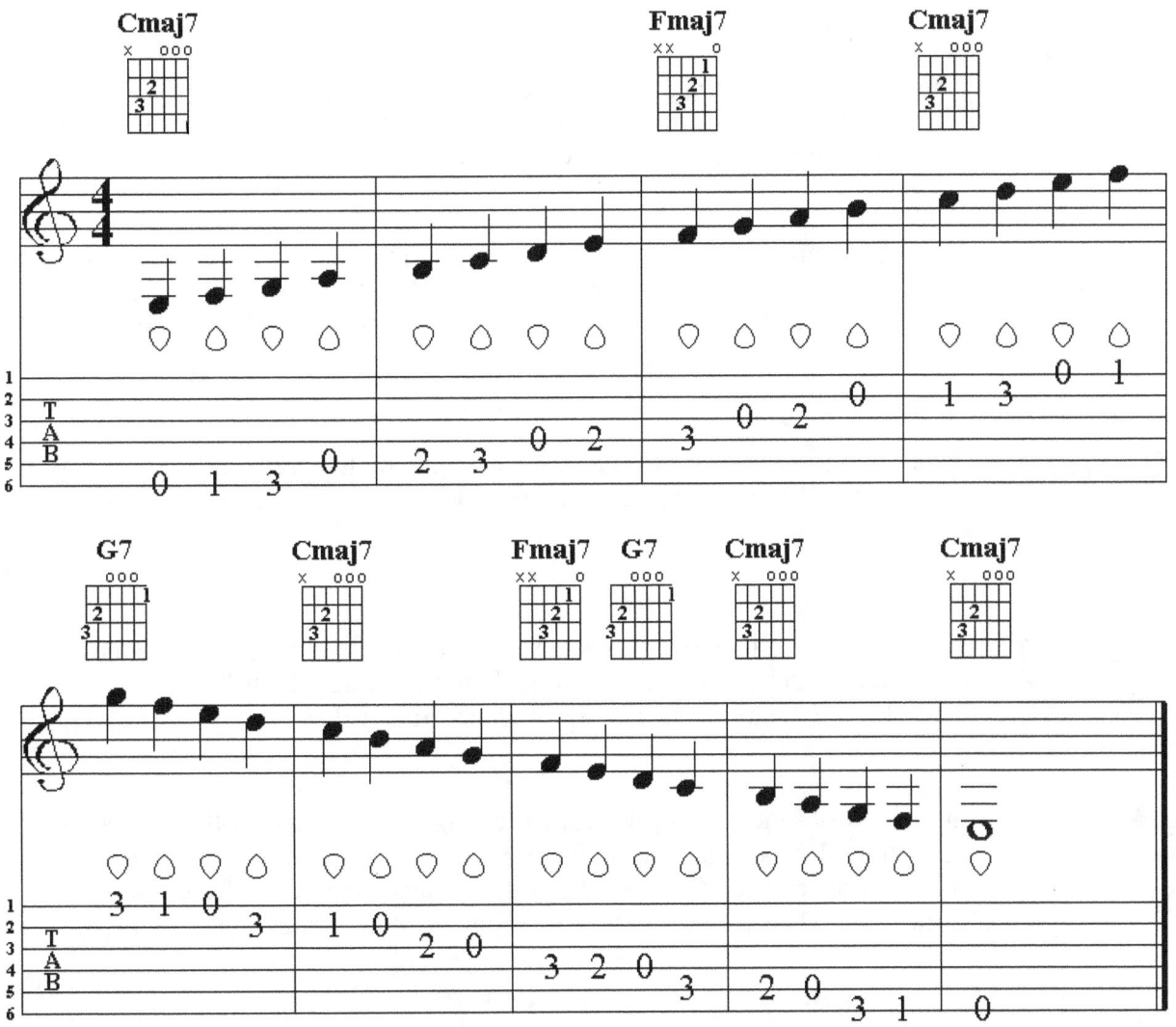

Guitar Expressions

<> Embellishments are string manipulations that create effects, which are used for expression

Bend - With the picking hand pick the string while the fretboard hand is holding the string down on the fret. Push the string upwards anywhere from a half step to two whole-steps. This creates a smooth raised shift in pitch.

Bend and Release - Pick and bend the string as described above, then slowly return to the starting point. This allows for the note to be raised and lowered in pitch smoothly.

Pre-bend - Silently bend the string before picking it, now strike the string, and then slowly lower the string. This lowers the pitch by the amount of the pre-bend. This sounds like a whale cry.

Vibrato - Strike the string then vibrate it by bending the fretted string up and down quickly with a rapid fret board handed movement or by a shaking side-to-side movement of the fretboard hand.

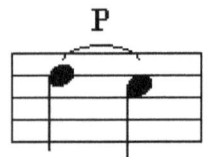
Pull Off - While pressing down on the fretted note with a finger of the fret board hand, pick the string, and then pull off the fretboard hand finger from the fretted note. This allows two notes to be played while picking the string only once.

Hammer On – Strike the string with a finger of the fretboard hand hard enough on the fretboard to make the note sound. This makes the note sound without picking the string.

Hammer On and Pull Off - This is the technique for producing a trill sound, a fast shift in pitches with or without picking the string. The trill will be played for the duration of the designated note time value.

Slide or Gliss - Pick the string while pressing a fretted note with a finger of the fretboard hand, then, while continuously pressing down on the string, slide the finger of the fretboard hand up or down the neck of the guitar to another fret. This can also be done with two or more strings simultaneously.

E7 Twelve Bar Blues

Licks & Expressions

Notes

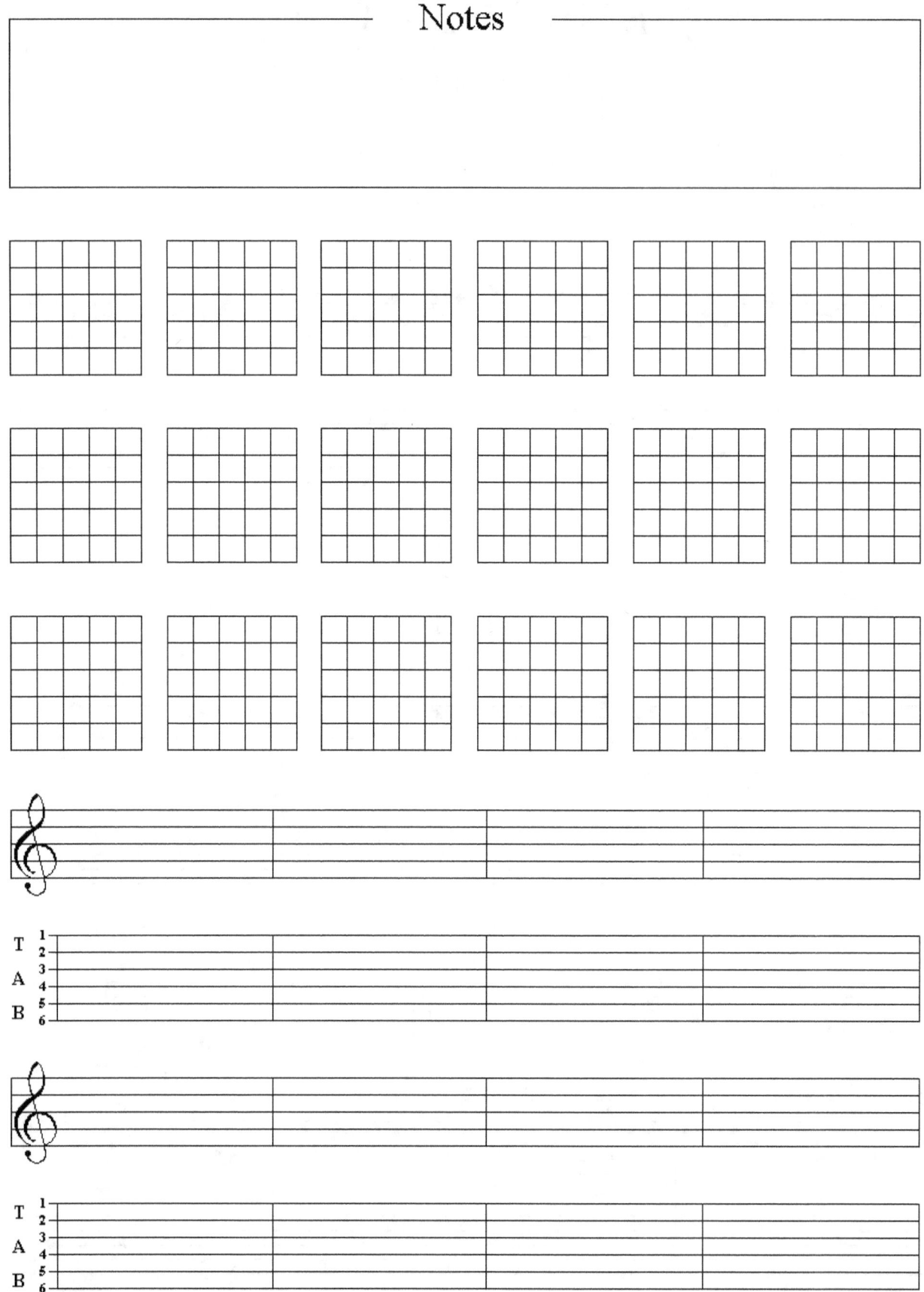

Chapter 3

Notation

Instrument Ranges

Treble And Bass Clef Staves With Notes

This diagram is useful as an overview reference. The piano is an excellent visual example of the major scale: C - D - E - F - G - A - B - C, repeated six octaves on the white keys. The numbers over the white keys are the vibrations per second that distinguish that notes pitch from any other. Notice the natural half steps, no black keys between E, F and B, C.

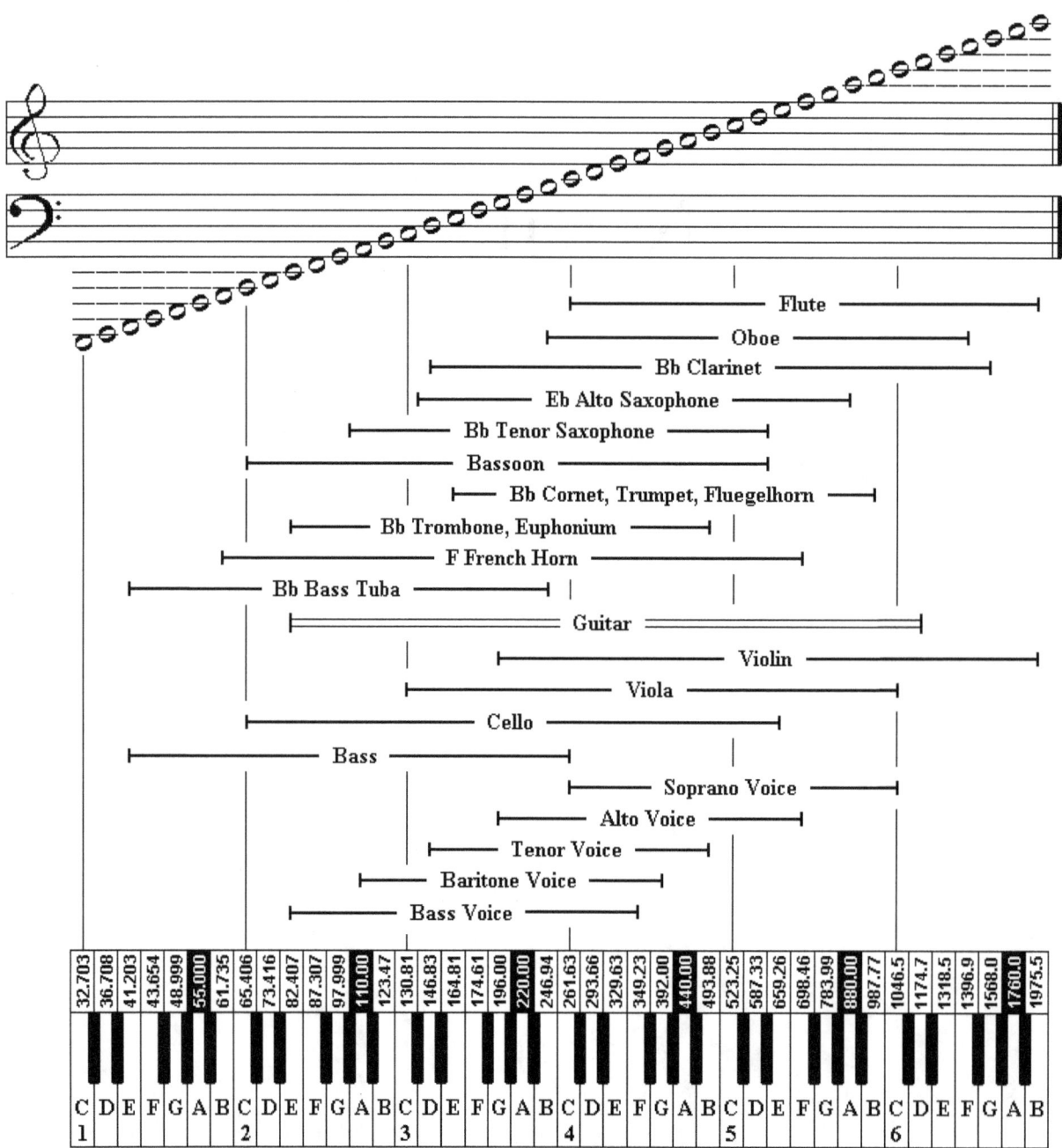

Tones

A tone is the sound we hear when a note is played. Each tone has a specific frequency or vibration that defines it. Each of these frequencies are assigned a letter name for communications sake. The letters of the musical alphabet are: A B C D E F G. There are only seven letters of the musical alphabet. After we get to G it starts all over again at A, only this time an octave higher in pitch. To understand this look at the piano diagram below and notice that the A1 piano key has a number 55 above it. This means there are 55 vibrations of the string moving back and forth per second when this tone is sounded.

Bass (low) = less vibrations per second.   Treble (high) = more vibrations per second.

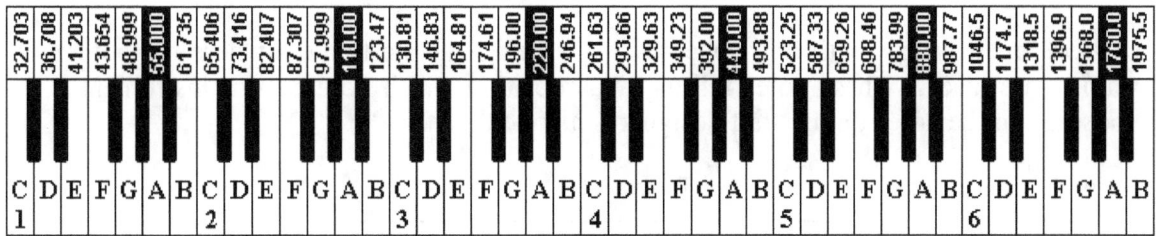

One vibration is equal to the string moving back and forth once. This can be seen in the waveform diagram below between points A and B.

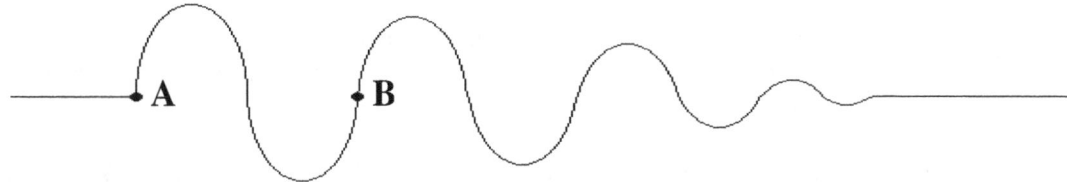

This is known as one cycle or one hertz. The human hearing range is approximately between 20 hertz (20Hz) and 17,000 Hz (17kHz). Quality stereo systems are rated at 20Hz to 20kHz.

Now count up the piano keyboard starting from the A (A1) at 55. As you count A B C D E F G the next A (A2) has a number 110 above it. This means the A at 110 has twice as many vibrations as the A at 55 and being eight notes higher on the white keys it is referred to as being one octave higher in pitch. Since the pitch doubles itself in vibrations every eight notes, we are able to use the same letters and refer to the octaves as A1, A2, etc.

Let's now look at the guitar fret board below and see how this relates to its strings and frets:

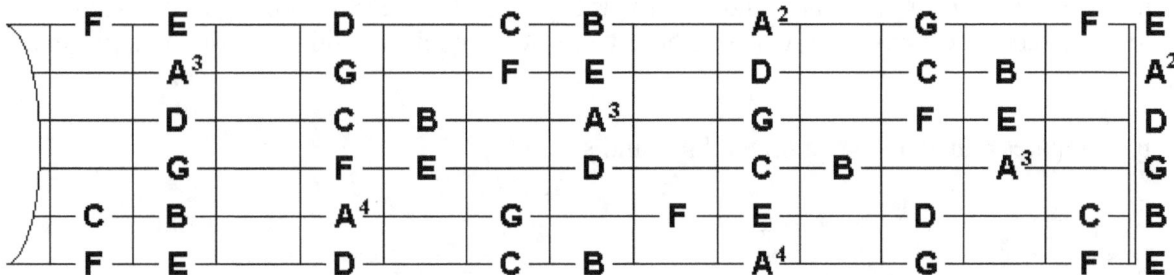

3-2

Notation

There are two standard ways of writing down music: 1) Notation which originated during the Greek era by Pythagoras is a way for the information of a song to be written down so it can be read, played and learned. 2) Tablature an ancient form of music notation is a diagram that simply shows the six strings of the guitar that reveals, by fret numbers, where the fingers are to be placed on the strings and frets. Tablature requires standard notation to reveal the notation timing. Tab also does not reveal the visual interval distances of the notes in the song, which is essential for a deeper understanding of the music. This could be compared to a digital clock, which tells you the time but doesn't give you its visual time of day like the analog clock with its hands does. Since tab is self-explanatory we'll turn our attention to notation.

In Diagram1 there are five lines with four spaces. This is called the staff and is where the notes, which have letter names, are placed. These notes tell us by association which note on our instrument is to be played. The position of the notes on the staff designates its pitch name.

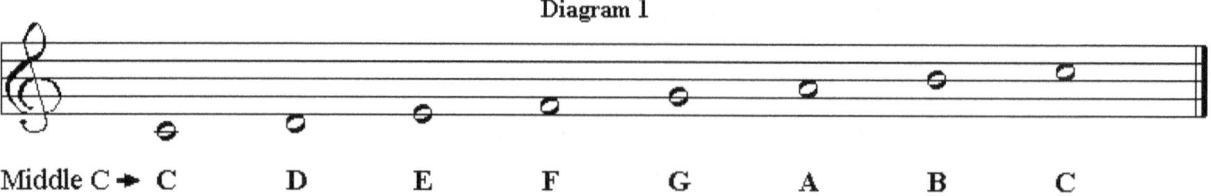

When the notes go above or below the staff they are placed on ledger lines. The middle C note below the staff in Diagram 1 is an example of a ledger line. This keeps the notation page uncluttered of unnecessary lines when there are no notes on them and is also easier to read.

Using the seven letters of the alphabet A B C D E F G it can be seen below in Diagram 2 that starting with the bottom line E, the lettered note names proceed up the staff through the musical alphabet: E F G A B C D E F. To make it easy to memorize: the spaces spell **F A C E** and the line letters are E G B D F, the first letters of **Every Good Boy Does Fine**.

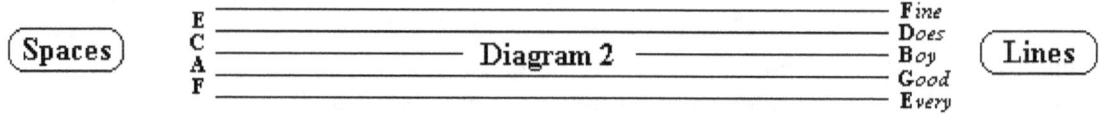

Since there are several ranges that different musical instruments play in, it is necessary to place a clef sign at the beginning of the song. This lets the musician know if the music being read is in the correct range for that instrument. The clef the guitarist uses is mainly the treble clef. Since a considerable amount of music is written for the piano and not for the guitar, it is helpful although not essential, to read both the treble and bass clefs. This will also help you to communicate with both the bass player and the pianist.

The clef sign designates which notes are on the lines and spaces.

Notation And The Guitar

The notes on the staff are symbols that tell us where those notes are to be played on the guitar fret board. The Phrygian mode in the Key of C is used in the first diagram below for this lesson.

1) The guitar grids display the note names on the open strings or in the frets as they are to be played on the guitar.

2) The letter note names displayed on the guitar grids are the names of the notes, which are found on the staff directly below the guitar grids.

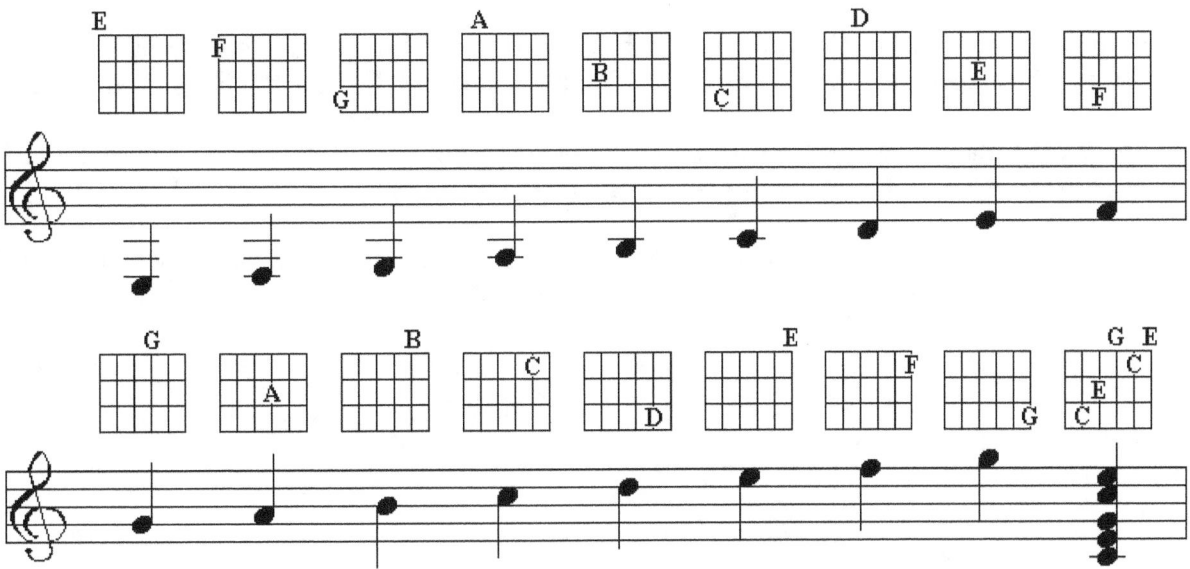

Memorization is the best way to learn notation and its relationship to the guitar. To memorize this lesson, play it repeatedly on the guitar while saying the names of the notes out loud. To keep your fingers from getting tangled up and to keep from having to constantly look at your hand to see where your fingers are supposed to go, use the correct fingers in the scale pattern. This way you can read the music as you play the guitar. Refer to the fret board hand fingerings as shown on page 2-3. Use the flat-picking technique of the picking hand for sounding the strings.

The overview reference of the guitar diagram is shown below with the Phrygian mode in the open position. You are playing in the open position if any of the notes of each string of the scale are played open, or in other words, without pressing down a string in a fret with a finger.

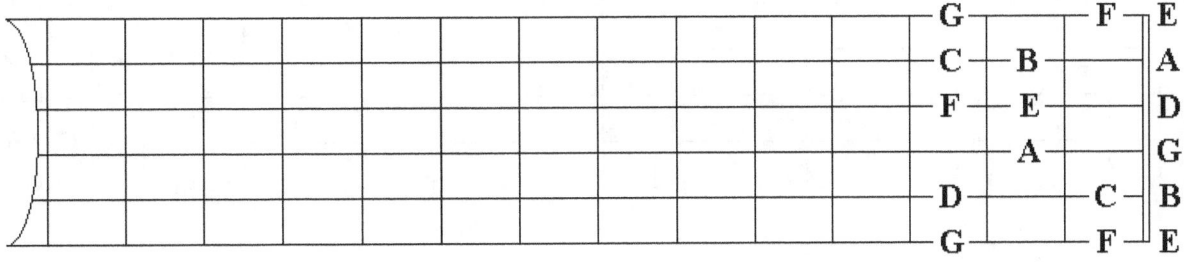

3-4

Ledger Line Notation

When the notation is placed below the staff the notes are placed on ledger lines. This is so when the notes are not needed the ledger lines are removed and the staff is still five lines and four spaces which keeps the appearance tidy without a lot of extra clutter on the page making for easier reading.

There is a symmetry happening that when seen, will make it easy to know the notes on the ledger lines below the staff. On Page 3 we learned that the notes in the **spaces** rhymed with **face**, which are the note names, **F - A - C - E** from the bottom to the top space of the treble clef staff. We also learned that the **lines** rhymed with **fine** which is the last word in the clever way of remembering the notes on the lines, **E**very **G**ood **B**oy **D**oes **F**ine, from the bottom to the top line of the treble clef staff.

When we look at the notes on the ledger lines below the treble clef staff, it just so happens that the spaces between the ledger lines are **E - G - B - D - F** and the lines are **F – A - C - E**. They are reversed.

It can also be seen that the ledger lines above the treble clef staff have reversed their order as well, the spaces between the ledger lines are **E - G - B - D - F** and the lines are **F – A - C - E**.

As you look further up the scale it will be found that they flip again. They alternate. They alternate from octave to octave.

This insight will help you in your reading endeavors allowing you to be a more efficient reader therefore a faster reader of musical notation.

On The Guitar

Corresponding with the notes on the staff in the diagram above, the diagram below shows the same notes on the guitar laterally in the open position and ascending linearly up the 1st string.

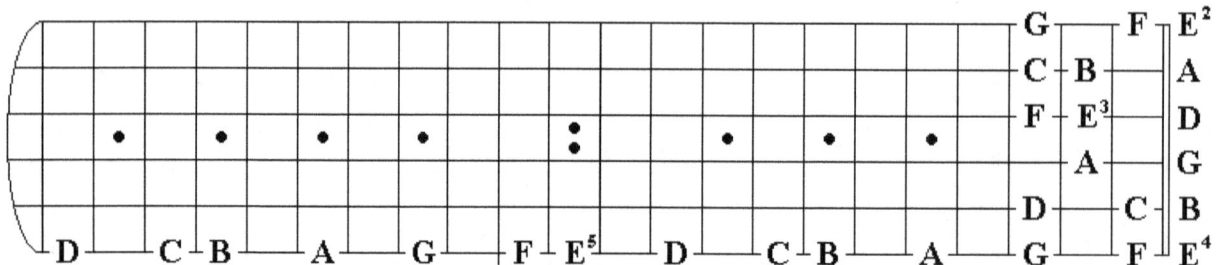

Where's Middle C ?

Diagram 1 shows the notation format for the pianist. It has the treble and bass clefs for the right and left hands of the pianist with middle C in the center of the two staves, which corresponds, with middle C in the middle of the piano. This is the format that the guitarist will generally encounter in sheet music only with guitar chord grids added above the staves to play along with. Although the guitar is considered a treble clef instrument with middle C on the first fret of the second string most of our playing is actually in the bass clef. **Diagram 2** shows what the sheet music would look like if only the treble clef we're used. The excessive ledger lines below the staff of the pitches the guitarist uses most often would be difficult to negotiate. **Diagram 3** shows in two ways how guitarists over the passage of time have compensated for this dilemma. 1) The 8 under the treble clef sign signifies that the notation has been transposed up an octave on the staff. Only the notation has been transposed, the pitches remain the same. This makes the notation more centered in the staff for ease of reading resolving the notation problem we encountered in diagram 2. 2) With middle C still being physically played on the first fret of the second string the guitarist would now play mostly in the upper register of the guitar and once again in all those ledger lines only this time above the staff. To resolve this dilemma, this time it is the guitar that is mentally transposed down an octave with middle C now being played an octave lower on the third fret of the fifth string. The guitar is now also more centered on the staff for ease of reading.

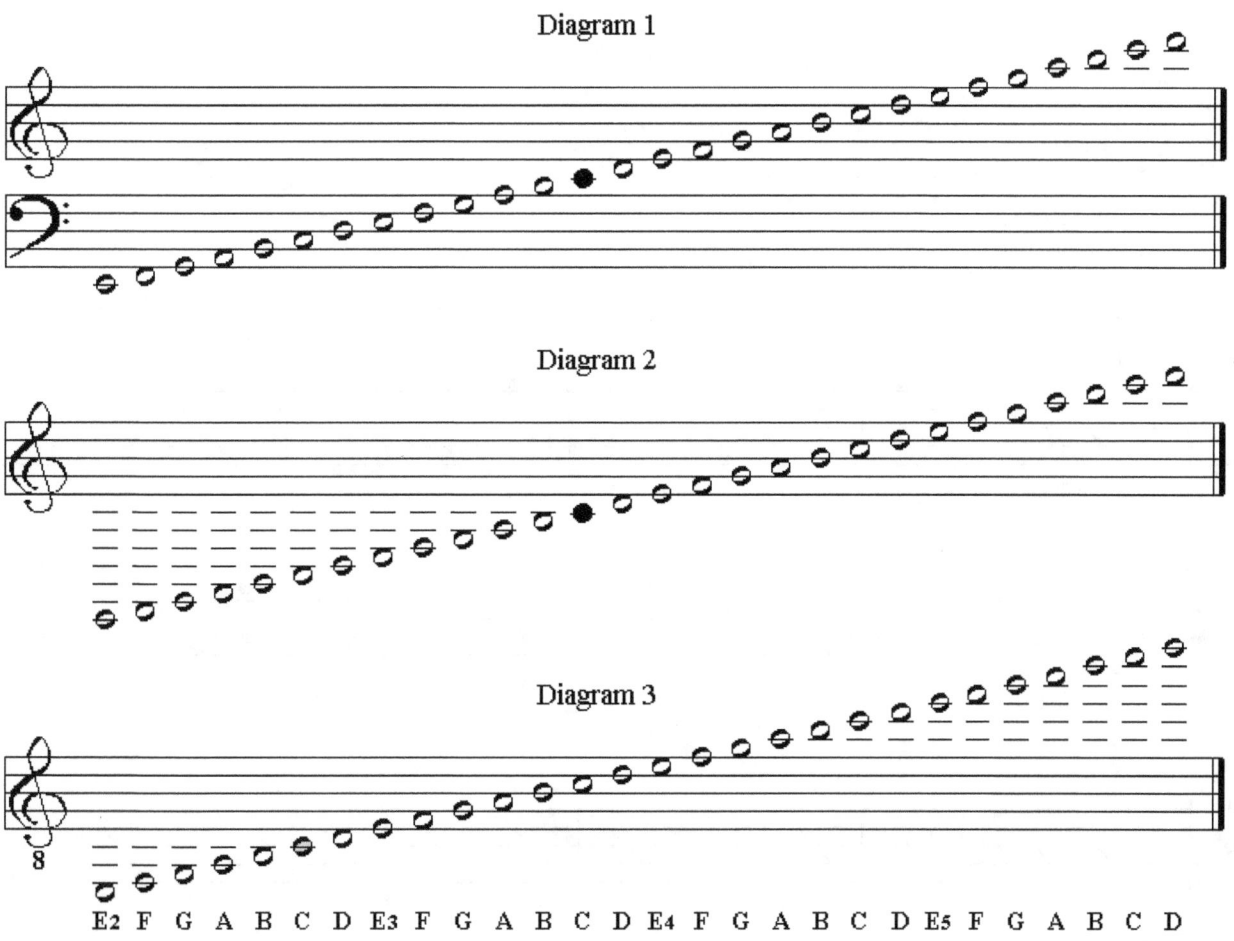

3-6

There are many forms music can take. The form shown below is a good example of a middle of the road form to learn from. Because of the repeated verses that have the same music but different words, little symbolic signs have been created with Italian words and acronyms to tell you where to go. If there were no repeats the music would require eight or so sheets rather than the usual two or three. After the title, authors and tempo/feel information the song starts with an **Introduction** of four bars. The **Verse** section with twelve bars/measures has three verses with a repeat and Dal Segno (It., Sanyo) sign. So we'll play the twelve bars of the **first verse** until we come to the **first ending** which has two bars and a repeat sign which directs us back to the repeat sign at the beginning of the **second verse** Play through the twelve bars of the second verse this time going directly to the **second ending**, bypassing the first ending. Continue on through the two bars of the second ending and play the twelve bars of the **bridge** where you'll find the *D.S. al Coda* together with a Dal Segno sign, which means return to the sign. This will take us back to the Dal Segno sign at the beginning of the **third verse**, which we'll play through the twelve bars until we come to the *To Coda* sign that will take us directly to the *Coda* sign of the **ending section.** Play the four bars of the ending section, make a dramatic ending and you are *Fine*.

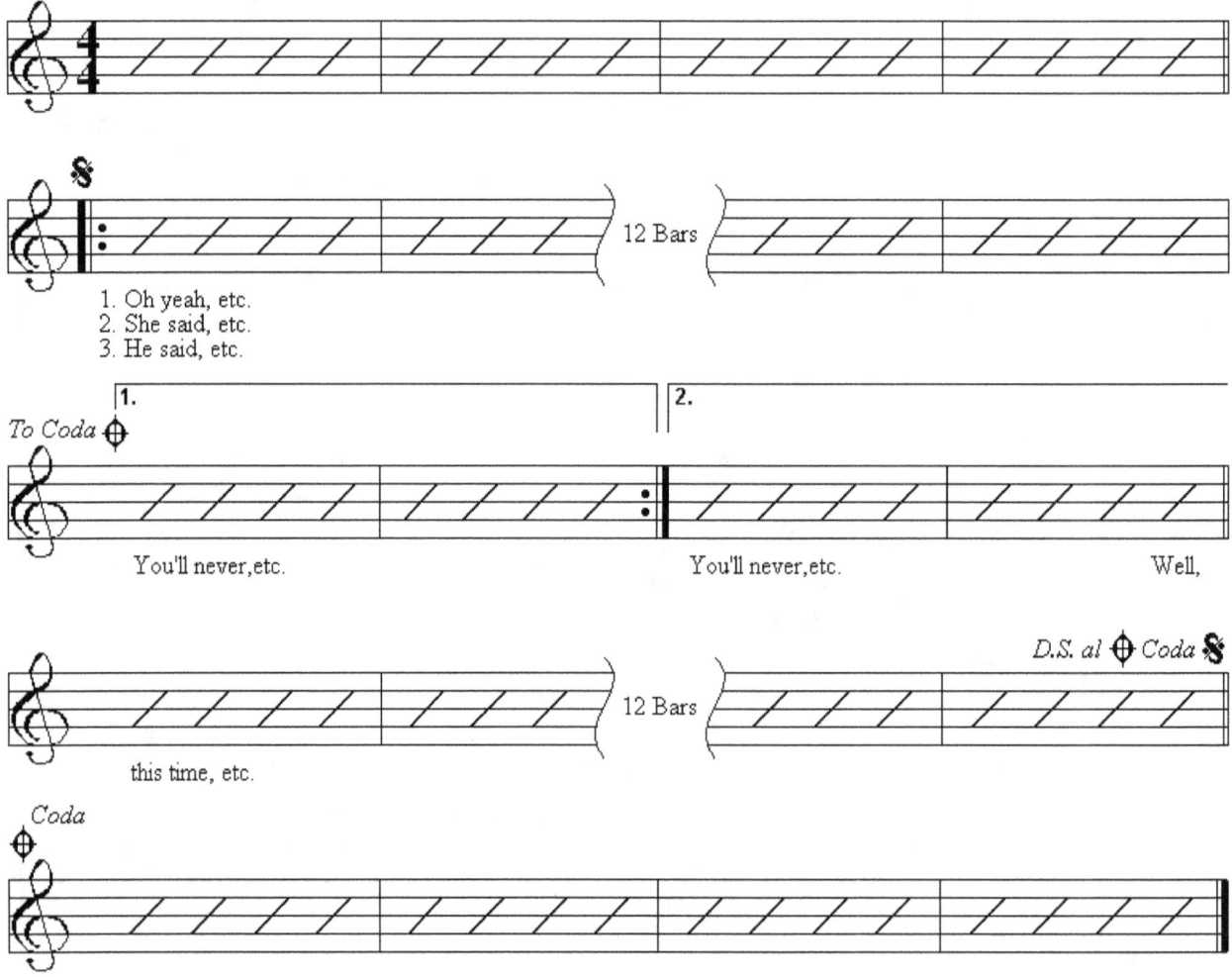

Form is important since it gives us an outline with which to follow. Since different parts or sections of the song are variations on the original theme, which is usually presented in the first verse, the sections of the form help us to keep the song organized. Music can be complex and our hearing can deceive us, so by being organized through the form, the song can be followed easier, which in turn helps us to understand the song better. Form is used as a reference.

The form of the example song on the previous page is: A A B A. The A sections are verses 1, 2, and 3 and the B section is the bridge. If there was an instrumental, which is a solo based on the melody/theme of the verses, this would be called section C and the form would then be defined as A A B C A. This could also change simply by changing the order in which the sections are played. It can be seen that when a new section is added to a song it would generate a new arrangement, which in turn creates a new form. There are many forms to be found in our rich musical heritage.

Tempo

<> Tempo is the rate of speed a musical piece is played and is expressed in Beats Per Minute (BPM). For Example:

If a composition were to be played at ♩ = 60 in 4/4 time, there would be sixty beats per minute counted with a quarter note equaling one beat.

<> A Metronome is a device that makes steady click sounds in a specific time frame which can be set to various tempos.

<> Metronome markings with the Italian names define the different tempos in BPM.
(Settings can vary between different metronomes.)

    40 - 49 *Largo* - very slow.
    50 - 60 *Larghetto* - a little faster than Largo.
    61 - 65 *Lento* - slow.
    66 - 71 *Adagio* - slow, between Lento and Andantino.
    72 - 76 *Andantino* - a little slower than Andante.
    77 - 107 *Andante* - moderate, walking speed.
    108 - 120 *Moderato* - moderate.
    121 - 149 *Allegretto* - moderately fast, a little slower than Allegro.
    150 - 168 *Allegro* - fast.
    169 - 199 *Presto* - very fast.
    200 - 208 *Prestissimo* - as fast as possible.

<> *Accelerando* - Gradually play faster.

<> *Retardando* - Gradually play slower.

<> Dynamics - the various degrees of volume (loudness), which is essential in the expression of emotion:

PP = *Pianissimo* - very soft.
P = *Piano* - soft.
MP = *Mezzo Piano* - moderately soft.
MF = *Mezzo Forte* - moderately loud.
F = *Forte* - loud.
FF = *Fortissimo* - very loud.

 = *Crescendo* - a gradual increase in loudness.

 = *Diminuendo* - a gradual decrease in loudness.

Symbols

Staccato - Cut the note short leaving a gap between it and the next note.

Legato - A curved line drawn over two or more notes of different pitch indicates to play in a smooth and connected manner. Also called a **slur**.

= **Fermata** - Hold the note longer than its original value. Often found at the end of a song.

> = **Accent** - Play the note a little louder.

Repeats

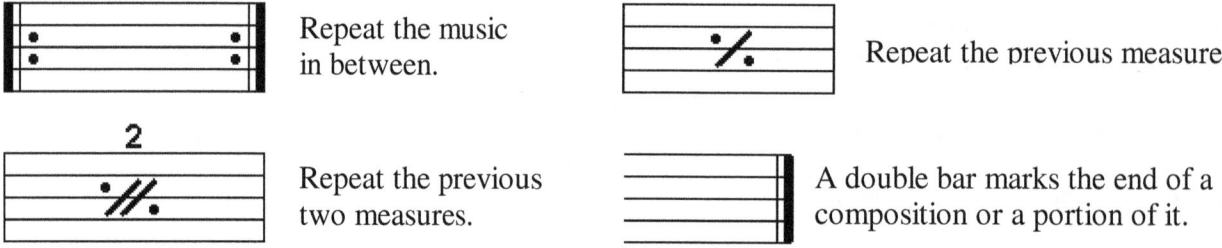

Repeat the music in between.

Repeat the previous measure.

Repeat the previous two measures.

A double bar marks the end of a composition or a portion of it.

Finger Picking

Picking The Strings

Picking Hand

The Picking Hand diagram letters are of Spanish origin, and are used for reference in notation, instructing the musician as to which fingers are to pick which strings. The picking and strumming hand fingernails should be long enough so they can be just seen when looking at the palm of the hand. This allows the flesh of the end of the finger and the fingernail to contact the string in equal amounts, which will give the string a balanced warm yet bright sound.

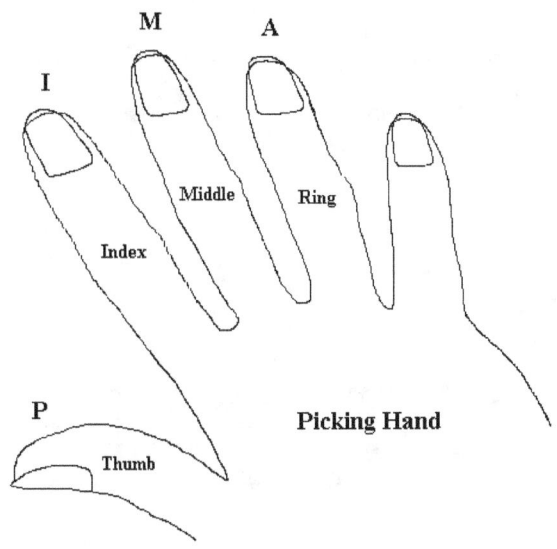

P = Pulgar (Thumb)
I = Indicio (Index)
M = Mayor (Middle)
A = Anular (Ring)

Finger Picking Form

The Finger Picking Form diagram shows the proper position of the picking hand in relation to the guitar. When picking the strings, keep the hand level and steady, moving only the fingers - not the whole hand over the sound hole with the fingers lightly striking or skimming the top of the strings making contact with both the flesh and the nail. Be careful not to "claw" the string from underneath and pull up as this action will slow you down because your hand will be pulled away from the strings making it difficult to return quickly and accurately to the next string to be played. The fingers should remain, when not in action, hovering just above the strings.

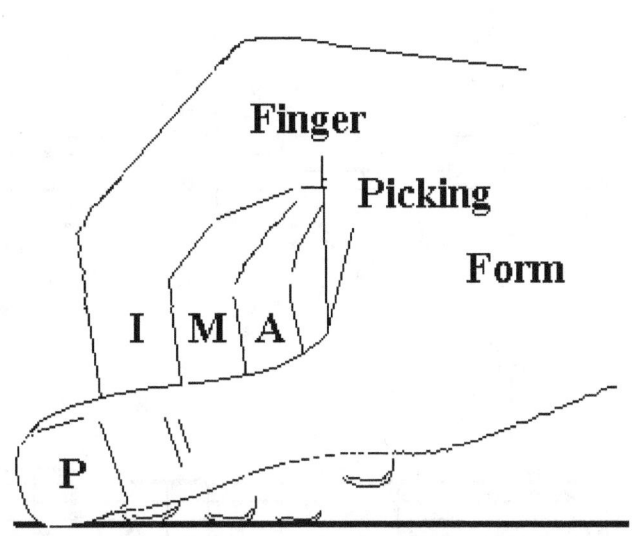

Arpeggio Study

The Arpeggio Study is a basic picking technique using the five basic chords with one variation, the E7 chord, for taking the student through the first step in developing a picking style. The straight forward P - I - M - A - M - I finger picking done twice on each chord helps to get established on each chord before changing to the next. The thumb plays the root of each chord producing a strong bass line. In the chords G, E and E7 the fifth string is not played so there is a jump from the sixth string, played by the thumb (P) and the fourth string, played by the first (I) finger.

The triplet is an interesting rhythm with three eighth notes played in each beat. The way they are counted is: one-trip-let, two-trip-let, three-trip-let, four-trip-let - for each measure.

Finger pick slowly and evenly to a metronome or computerized song generator speeding up only when the chord changes can be made smoothly.

Chapter

4

Time Signatures

Rhythm

The staff is divided by vertical lines called bar lines into portions called either measures or bars. Each measure is given a measurement of time by the time signature.

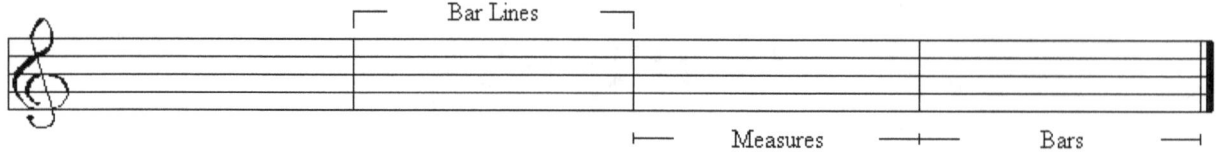

Time Signatures

Since the staff is divided into measures for the measurement of rhythm, a time signature is placed to the right of the clef sign at the beginning of the song to inform us as to how many beats will occur in each measure (top number) and which note will receive one beat (bottom number). The most commonly used examples shown below will get you acquainted.

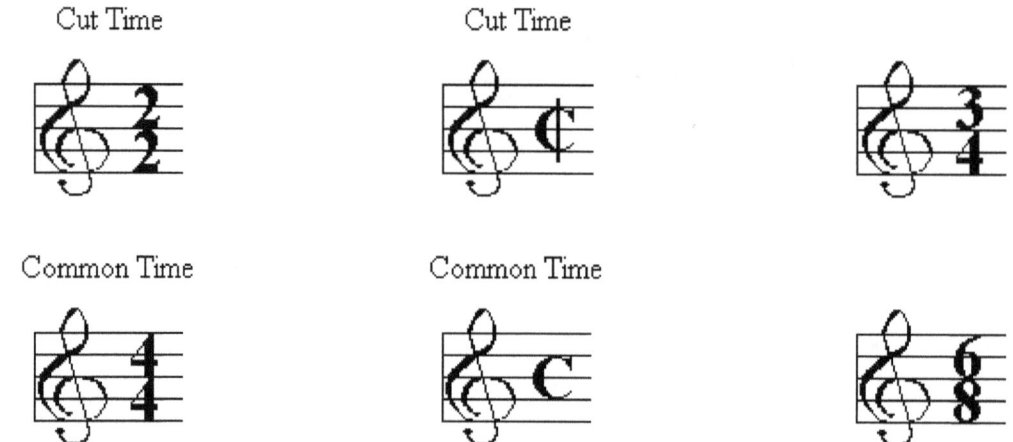

The time signature examples shown below follow the same rules as the time signatures shown above but are more complex thus allowing for more rhythmic freedom.

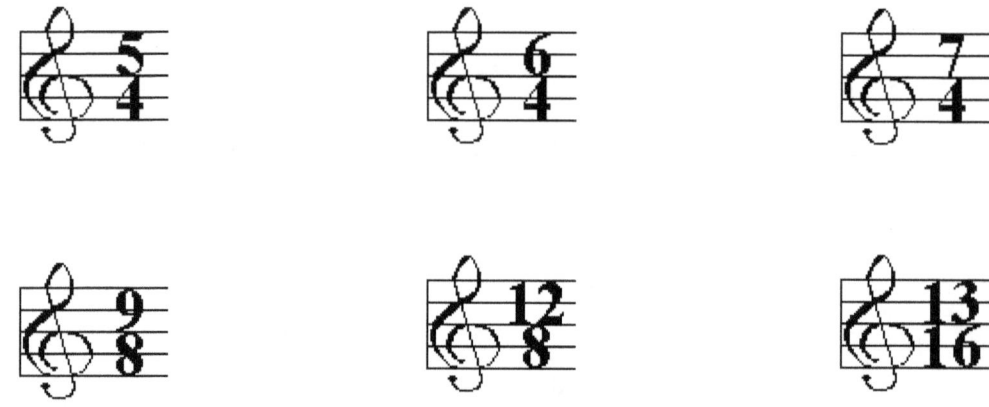

The bottom number must be one of the seven note time values: 1/1, 1/2, 1/4, 1/8, 1/16, 1/32 or 1/64. The top number can be what ever you want. Of course you'll have to to be able to play it!

Notes And Rest Values

In Common Time

The notes are placed on the staff:

Notes

The staff is divided into measures of time. Each of the seven types of notes are given a time value so we will know how long the duration of each note will sound for within each measure.

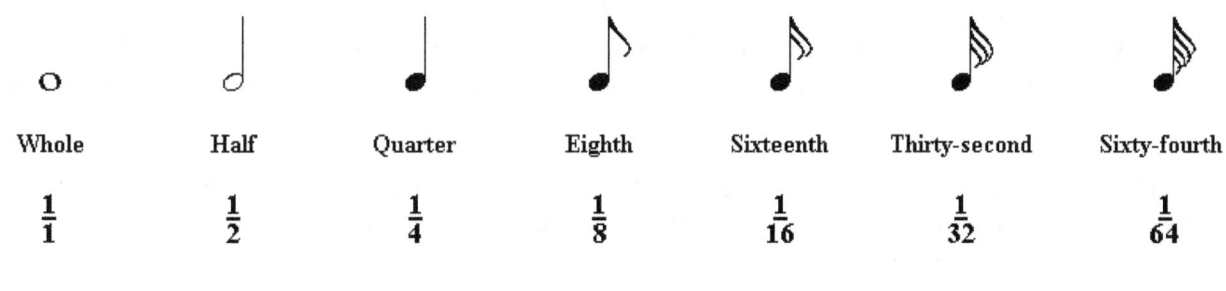

Rests

Rests are the silent counterpart of notes and are also given a time value.

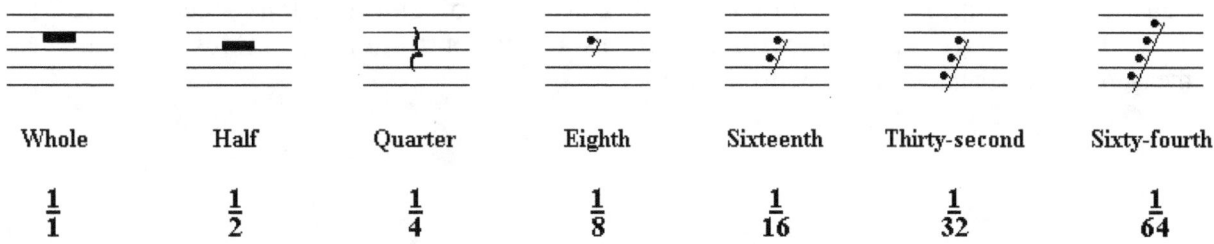

Note Time Value Divisions

In Common Time

Rhythm is the arrangement of beats in a measure of time. We can endlessly arrange the different notes within the measures of songs to create interesting and varied rhythms of music.

In the Note Time Value Divisions diagram the seven types of notes are displayed.

Below are the seven types of notes with their defining qualities.

Whole Note: Sounds for four beats. Strike the string once and let it sound for four beats while counting 1 - 2 - 3 - 4. This equals one whole note played within four beats.

Half Note: Sounds for two beats. Strike the string once and let it sound for two beats while counting 1 - 2. This equals one half note played within two beats. Two half notes equal a whole note.

Quarter Note: Sounds for one beat. Strike the string once and let it sound for one beat while counting 1. This equals one-quarter note played within one beat. Four-quarter notes equal a whole note.

Eighth Note: Sounds for a half of one beat. Count 1 while striking the string twice within the one beat and count one – and. This equals two eighth notes played within one beat. Eight, eighth notes equal a whole note.

Sixteenth Note: Sounds for a quarter of one beat. Count 1 while striking the string four times within the one beat and count one - e - and – a. This equals four sixteenth notes played within one beat. Sixteen, sixteenth notes equal a whole note.

Thirty-Second Note: Sounds for an eighth of one beat. Count 1 while striking the string eight times within the one beat and count one - e - a - a - and - e - a – a. This equals eight thirty-second notes played within one beat. Thirty-two, thirty-second notes equal a whole note.

Sixty-Fourth Note: Sounds for a sixteenth of one beat. Strike the string sixteen times within one beat and since it is to fast to count each strike, it must be felt. This equals sixteen sixty-fourth notes played within one beat. Sixty-four, sixty-fourth notes equal a whole note.

To help with the mathematical equations, it might be useful to compare the notes to a ruler: a whole note equals an inch, a half note equals a half an inch, a quarter note equals a quarter of an inch, an eighth note equals an eighth of an inch, a sixteenth note equals a sixteenth of an inch, a thirty-second note equals a thirty-second of an inch and a sixty-fourth note equals a sixty-fourth of an inch. Music is mathematical. Each measure must balance and equate to the whole.

Note Time Value Divisions

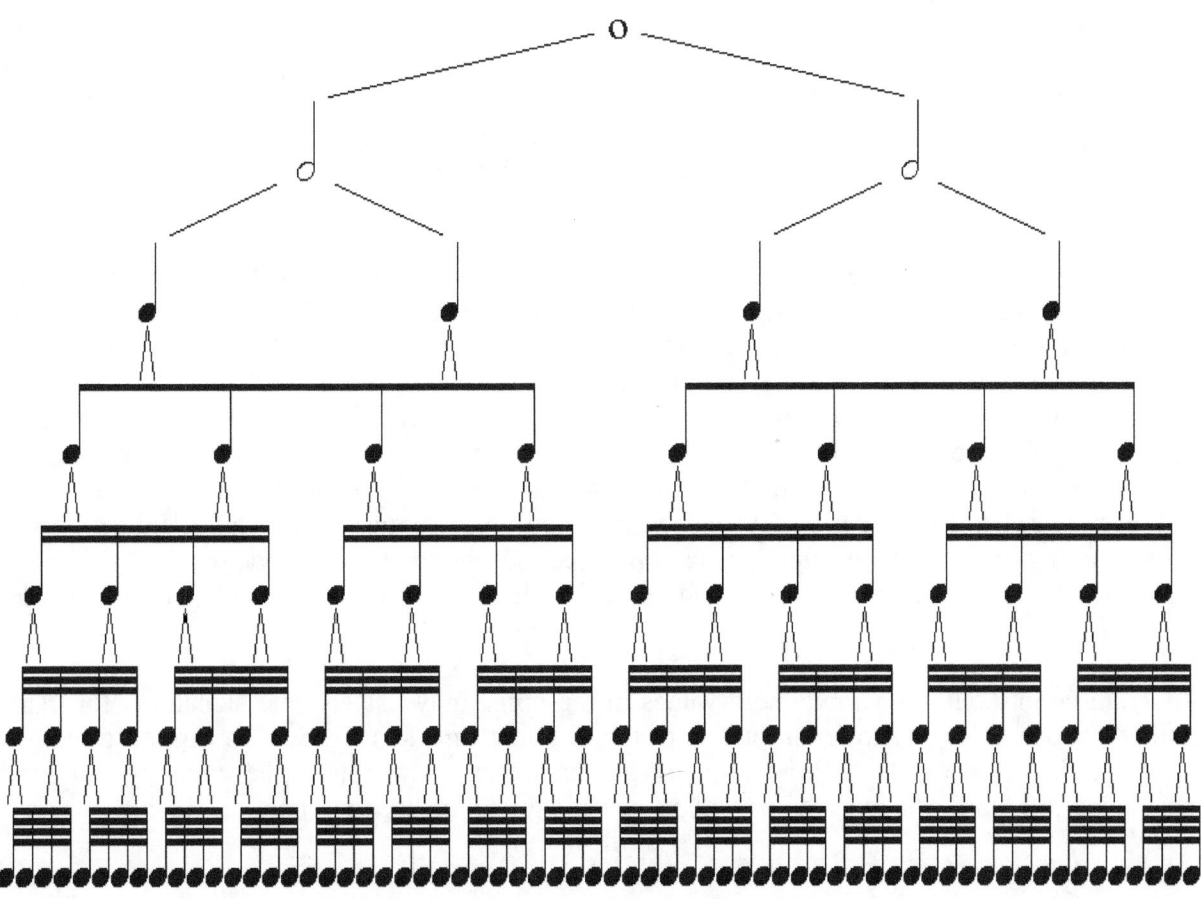

Time Signatures

Time signatures, consisting of an upper and lower number, are placed at the beginning of a composition indicating how many beats will be in each measure and what note will receive one beat.

<> The upper number indicates the number of counts or beats within each measure.

<> The lower number indicates what note receives one beat.

In the notation diagram on the following page everything is based on the whole note having four beats while the quarter note has one. This is known as common time and is so called because it is the standard time or basic equation from which all the other time signatures are based. Look to the diagram at measure nine. The equation 4/4 or common time tells us by the top number 4 that there are four beats in each measure. The bottom number 4 is a 1/4, which means the quarter note receives one beat. Let's now look at the 3/4 time signature at measure seventeen. The upper number tells us there are three beats in each measure and the bottom number once again means the quarter note receives one beat. At measure one the time signature 2/2 indicates that there are two beats to the measure, as shown by the top number and the bottom number 2 which is 1/2 tells us the half note receives one beat. At measure twenty-five the time signature 6/8 designates six beats to the measure with the eighth note receiving one beat. The upper number is easy to understand as it always indicates the number of beats in a measure. It can be any number you want but for practical and playable reasons 2, 3, 4, 6, 8 and 12 are the more common beats in a measure with 5 and 7 being interesting, but less used. The lower number is simply a fraction of the whole. If the bottom number is a four, it is a fourth of a whole or a quarter, which means the quarter note receives one beat. If it is a two, it is a half of a whole or a half, then the half note receives one beat. If it is an eight, it is an eighth of a whole or an eighth and the eighth note receives one beat. The bottom number can only be of the seven of notes. The half, quarter, eighth and sometimes the sixteenth note types are the most used while the whole, thirty-second and sixty-fourth note types are impractical.

The different time signatures are one of the main contributing factors that sets Western music apart from Eastern music. Each time signature gives the music a different rhythmic feel. For some examples: 4/4 and 3/4 are regularly used in popular, rock, folk, country, blues and classical music with the accent or emphasis played on the one and three while the two and four beats are referred to as the back beat. 3/4 time gives the waltz its one - two - three, one - two - three feel with the accent on the one beat. 2/2 time is often called half time or cut time as it cuts 4/4 time in half and is used for marches; left, right, one, two, left, right, one, two. 2/2 time is half as slow as 4/4 time when played at the same tempo. 6/8 time is twice as fast as 3/4 time when played at the same tempo and is commonly found in Jazz with its one, two, three, four, five, six swing, eighth note triplet feel accenting the one and four beats. The time it takes to play each of the eight measures in 3/4 and 6/8 is the same; it's the beat that plays half as slow or twice as fast.

The diagram counts out the various note values in the commonly played time signatures for clarity of understanding. The best way to learn the feel of the different time signatures is to turn on a metronome to a slow setting of about 66 BPM and clap your hands for each note while counting out loud the numbers below the staff. The metronome will be a steady guide for keeping time.

Dotted Notes

A dotted note is an abbreviated expression that is half again the value of the note itself.

For example, the whole note has a value of four beats. The dot following the whole note has a given value of two beats, which is half of the value of the whole note. Add the two together and the dotted whole note will sound for six beats.

The whole note tied to the half note on the right of the equation is what the dotted whole note would look like if it were written out in its full expression.

The dotted note eliminates excess notation for ease of reading.

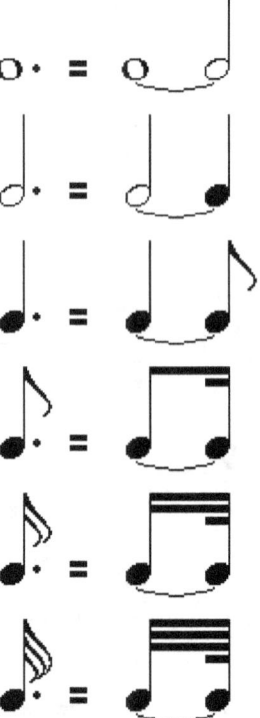

Shuffle Notation

The shuffle is an eighth note triplet feel (1) with the middle eighth note removed (2). It is notated as a triplet with a quarter note and an eighth note (3). Musically it is written as eighth notes with a note of instruction at the beginning of the song (4). This informs the musician that the eighth notes get a triplet feel.

The music is written this way (4) for the ease of reading since it would make the score too busy having all the quarter and eighth note triplets.

The Twelve Bar Blues

The twelve bar blues is the basic form for the blues. There are many blues forms that range from eight bar, twelve bar, sixteen bar, twenty-four bar to thirty-two bar blues. The blues stand on their own as a style of music and also function as the entry level for Jazz. The five songs, utilizing variations of the five basic chords, presented in this chapter gives the student the experience of playing the twelve bar blues in five different keys around the circle of fifths.

The slashes represent quarter notes. Each slash will be a down stroke of the strumming hand. Use the strumming hand technique learned on page 1-8. When the chord changes become smooth, play the songs with the shuffle feel. To understand how this feels, first clap your hands together while simultaneously counting triplets: one - trip - let, two - trip - let, three - trip - let, four - trip - let. Do this until you can comfortably keep the rhythm. Second, leave out the middle eighth note (trip) while clapping your hands together and simultaneously saying: ta - - - ta - ta - - - ta - ta, etc. Now that you understand the rhythm strum it on your guitar.

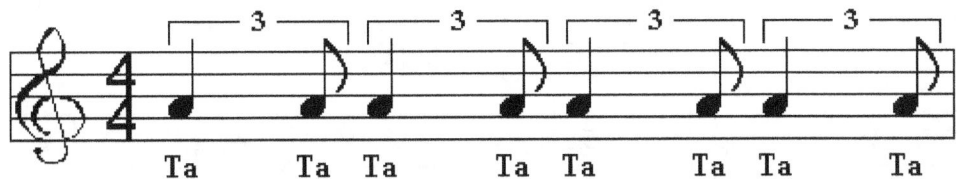

The tempo shown is the maximum speed in which the songs should be played. Start the song with a tempo as slow as 30 if necessary to be able to make the chord changes in time. If you are experiencing difficulty changing between two chords, which most students will, practice those two chords back and forth with each chord having one beat until the change can be done smoothly.

E7 Shuffle

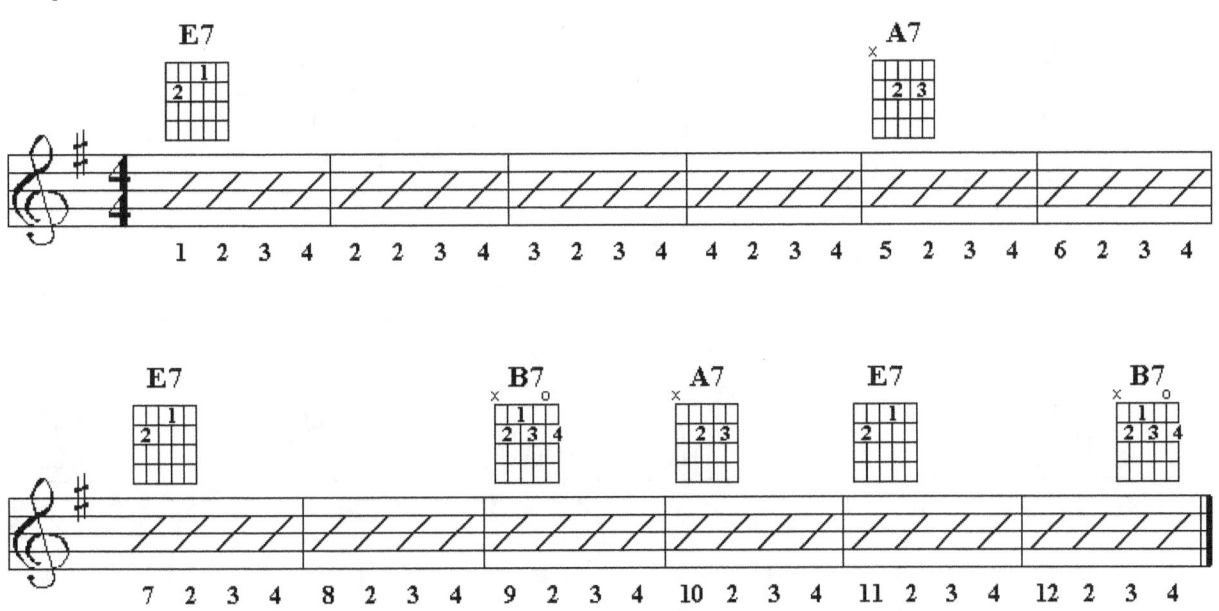

A7 Shuffle

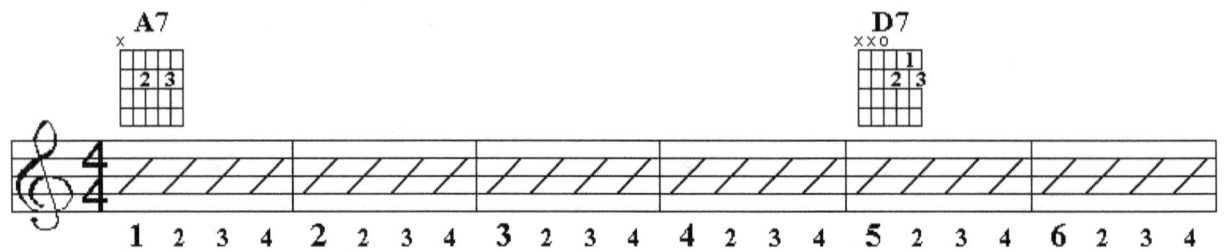

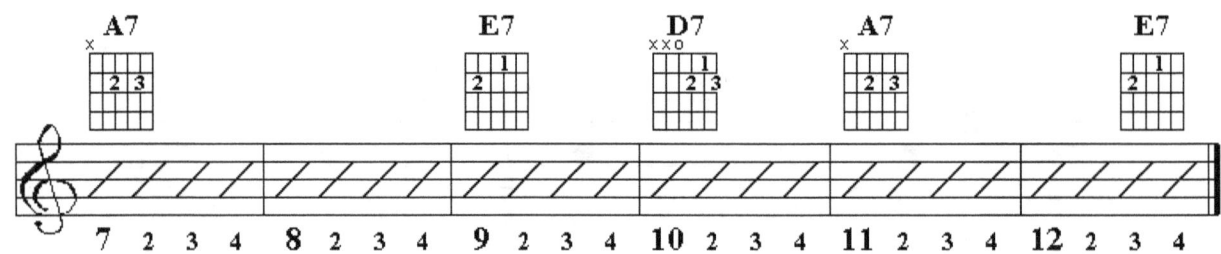

D7 Shuffle

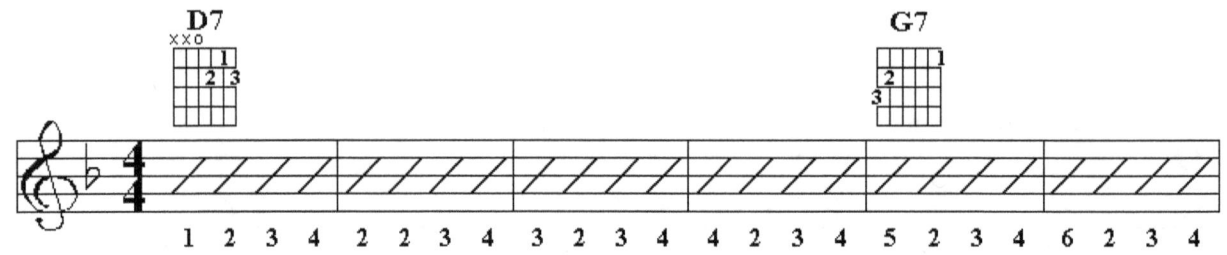

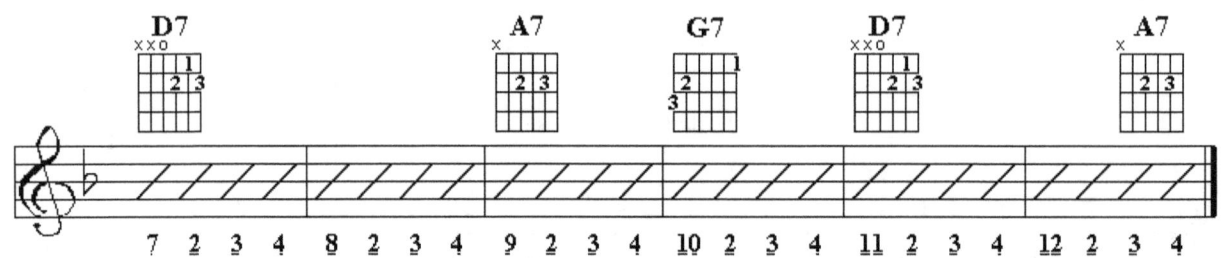

G7 Shuffle

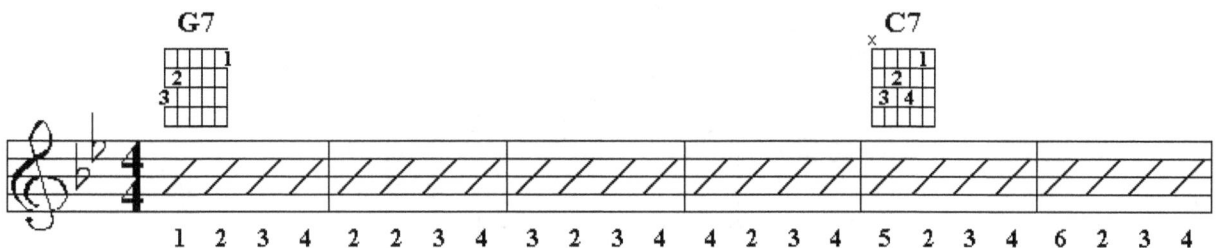

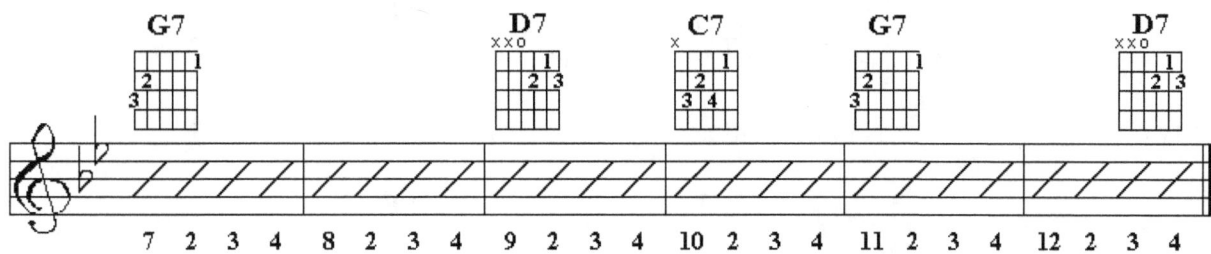

C7 Shuffle

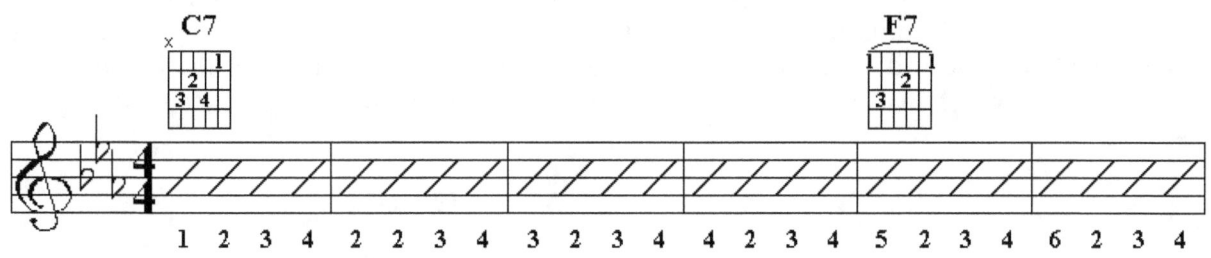

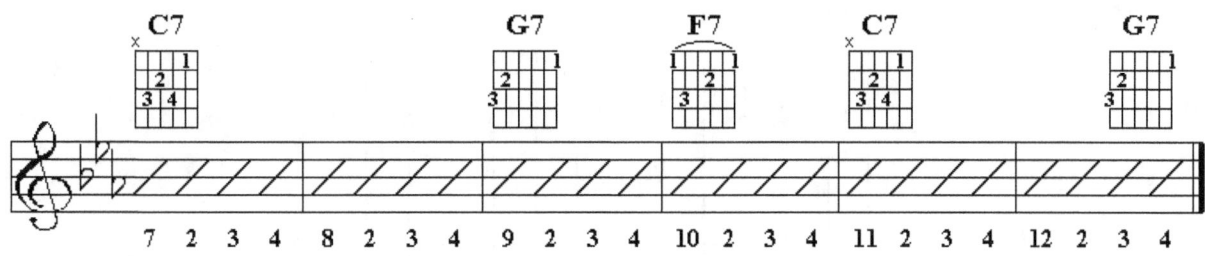

The Moveable E And A Forms

The E chord and the A chord are two of the easiest chords to play in the open position.

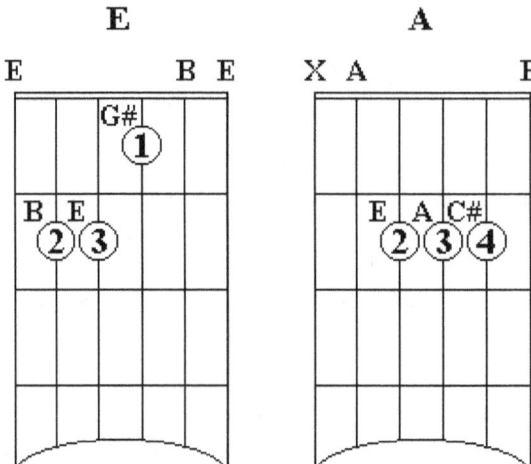

These two chords like all chords form a pattern. This pattern is called a form.

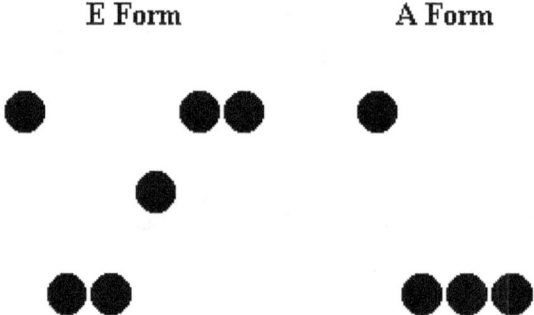

By replacing the nut of the guitar in the open position with our first finger we can take these forms, now called bar chords, move them up the neck of the guitar and play them in all twelve keys. The only thing that changes will be the chord name. The E and A barred forms are the easiest of the five basic barred chord forms to play, which makes them the most popular. They require regular practice to strengthen the muscles.

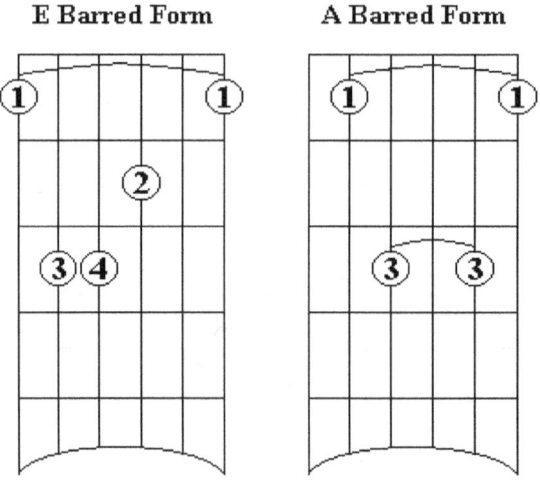

4-11

A7 Shuffle Barred

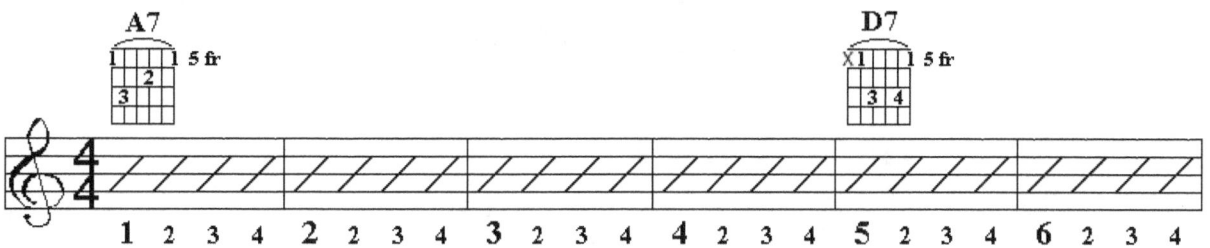
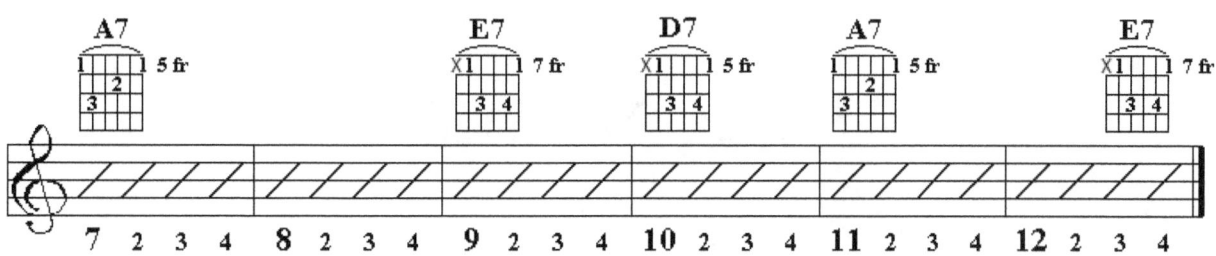

E7 Shuffle Barred

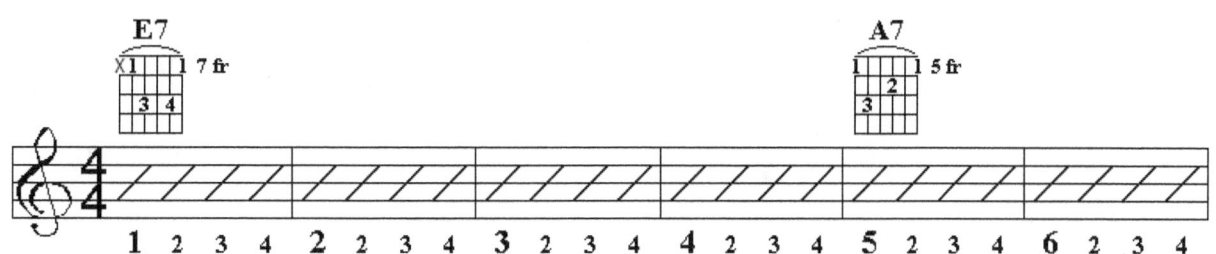
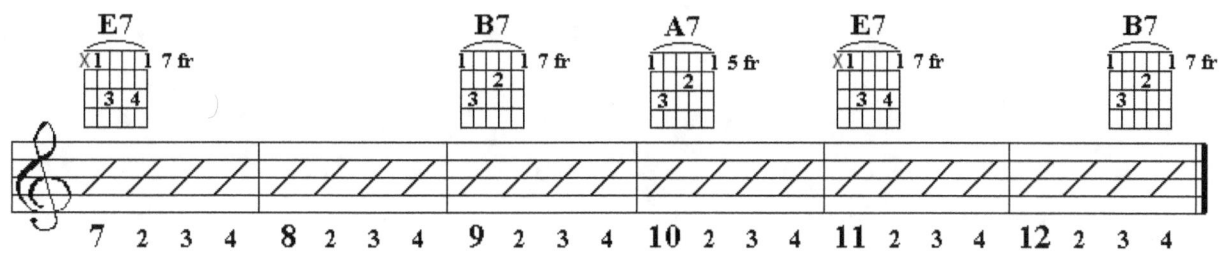

Chapter

5

Technique

How To Do It

Finger Picking The Strings

Finger picking on the guitar is pure pleasure, that is, once you get the hang of it. The exercises in this book are geared to do just that; to be able to play a song fluidly, interchanging between finger picking, flat-picking or strumming with ease. The exercises listed below are for the finger picking hands technical development of finger independence. It is advisable that the student practices the scales, modes and technical exercises in this text with each of these alternating finger exercises if a high level of excellence is desired.

Alternate thumb and index fingers:	P I P I	etc.	Clean, unique and very fast.
Alternate index and middle fingers:	I M I M	etc.	Traditionally classical.
Alternate middle and ring fingers:	M A M A	etc.	Good exercise for finger picking.
Alternate index and ring fingers:	I A I A	etc.	Good exercise for finger picking.
Alternate ring and index fingers:	A I A I	etc.	Reverse of # 4 above.
Alternate ring and middle fingers:	A M A M	etc.	Reverse of # 3 above.
Alternate middle and index fingers:	M I M I	etc.	Reverse of # 2 above.

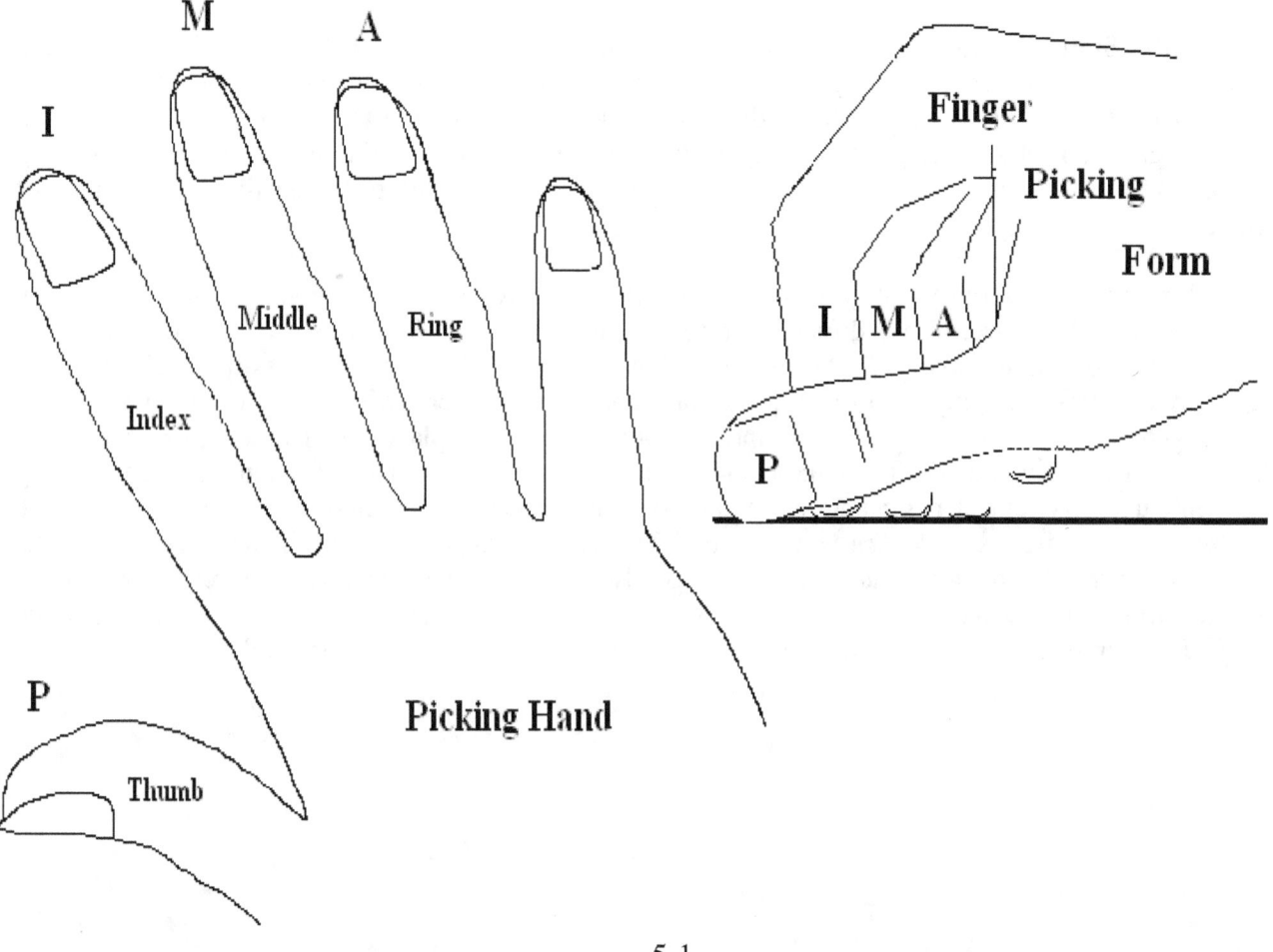

Technique Builder

Chromatic scales can be used in any style of music but are predominately used in jazz and jazz related styles such as blues, and fusion. In our Western system of music the chromatic scale is the mother scale in which there are twelve tones, each half on the guitar. From the chromatic scale all other scales are created. The chromatic exercises on the following page are an excellent way to develop independent fretboard hand finger technique, regardless of any style of music you intend to play. Practice each exercise using all the picking techniques previously learned on pages 1-8 and 5-1, which is the best method to developing the picking hand. Play slowly! Play evenly - use a metronome.

Linear: Play the E on the open sixth string, then proceed with the first finger on the first fret, second finger on the second fret, keeping the fingers on the string until all four fingers have played their notes, then shift to the second hand position, again starting with first finger, only now on the A of the fifth fret, continue again until all four fingers have played their notes, then shift to the third hand position starting at C# on the ninth fret. When the fourth finger has reached the twelfth fret, in the third hand position, slide the fourth finger up one fret, a half step to the thirteenth fret, releasing the rest of the fingers, then slide it back to the twelfth fret and proceed by descending through the three hand positions in reverse, only this time, keep one finger on the fret board at a time, releasing each finger as you descend the fret board, returning to the open E note. The shift change between the hand positions should be smooth and without any interruptions. Practice each string individually, then, ascend and descend all six strings in one continuous movement, beginning and ending on the sixth string open E. The crossing over to each string should also be smooth and without any interruptions.

Lateral Shift: Start with the B note on the seventh fret of the sixth string with the first finger and proceed to play up the neck, once again keeping the fingers on the string until all four fingers have played their notes, then cross over to the fifth string while shifting down a fret and proceed in the same manner. Practice on all six strings, ascending and descending in one continuous movement beginning and ending on the sixth string. There is no shift between the second and third strings due to the tuning of the guitar.

Lateral Barred: This exercise will prepare you for playing chords with a melody, bass and lead within a position. Although this exercise is difficult due to the barre, stay with it, as this is truly one of the most powerful secrets of guitar playing. By laying and holding down the first finger across the neck on all six strings; play on the sixth string with the second, third and fourth fingers, with a slide up the neck by the fourth, keeping all the fingers on the string until all four fingers have played their notes, then cross over to the fifth string and proceed in the same manner. Practice on all six strings, ascending and descending in one continuous movement beginning and ending on the sixth string. It might be easier to start at the eighth fret since the frets are closer together there. To play a barre without the strings buzzing, let the weight of your fret board arm lead you as you gently pull down and backwards forcing the fingers against the fret board, while at the same time gently resisting with the finger picking arm against the body of the guitar. Take your time and be patient, most skilled guitarists have learned this.

Chromatic Exercises

Technique Builder

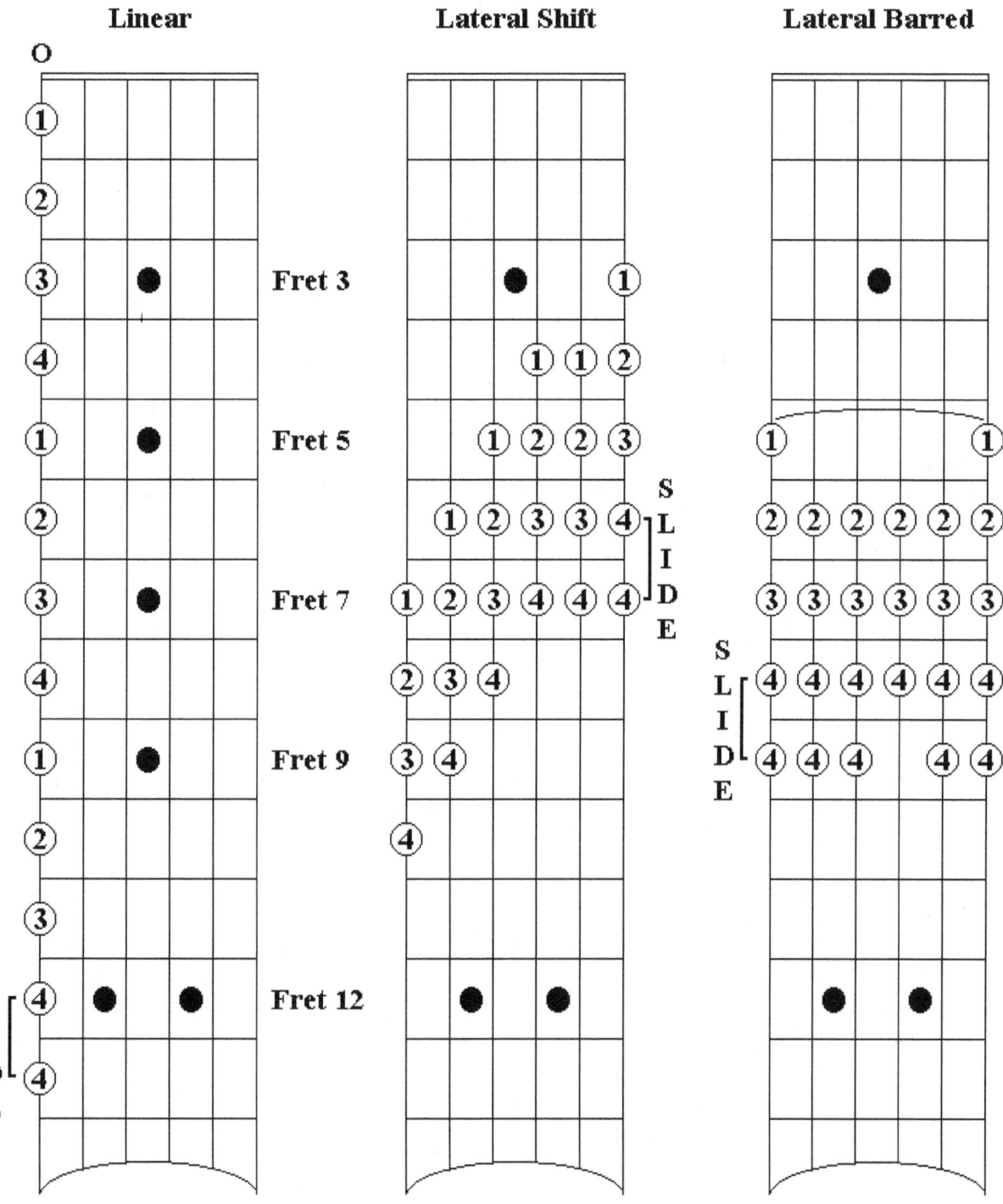

Chapter 6

Key Signatures

Circle Of Fifths

The circle of fifths on the outside of the circle is a convenient diagram that shows the progression of sharp keys in the order that they develop. As you move clockwise around the circle of fifths one sharp will be added to each key signature. C has no sharps, G has one sharp, D has two, etc.

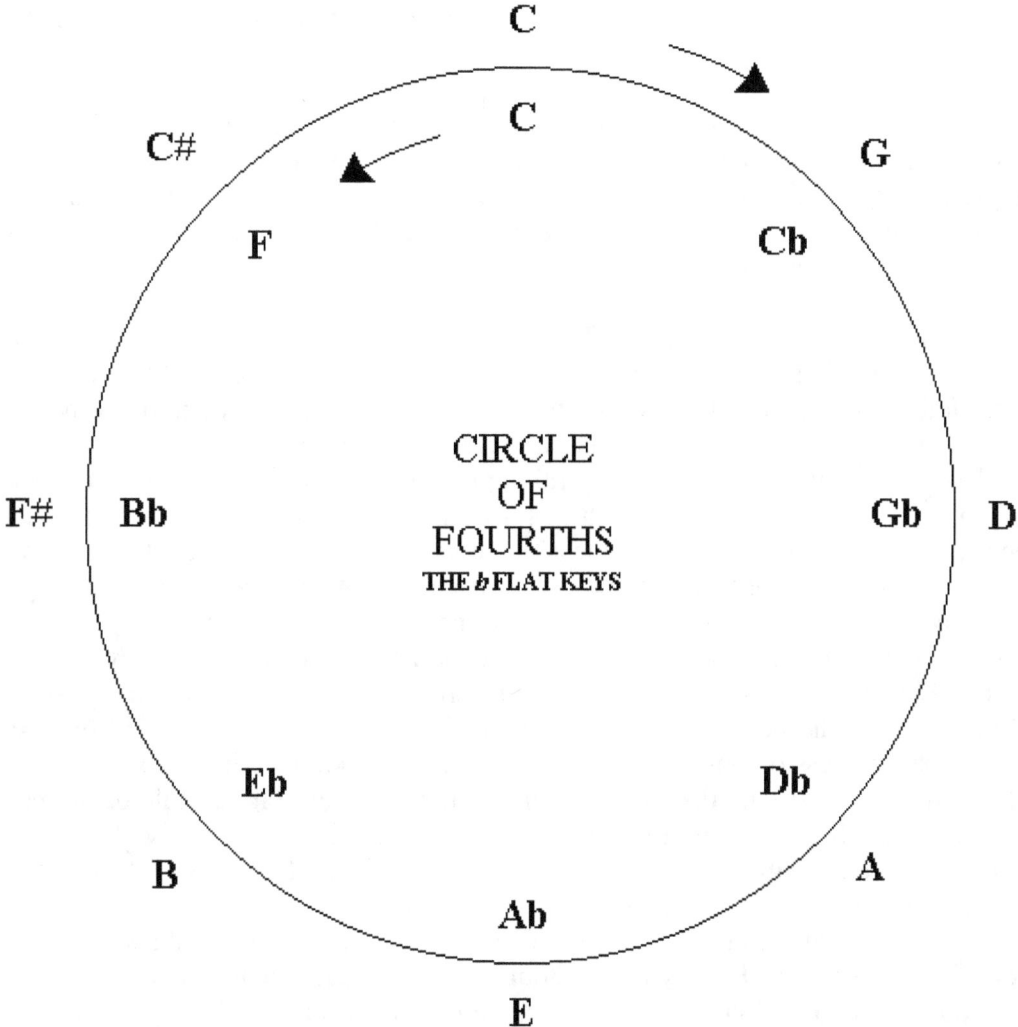

Circle Of Fourths

The circle of fourths on the inside of the circle is a convenient diagram that shows the progression of flat keys in the order that they develop. As you move counterclockwise around the circle of fourths one flat will be added to each key signature. C has no flats, F has one flat, Bb has two, etc.

Key Signatures

Up to this point we have used the C major scale, in the Key of C, to teach the lessons of this book. If this was all there was to it, our ability to write songs would be limited. The circle of fifths, with its various key signatures, is another factor that makes Western music unique from the music of the rest of the world. Music is used for different purposes, such as: Eastern music, which is repetitive with a strong rhythmic feel, uses a scale usually played monophonically, that is, a single melodic line so as to induce a trance like state for meditation. The idea is to leave the five senses and find the inner peace. Western music on the other hand is based in the five senses with the idea of expressing ones feelings through music. This way feeling can be shared and associated with others on an emotional level. To accomplish this, Western music requires different keys. There are two important functions key signatures give the guitarist:

1) The pitch of a song can be raised or lowered to different keys generally without changing the pattern of the melody or the chords. This way a song can be played in any key to accommodate a singers voice range by simply moving to the new position and generally play the same patterns of scales and chords just as it was done in the previous key. Also, some keys are better suited for fret board fingerings in certain guitar arrangements than others.

2) The second function is key modulation. This is rather technical and has not yet been but will be covered in depth so it is suggested to read this for the value of an overview, which will prepare you for the lessons that follow. Key modulation is used to enhance a song by moving into another key raising or lower the overall pitch of the song. This has a powerful effect that uplifts a song that is perhaps repetitious and needs a change. There are several approaches or passageways used to modulate into a new key: 1) Moving up chromatically one half step to a new key will give a lift to a song. The effect is likened to acceleration although the tempo doesn't increase. 2) A song can be intriguing by the seeming mysterious passage from one key to another giving a complexity to the song. One way this type of modulation is done is by entering into another key via the V7 chord of the new key. The circle of fifths and fourths are used for this purpose. To give an example let's say we're in the Key of C which has the chords C, F and G7 as its I, IV, V7 basic central chord progression. If I were to change the C chord to a C7 it would pull me into the new Key of F that has F, Bb and C7 as its I, IV, V7 basic central chord progression. Another and less obvious passage sound wise is to modulate into another key via one of the minor chords from the chord scale that is also found in the new keys chord scale being modulated into. Once again we'll use the Key of C and the Key of F for an example. The chord scale of the Key of C is: C, Dm, Em, F, G7, Am and Bm. The chord scale of the Key of F is: F, Gm, Am, B, C7, Dm and Em. It can be seen that Dm, Em and Am are chords common to both keys and can be used as passage ways for modulation. From the Key of F to the Key of C is five steps; F, G, A, B, C which is one part of the circle of fifths. From the Key of C to the Key of F is four steps; C, D, E, F which is one part of the circle of fourths. By modulating into various keys via the circle of fourths and circle of fifths some exciting and intriguing musical passages can be expressed and experienced.

In Western music the natural key signature is the Key of C, which has no chromatic signs. To keep the symmetry of the scales as they change from to key certain notes must be forced up or down a half step. This is one way Western music reflects Western philosophy. On the other hand Eastern music is asymmetrical without anything forced, reflecting the Eastern philosophy of accepting things as they are in the seeming chaotic events of life within which there is a perfectly peaceful core.

The Key Of C

The Key of C is easy. It has no key signature. That is because it is the natural key. The Key of C has natural half steps between the third, fourth and seventh, eighth degrees as shown on the staff:

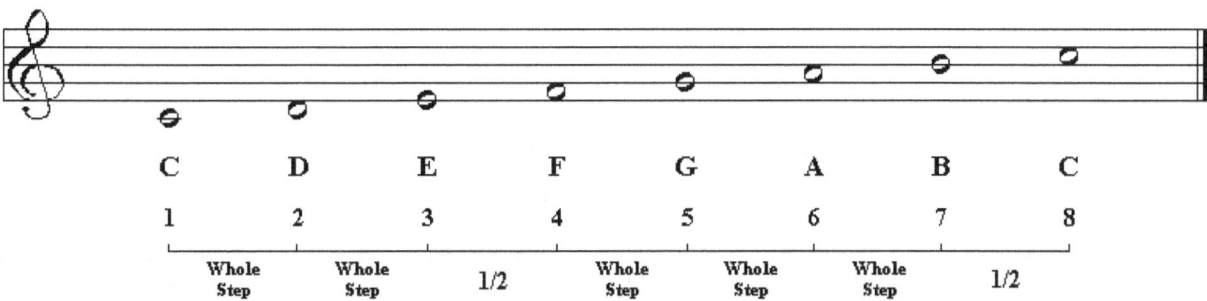

This can clearly be seen on the piano keyboard. The white keys are the C major scale repeated six times over six octaves with the natural half steps E, F and B, C occurring where there are no black keys. The black keys are half steps. If you were to play all the white and black keys one after the other from left to right, you would be playing the chromatic scale.

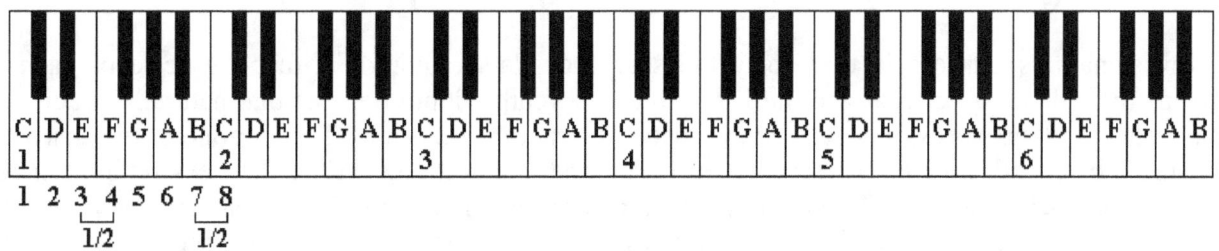

Now it should be understood that when looking at the guitar without the sharps and flats of the chromatic scale the guitar is in the Key of C. It can be seen that there are natural half steps occurring between E, F and B, C wherever they appear on the fret board. All of the rest of the notes are a whole step apart.

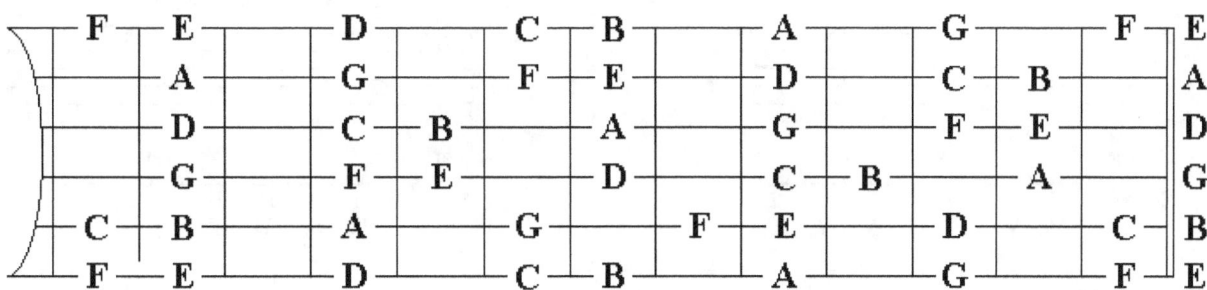

Key Signatures

The key signature designates which major key will be played. The key signature appears at the beginning of the song between the clef sign and the time signature and is comprised of:

Chromatic Signs

Sharp # raises the note one-half step.

Flat b lowers the note one-half step.

All notes, either on the lines or in the spaces of the staff that fall within the letter names of these chromatic signs will be raised or lowered one-half step. For example, in the Key of G there is an F# in the key signature. This means that all of the F notes in all of the octaves of the song will be raised one half step. This is done for the ease of reading. Otherwise all the F notes in the song would have to be written with an accidental (#) sharp sign in front of them, which would clutter the page with sharp signs.

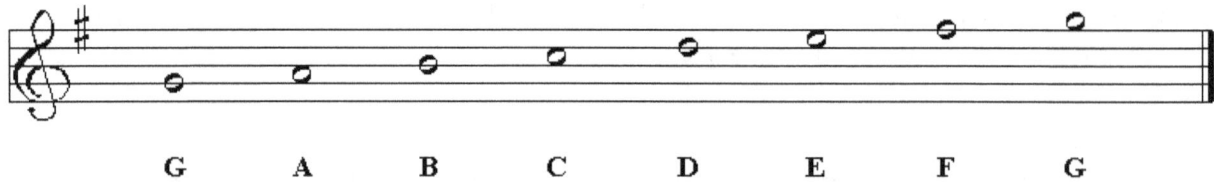

The key signatures purpose is to display the sharps or flats required so that the scale of each key maintains the half-steps between the third, fourth and seventh, eighth degrees that naturally occur in the major scale. In other words, to keep the symmetrical structure the same. This is done in the sharp keys by raising the seventh note of the scale in each key one half step and in the flat keys by lowering the fourth note in each key one half step. By placing a sharp or a flat in the key signature, this now forces that note one half step higher or lower respectively. For an example of this, the diagram below shows a comparison of the Key of C and the Key of G. The Key of G has one sharp and is the second key around the circle fifths after the Key of C. Count up five notes, C, D, E, F, G. C to G is an interval of a fifth. G is now the new Key and since F is the seventh degree of the G major scale and E to F is a natural half step which is now occurring between the sixth and seventh degrees, the F note must be raised one-half step to an F# so the sixth and seventh degrees will be a whole step and the seventh and eighth degrees will be a half step. This is necessary to maintain the half-steps between the third, fourth and seventh, eighth degrees so the major scale sound we're familiar with will remain the same in all keys with only the pitches changing.

 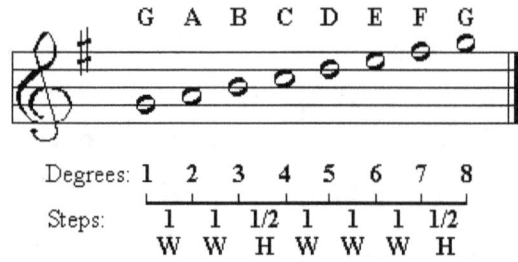

Key Development Study

ASSIGNMENT: 1) Write the note names below the notes of the staff with the chromatic signs in each key showing the notes that are sharped or flatted. For example: The notes of the Key of G would be written below the staff as: G A B C D E F# G. 2) With a V, show where the half steps are at the third, fourth and seventh, eighth degrees in each key. Notice that the half steps between the third, fourth and seventh, eighth degrees are maintained in each key by the key signatures.

Melody Study

The melody is derived from the major scale. It is individual notes played in succession one after the other of varied pitches and rhythmic values.

On the following five pages a simple song is presented in five keys around the circle of fifths. The song is a good example of how the melody is derived from the major scale. The song is easy enough for the beginner to play since the melody ascends and descends the major scale with little variation. Playing the same song in five different keys brings home the idea of different keys and key signatures.

Exercise

This is a good exercise for using the flat-picking technique. Start with the Melody Study in the Key Of C and play the C Major Scale ascending and descending to get a feel of the scale. With the flat pick or your finger play the first C note with a down stroke just lightly brushing the pick over the string. Next, use an up stroke of the pick or finger on the second D note. Continue alternating the up and down stokes of the pick or finger with each note you play moving smoothly without hesitation from one string to another. Remember to keep your remaining fingers relaxed in the palm of your picking hand, rotating the hand and arm together as you flat pick. Do not rest your fingers on the face of the guitar.

The two guitar diagrams below the staff will assist in reading the notes on the staff. The left diagram shows the names of the notes and the right diagram shows the correct fingers to use.

Now play the melody of the song Row Your Boat at the bottom of the page with the same technique used on the C Major Scale exercise.

Continue to practice the song by playing it in the other four keys.

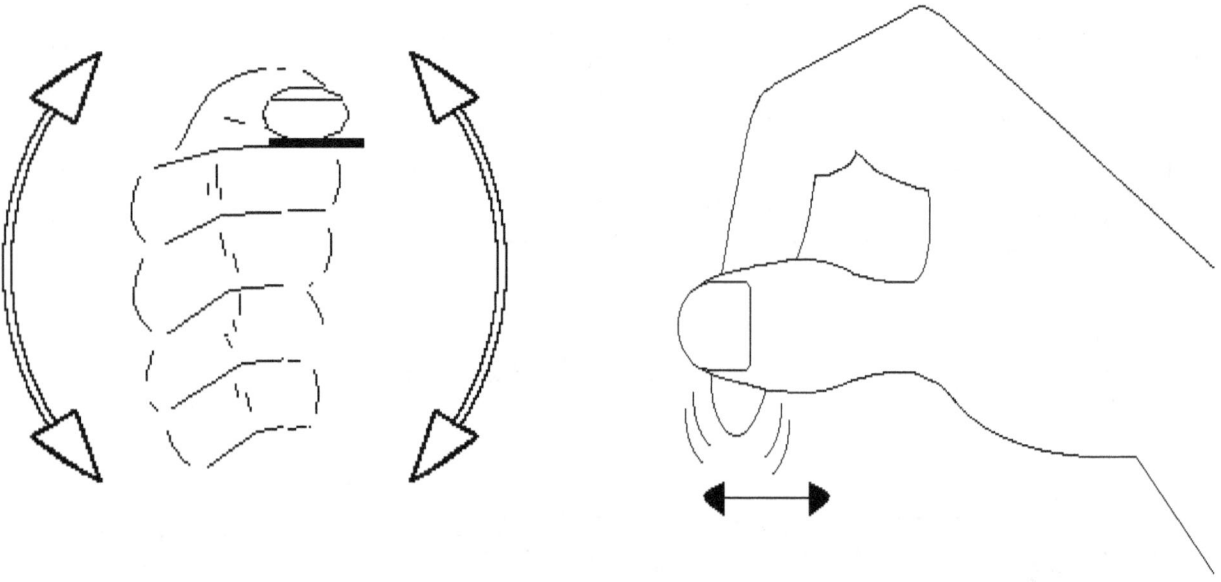

Melody Study

Key Of C

C Major Scale

C Major Scale

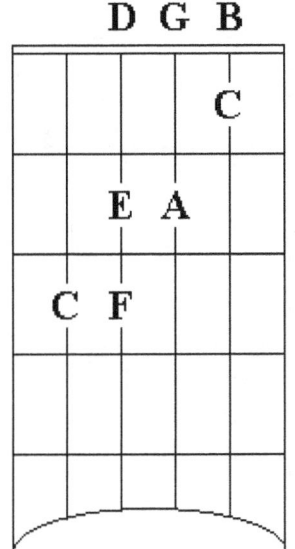
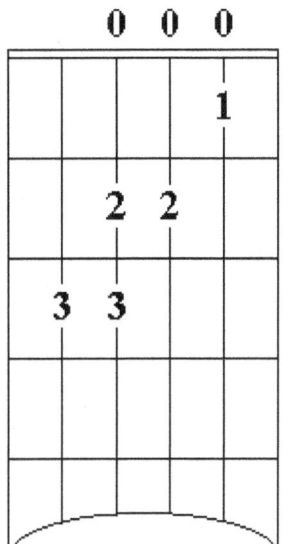

Row Your Boat

Melody Study

Key Of G

G Major Scale

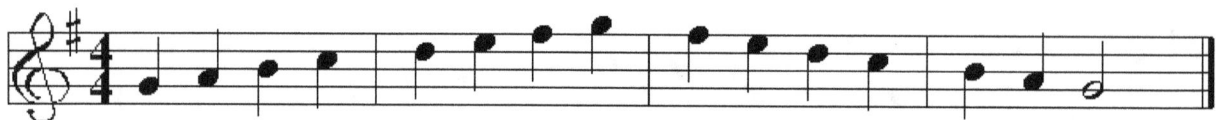

G Major Scale

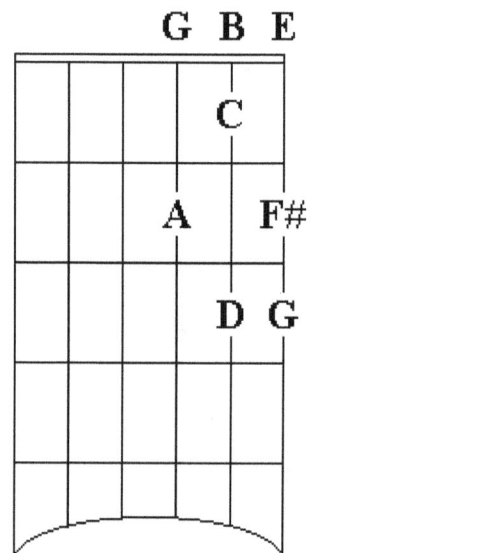
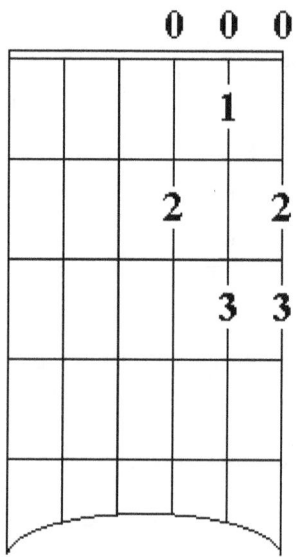

Row Your Boat

Melody Study

Key Of D

D Major Scale

D Major Scale

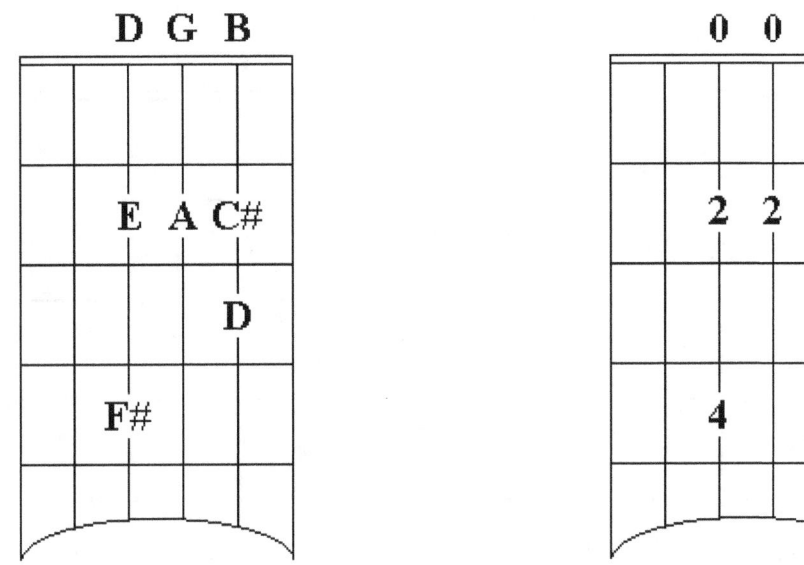

Row Your Boat

Melody Study

Key Of A

A Major Scale

A Major Scale

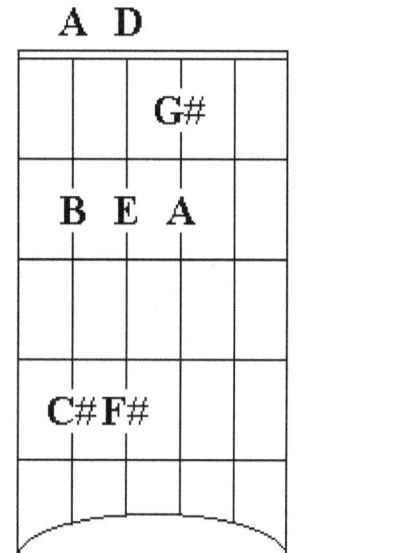
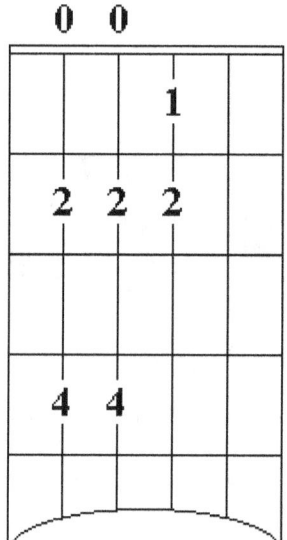

Row Your Boat

Melody Study

Key Of E

E Major Scale

E Major Scale

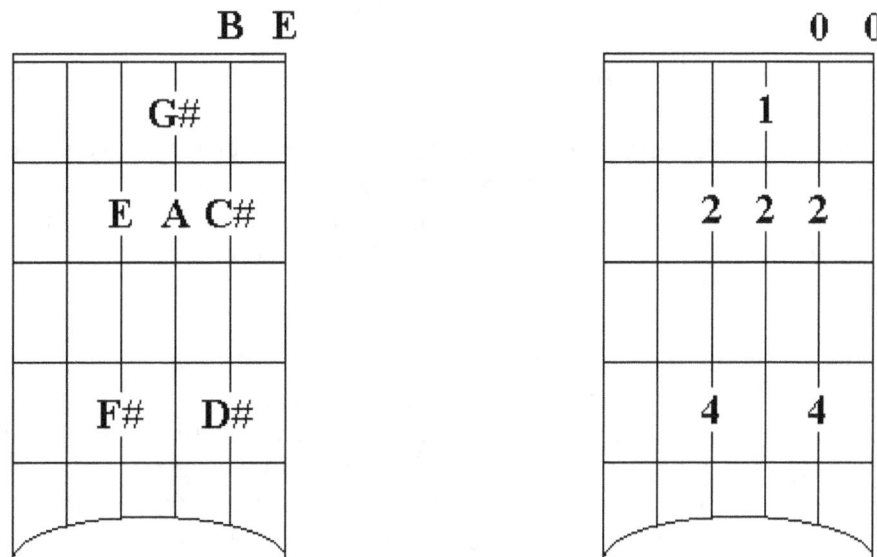

Row Your Boat

Accidentals

Accidentals are a way for the composer/songwriter to alter the major scale within the key of a song. They allow the usage of the chromatic scale incrementally within a song making it more flexible for creative expression by offering a larger variety of interval relationships. This expands the listeners hearing beyond the basic scale usually resulting in an interesting song or at the very least something that is different. There are five accidentals available for your playing pleasure:

    Sharp # raises the note one-half step.

    Flat *b* lowers the note one-half step.

    Natural ♮ cancels the sharp or flat restoring the note to its original pitch.

    Double Sharp X raises the note two half steps.

    Double Flat *bb* lowers the note two half steps.

Notice that the sharp # and flat *b* signs serve double duty as accidentals and as chromatic signs.

The accidentals will alter a notes pitch and all of its octaves within the measure they are placed in. Altered notes within a measure can be altered again by another type of accidental once again changing that notes pitch and all its remaining octaves in that measure. The end of a measure nullifies the accidental unless the altered note is tied to another note in the following measure which will affect that note and all of its octaves until the end of that measure.

The diagram below will help clarify this. The naturalized F quarter note at the end of the third measure is tied to the first eighth note of the fourth measure. All the F notes in the fourth measure will be natural due to the influence of the tied natural F note coming in from the third measure so it is necessary to place an accidental sharp sign on the next F note if the composer wants the remaining F notes in that measure to return to the status of the key signature. In the fifth measure the F note is once again altered by a natural sign which casts its spell over all the remaining F notes in that measure until the sixth measure arrives nullifying the natural accidental sign and the F note returns to the influence of the key signature once again.

Study

Notes

Alternate Picking

The Alternate Picking exercise is an advanced picking technique. It actually comes from the banjo style of picking using only the thumb (P), index (I) and middle (M) finger of the picking hand. Once you get the feel of its syncopated liveliness you'll recognize its usage in many styles, especially country rock. It is more advanced than the Arpeggio Study and will require patience and concentration.

1) Notice the first beat in each measure is a quarter note and the rest are eighth notes. This will cause a syncopated feel due to the interaction between the quarter note and the following eighth note in each measure. This is the feel that gets people up to dance. It is characteristically similar to the syncopated strumming shuffle feel of the Blues (see Pages 4-7 & 4-8).

2) Observe that the thumb alternates between two notes on two different strings throughout the exercise. The thumb plays only the down beats and is counted as: **One - two - three – four**. Play through the entire exercise with only the thumb first to learn the alternating pattern. Next just play the three eighth notes in each measure with your middle (M) and index (I) fingers alternating on their two adjacent strings. When you are comfortable with the thumb playing its part and your fingers doing theirs add it all together and play slowly, increasing the tempo only as your ability allows. The over-all count is: **1   2 + 3 + 4 +** for each measure.

Once you have slowly achieved getting the thumb and fingers to play smoothly by feel, beyond thinking, then you can bring the song to life by picking up the tempo to 120 BPM and making your fingers "dance".

Alternate Picking

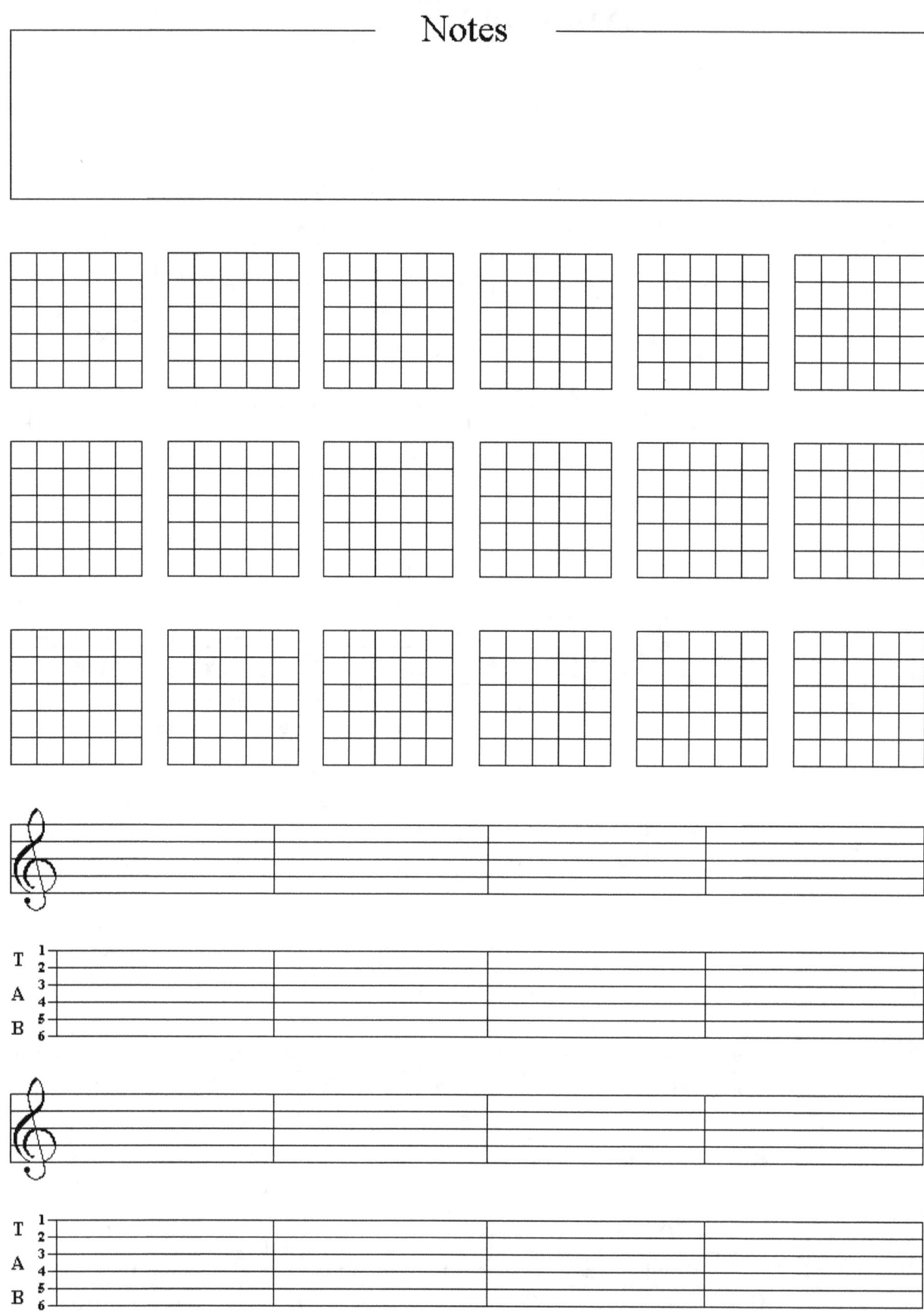

Chapter

7

Chord Harmony

Scale Degrees

Become familiar with the scale degrees since they are used to build chords, develop melodies, harmonize and communicate ideas. It is equally important to remember that there is always a half step between the third, fourth and seventh, eighth degrees of the major scale.

Intervals

An interval is the distance between two pitches identified by their position in the scale that build on and reference each other for meaning.

- Root to Minor Second: a tense, suspenseful sound used a lot in drama to create a fear effect.
- Root to Major Second: a suspended sound, the SUS 2 is hanging as if floating waiting to resolve to the root.
- Root to Minor Third: the sound used for the negative emotions: sad, lonely, funerals, failure, the blues, etc.
- Root to Major Third: the positive sound found in happy songs, patriotic songs, inspirational songs, weddings, etc.
- Root to Perfect Fourth: also a suspended sound, the SUS 4 is hanging as if floating waiting to resolve to the major third.
- Root to Augmented Fourth: a tritone, three whole steps from the root, sounds mischievous and is known as the "devils triangle".
- Root to Diminished Fifth: same as the augmented fourth, enharmonically spelled as F# and Gb.
- Root to Perfect Fifth: a positive sound wanting to resolve to the root.
- Root to Augmented Fifth: the sound of tension wanting to resolve up to the major sixth or down to the perfect fifth.
- Root to Minor Sixth: same as the augmented fifth, enharmonically spelled as G# and Ab.
- Root to Major Sixth: a positive and contented sound, easily resolving into the perfect fourth.
- Root to Minor Seventh: a tension sound that wants to resolve to the fourth either directly or by "walking" down the major scale.
- Root to Major Seventh: known as the leading tone because it wants to resolve to the root or the octave.

The ninths, elevenths and thirteenths are called color tones and are used in jazz and avant-garde types of music. The blues uses the ninth frequently. The color tones when played will generally have the seventh tone, either major or minor, present in the chord. If there is no seventh the chord will be written as: Cadd9 for example.

Notice that the ninth, eleventh and thirteenth tones are the same note names as the second, fourth and sixth with the difference being they are an octave higher and even though they still retain their characteristic intervallic sound qualities, the greater interval creates a spacious, airy effect.

Scale Degrees

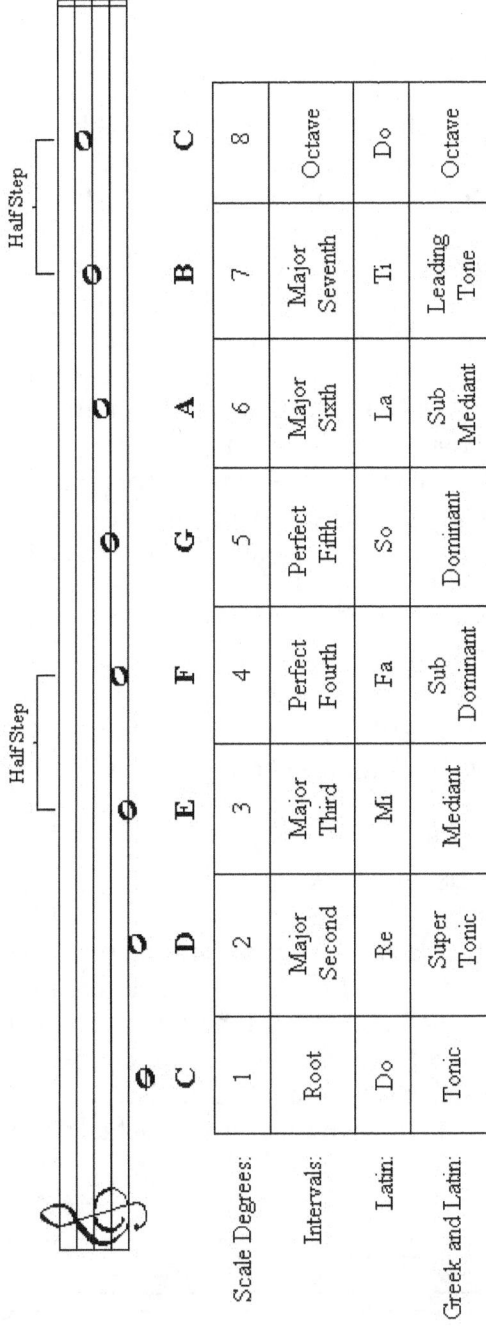

Intervals

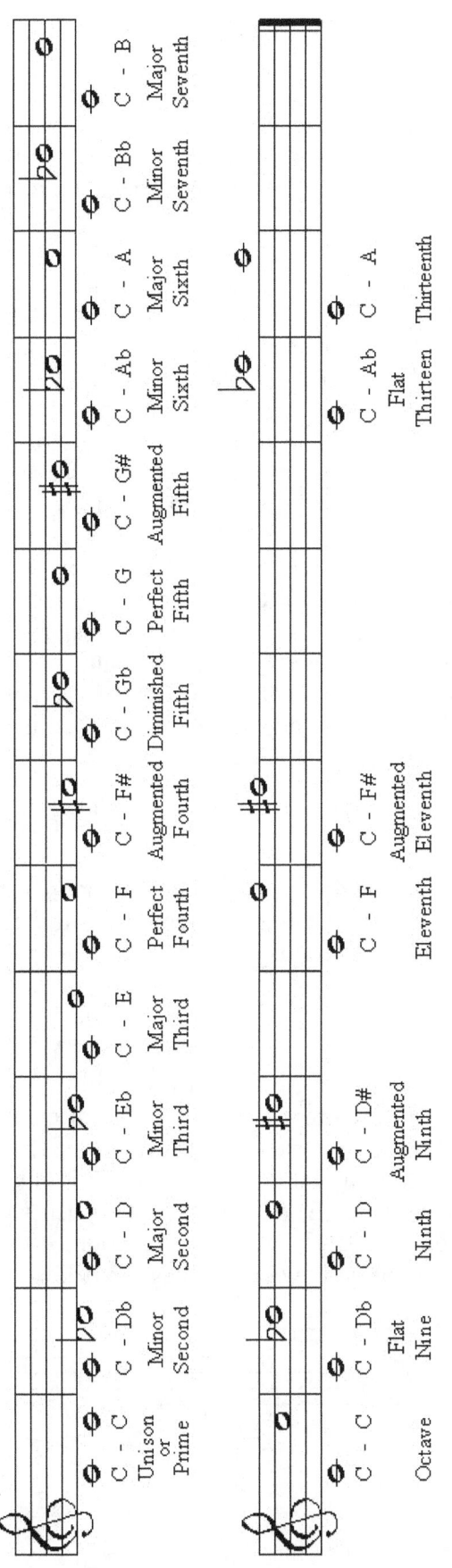

Chord Harmony

Chords are specific notes that are derived from specific degrees of the major scale and played together in unison by strumming or one after another as arpeggios. Chords are triads made up of intervals of thirds. The C chord for example is made up of the notes C - E - G, which are derived from the 1 - 3 - 5 degrees of the C major scale: C - D - E - F - G - A - B - C.

The major chord scale is developed from the major scale. Since there are seven notes in the major scale there will be seven chords developed from it. To understand this look at Diagram 1A on page 7-4. In the Key of C begin with the root note C and count up the alphabet: C is 1, D is 2 and E is 3. The distance between C and E is an interval of a third. NOTE: always count the root or first note as one and using the digits on your hand to count with, always start with the thumb. To harmonize the <u>entire</u> C major scale as intervals of thirds, count up eight notes to the octave E and imagine taking this octave from E to E and putting it on top of the C major scale as shown in Diagram 2. What we have done is to place the C major scale starting on E on top of C major scale starting on C, which harmonizes it in intervals of thirds. This makes the bottom half of the chords. Next, turn to the E in Diagram 1B and count up the alphabet: E is 1, F is 2 and G is 3. The distance between E and G is also a third interval. To harmonize the <u>entire</u> C major scale as triads or chords, count up eight notes to the octave G and imagine taking this octave from G to G and putting it on top of the C major scale that has already been harmonized with intervals of thirds as shown in Diagram 2 and the result is Diagram 3. What we have done is to place the C major scale starting with G on top of the C major scale previously harmonized in intervals of thirds to now form triads or chords. This adds the top half and completes the basic triad. A major scale that is harmonized in thirds to form chords is called a major chord scale.

Sevenths And The Color Tones

Diagram 4 reveals that we can harmonize chords with sevenths, which is also an interval of a third. The color tones; ninths, elevenths and thirteenths which are also third intervals can be developed on top of triads in the same manner.

Two Intervals Of Thirds Make A Fifth?

As we have just learned it is true for all chords that by placing a note a third interval over the root, we create a harmony of a third. By placing another note an interval of a third above that third interval, we now create a triad or a chord. Within the triad there are two intervals of a third, which would seem to total an interval of a 6th but in reality it is only an interval of a 5th from the root. By taking the first interval of a third: C to E, (C - D - E) and then starting the second interval of a third, E to G from E again and counting E - F - G the E was counted twice which means only five tones where actually used: C - D - E - F - G as is shown in the diagram below.

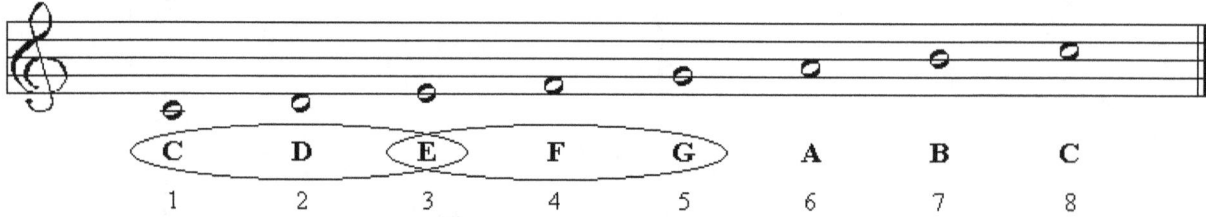

Chord Harmony

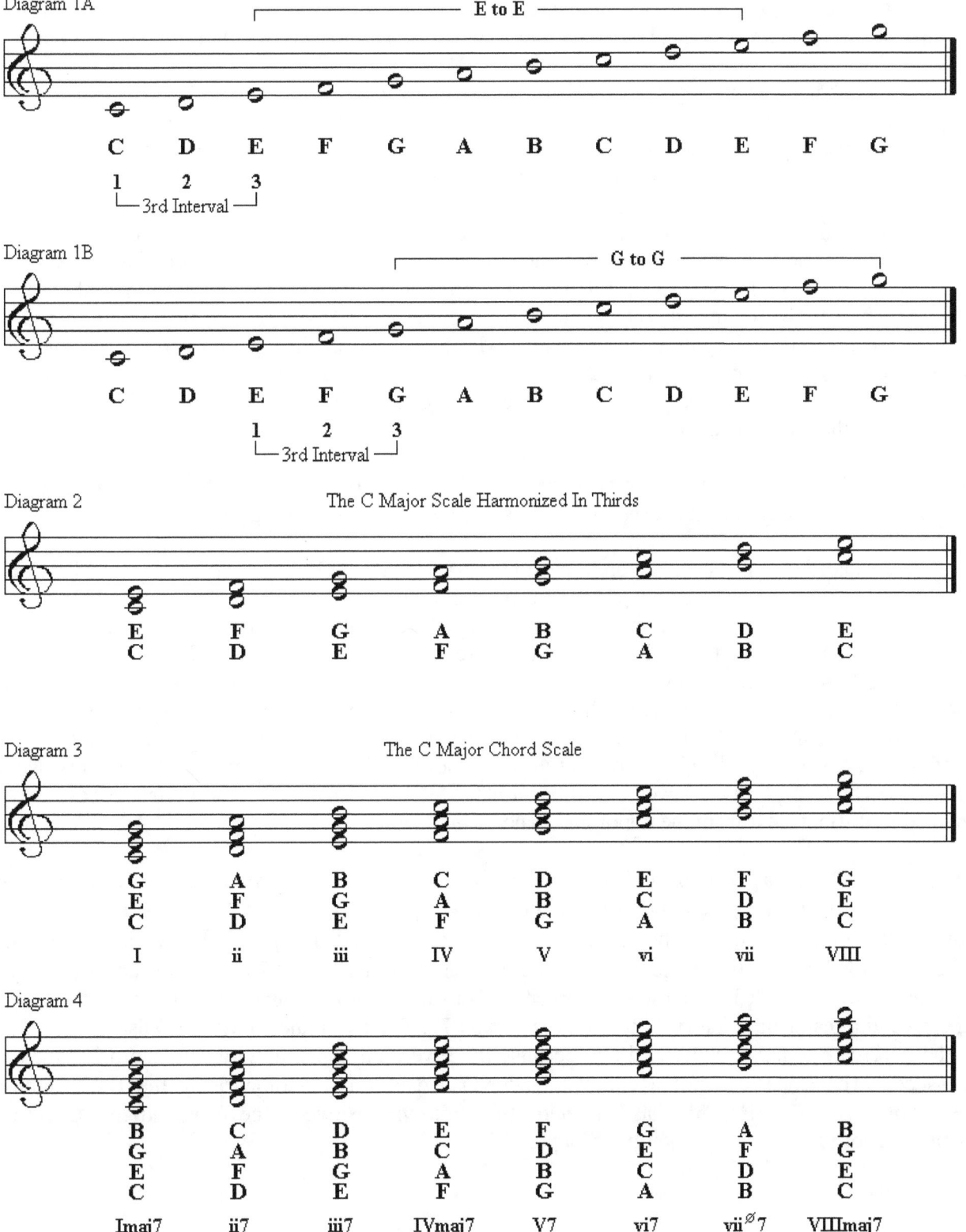

The Major Chord Scale

Notice that the C Major Chord Scale in diagram 3 on page 7-4 can also be presented in chord grids as shown on page 7-6. Here is a visual presentation of the working application taught on pages 7-3 and 7-4.

Look at the C chord grid on page 7-6 and compare its notes to the notes in the C Major Scale diagram in the upper left of the page. The chords notes are C - E - G - C - E. The extra C and E notes are octave tones that are used to make the chord fuller in sound. The basic C chord contains the notes C - E - G, which are the 1 - 3 - 5 degree tones of the C major scale.

Going up the scale, D is the second degree of the C major scale therefore the D minor chord is also the second degree of the C major chord scale. Once again, since chords are made up of thirds derived from the major scale, the D minor chord starting with the root note D and going up a third to F and then from F up another third to A, we find the D minor chord is made up of D - F - A. Now compare the D minor chord on page 7-6 to the notes in the Phrygian Mode diagram in the upper right of the page. In this example it is found that the notes in the Dm chord grid: D - A - D - F, do not have to be in the same order as the triad: D - F - A shown on page 7-4. The only way chords will remain in their basic order: root - 3rd - 5th, is to play them linearly as shown in Chapter 18.

When you reach the Fmaj7 chord, the basic triad F - A - C is expanded to F - A - C - E to make a major seven chord. The IVmaj7 chord is used in the classical, jazz and sometimes pop/rock.

Next, the G7 chord has also been expanded from the basic triad of G - B - D to G - B - D - F, which is a dominant seven chord. With the exception of heavy metal and punk rock, The V7, dominant seven chord is found in most styles of music although occasionally the seventh note may be dropped using only the triad. Why is it called dominant? The G7, dominant seven chord is made-up of the 1 - 3 - 5 - 7 tones of the major scale. Between the root and the 3rd there are two whole steps making the chord major and between the 5th and the 7th there is a whole step and a half step (1½ steps) making the seventh minor. Because the 3rd of the chord is major it cannot be called a minor seventh. In comparison, the Gm7, minor seventh chord has a minor 3rd (1½ steps) between its root and 3rd and a minor 3rd (1½ steps) between the 5th and 7th. The Gmaj7, major seven chord has a major 3rd and a major 7th. The dominant seven chord is so named to distinguish it from the minor and major seven chords.

Last, the $B^{\emptyset}7$ chord has been expanded from the basic triad of B - D - F to B - D - F - A which is a half diminished chord. With the exception of heavy metal and punk rock the $vii^{\emptyset}7$ chord is found in all styles of music although occasionally the seventh note may be dropped using only the diminished triad. The $B^{\emptyset}7/D$ chord is inverted (see page 7-14) with the same notes as the $B^{\emptyset}7$ only arranged differently with the 3rd in the root. The half diminished seven chord is made up of two minor third intervals from the root to the 5th and a major third interval between the 5th and 7th. The two minor third intervals between the root and the 5th create a diminished chord and because the seventh is a major third, the chord is called a half diminished seven since it is not a completely diminished chord. In comparison, the $B^{\circ}7$, diminished seven chord: B - D - F - Ab, has all minor third intervals between the root and the seventh. The diminished chord is explained in depth in Chapter 17.

C Major Chord Scale

Open Position

Key Of C

C Major Scale 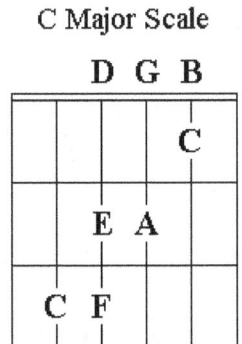 Scale Degrees 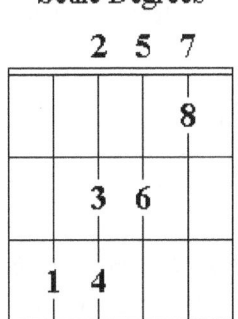 Phrygian Mode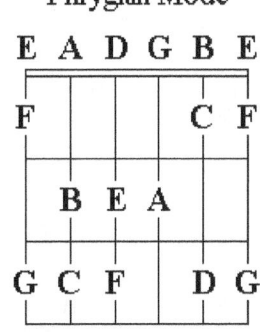

I
C
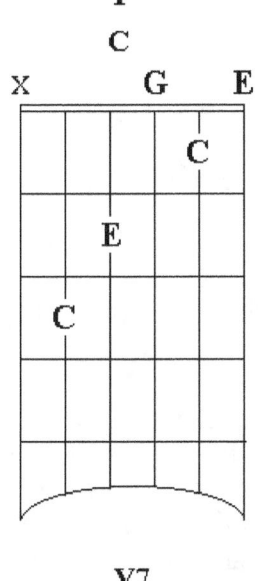

ii
Dm
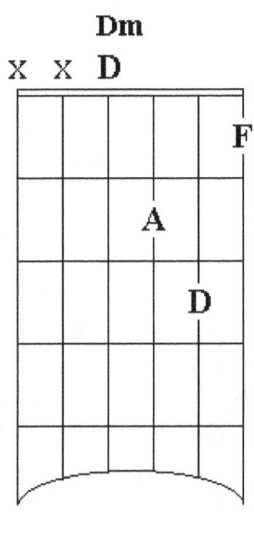

iii
Em
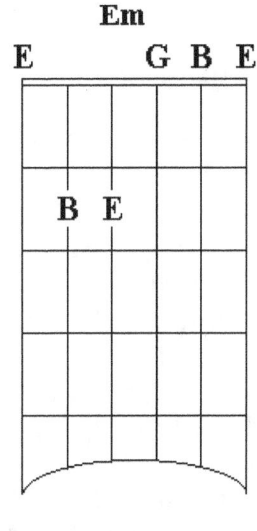

IVmaj7
Fmaj7
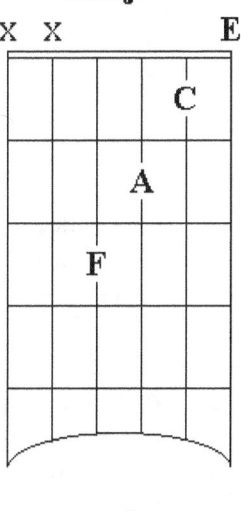

V7
G7
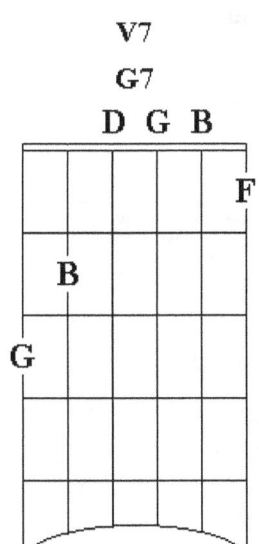

vi
Am
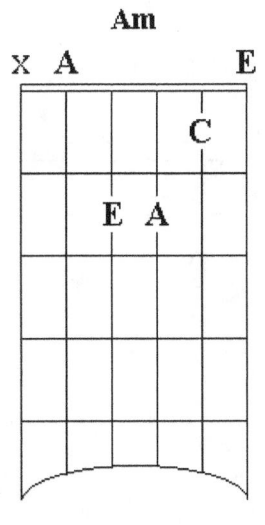

vii⌀7
B⌀7
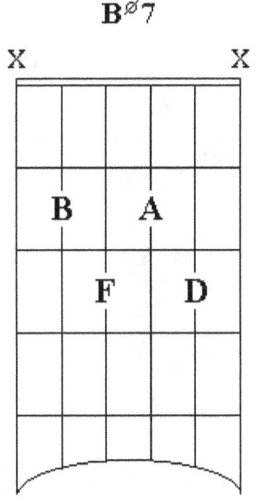

vii⌀7
B⌀7/D
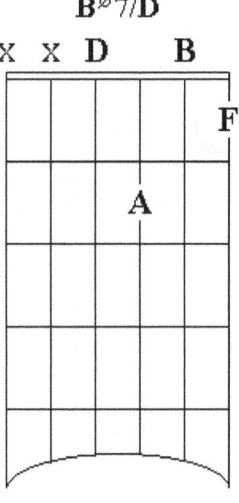

7-6

Major And Minor Chords

Why is it that when the major scale is harmonized into a major chord scale four of the chords are major and four chords are minor?

MAJOR - minor - minor - MAJOR - MAJOR - minor - minor - MAJOR

When the major scale is harmonized in thirds to form chords, the interval between the root and the third within the chords of the major chord scale vary between two whole steps and one and a half steps, as seen in the C Major Chord Scale diagram below.

Since chords are harmonized from the major scale, the different whole and half steps within each of the chords is the *direct result of the placement of half steps between the third, fourth and seventh, eighth degrees of the major scale*. If the interval is two whole steps or a major third, the chord is then major. If the interval between the root and the third is one and a half steps or a minor third, the chord is minor. Half steps between the third, fourth and seventh, eighth scale degrees is the structure of the major scale and is the reason Western music sounds the way it does. Each culture in the world has a unique sound to its music, which is directly due to the placement of the whole and half steps in the scales.

Why is the major chord scale in the order of:

MAJOR - minor - minor - MAJOR - MAJOR - minor - minor – MAJOR?

Let's take a look at the first chord in the C Major Chord Scale diagram. It is a C major chord harmonized with the 1 - 3 - 5 degrees of the C major scale, which are the notes: C - E - G. C to D is a whole-step and D to E is also a whole-step. This C chord is major because it has a major third interval of two whole-steps between its root note C and E. Now let's look at the second chord in the diagram. It is a Dm chord which is built upon the 2 - 4 - 6 degrees of the C major scale which are the notes D - F - A. Now D to E is a whole-step and E to F is a half step. This means that the Dm chord is minor because it has a minor third interval of one whole-step and one half step between its root note D and F. It is these whole and half step intervals between the root and third notes of the chords of the major chord scale that causes them to be M - m - m- M - M - m - m- M. This is directly due to the whole - whole - half - whole - whole - whole - half steps of the major scale in which the half steps occur between the third, fourth and seventh, eighth degrees.

C Major Chord Scale

2 G E C	1½ A F D	1½ B G E	2 C A F	2 D B G	1½ E C A	1½ F D B	2 G E C
Roman Numerals: I	ii	iii	IV	V	vi	vii	VIII
Chord Names: C	Dm	Em	F	G	Am	B°	C
Chord Numbers: 1	2	3	4	5	6	7	8

Circle Of Fifths

The circle of fifths on the outside of the circle is a convenient diagram that shows the progression of sharp keys in the order that they develop. As you move clockwise around the circle of fifths one sharp will be added to each key signature. C has no sharps, G has one sharp, D has two, etc.

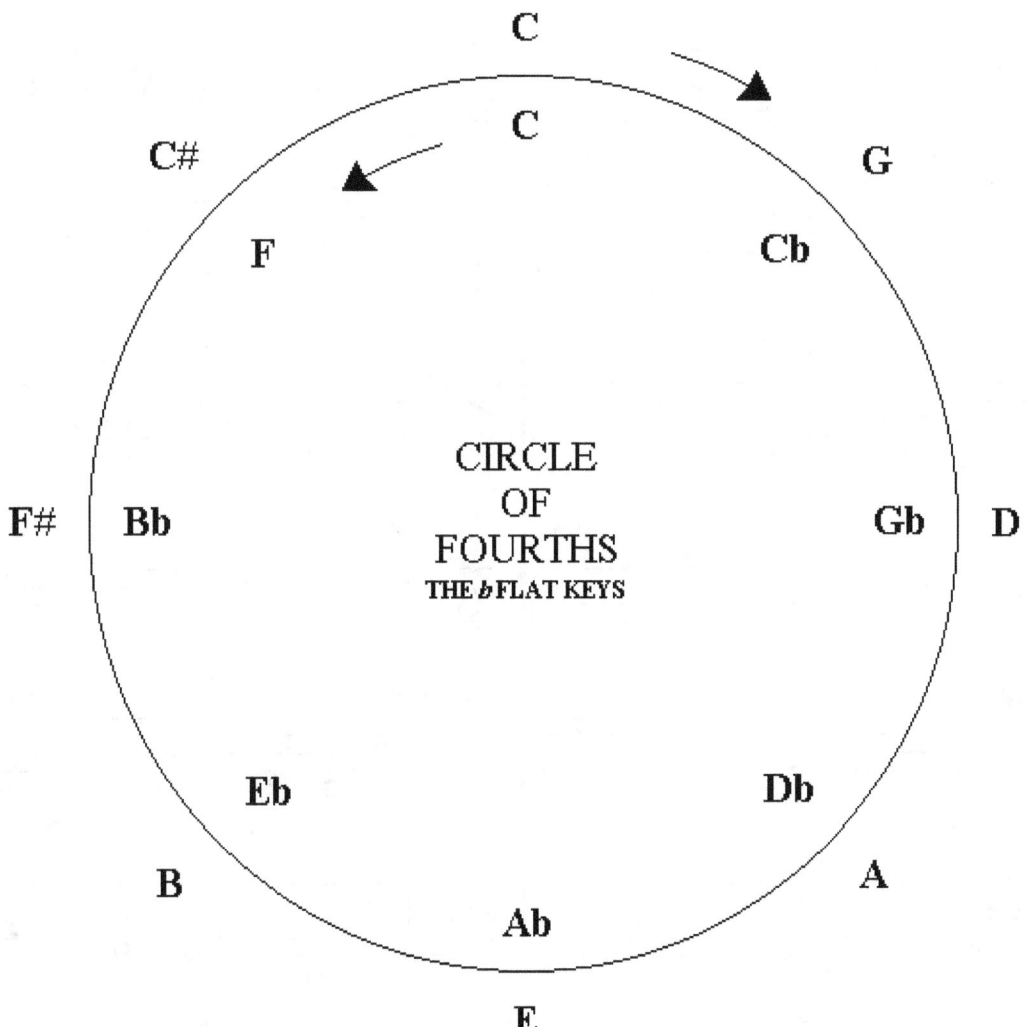

Circle Of Fourths

The circle of fourths on the inside of the circle is a convenient diagram that shows the progression of flat keys in the order that they develop. As you move counterclockwise around the circle of fourths one flat will be added to each key signature. C has no flats, F has one flat, Bb has two, etc.

Chord Development Study

Circle Of Fifths – Sharp Keys

ASSIGNMENT: 1) In the Major Scale diagram write in the note names and the half steps of the scale for each key. 2) In the Major Chord Scale diagram write in the notes, chord names and the whole and half steps between the root and the third interval of each chord in each major chord scale. Use the C major scale and the C major chord scale examples as a reference. This exercise will help the student understand the development of the major chord scale that is harmonized from the major scale in the sharp keys.

7-9

Chord Development Study

Circle Of Fourths – Flat Keys

ASSIGNMENT: 1) In the Major Scale diagram write in the note names and the half steps of the scale for each key. 2) In the Major Chord Scale diagram write in the notes, chord names and the whole and half steps between the root and the third interval of each chord in each major chord scale. Use the C major scale and the C major chord scale examples as a reference. This exercise will help the student understand the development of the major chord scale that is harmonized from the major scale in the flat keys.

Chord Study

The Chord Study on the following page is a basic nursery rhyme song chosen for its simple yet interesting use of the C major scale and the C and G major chords. The song is played in the Key of C in the open position. The C chord is the root I chord and the G chord is the dominant V chord. Many of the old American folk songs used the simple I - V chord progression as it is easy to play and the melodies are simple yet catchy for remembering.

In measure one, the first phrase of the melody starts on the root C note and makes a statement of what the author of the song is wishing for us to do which is to: "Row, row, row your boat" or to carry our body, by ascending the C major scale one note at a time from the C note to the D note and then to the major third note E. Phrase 1 plays the interval of the root and major third of the C chord. In the second measure, the second phrase tells how and in what setting we are going to carry our being through life, which is by rowing "gently down the stream". This is done by continuing to ascend the C major scale from the major third E note with only a quick return to the major second note D for contrast before ending up on the perfect fifth note G. Phrase 2 plays the interval of the major third and the perfect fifth of the C chord. By using the first five tones of the C major scale: C, D, E, F, G and by emphasizing the 1, 3, 5 degrees of the C major chord which is played as accompaniment, the melody and the chords which are derived from the C major scale are in harmony and structurally strong. Also in Phrase 2 the G note allows for a quick chord change from the C chord to the G chord, which breaks the monotony. The variety creates interest.

In the third measure we return to the C chord. The third phrase uses rhythmically interesting triplets with three notes to a beat, this time taking us descending back down through the C major triad from the octave note C to the perfect fifth note G, the major third note E and the root note C all the while telling us what a "merrily, merrily, merrily, merrily" mood we should be doing all of this rowing in. While carrying our beings gently through life we are now informed that "life is but a dream" after all, as we continue to descend the C major scale, now under the influence of the G chord, from the perfect fifth note G to the perfect fourth note F, the major third note E, the major second note D and finally end on the root note C returning to the C chord in phrase four where we originally started the song from, telling us that we will end up at the same place as we began. The moral of the story is to be gentle and happy since nothing is real.

The song with its chords and melody is derived from the C major scale. The intervals of the major third E note and the Perfect fifth G note from the root note C are the plateaus that each phrase of the melody is reaching for with the lesser major second D note and perfect fourth note F being used as a connecting tones so the melody will be a continuous flowing event. The up and down movement of the melody is similar to the pitch changes found in our everyday vocal conversations.

Exercise

Strum the C chord as the first beat then with the alternating flat-picking technique continue playing the melody. Continue with the rest of the song in the same manner strumming each chord change as a beat with the melody continuing beyond it.

Chord Study

Key Of C

C Major Scale

C Major Scale   C Major Chord   G Major Chord

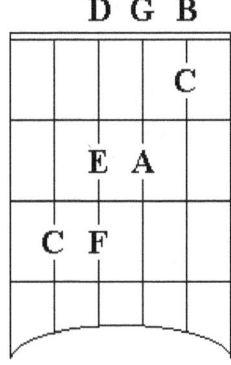 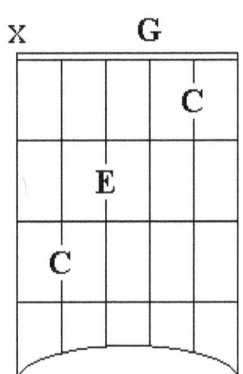 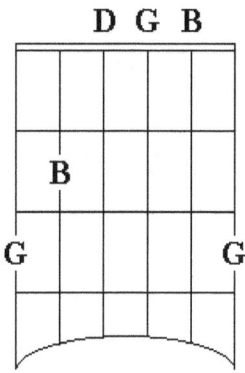

Row Your Boat

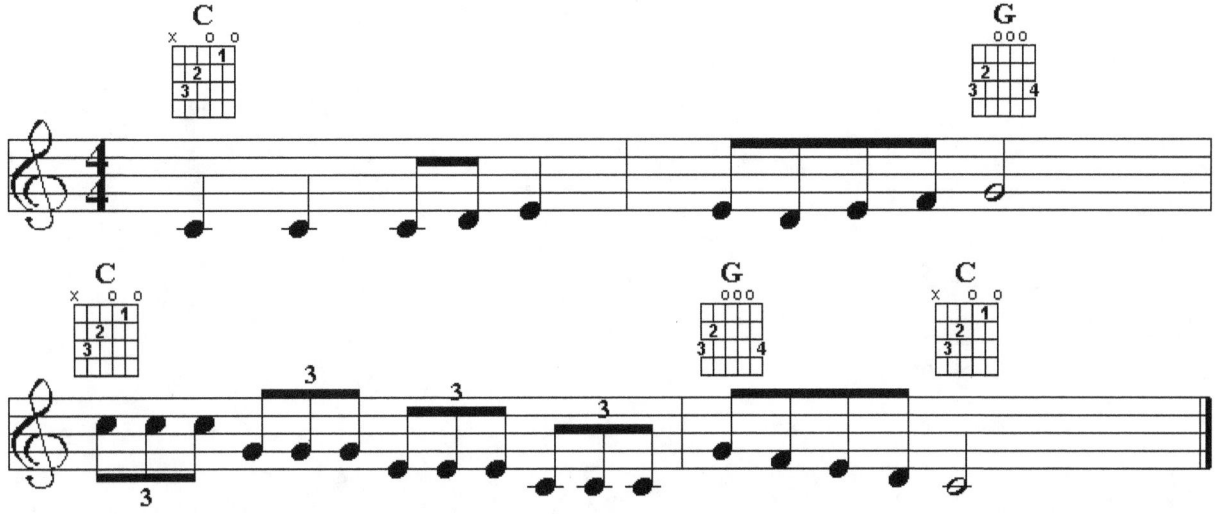

7-12

Notes

Chord Inversions

Chord inversions are for interest. There are first inversions and second inversions. The first inversion of a chord means to turn it upside down once. The second inversion means to turn it upside down again. The easiest way to understand this is by looking at the piano keyboard below:

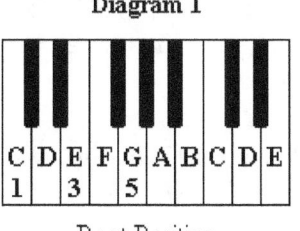
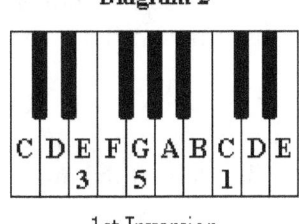
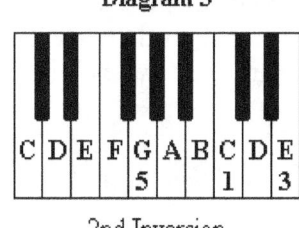

The C chord in Diagram 1 is: C – E – G. By moving the root note C one octave higher as shown in Diagram 2 the E note would then become the bass note. This is called a first inversion. If we were to move the E note one octave higher as shown in Diagram 3 the G note would then become the bass note. This would be called a second inversion.

The two B half diminished seven chords played on page 7-6 are shown below. Diagram 1 is the B half diminished seven chord in its root position with its root note B in the bass. The B half diminished seven chord in Diagram 2 is a first inversion with its third note D in the bass and its root note B has moved up an octave. The /D at the end of the chord name as shown in Diagram 2 means that the chord is inverted with the D note in the bass. Diagram 3 is added to show the B half diminished chord in its second inversion with its fifth note F in the bass and the third note D has moved up an octave.

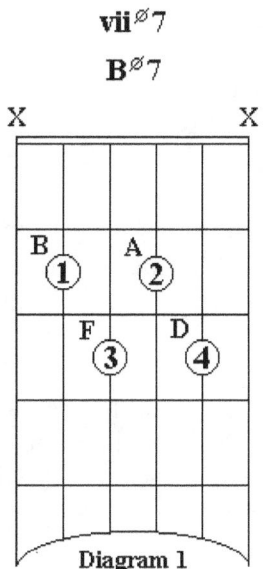
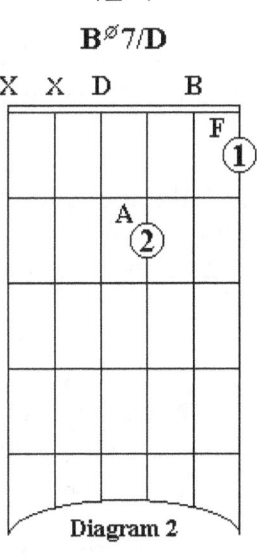
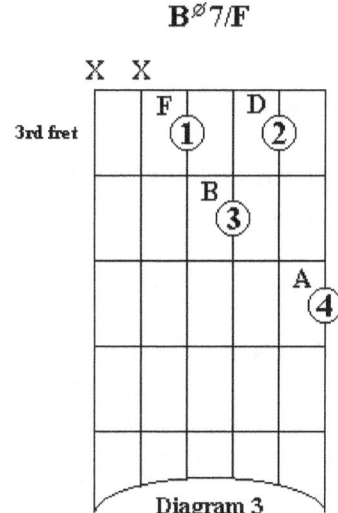

Chord inversions play a significant role in the creative process of music giving the guitarist more tools with which to create interesting arrangements. The same notes are being played but with their order being rearranged the sound is magically transformed by the variations.

Interval And Inversion Study

In measure 1 of the Delta Blues song, on the next page, it can be seen that in the first chord diagram labeled A7 there is an A7 chord posing in the D form. It can also be seen in the staff that there are only two notes of the chord actually being played. These two notes are the 5th (E note) and the 3rd (C# note) of the A7 chord. A basic chord requires three notes: the root, 3rd and 5th to be classified as a chord. If there are only two notes it is an interval.

The chord in this case does not need to have the root present because the bass player (your thumb in this song) is playing it in the walking bass line. This is the thinking process behind using intervals.

The walking bass line is derived directly from the Dorian pentatonic scale. This is confirmed by the fact that the Dorian mode follows the D form in the traditional Western format. Since we are playing only the 3rd and the 5th of the chord it doesn't tell us if it is a minor 7th (Am7), dominant 7th (A7) or major 7th (Amaj7) chord. Being that we are actually in the Blues Key of A7, in which we would basically play it as an A7 chord, now with the 7th tone eliminated we can now play it as though we are in the Key of A. The chosen Dorian mode is now played at the 2nd degree as it naturally occurs within the Key of A. This is how we can be creative and use all the tools (in this case knowledge) available to us to create new music just as the African/American did while in slavery.

The inversion occurs in measure six as D9/F# chord. This is simply a D9 chord with its 3rd (D – F# - A) in the bass. When the 3rd is in the bass it is a 1st inversion and when the 5th is in the bass it is a 2nd inversion. The purpose of inverting the D9 chord in this song is for the bass line step-up that connects the E chord chromatically up to the D9 chord. Using the chromatic scale to connect chords is a common occurrence in blues and jazz. The Beatles as a Pop group used the chromatic bass line in many of their songs.

The Delta Blues is a classic style of finger picking blues. The picking hand uses the thumb on the three bass strings (E – A – D) and the first and second fingers on strings 3, 2 and 1. This is the finger picking style used by the banjo player.

For the finger picking hand: In measures 1 through 5 use the first finger (i) on the 3rd string and the second finger (m) on the 1st string. In measures 6 through 10 use the first finger (i) on the 3rd string, the second finger (m) on the 2nd string and the third finger (a) on the 1st string except for the E7(#9) chord, which uses the inner four strings.

The fretboard hand finger numbers are presented next to the notes for guidance. The fret positions that each part of the song is to be played in are revealed in the TAB staff as well as the chord diagrams. The notation is presented for the students continuing reading improvement as well as for the timing, which TAB does not address.

The chord diagrams above the staff are presented to show the full standard chord from which the intervals are derived from; being that the song for the most part uses intervals, they are not what is actually being played.

Delta Blues

Traditional

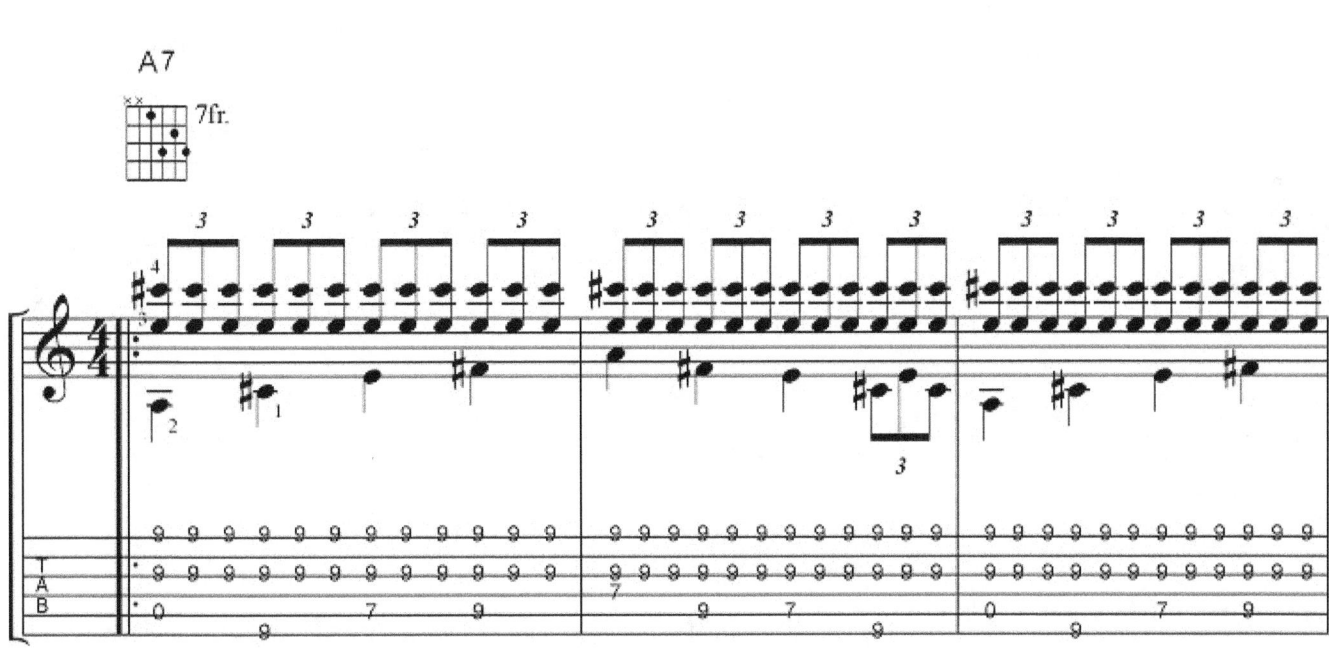
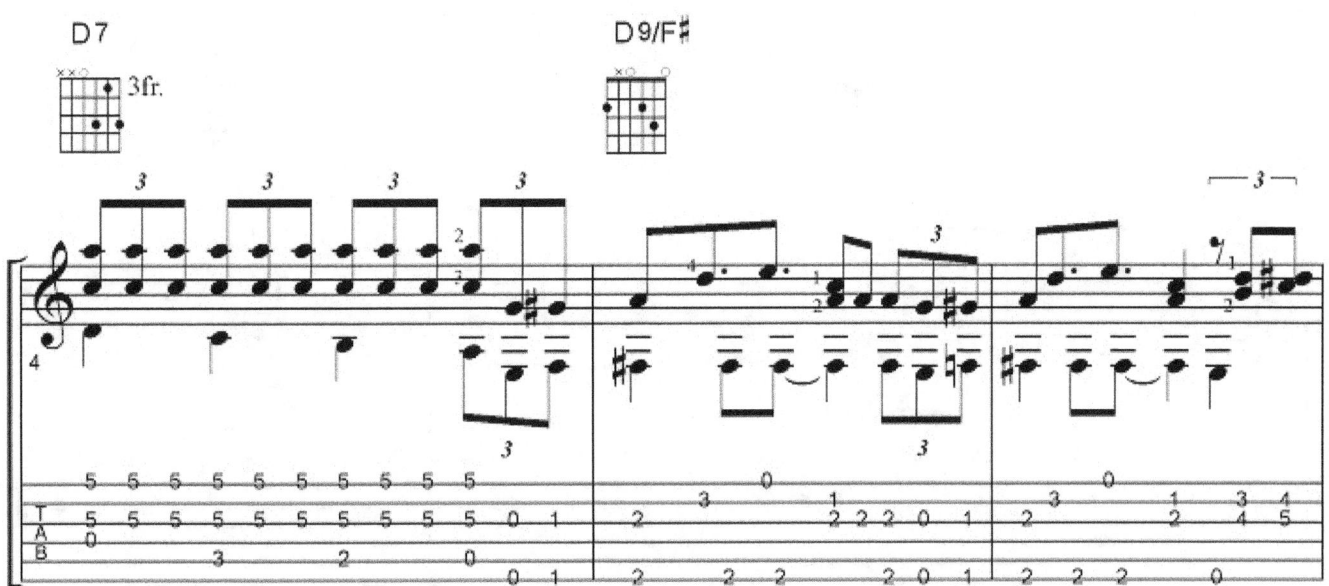

Delta Blues

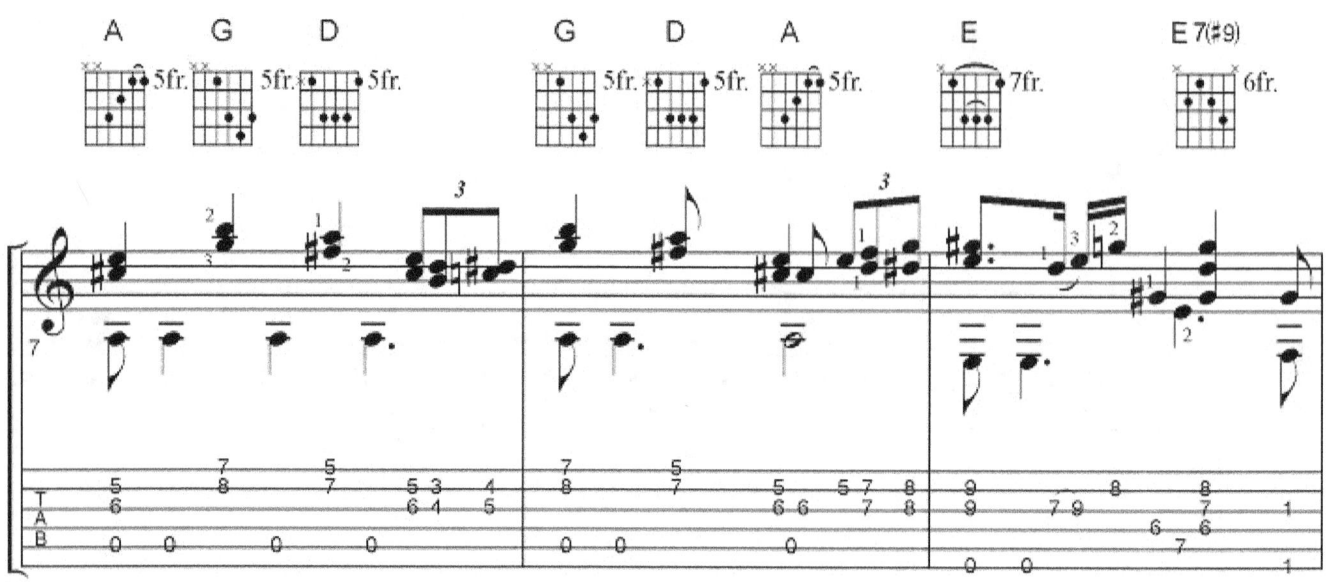
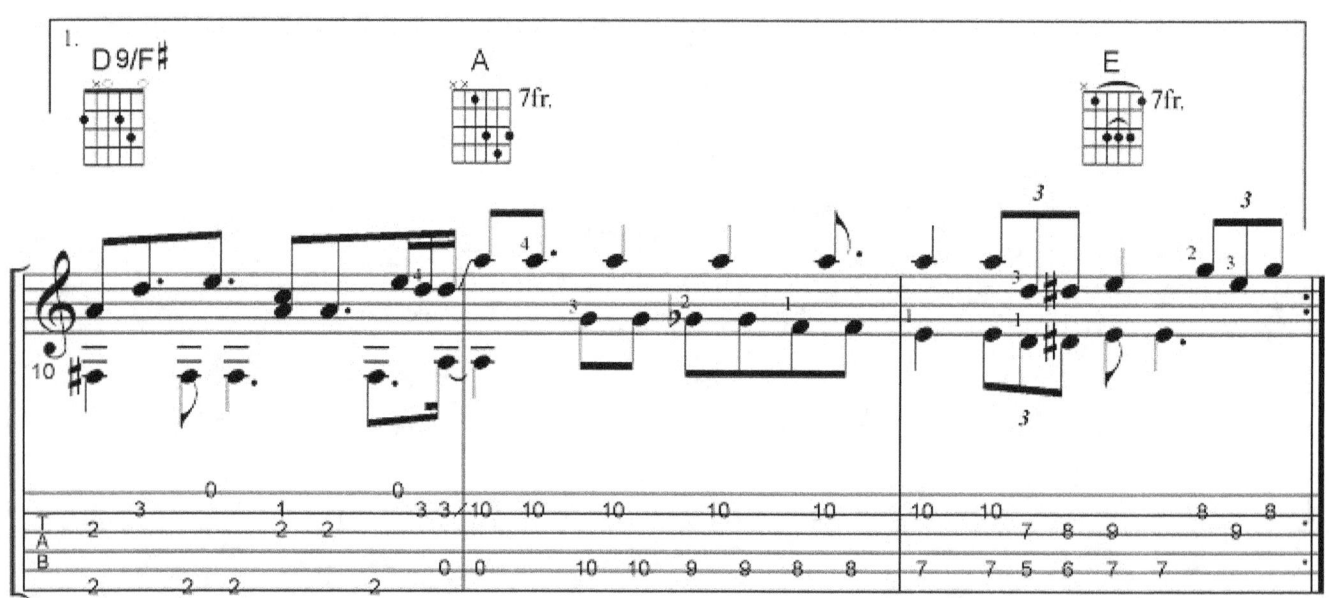

Delta Blues

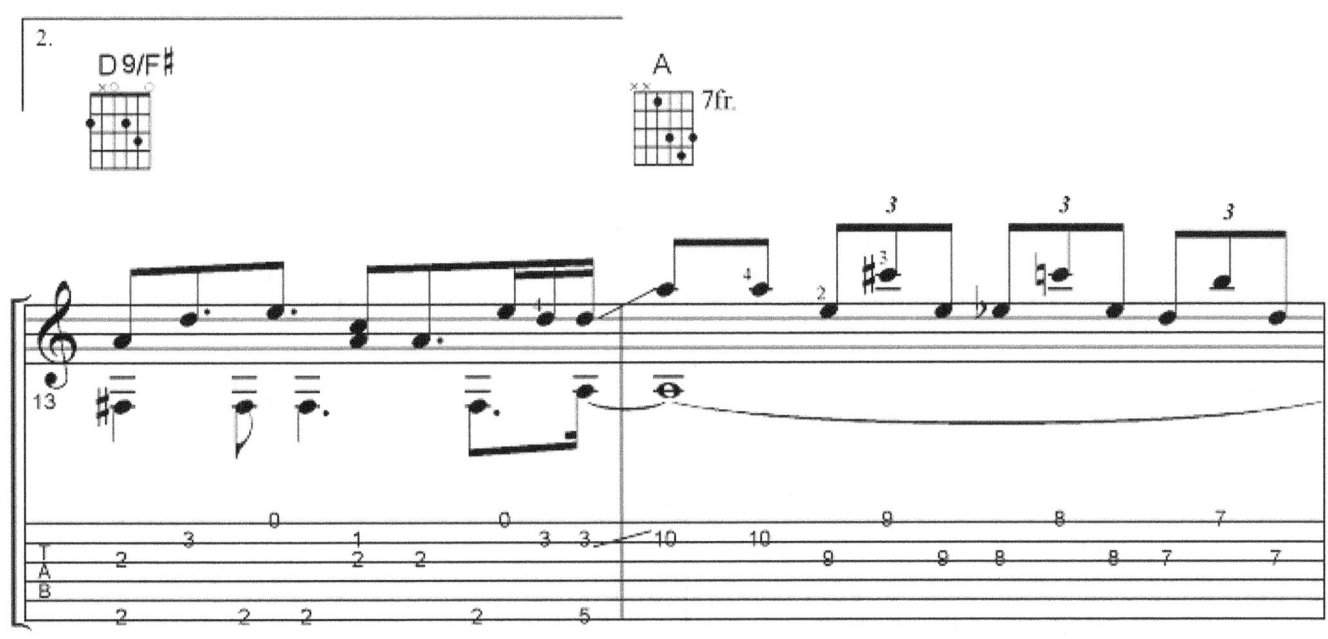

Notes

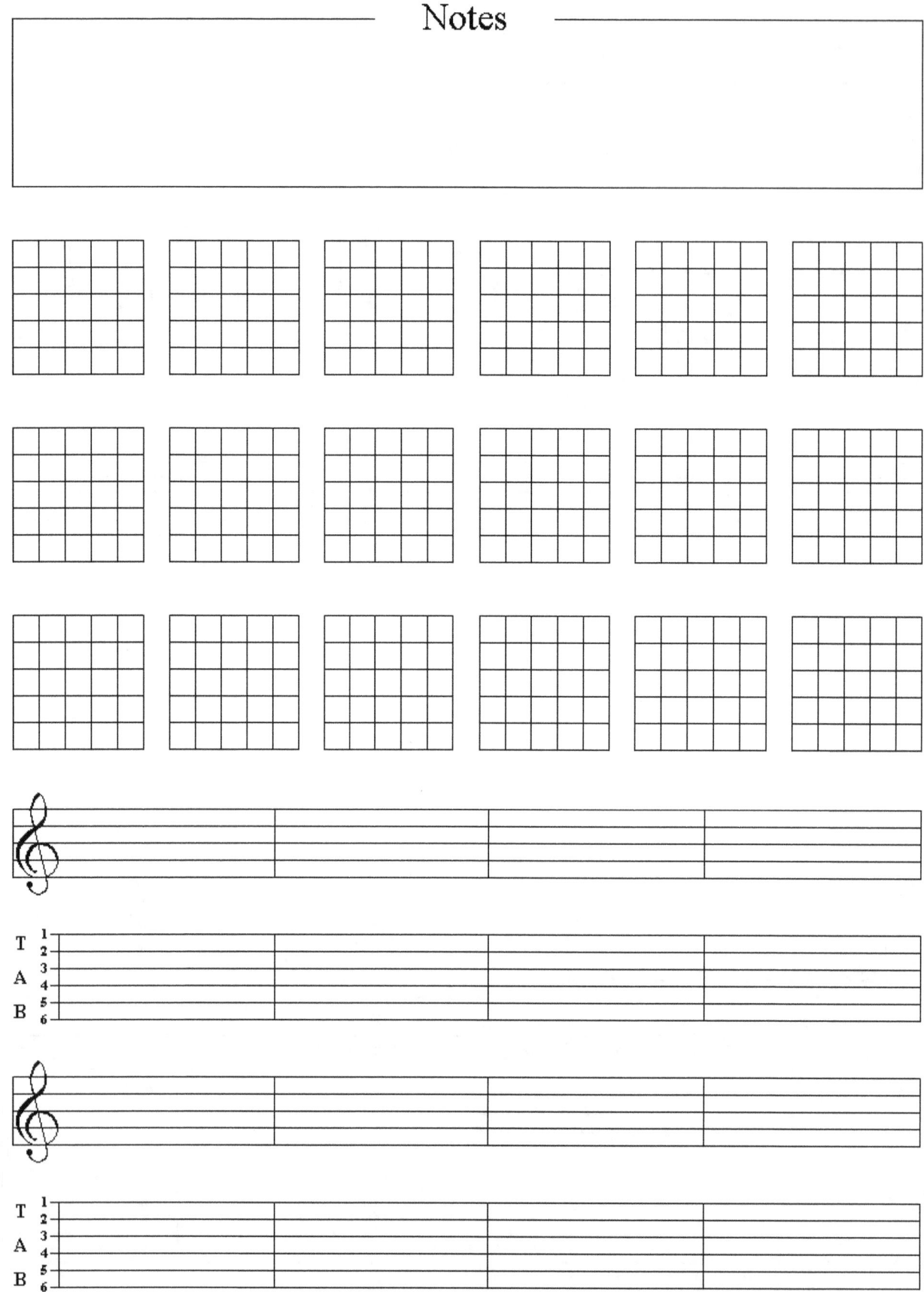

Section Three

Variations

Notes

Chapter 8

Modes In The Open Position

Modes

Webster's dictionary defines a mode as: a particular form or variety of something. This definition precisely describes the modes as they are applied to the guitar. The major scale is the *Something* and the modes, which are derived from the major scale, are the *Particular form or variety*. The eight tone C major scale is presented with dots defining the half steps between the third, fourth and seventh, eighth degrees for reference:

$$
\begin{array}{cccccccc}
C & D & E\bullet F & G & A & B\bullet C \\
1 & 2 & 3 \; 4 & 5 & 6 & 7 \; 8
\end{array}
$$

In the diagram below it can be seen that the scales that are built from each degree of the major scale, which is now displayed vertically, are called modes. The notes in all seven modes are the same as the notes in the C major scale. Each mode has its own name for identification purposes. The modes were named after the neighboring people and their communities surrounding Greece.

Modes are useful to the guitarist because of the placements of the half steps in each mode. Notice the symmetry of the modes created by the half steps that are designated by dots in the diagram below. The different half step placements create major or minor modes. The same rules apply to the modes that apply to the major scale: two whole steps between the root and the third interval equals a major third interval and one whole and one half steps between the root and the third interval equals a minor third interval. The modes by themselves sound just like the major scale they are derived from. It is not until the major and minor modes interact with the major and minor chords of the major chord scale that they will have their subtle yet powerful effect.

Major	8	C	D	E•F	G	A	B•C	VIII	Ionian Octave Mode
Minor	7	B•C	D	E•F	G	A	B	vii	Locrian Mode
Minor	6	A	B•C	D	E•F	G	A	vi	Aeolian Mode
Major	5	G	A	B•C	D	E•F	G	V	Mixolydian Mode
Major	4	F	G	A	B•C	D	E•F	IV	Lydian Mode
Minor	3	E•F	G	A	B•C	D	E	iii	Phrygian Mode
Minor	2	D	E•F	G	A	B•C	D	ii	Dorian Mode
Major	1	C	D	E•F	G	A	B•C	I	Ionian Mode

Degrees ⌐   ⌐ C Major Scale   Degrees ⌐

The Modes diagram on the next page shows the half step patterns of the modes on the staff in the Key of C. Although the other keys are not shown, it should be realized that the same half step patterns occur in all twelve keys. This pattern frequency is due to the symmetry of the major scale.

Modes

A Half Step Study In The Open Position

Key Of C

I	Ionian Mode	Major	C D E F G A B C
ii	Dorian Mode	Minor	D E F G A B C D
iii	Phrygian Mode	Minor	E F G A B C D E
IV	Lydian Mode	Major	F G A B C D E F
V	Mixolydian Mode	Major	G A B C D E F G
vi	Aeolian Mode	Minor	A B C D E F G A
vii	Locrian Mode	Minor	B C D E F G A B
VIII	Ionian Octave Mode	Major	C D E F G A B C

8-2

Seven Modes & Five Basic Chord Forms

Open Position

Study: Page 8-4 is a study of the seven modes and their relationship with the five basic chords in the open position of the guitar. In the diagram on page 8-4 each chord is in its own key with an accompanying mode directly below it. It can be seen by the circled notes that each chord has a unique form and is an integrated part of its accompanying mode. This association between the chord and mode is useful as a location reference guide when playing.

Example 1. Let's take a look at the C chord diagram with the Phrygian mode below it. In the Key of C the C chord form will always be played in the open position. The Phrygian mode that starts from the third degree note E of the C major scale will always be the accompanying mode. This is because the Phrygian mode is always the third degree of any major scale. The third degree of the C major scale is E. Let's count up the C major scale: C - D - E - F - G - A - B - C. In the Key of C, in the open position of the guitar, the first note the Phrygian mode would start on is the open note E of the sixth string.

Example 2. Now let's look at the G chord diagram with the Aeolian mode below it. In the Key of G the G chord form will always be played in the open position. The Aeolian mode that starts from the sixth degree note E of the G major scale will always be the accompanying mode. This is because the Aeolian mode is always the sixth degree of any major scale. The sixth degree of the G major scale is E. Let's count up the G major scale: G - A - B - C - D - E - F# - G. In the Key of G, in the open position of the guitar, the first note the Aeolian mode would start on is the open note E of the sixth string.

Example 3. How do we relate this to our everyday playing of the guitar? Let's say we're in the Key of D and playing a I - IV - V7 chord progression using the D, G and A7 chords in the open position and we want to improvise a solo using a mode also in the open position. Since the open note E is the first note on the sixth string in the open position and the second degree of the Key of D is E, the Dorian mode is the correct choice since it is derived from the second degree of the D major scale: D - E - F - G - A - B - C - D.

Continue with the Mixolydian mode and it's A form in the Key of A and the Ionian mode with its E form in the Key of E to complete the five basic chords with their accompanying modes. Notice that the Phrygian mode is the natural mode without any sharps or flats from which the next four modes vary by adding one sharp each as we journey around the circle of fifths. Finish with the Lydian mode that shares the A form with the Mixolydian mode and finally the Locrian mode that shares the E form with the Ionian mode.

PRACTICE: On page 8-5 play the C chord then practice the Phrygian mode ascending and descending three times without stopping using the finger picking techniques learned on page 5-1. Continue with each of the chords and their modes in the same manner. Memorize these patterns as they are the foundation from which all of your improvisation will stem from.

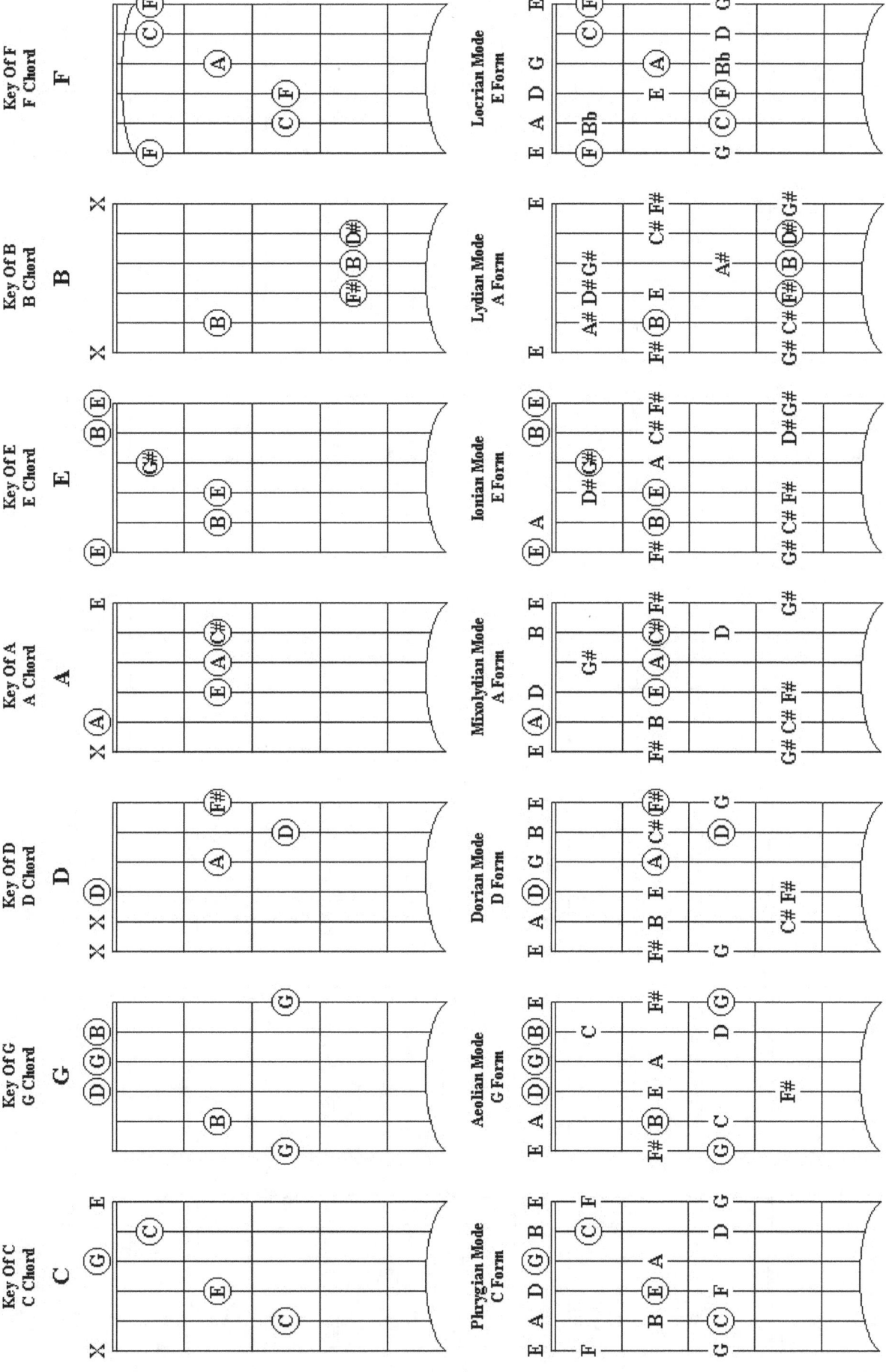

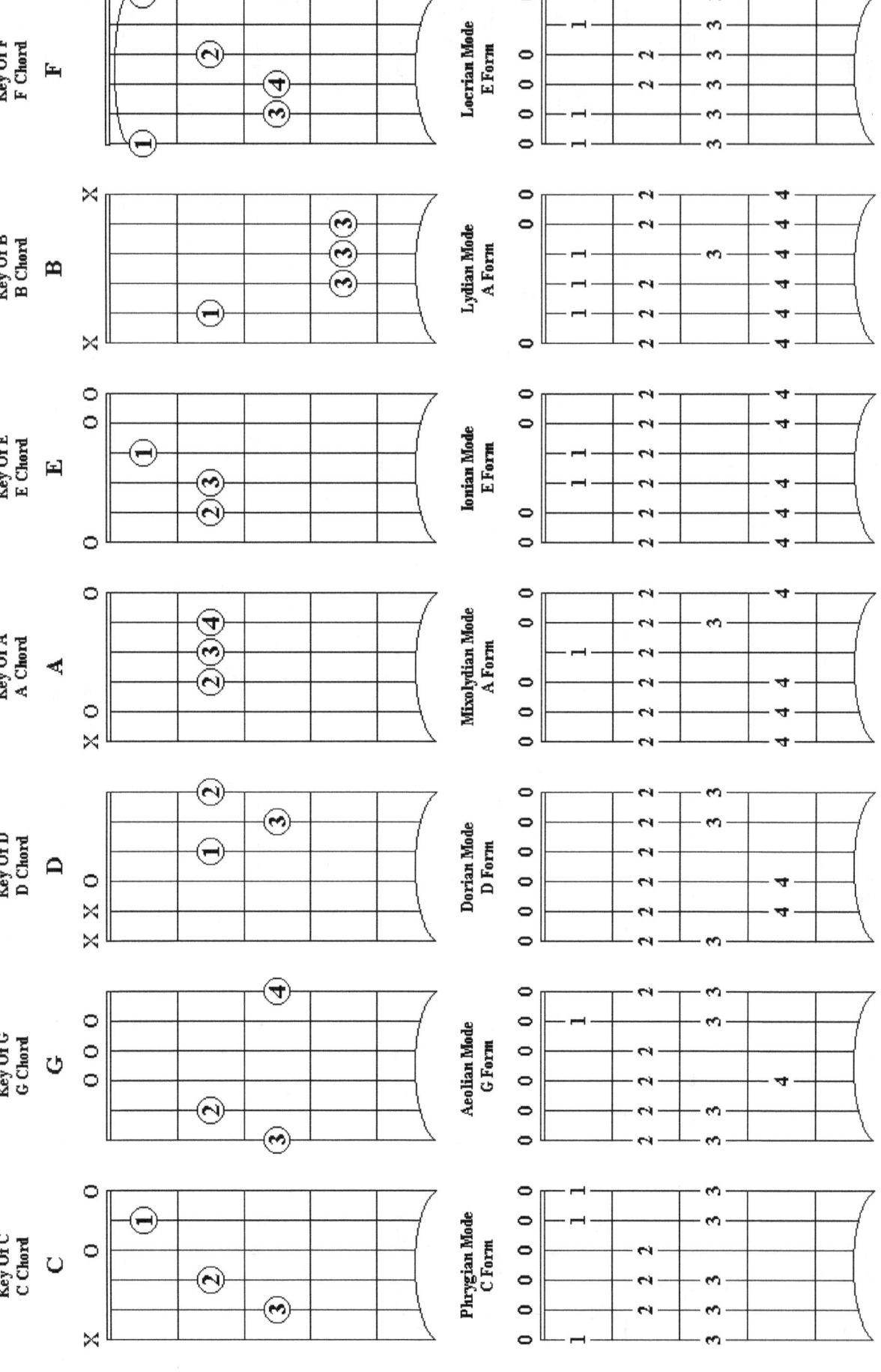

Notes

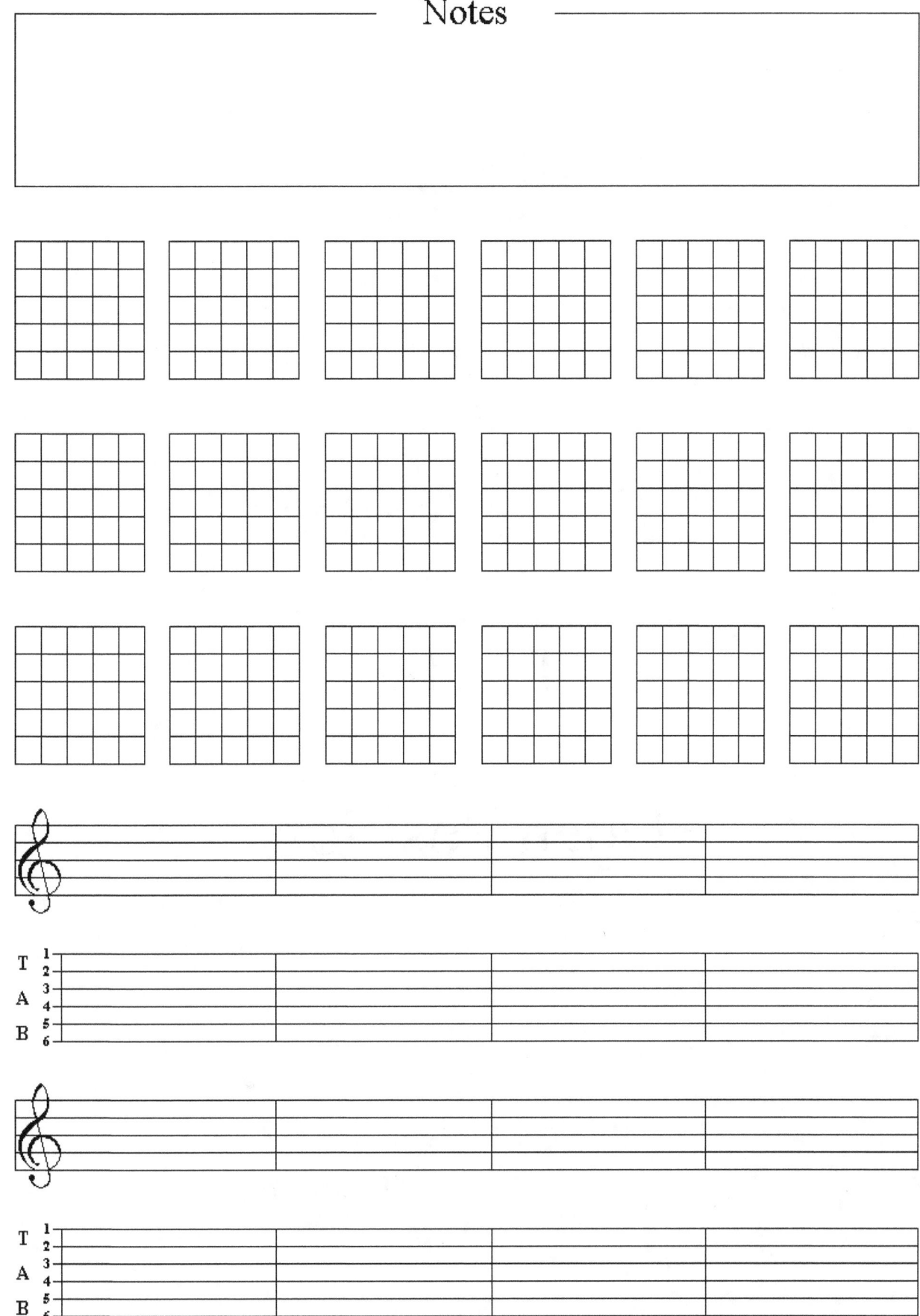

Chapter 9

Chord Scales

In The

Open Position

Chord Scales

Open Position

In this section we'll learn and play the chord scales in the open position that are built from each degree of the major scale in the five basic chord keys: C - G - D - A - E.

Remember that the chord, the chord scale and the mode are derived from the major scale.

Review: In the Key of C when the C chord is being played in the open position, the Phrygian mode will be played. In the Key of G when the G chord is being played in the open position, the Aeolian mode will be played. In the Key of D when the D chord is being played in the open position, the Dorian mode will be played. In the Key of A when the A chord is being played in the open position, the Mixolydian mode will be played. In the Key of E when the E chord is being played in the open position, the Ionian mode will be played.

Now look at the Phrygian Mode – Open Position – Key Of C diagram. The C Major Scale, C Major Chord and Phrygian Mode diagrams are shown with notation. On the facing page in the C Major Chord Scale Open Position diagram there are eight chords that are derived from the major scale: C - Dm - Em - Fmaj7 - G7 - Am - B half diminished 7 and an additional 1st inverted B half dim.7 chord since it is also in the open position thus providing us with more tools to play with. The other four keys will be presented in the same manner.

Exercise

Play each of the modes and chord scales ascending and descending as outlined below.

1) Strum the chord - saying out loud the chord name.

2) Play the mode - saying out loud the note names. Memorize.

3) Strum the chords of the chord scale - saying out loud the chord names. Memorize.

4) Finger pick (P-I-M-A) the chords of the chord scale - saying out loud the chord names.

Advice

When strumming or finger picking these chords, start with the root note first. Take the C chord for example, strike the C note on the third fret of the fifth string first then follow through with the rest of the chord. When strumming, most of the time a chord, in a rhythmic pattern, is approached from the bass note and played through to the treble note, which is done by a downward stroke of the pick. If finger picking, the thumb is played first then the fingers follow. For the fret board hand, place each finger one note at a time on the chord starting with the bass string and playing through to the treble string of the chord. This will make it easier to play the chord. For tone, playing the chord from the bass note to the treble note gives a full, warm sound to the chord. Try the reverse by strumming or finger picking a chord from the treble notes to the bass notes for a different effect.

Phrygian Mode

Open Position

Key Of C

C Major Scale

C Major Scale   C Major Chord   Phrygian Mode

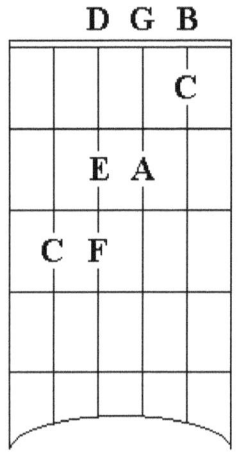 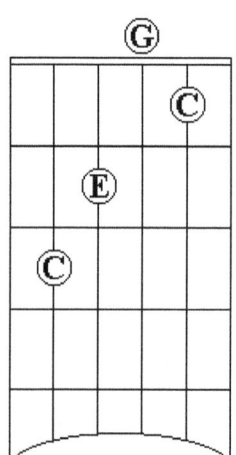 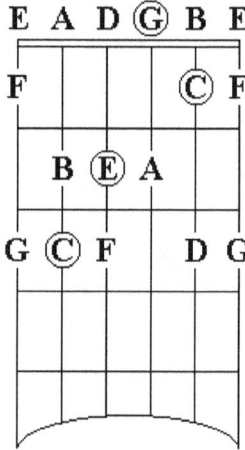

Phrygian Mode

C Major Chord Scale

Open Position

Key Of C

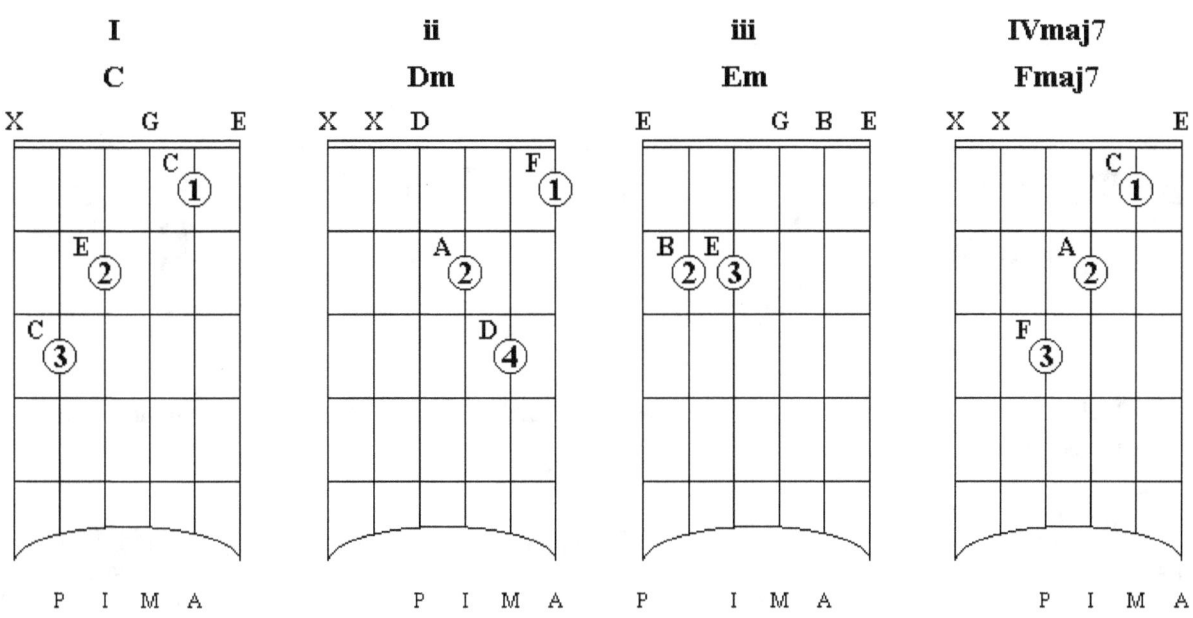

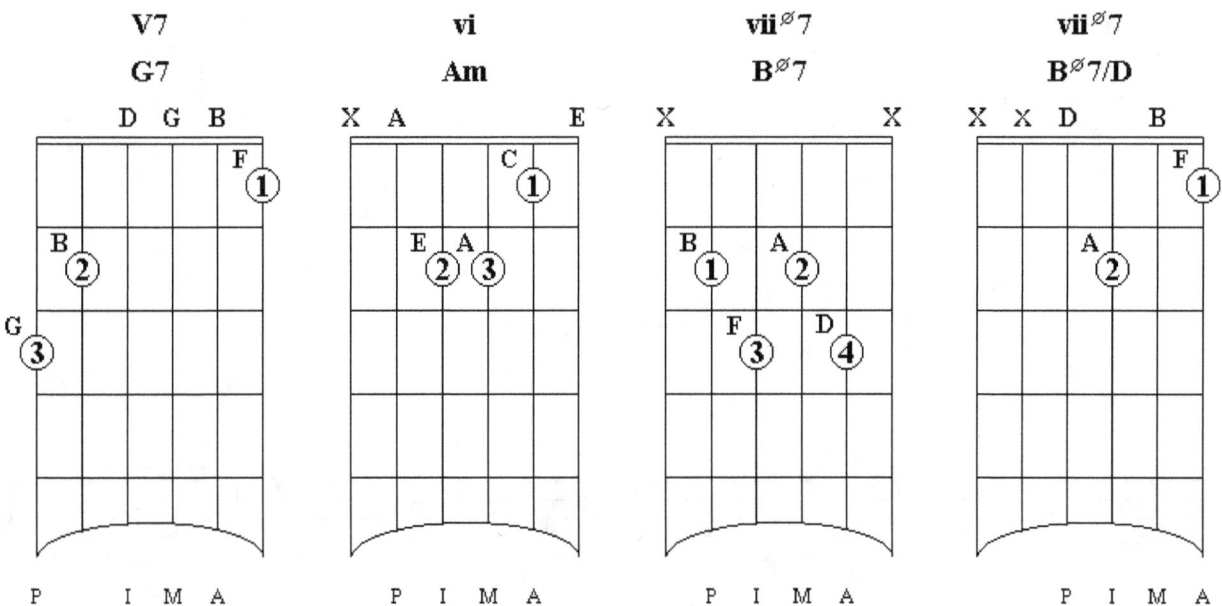

Aeolian Mode

Open Position

Key Of G

G Major Scale
Two Octaves

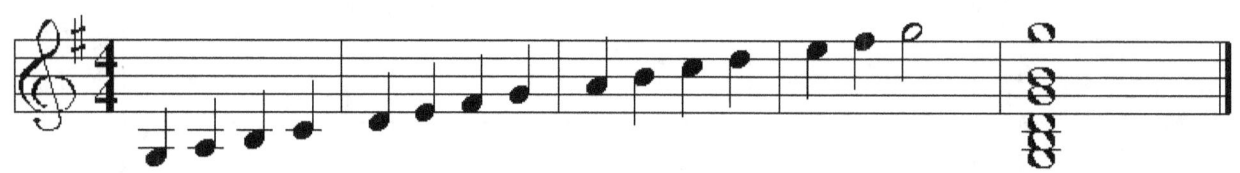

G Major Scale
Two Octaves

G Major Chord

Aeolian Mode

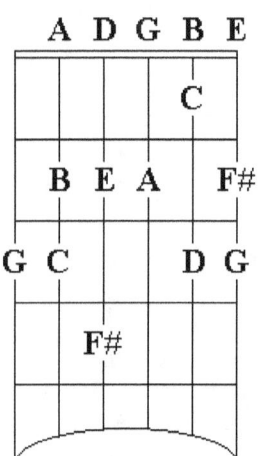 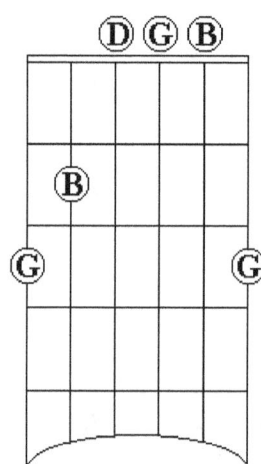 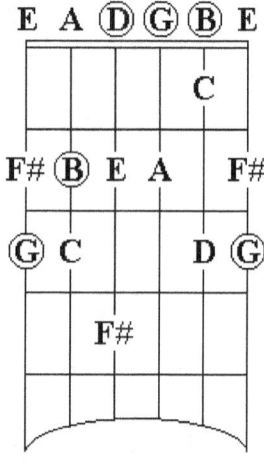

Aeolian Mode

G Major Chord Scale

Open Position

Key Of G

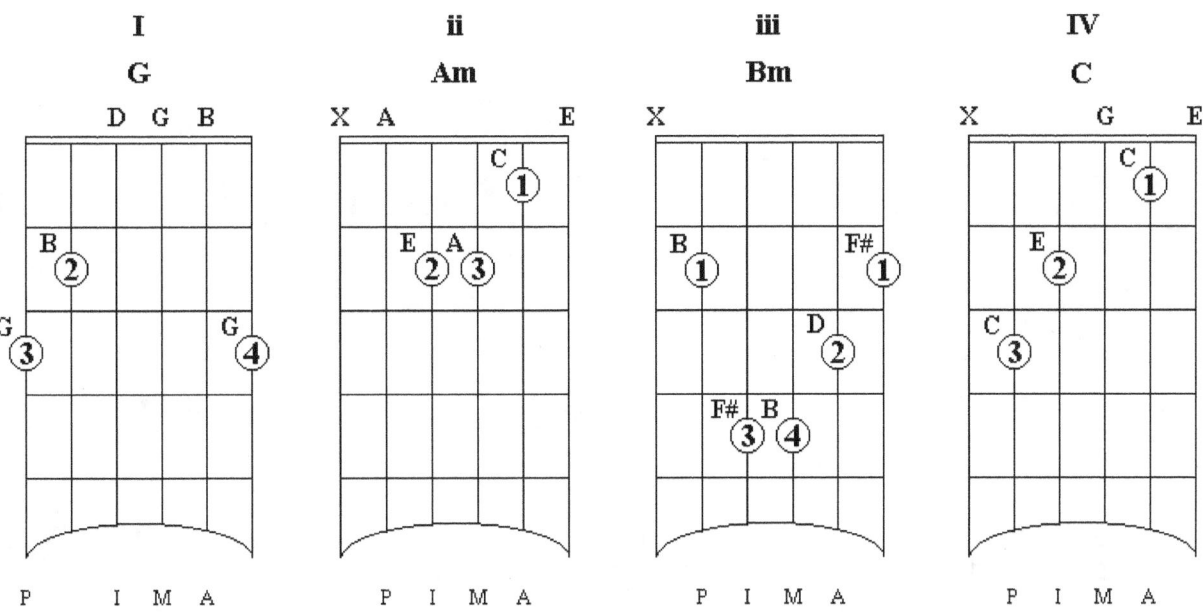

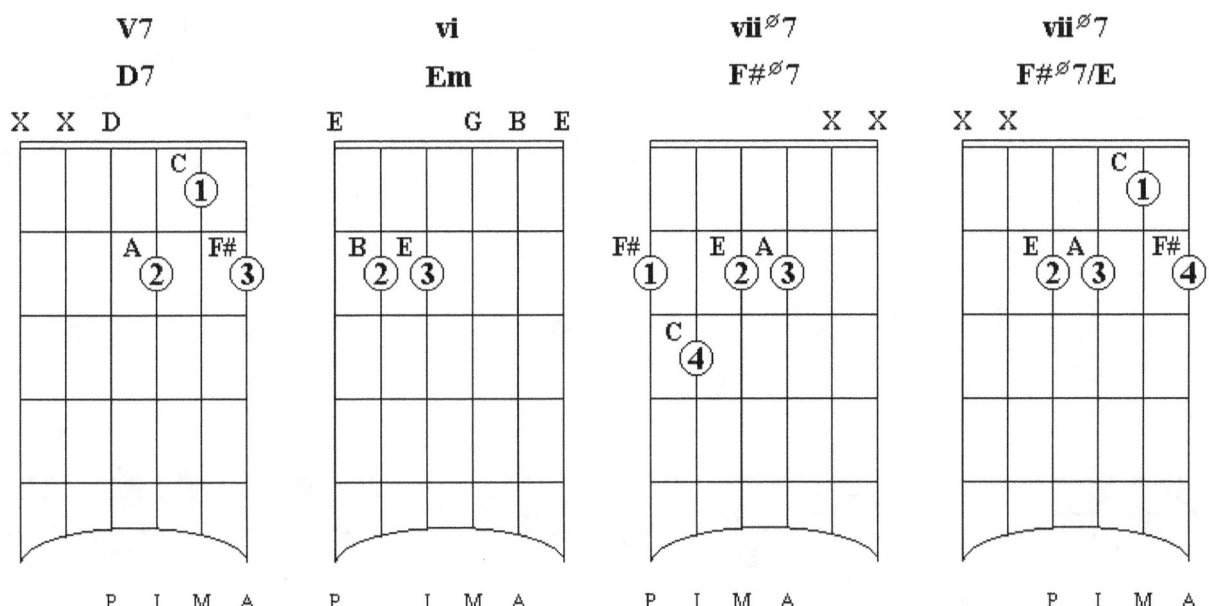

Dorian Mode

Open Position

Key Of D

D Major Scale

D Major Scale   D Major Chord   Dorian Mode

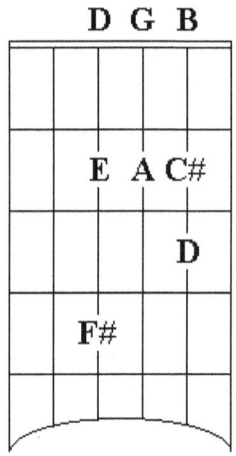 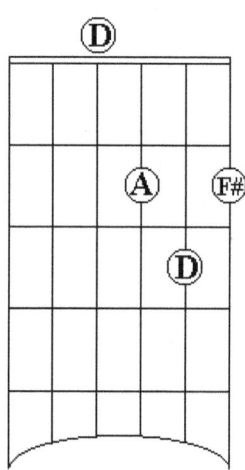 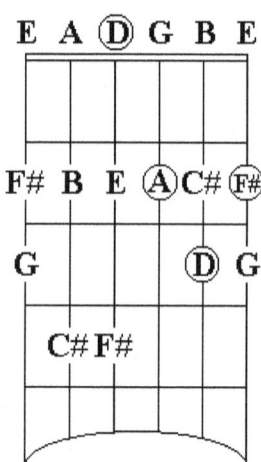

Dorian Mode

D Major Chord Scale

Open Position

Key Of D

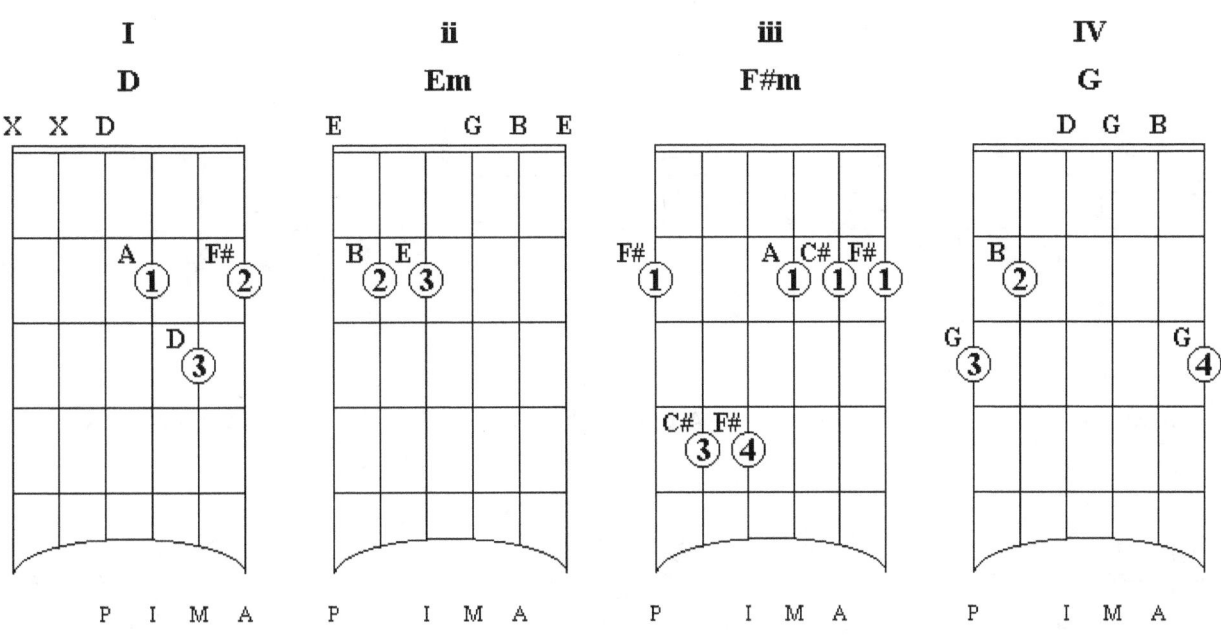

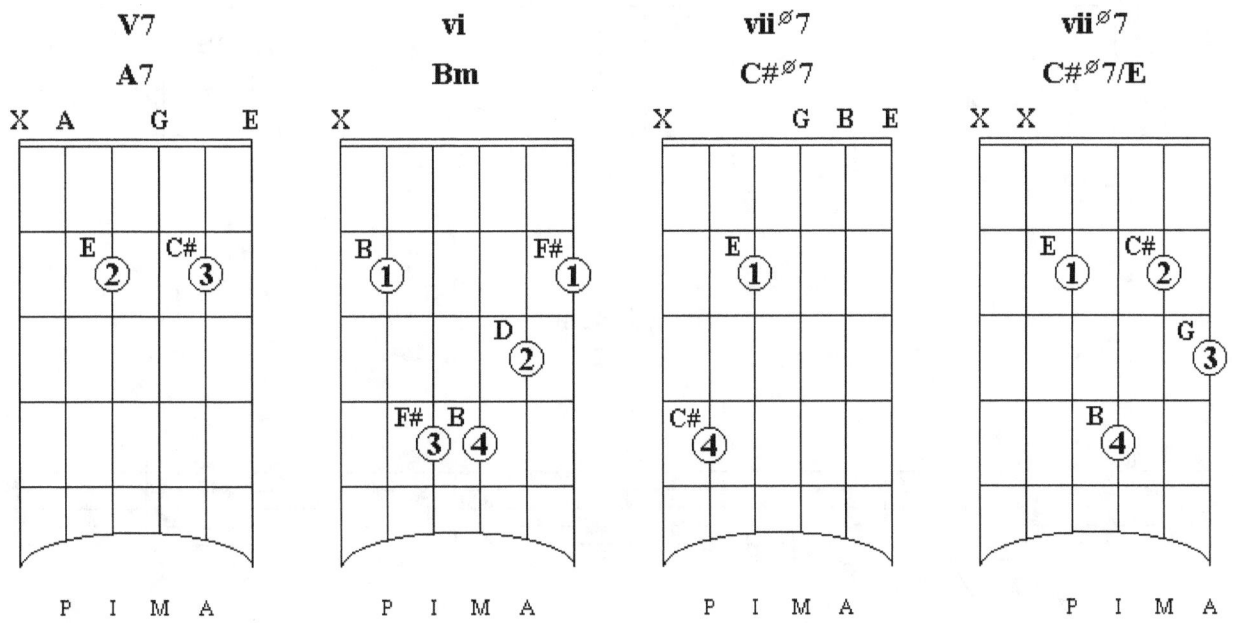

Mixolydian Mode

Open Position

Key Of A

A Major Scale

A Major Scale   A Major Chord   Mixolydian Mode

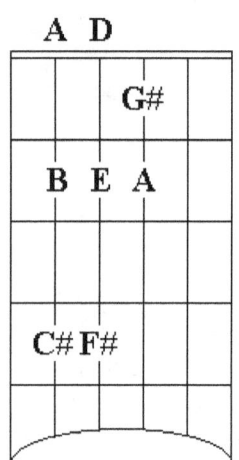 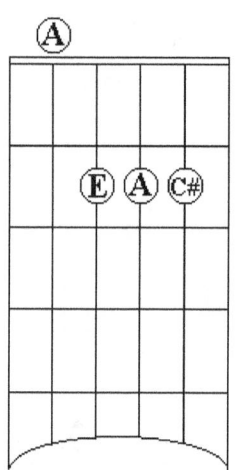 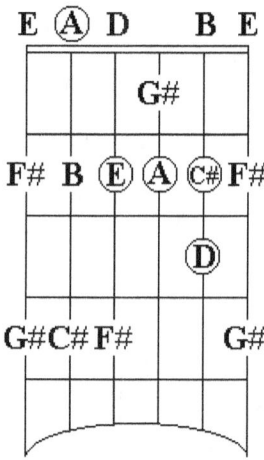

Mixolydian Mode

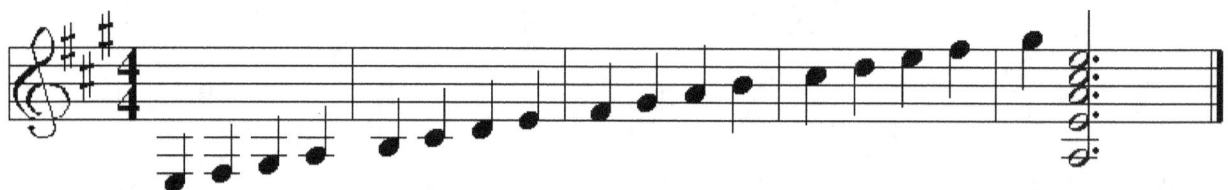

A Major Chord Scale

Open Position

Key Of A

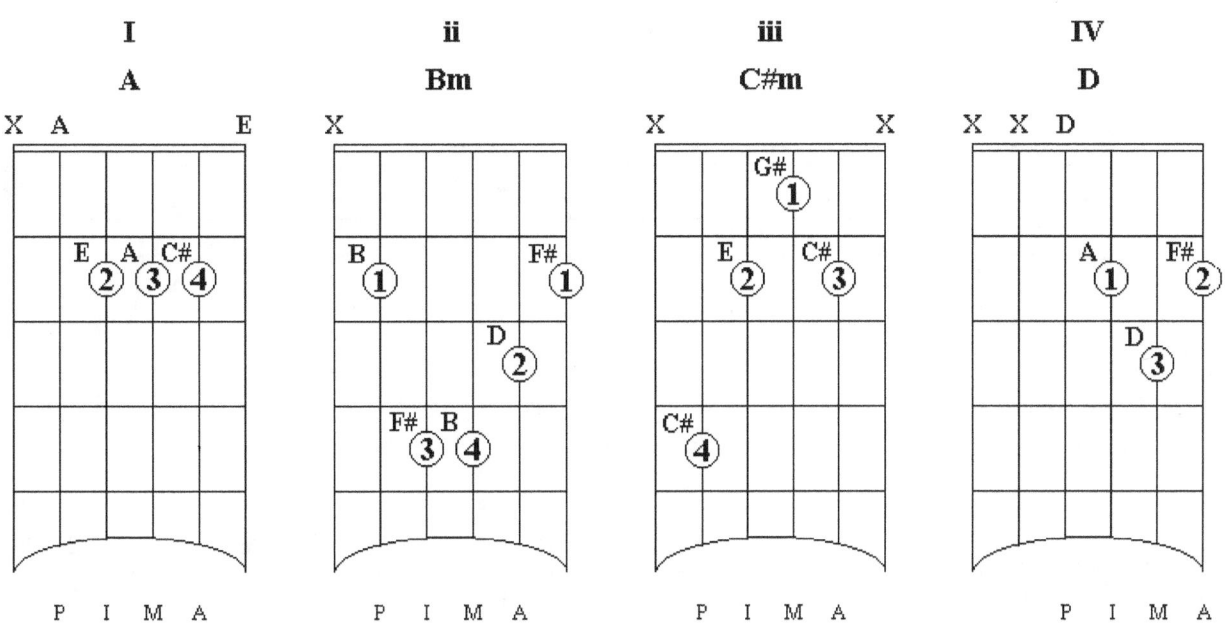

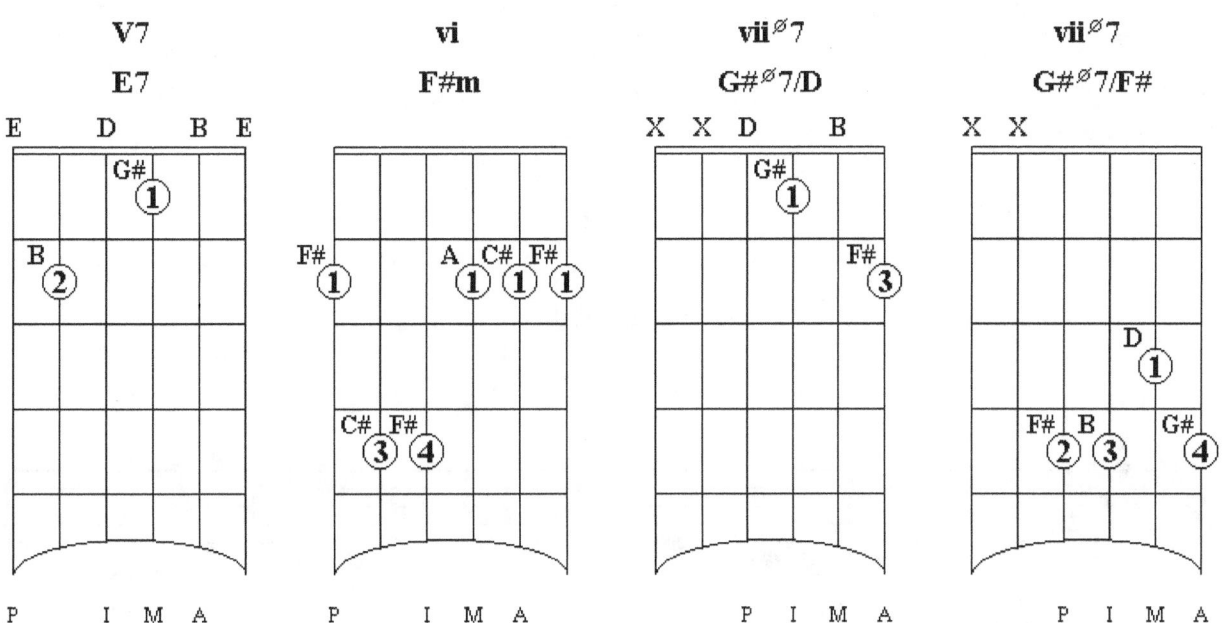

Ionian Mode

Open Position

Key Of E

E Major Scale
Two Octaves

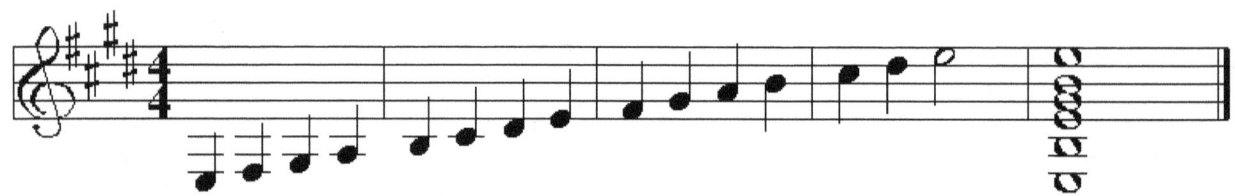

E Major Scale
Two Octaves

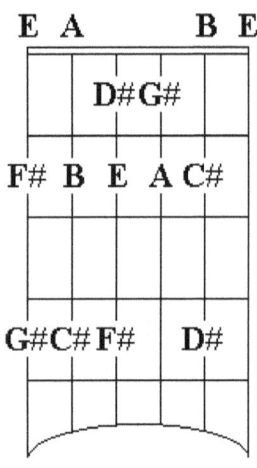

E Major Chord

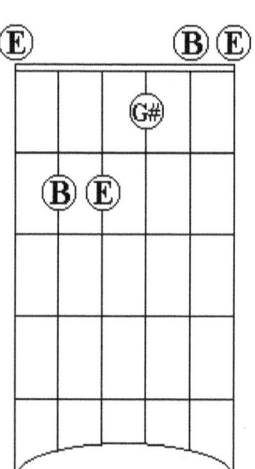

Ionian Mode

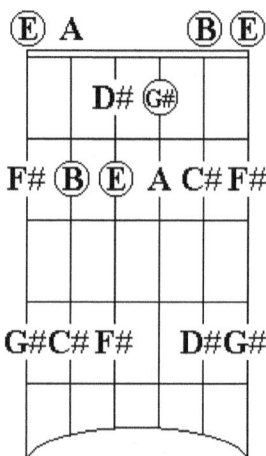

Ionian Mode

E Major Chord Scale

Open Position

Key Of E

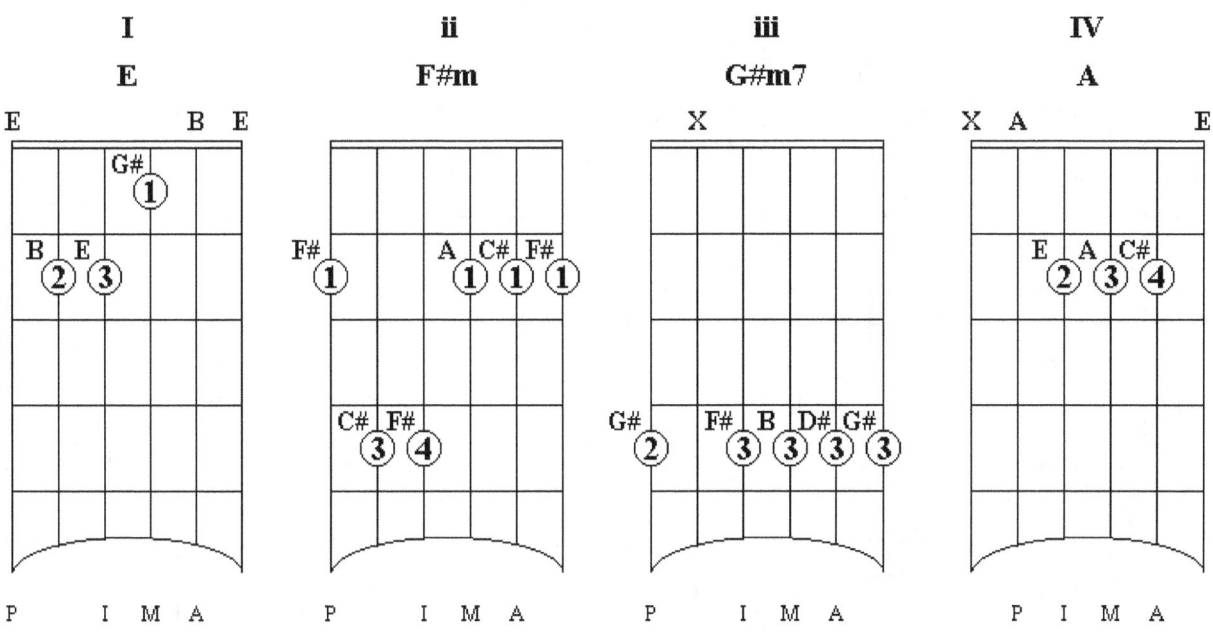

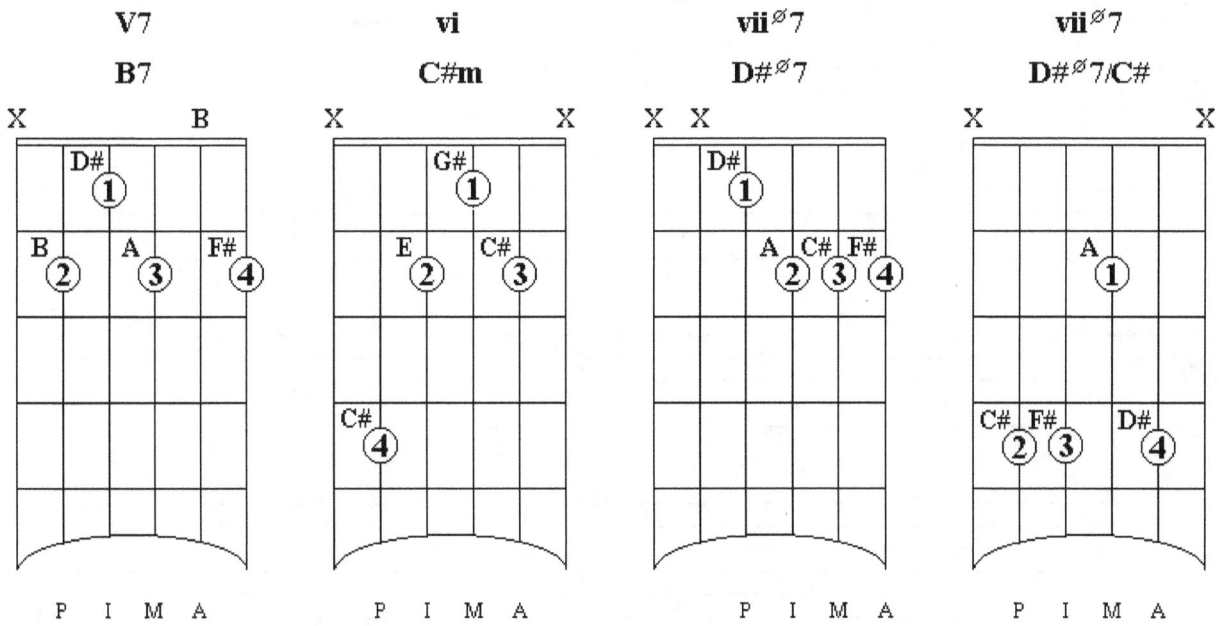

Notes

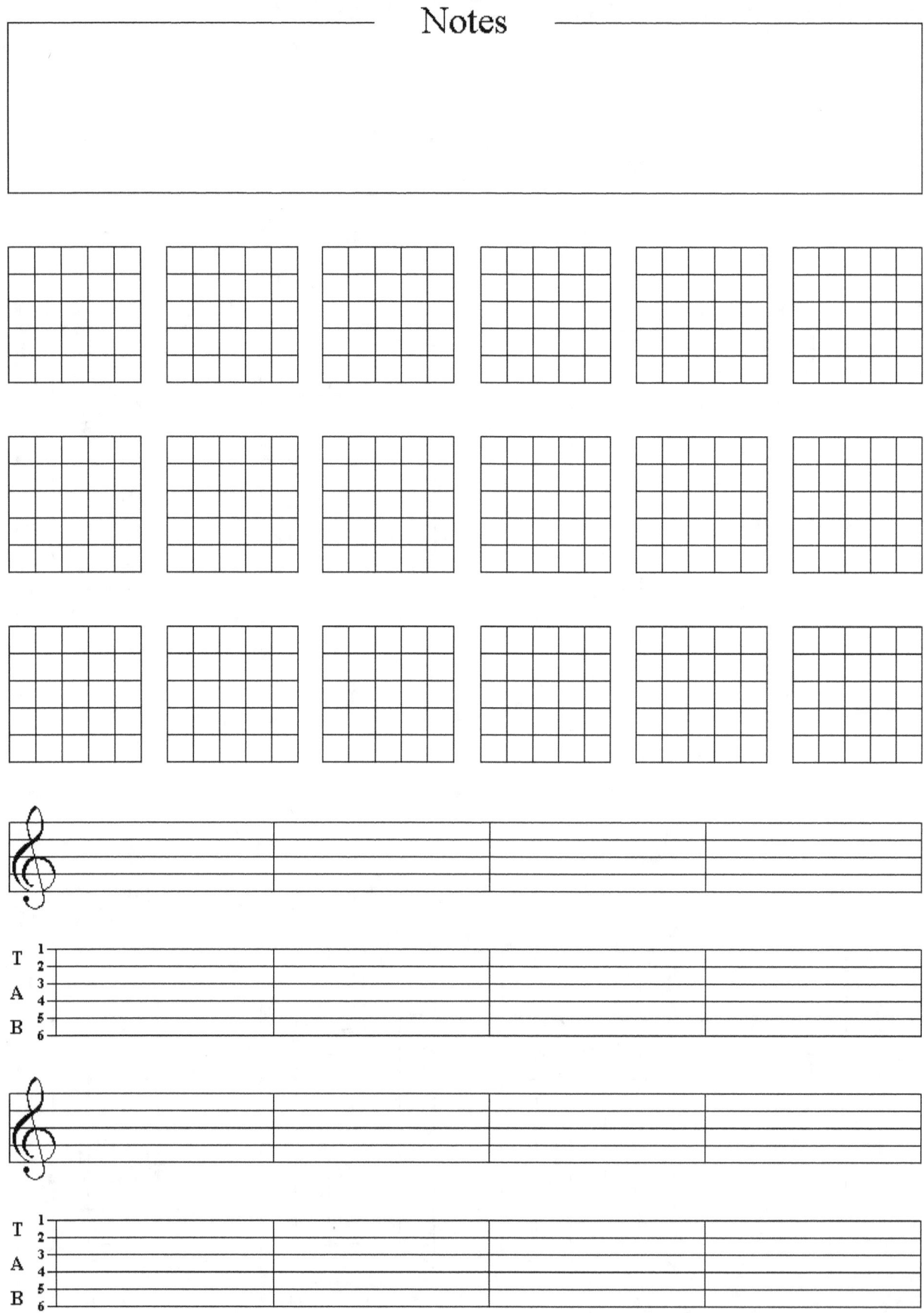

Chapter 10

Modes In The Moveable Position

Modes In The Moveable Positions

Key Of E

The Modes In The Open Position chapter presented the modes in seven different keys. In this chapter the modes are now presented in the moveable positions in the order of Ionian, Dorian, Phrygian, Lydian, Mixolydian, Aeolian, Locrian and the octave Ionian in one key. This means that by replacing the nut of the guitar with the first finger we can play the seven modes spanning the neck of the guitar from the open position upwards to the sixteenth fret giving us seven different patterns for finger variations of the same notes to express ourselves in one key of a song. The guitar is the only instrument that has this much flexibility and variety.

Ionian Mode - The Ionian mode begins on the first degree of the major scale which in the Key of E is E of the open sixth string and plays through to the G# on the 3rd fret of the first string. In the Key of E the open position is the first position.

Dorian Mode - The Dorian mode begins on the second degree of the major scale which in the Key of E is F# on the 2nd fret of the sixth string and plays through to the A on the 5th fret of the first string. In the Key of E the 2nd fret is the second position.

Phrygian Mode - The Phrygian mode begins on the third degree of the major scale which in the Key of E is G# on the 4th fret of the sixth string and plays through to the B on the 7th fret of the first string. In the Key of E the 4th fret is the third position.

Lydian Mode - The Lydian mode begins on the fourth degree of the major scale which in the Key of E is A on the 5th fret of the sixth string and plays through to the C# on the 9th fret of the first string. In the Key of E the 5th fret is the fourth position.

Mixolydian Mode - The Mixolydian mode begins on the fifth degree of the major scale which in the Key of E is B on the 7th fret of the sixth string and plays through to the D# on the 11th fret of the first string. In the Key of E the 7th fret is the fifth position.

Aeolian Mode - The Aeolian mode begins on the sixth degree of the major scale which in the Key of E is C# on the 9th fret of the sixth string and plays through to the E on the 12th fret of the first string. In the Key of E the 9th fret is the sixth position.

Locrian Mode - The Locrian mode begins on the seventh degree of the major scale which in the Key of E is D# on the 11th fret of the sixth string and plays through to the F# on the 14th fret of the first string. In the Key of E the 11th fret is the seventh position.

Octave Mode - The octave mode begins eight degrees above the open position which is always the 12th fret and plays through to the G# on the 16th fret of the first string. The octave mode repeats the open position mode an octave higher.

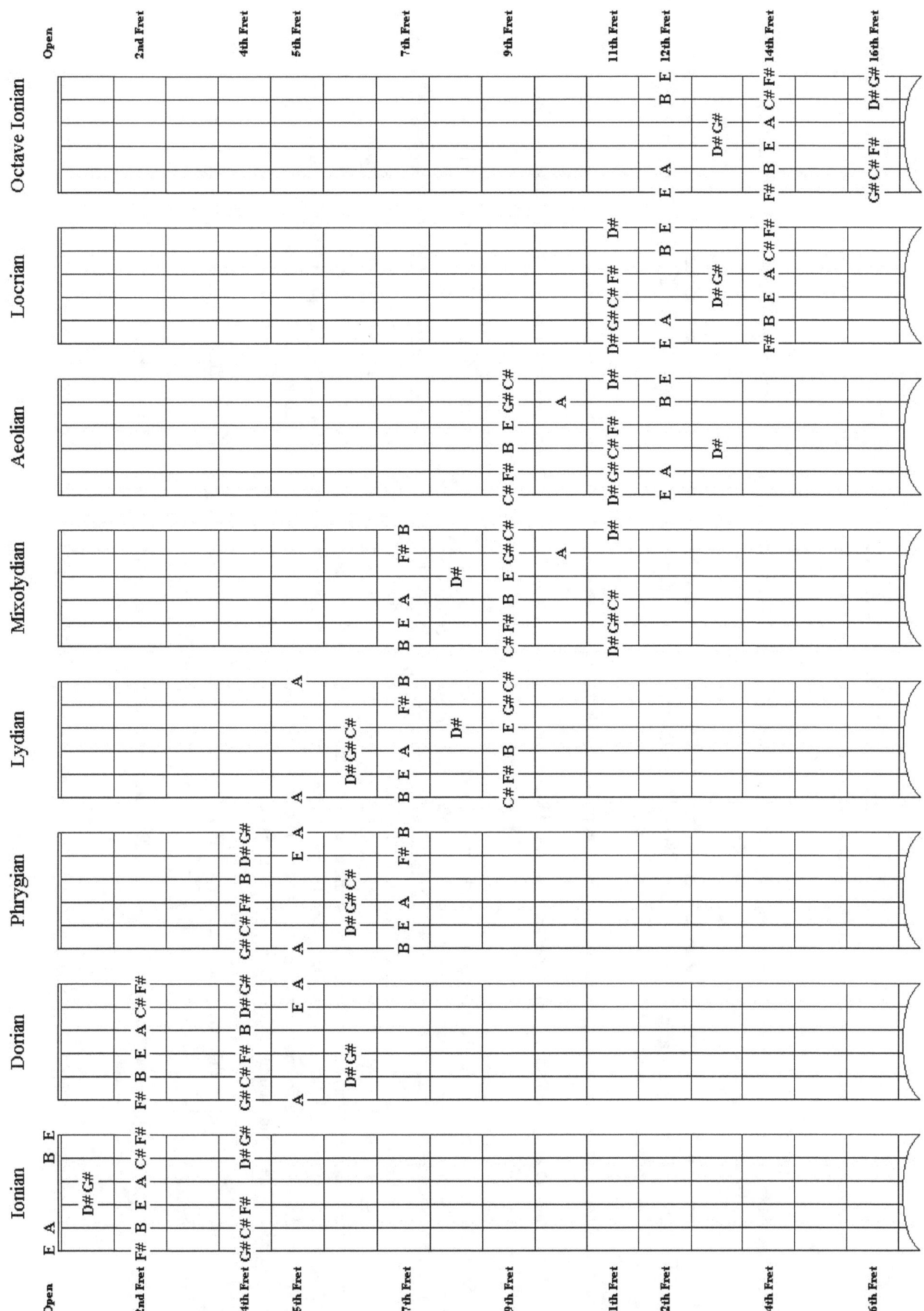

Modes In The Moveable Positions

Practice

In the diagram below the letter note names have been replaced with finger numbers. The finger numbers are for your fret board hand fingers. The finger numbers will guide you through the modes as you play them ascending and descending on the neck of the guitar.

The modes are the foundation of patterns from which all your playing will take place. Practice these seven modes until they are memorized and they will give you greater technical ability to play your guitar as well as provide you with well-traveled territory in which all melodies, chords, solos and improvisations take place. No longer will you be guessing as to where to place your fingers.

At first we'll concentrate on the fret board hand so use whichever picking hand technique is comfortable for you at this time.

The finger numbers are presented to keep your fingers playing in a logical order so they will not get tangled up with each other and also to provide consistency for ease of hand to mind memorization.

1) Start with the Ionian mode in the open position and play it ascending and descending. Next move up to the Dorian mode on the 2nd fret and play it ascending and descending. Continue with the Phrygian mode on the 4th fret and play it ascending and descending. Notice the natural half step between the third degree Phrygian mode and the fourth degree Lydian mode. The Lydian mode is the only mode that will shift as you are playing it. Play the 1 - 3 - 4 fingers starting with the 5th fret on the sixth string then shift up a half step to the 6th fret of the fifth string and play the 1 - 2 - 4 fingers. When you get to the first string you'll need to shift back down to the 5th fret with the first finger and play the 1 - 3 - 4 fingers to complete the Lydian mode ascending. Descending the Lydian mode will be the same procedure only in reverse. The Mixolydian, Aeolian and Locrian modes are straight forward so continue by playing them each in turn ascending and descending. Notice the natural half step between the seventh degree Locrian mode and the eighth degree octave Ionian mode. The octave Ionian mode on the 12th fret is the same pattern as the Ionian mode in the open position. Because the octave Ionian mode is on the 12th fret the first finger replaces the nut that is in place on the guitar for the Ionian mode in the open position. Because of this difference the fingerings of the octave Ionian mode and the Ionian mode in the open position will be different.

2) Once you are comfortable with the fret board hand playing the modes begin to concentrate on your picking hand. Use the alternating flat-picking or chicken pickin' technique explained in Chapter One and each of the finger picking P - I - M - A techniques explained in Chapter Five.

Good! Practice at least fifteen minutes a day. Better! Practice fifteen minutes several times a day. Best! Get lost in it all day, everyday.

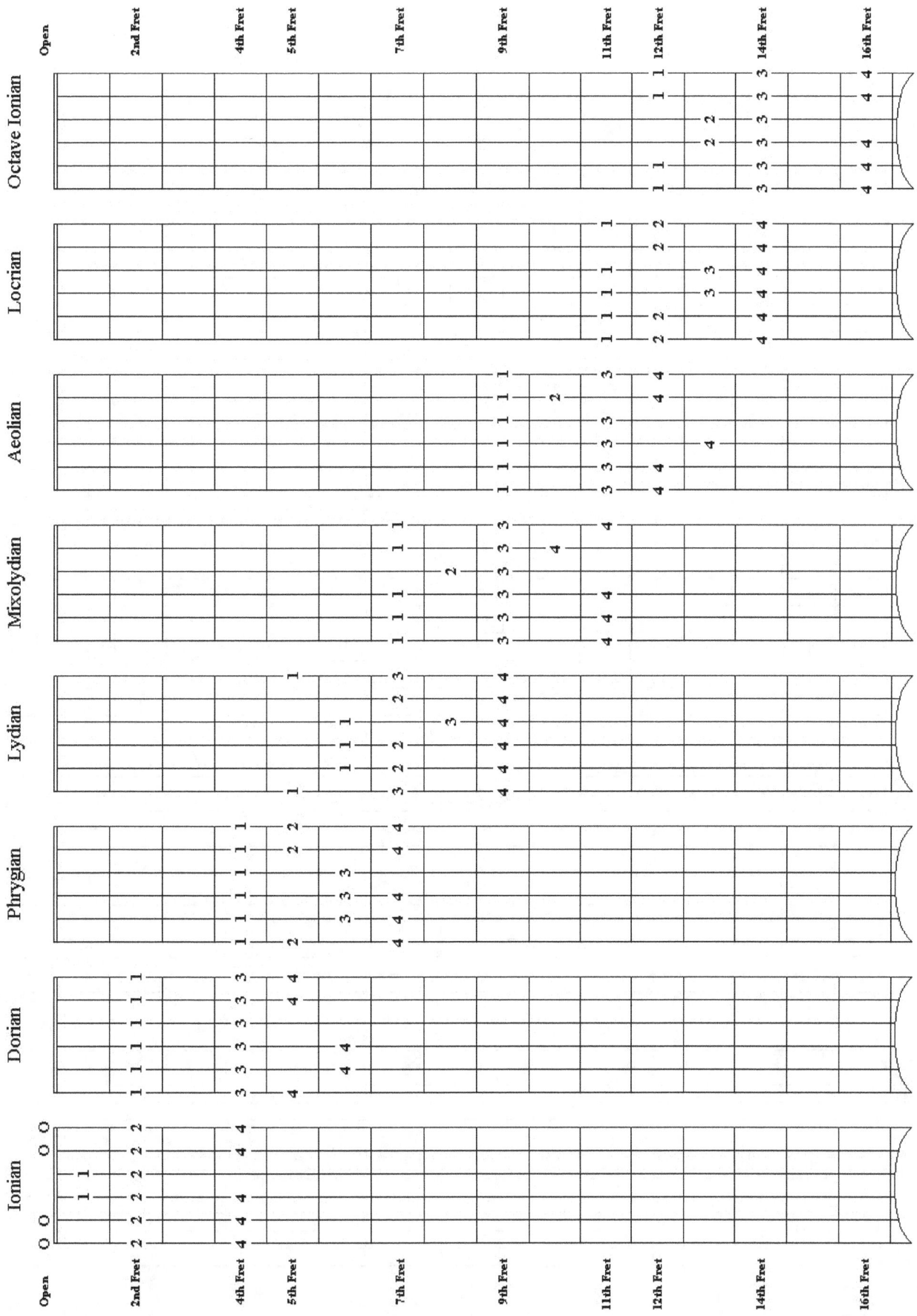

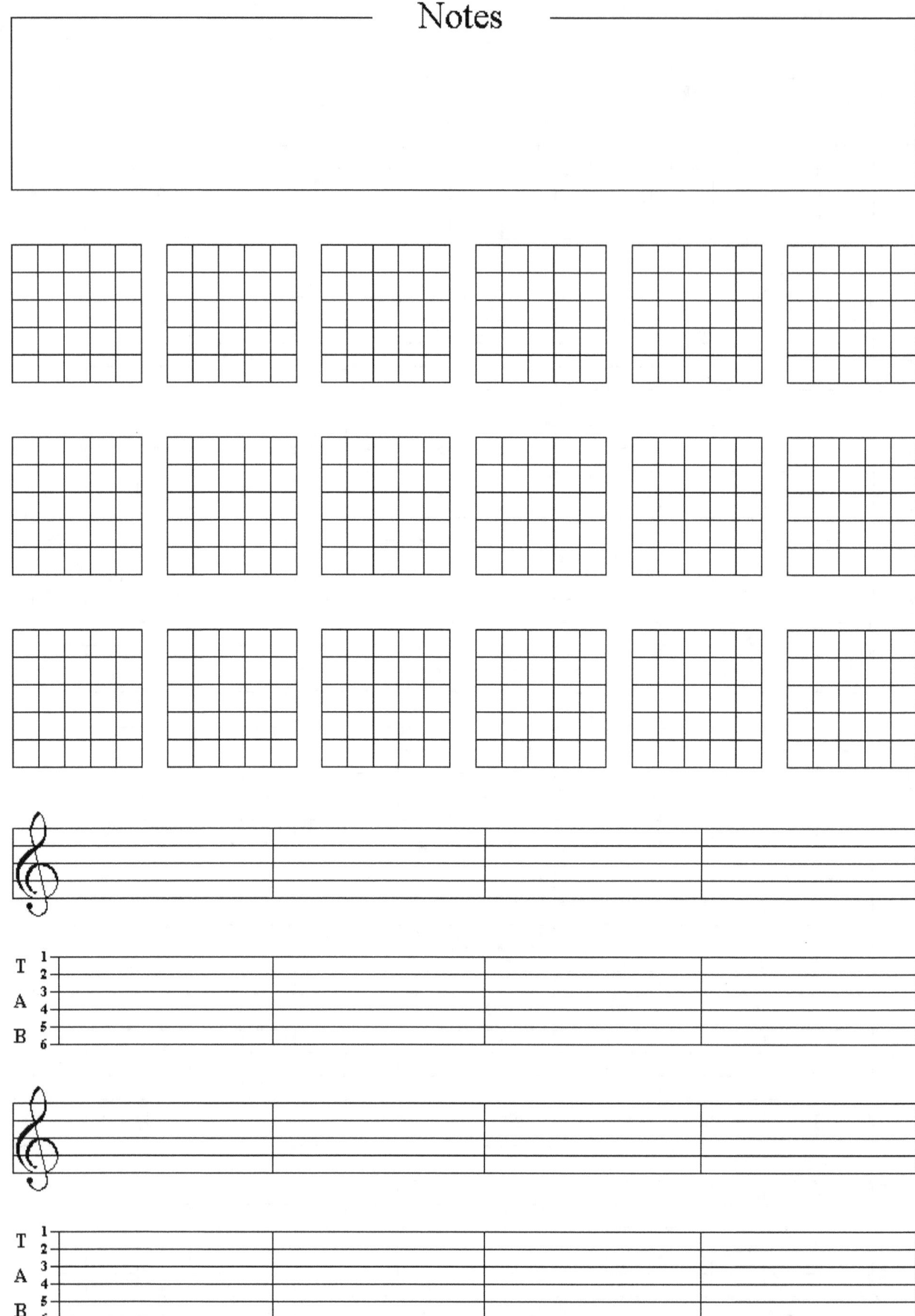

Chapter

11

Moveable Chords

Moveable Chords

With chords in the open position of the guitar understood let's now explore the chords on the rest of the guitar fret board. In this chapter we will learn that the five basic chords previously learned in the open position can be moved up the neck of the guitar fret board and still retain their same forms. It will also be found that the major chord scales of the five basic chord keys C, G, D, A and E can also be moved up the neck of the guitar fret board and still retain their same forms as well.

When the chord form is played by replacing the nut of the guitar with the first finger, the same chord form can then move up and down the neck of the guitar to different fret positions and still retain its' form. Because the first finger replaces the nut the moveable chord form will now be played with different fingers and the letter note names of the chords and the chord name will change according to the notes on the fret board in the different fret positions the chords are in.

To understand this better, let's look at the chords in the Five Basic Chords diagram. Take the C chord in the Open Position section. Notice the fingers used are 1, 2 and 3 with the third string note being played open because of the nut. Now look down at the C# chord in the Moveable section and notice that the chord is the same C form only now its shown with the 2nd, 3rd and 4th fingers and the first finger is used on the third string to replace the nut on the first fret. By moving the C up one half step which is one fret, it now becomes a C# chord. Now move the C form up one more fret and it becomes a D chord. Each of the five basic chords can be played in this manner up the Chromatic scale in all twelve keys. Since both the open and moveable chords are used in playing, both fingerings are useful to learn.

Being able to move up the neck of the guitar is a liberating experience that opens up infinite possibilities for creative expression. With these possibilities comes the need to train our fingers and memory through exercises to be able to technically perform the songs we want in our repertoire.

Because the moveable chord forms are advanced due to their fingering they should be approached first playing one note at a time in the style of arpeggio and later as skill permits play the chord by holding down all the fingers of the chord at once. For example, play the root note of the C form on the fifth string first with the fourth finger then lift it off the fifth string at the same time as the third finger comes into play on the fourth string. Continue by lifting the third finger off the fourth string at the same time the first finger plays the note on the third string. As you are lifting the first finger off the third string the second finger will be pressed down on the second string. In summary, the chord is played one note at a time by lifting each finger off the string as the next finger is pressed down from the bass strings to the treble strings. When playing the moveable G chord form leave the partially barred first finger down while playing through the three notes. The same approach applies to the moveable A chord form.

Playing chords in arpeggio is a technique used by soloists that breaks the linear sound of scale passages to create a more interesting solo. Arpeggio playing causes the notes to jump across the strings sounding larger intervals while playing scales moves the fingers up and down the strings generally in whole and half step intervals. A good solo will integrate chord arpeggios and scales.

Five Basic Chords

Open Position

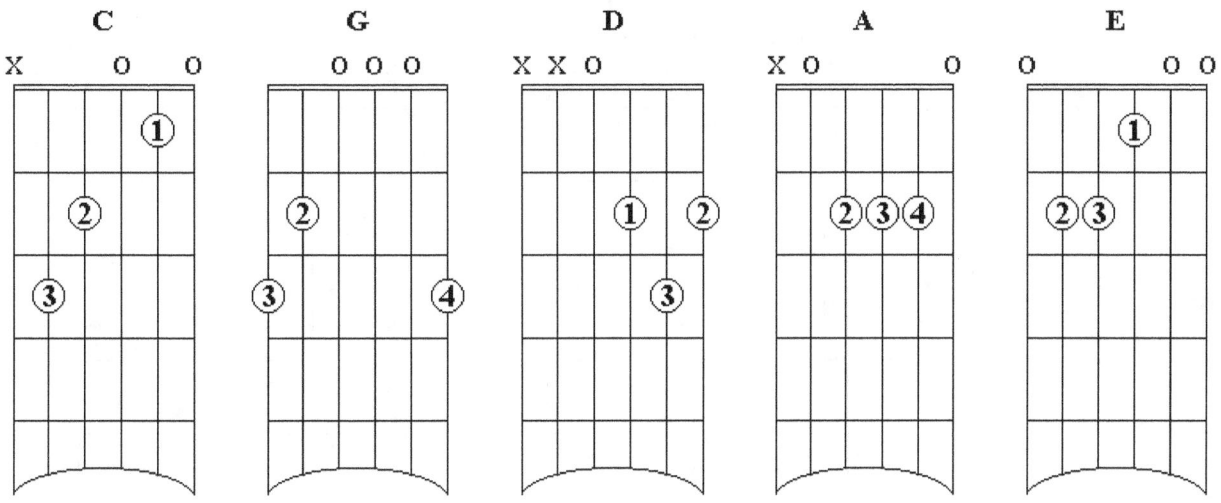

Moveable

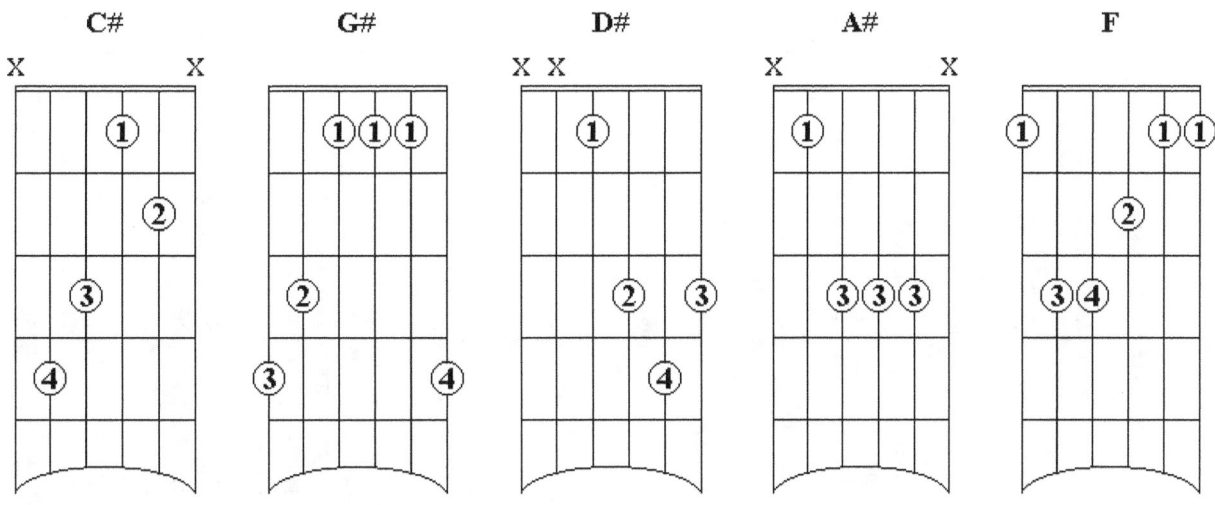

C – A – G – E – D

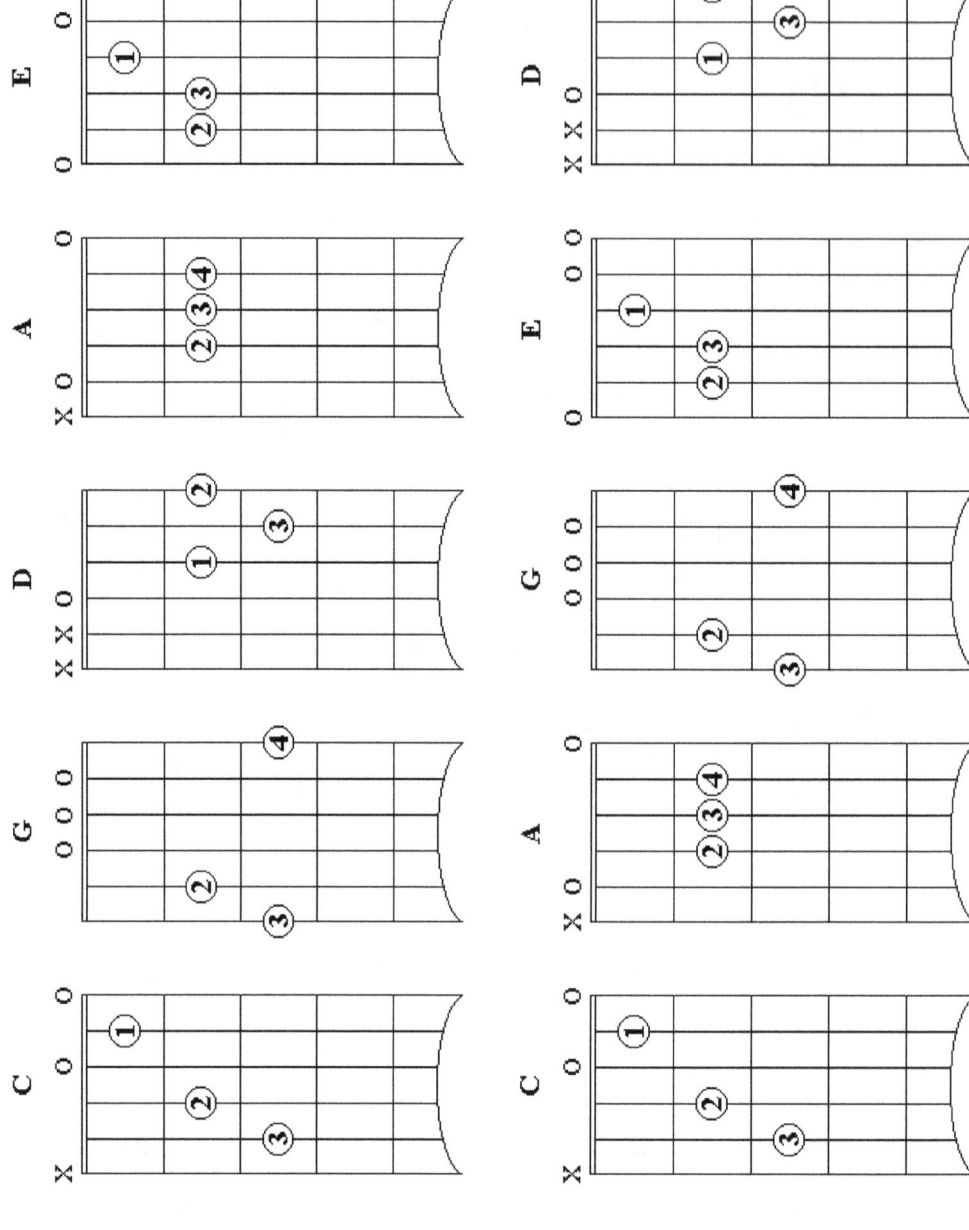

Here's a neat reference trick!

Look at the five basic chord forms C - G - D - A - E below as previously learned and rearrange their order to C - A - G - E - D.

Now look at the C - A - G - E - D diagram on the following page.

It is found that the chord forms C, A, G, E, D follow each other up the neck of the guitar.

They are all C chords by name due to the letter note names that form the chords in the fret positions they are found in.

We now have location markers for which modes and chords to play in each specific position on the guitar.

The C - A - G - E - D sequence works the same in all twelve keys.

Amongst the array of six strings and twelve frets there is a sequence of chord forms that provide us with position markers.

The C - A - G - E - D system is one of a kind as there is no other orderly reference system known.

The C - A - G - E - D system makes it easy to remember.

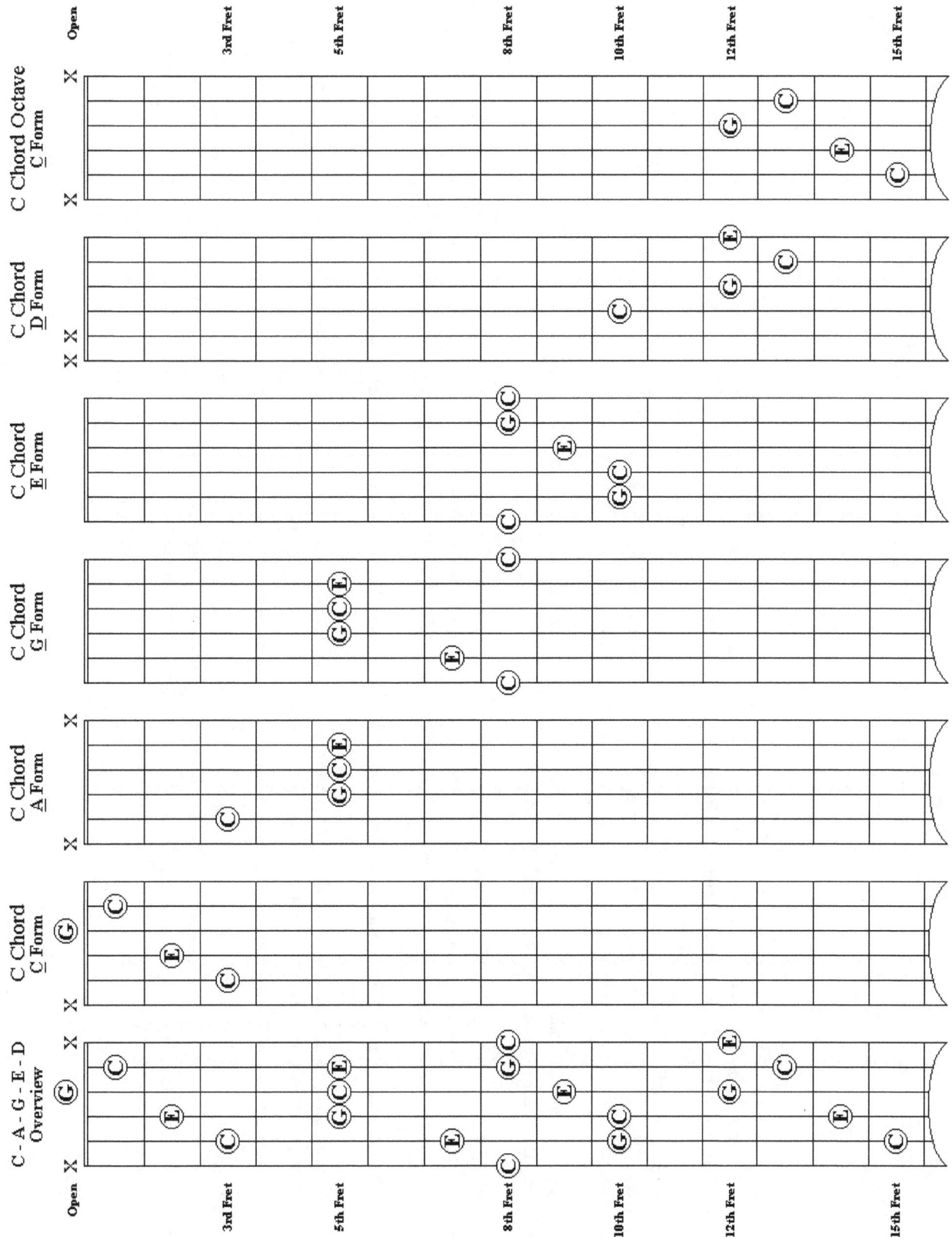

C – A – G – E – D And The Modes

Key Of C

Now that we understand that the C - A - G - E - D sequence has an order that defines the fret board as location markers let's see how it fits into the modes that are the pattern foundation in which all of our melodies, chords, solos and improvisations take place.

The C - A - G - E - D AND THE MODES diagram below is in the Key of C which presents with clarity the C - A - G - E - D sequence from the open position to the twelfth fret of the modes without a break in its continuity so it can be seen from the C form right on through to the D form as well as the octave C form. Eight guitar fret boards are presented so each mode can be seen in its entirety as the modes progress up the fret board.

Notice that there are seven modes and only five basic chords with the A form sharing itself with the Lydian and Mixolydian modes and the E form sharing itself with the Locrian and Ionian modes. This is due to the size and closeness of these modes.

It should be realized that there are several different ways to play the finger patterns of the modes. It is one of the purposes of this book however to simplify the modes and to this end the patterns presented here are believed to be, after much thought and playing experience, the most logical to learn and play. It will be seen in Chapters Thirteen and Fourteen when the Pentatonic, Hexatonic and Octatonic scales are derived from the modes that the significance of their patterns are fully realized.

The C - A - G - E - D AND THE MODES diagram below is an overview for understanding. Practice will begin in Chapter Twelve.

The lesson to be learned here is that the C form will always be present with the Phrygian mode, the A form will always be present in the Lydian and Mixolydian modes, the G form will always be present with the Aeolian mode, the E form will always be present in the Locrian and Ionian modes and the D form will always be present with the Dorian mode.

Since confusion can arise as each of the five basic chord forms can be played as the I chord, the IV chord and the V chord in each key it needs to be clarified that only the I chord applies to the C - A - G - E - D sequence and the modes. For example, the same C chord form in the Key of C can be played as the C chord, F chord and G chord linearly up the neck of the guitar. It would only be the C chord of the C form that would be present in the Phrygian mode and C - A G - E - D. If the song is in a minor key than the root chord of the parent key.

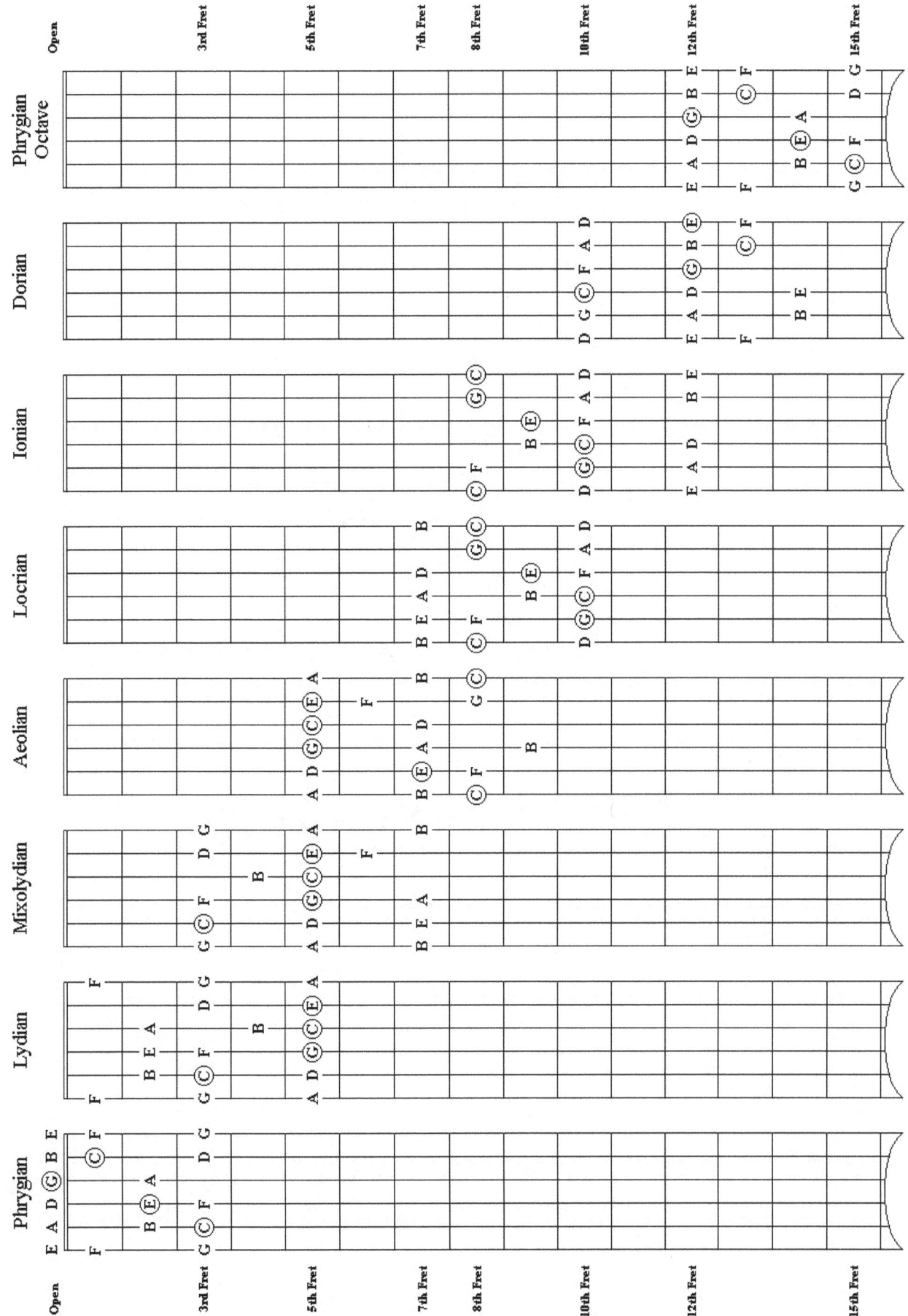

Chapter 12

Chord Scales

In The

Moveable Position

Chord Scales

Moveable Positions

In this section we'll play the five major chord scales plus the octave in the open and seven moveable positions. The student will also learn how the melody of a song intertwines through the modes and chords naturally positioning the finger movements for improvisation. Of the seven modes, the Lydian and Mixolydian modes share the A chord form and the Locrian and Ionian modes share the E chord form thus requiring only five major chord scales.

The chord forms sequence: C - A - G - E – D reveals its importance here as location guides on the guitar. For example, look at the C form on pages 12-3 and 12-4. There is the Phrygian mode and seven specific chord forms, all of which are derived from the major scale and associated with the C form. This applies to all twelve keys.

Review: The modes sequence of the major scale: Ionian - Dorian - Phrygian - Lydian - Mixolydian - Aeolian - Locrian and the Octave will always be in this same order in all twelve keys. It is essential to practice the modes with their associated chord forms and major chord scales in all keys to become familiar with the feel of the different positions. It is not enough to memorize and play in only one key. Start with the Key of E then F, F#, G, G#, A, A#, B, C, C#, D and D#.

Since the C - A - G - E - D forms are utilized as reference points on the guitar, it doesn't matter which one you start with, always remember that whatever chord form is in the position your playing, the other four chord forms with their respective modes and major chord scales are surrounding it. With the modes and chord scales memorized and practiced in all twelve keys, you will always know where you are at any time.

Improv 101

Improvisation is the spontaneous creation of music. Because improvisation is based on the melody theme the improviser must know the melody to be able to improvise around it.

Prior to the infusion of Blues into the Western musical system, improvisation was merely a flurry of notes added to the song in-between melody phrases, which were derived from the major scale of the key of the song that it was being played in. Spanish music with its' fiery style of playing is a good example of this type of improvisation.

When the Blues entered the scene, improvisation was redefined. Having a lead section in a song became typical. This means that a musician can take a lead part in a song and improvise upon the melody theme expressing themselves musically. This expression comes from our every day life's experiences that are absorbed into our sub-conscious minds, which is then recalled at a later time presenting itself uniquely from the musician's perception of life.

Looking back at Page 11-6 there are eight modal positions including the octave that the melody can be played in. This also means that there are eight modal positions including the octave that the musician can improvise in.

Now looking forward to Page 12-5 the song Scarborough Fair, an old traditional folk song from Europe of past, is presented for its simplicity in the Key of C since it has no sharps (#) or flats (b) so the student can learn the note names and grasp the essence of the melody and its finger arrangements. Reading notation is a significant part of the creative improvising procedure as the interval distance between the notes on the staff reveals the interval distance within the modes and the chords on the guitar. Every melody is intertwined within the mode and chord structures. If a melody were to follow only the mode it would be boring. However, by utilizing the intervals of chords and the playing across the strings, the melody becomes much more interesting. The melody utilizes both the modes and chords. This is an important insight to successful reading of notation and creative improvisation. Memorize the notes on the staff (Pages 3-3 & 3-4) as well as on the guitar and have a picture of the mode in your minds eye so you will be able to see the melody on the guitar before you play it. This eliminates guessing, gives you a deeper insight into the guitar and will make your playing smoother. It does take practice and the going will be slow at first but the end result will be well worth the effort.

As you play the melody of Scarborough Fair in the eight positions on the proceeding pages pay close attention to the finger numbers. The correct fingering is essential to playing with ease, which in turn produces a smooth performance. The finger movements will automatically lend themselves to improvising by revealing the chord and modal playing that is occurring as the melody is being played. Although this exercise at first appears to be only reading the melody, it is the perfect exercise to get in on the very ground floor of improvising.

Practice

Beginning on pages 12-3 and 12-4 practice the root chord, mode and major chord scale then play the Scarborough Fair Phrygian Mode Open Position song on page 12-5. Proceed through each of the positions one step at a time. It is advisable to reference: C-A-G-E-D And The Modes from page 11-6. Pay attention to your picking hand technique whether you use a flat pick, finger picking or the Chicken Pickin' form.

How To Do It

Pick the root chord then without stopping; fingerpick or flat pick the mode ascending and descending, picking the chord scale ascending and descending and last pick the root chord again. Practice this three times in one continuous movement for each chord scale position.

To practice the modes in the finger picking style use down strokes of the thumb (P) on the three bass strings: E - A and D, and alternating strokes of the index (I) and middle (M) fingers in the three treble strings: G - B and E. This is classical style and is a very fast and effective picking hand technique. To practice the modes in the flat-picking style use alternating up and down strokes. The student should also practice the modes with all of the finger picking exercises learned in Chapter Five.

The chords in the open position major chord scale are played as arpeggios in the smooth and flowing legato style. The chords in the moveable major chord scales are played as arpeggios by playing the notes of the chord one after the other as staccato by releasing each finger of the fret board hand before playing the next note. This is an excellent exercise for finger independence. The picking hand plays only the four strings of the notes presented in the pattern of P - I - M - A for each chord in the major chord scale.

Phrygian Mode

C Form

3rd Degree Of The Major Scale

Key Of C

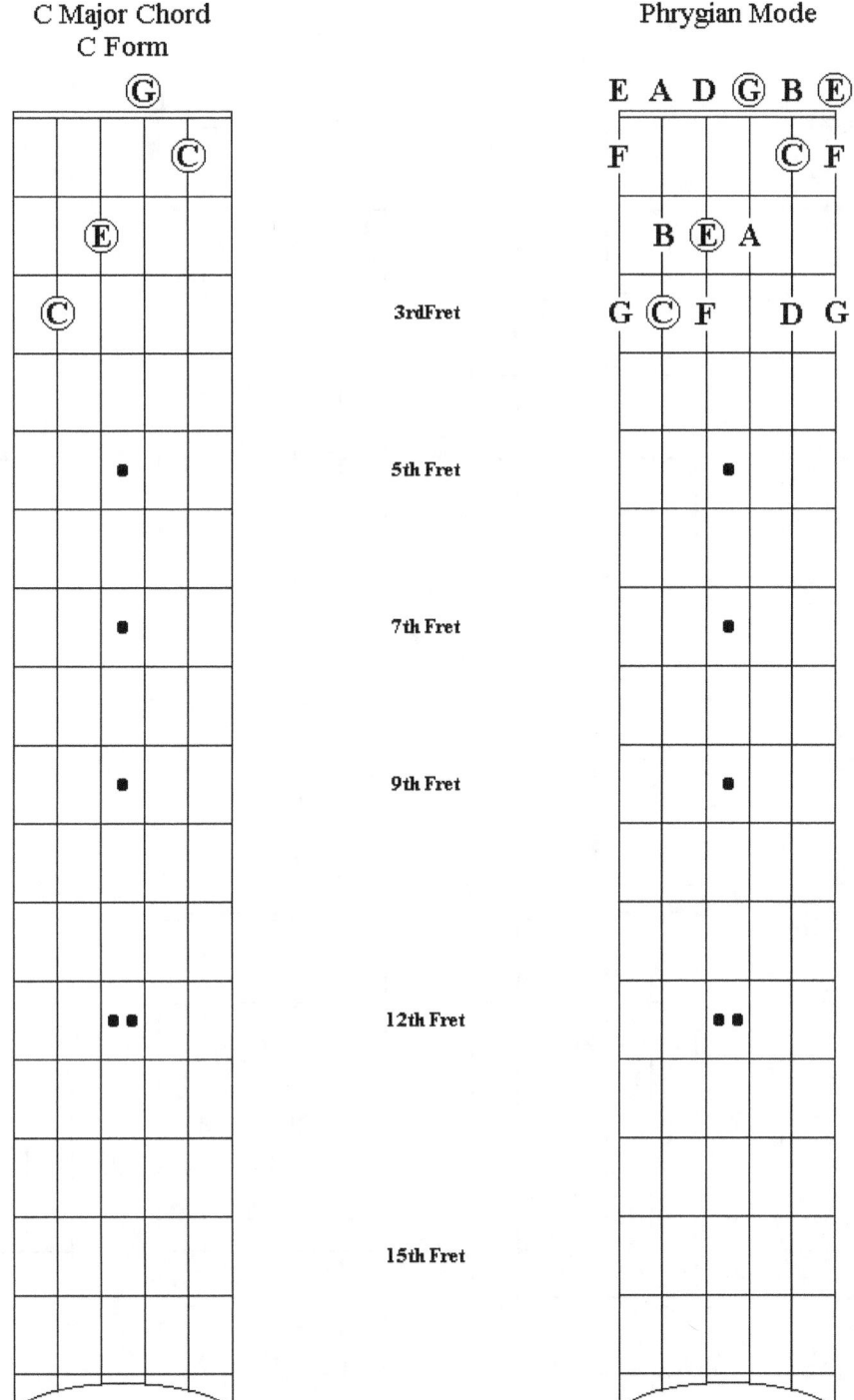

C Major Chord Scale

C Form – Phrygian Mode

3rd Degree Of The Major Scale

Key of C

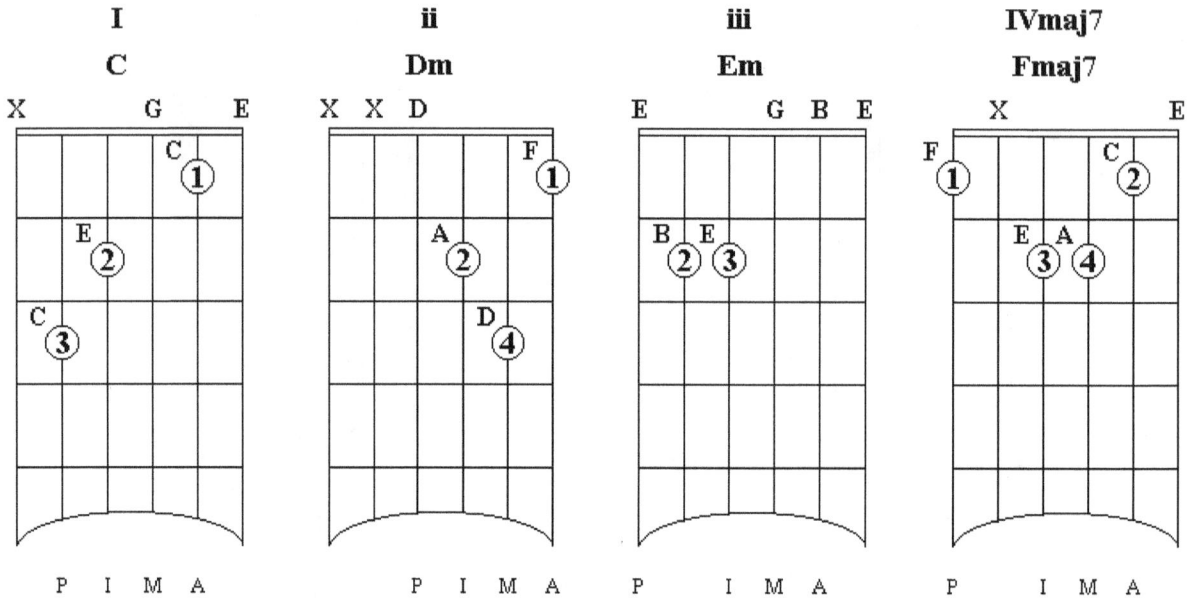

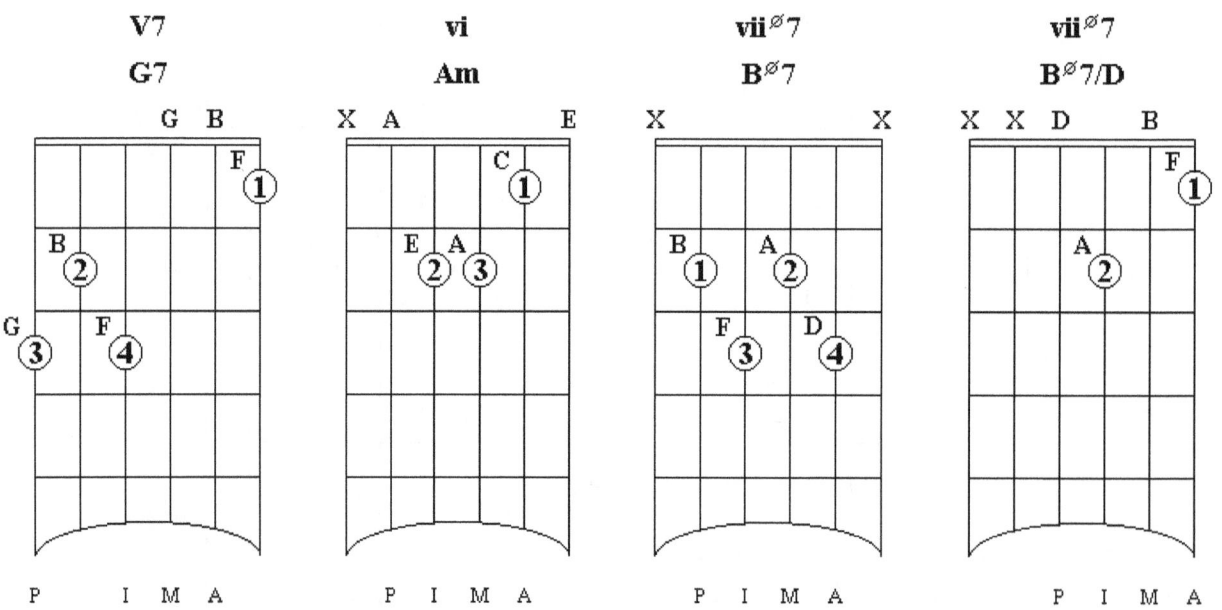

Scarborough Fair
Phrygian Mode - Open Position

Anonymous

Lydian And Mixolydian Modes

A Form

4th And 5th Degrees Of The Major Scale

Key Of C

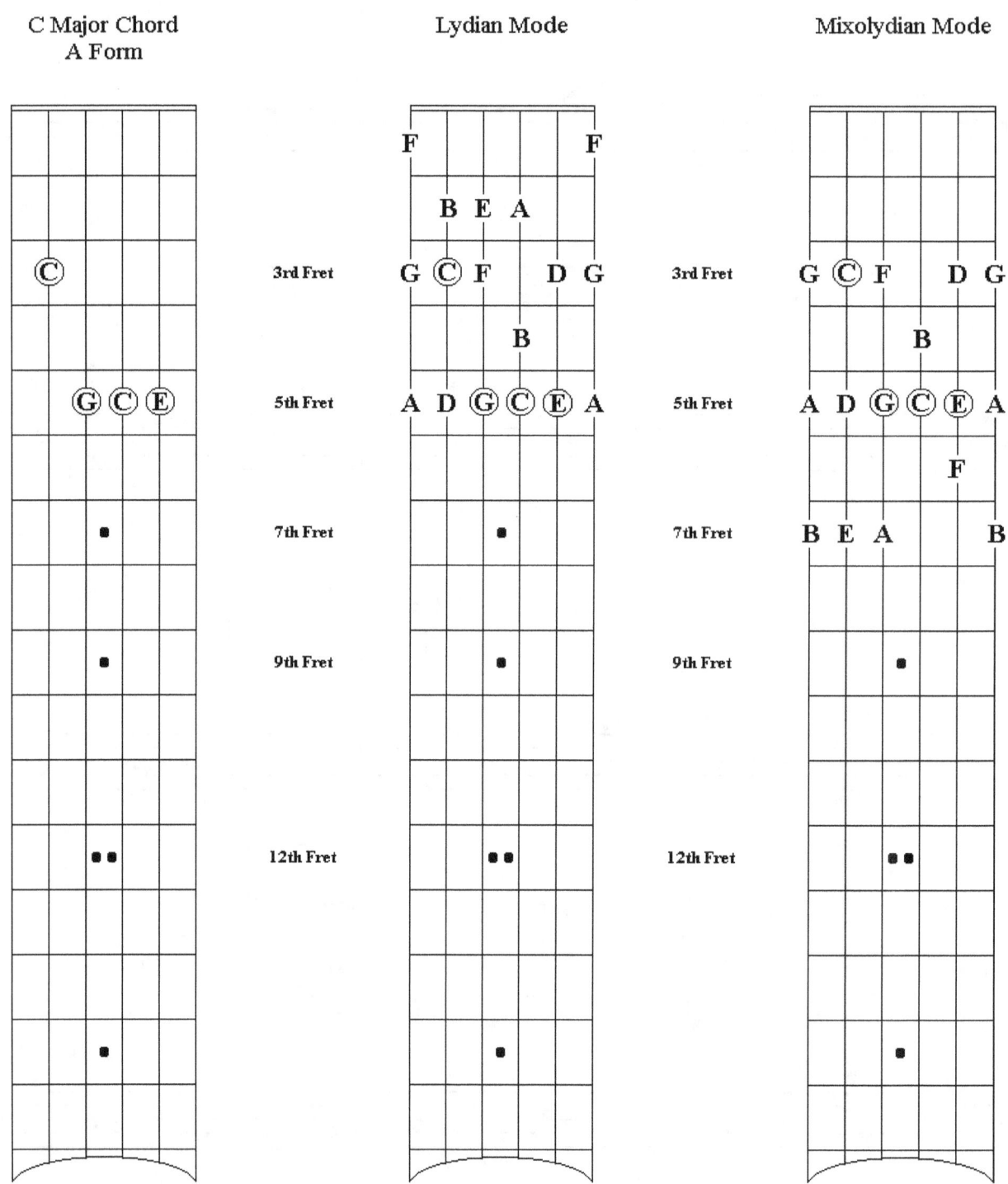

C Major Chord Scale

A Form – Lydian And Mixolydian Modes

4th And 5th Degrees Of The Major Scale

Key Of C

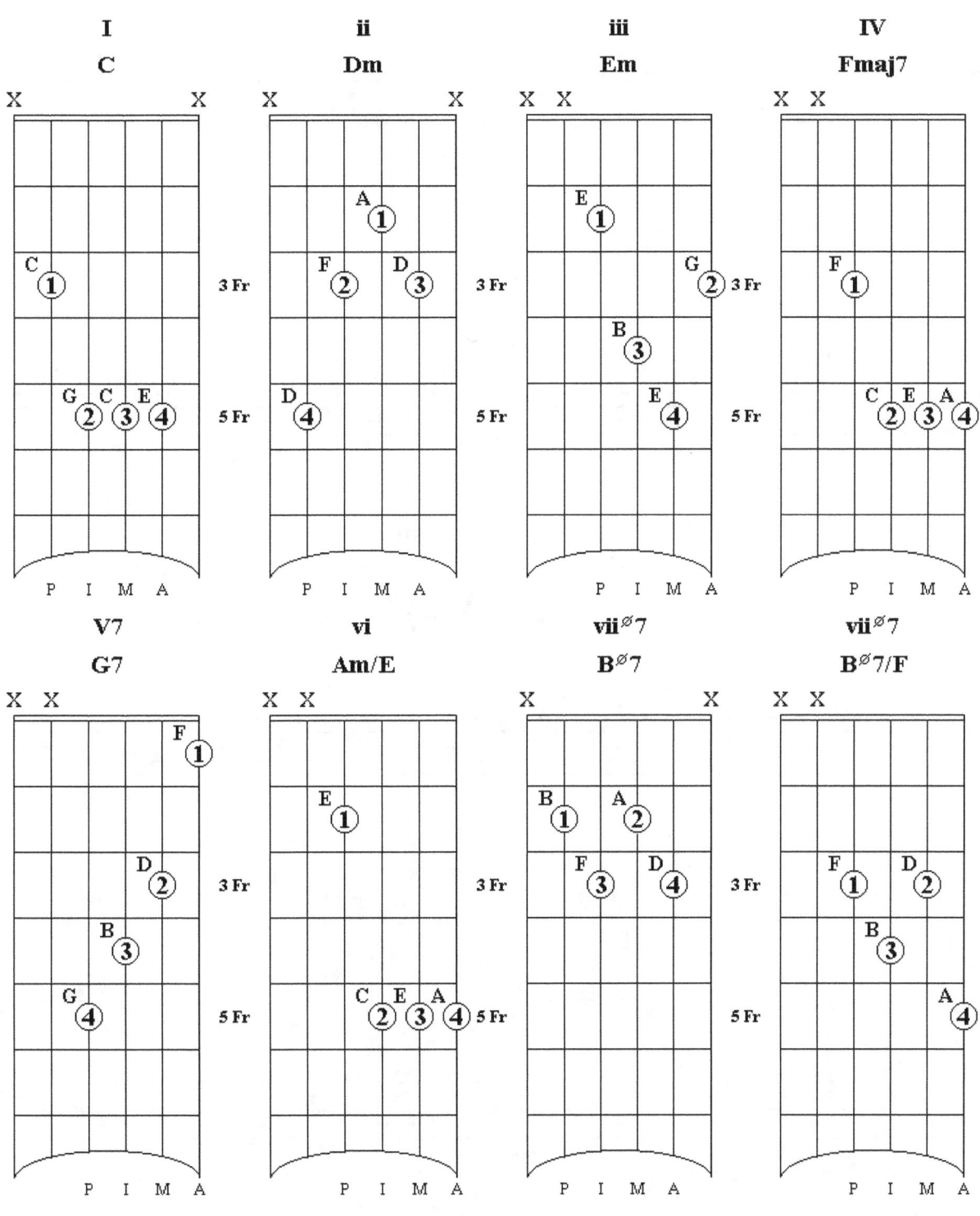

Scarborough Fair
Lydian Mode

Anonymous

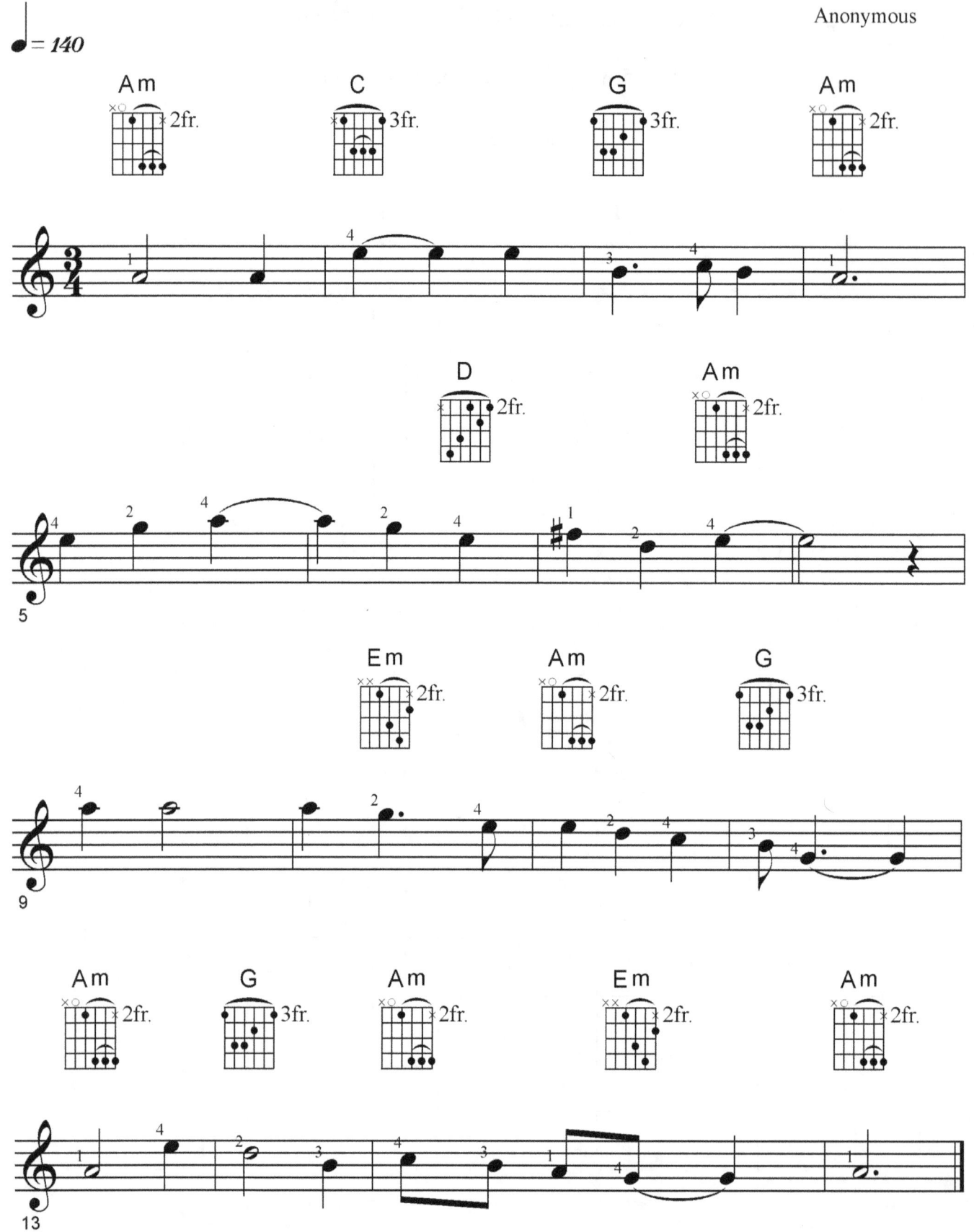

Scarborough Fair
Mixolydian Mode

Anonymous

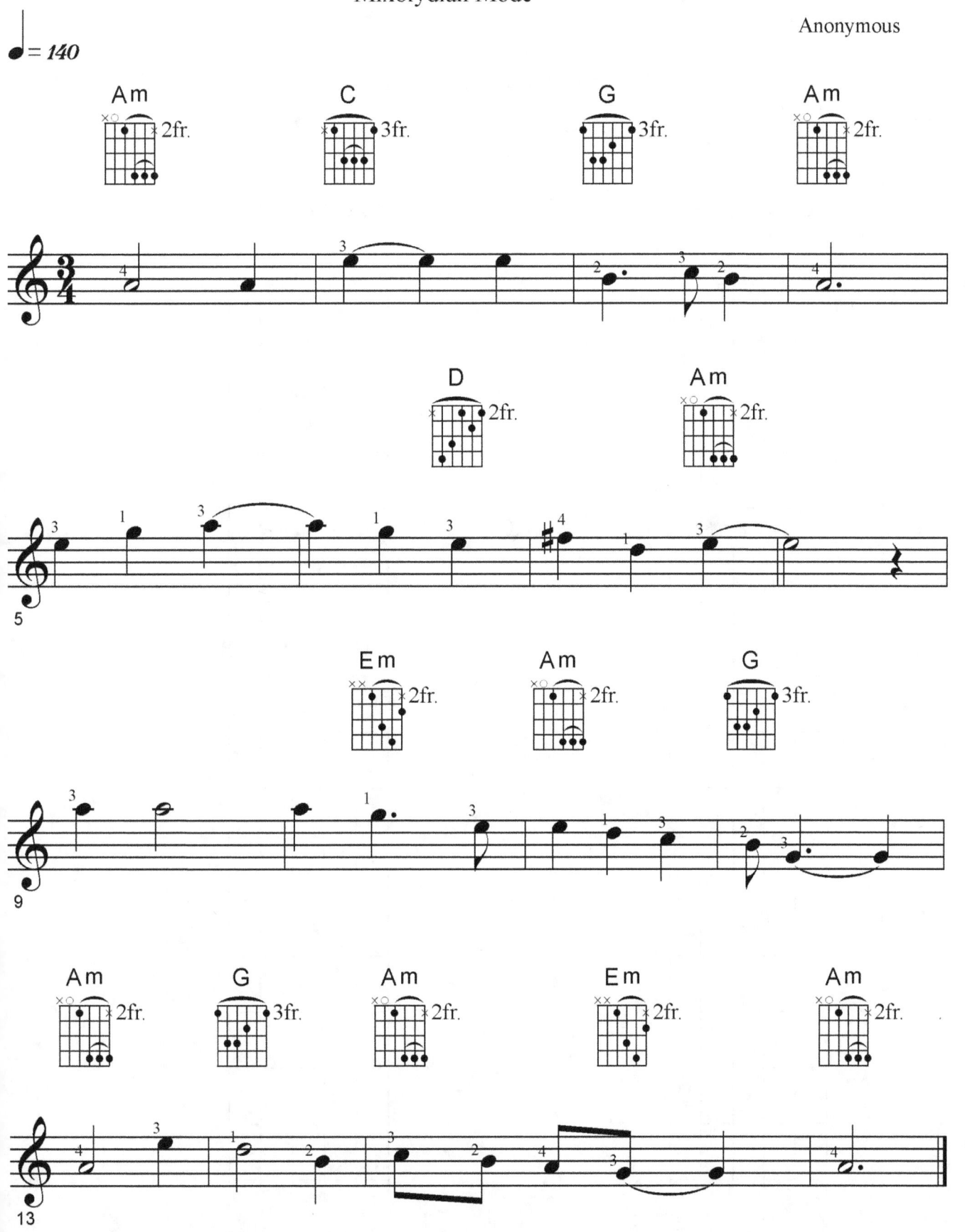

Aeolian Mode

G Form

6th Degree Of The Major Scale

Key Of C

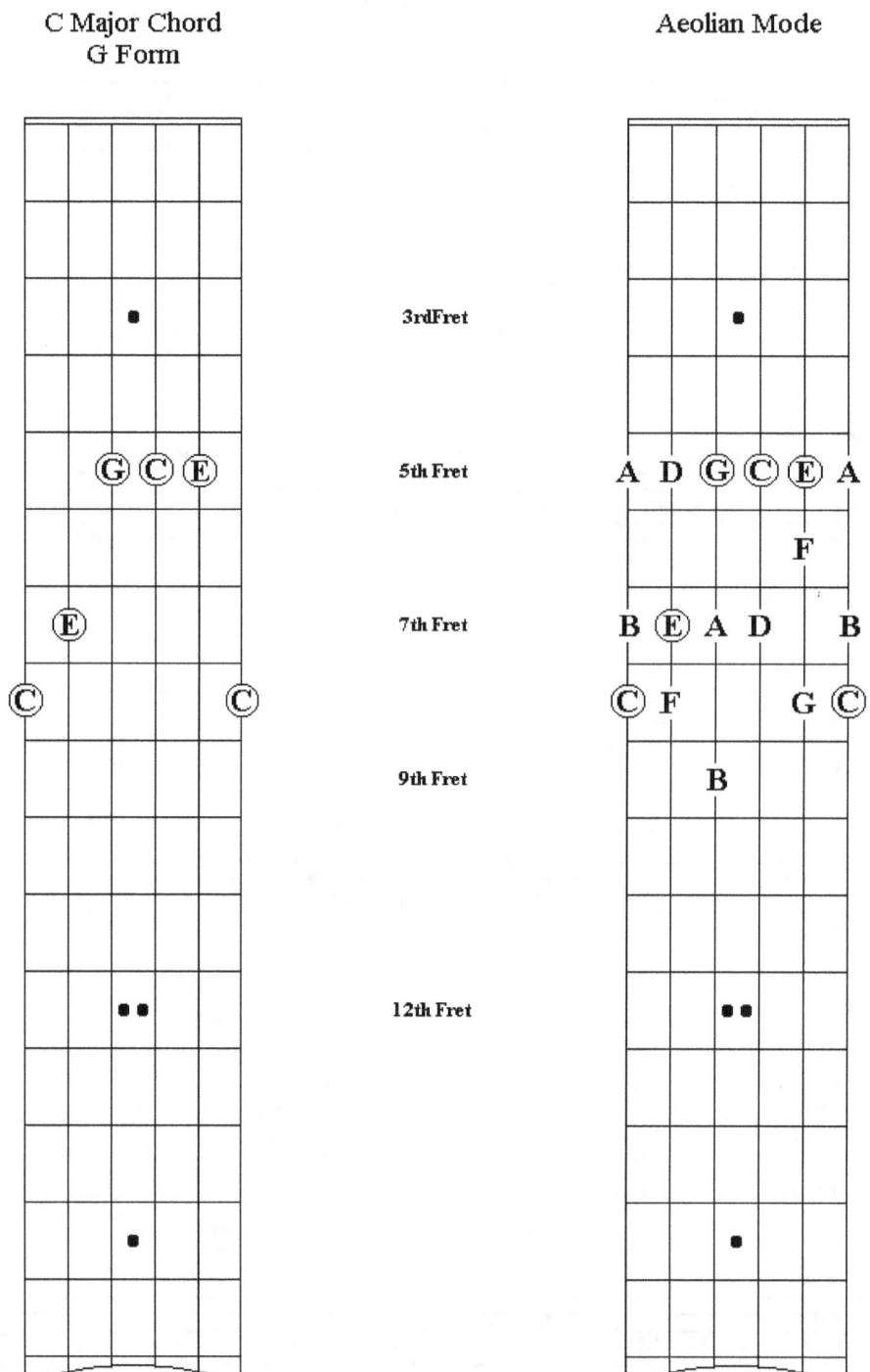

12-10

C Major Chord Scale

G Form – Aeolian Mode

6th Degree Of The Major Scale

Key of C

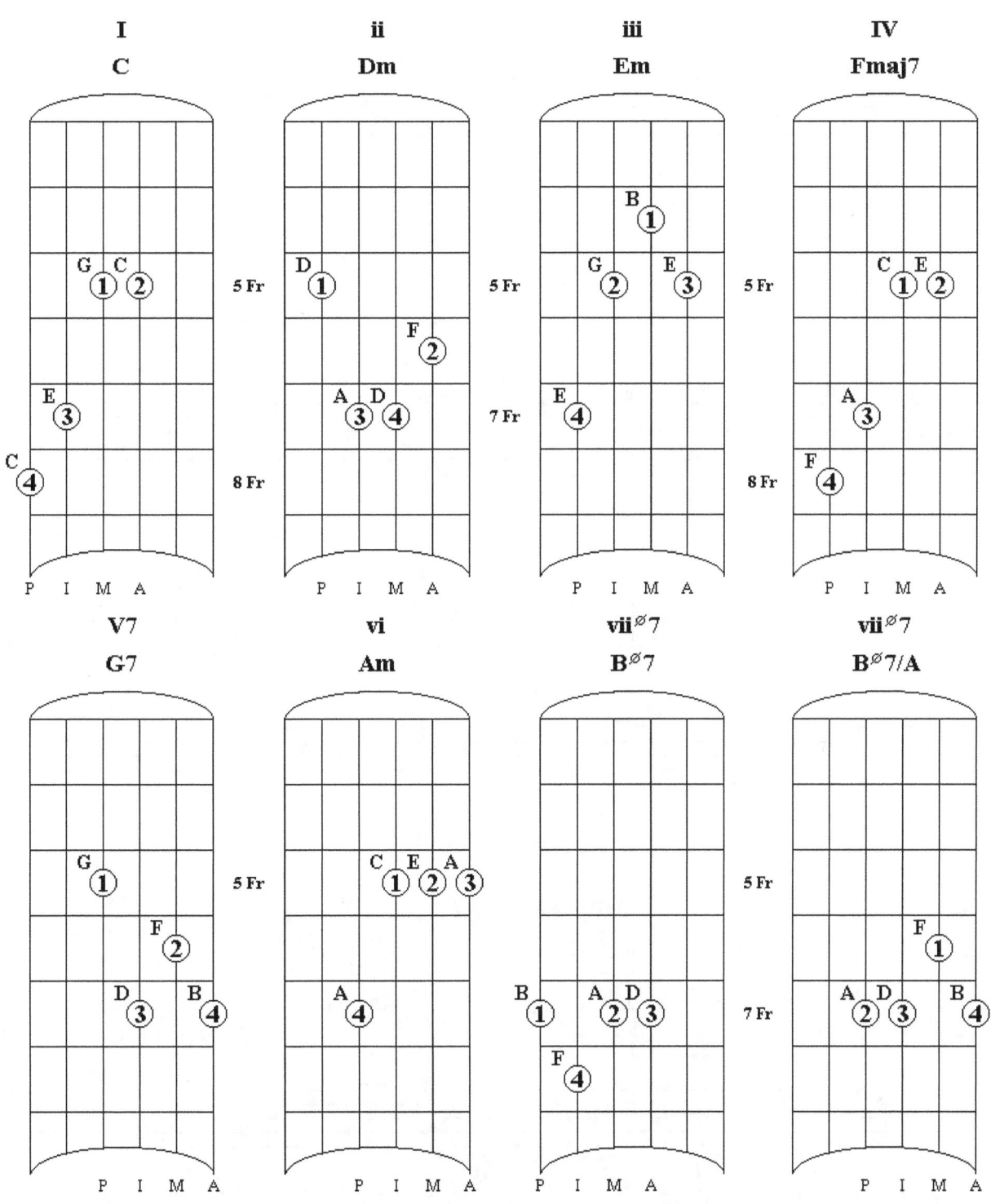

12-11

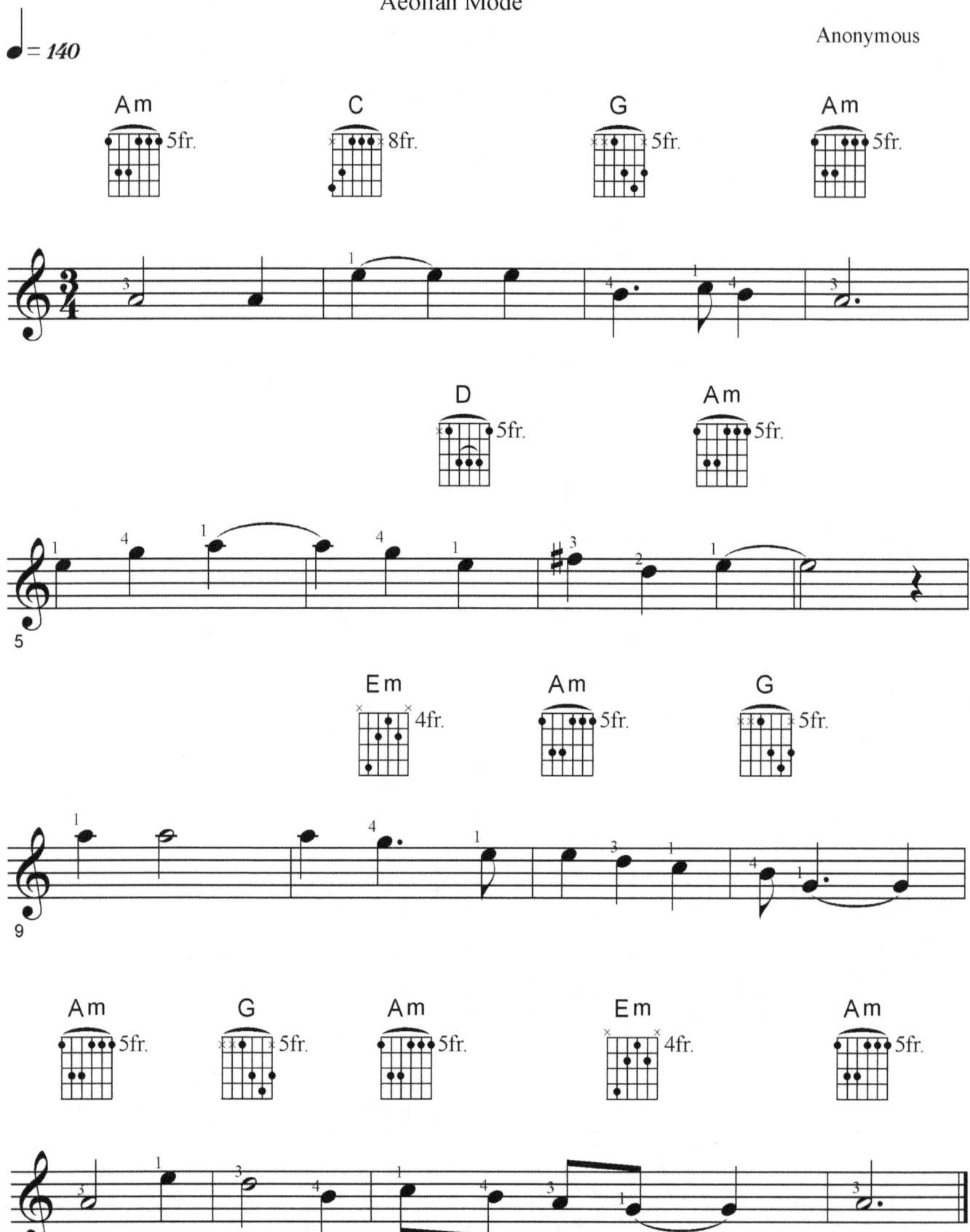

Locrian And Ionian Modes

E Form

7th And 8th Degrees Of The Major Scale

Key Of C

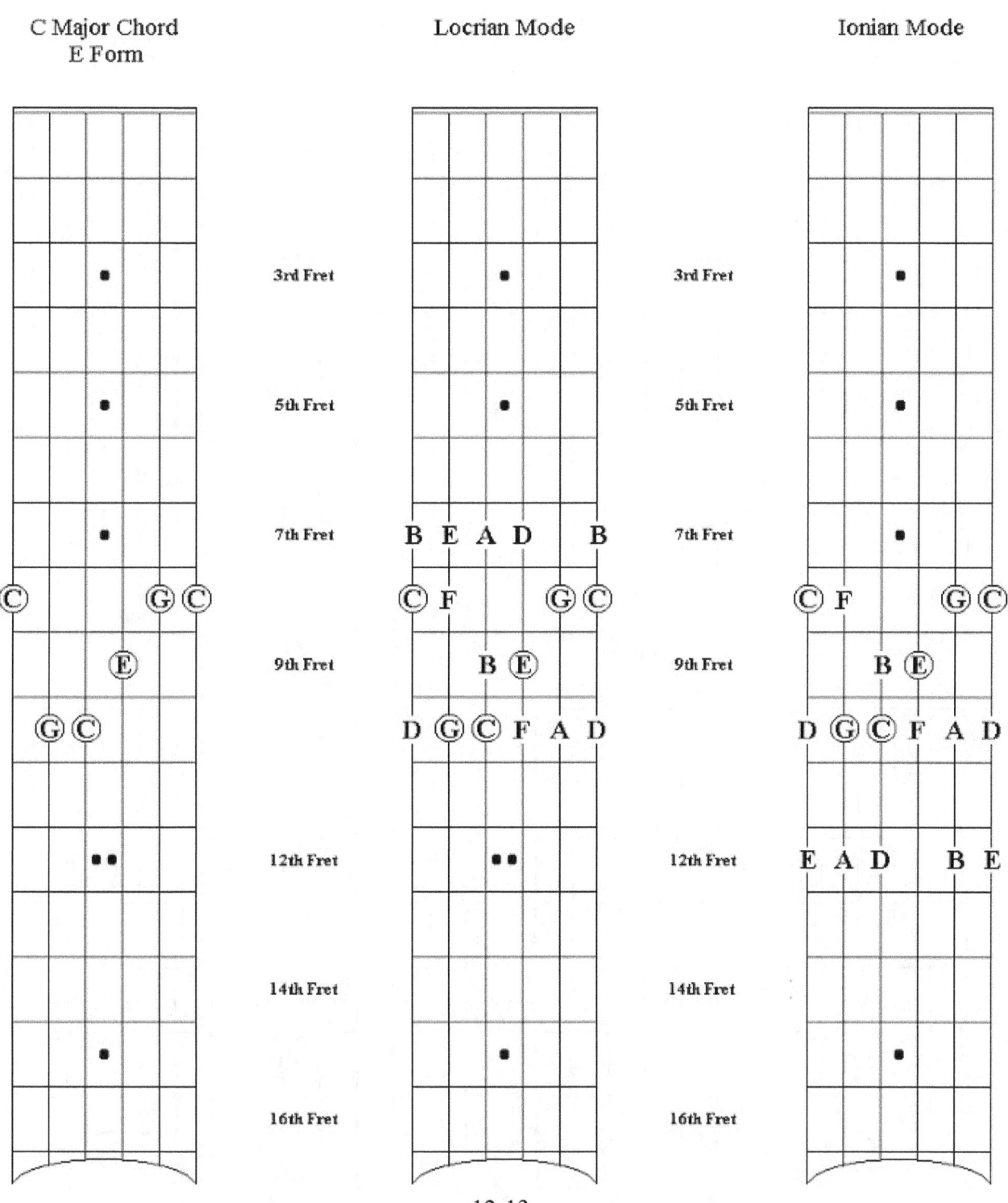

12-13

C Major Chord Scale

E Form – Locrian And Ionian Modes

7th And 8th Degrees Of The Major Scale

Key of C

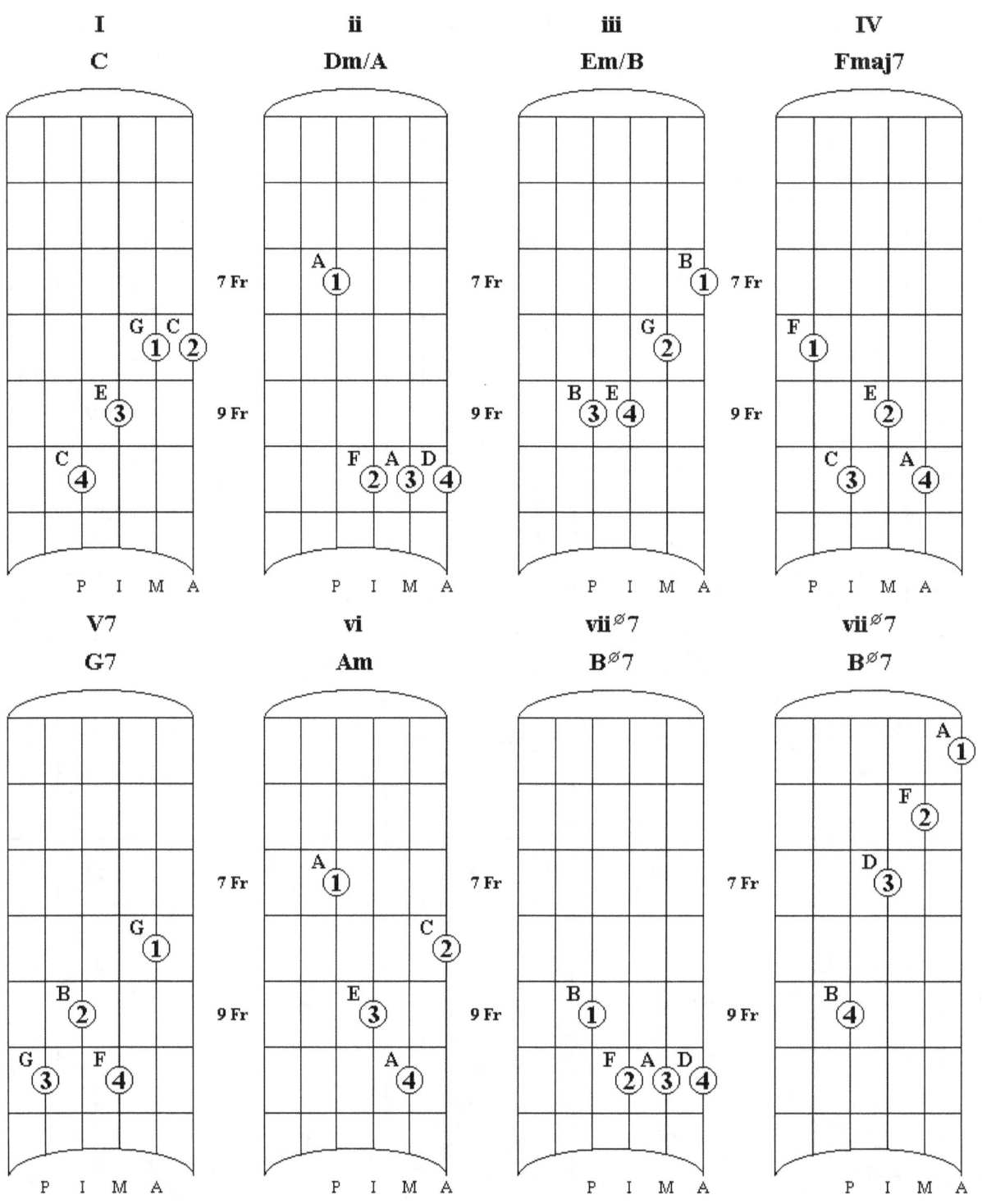

Scarborough Fair
Locrian Mode

Anonymous

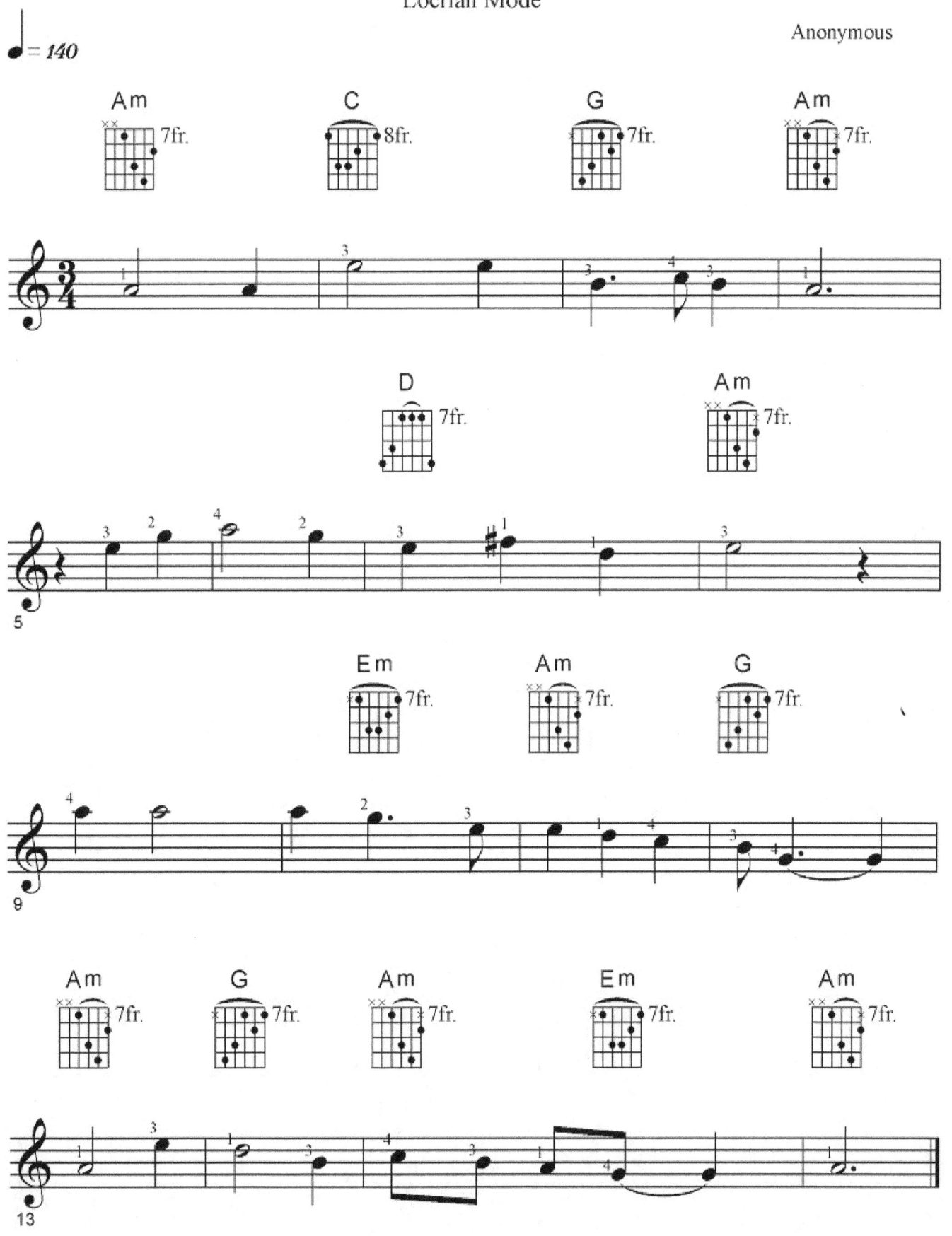

12-15

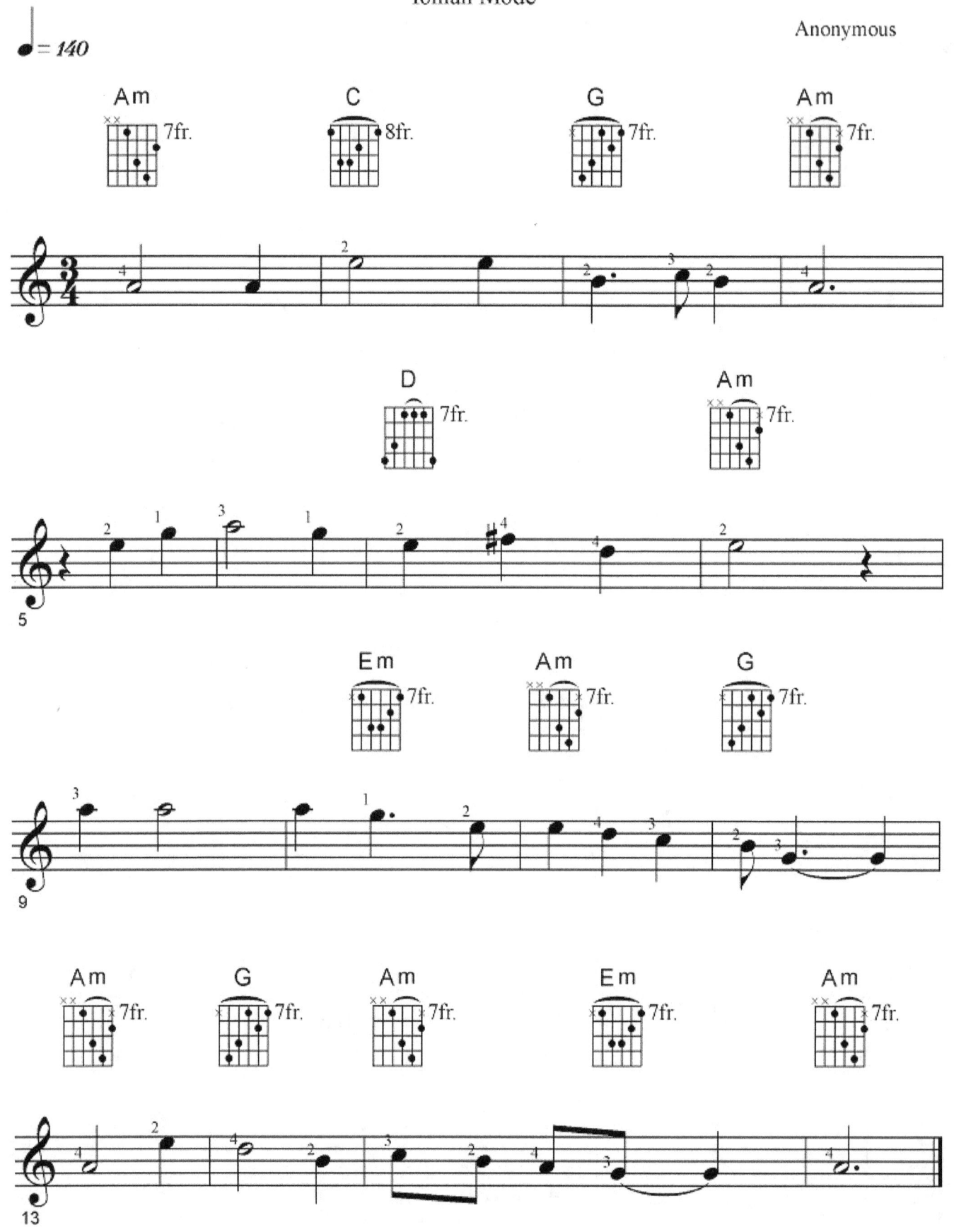

Dorian Mode

D Form

2nd Degree Of The Major Scale

Key Of C

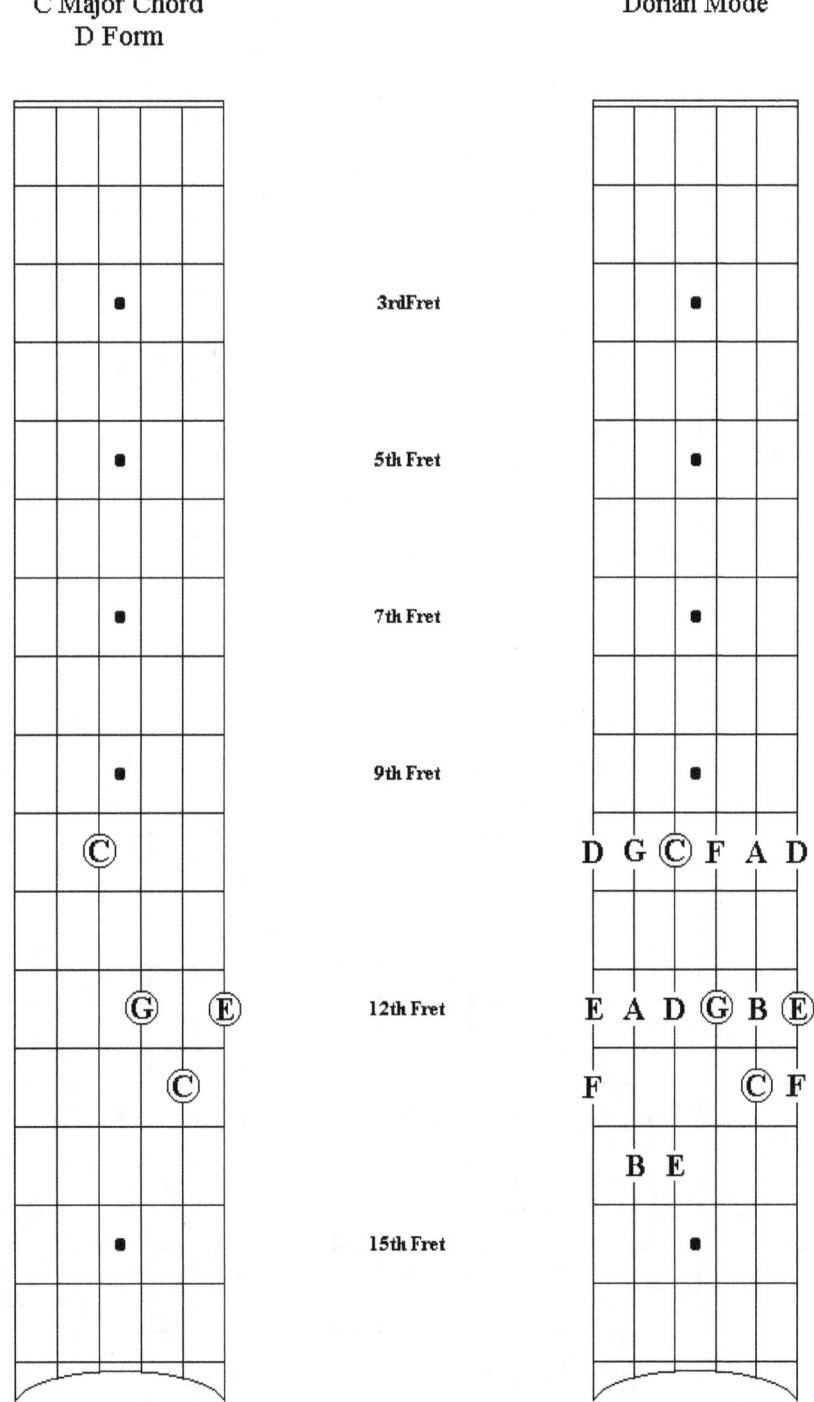

C Major Chord Scale

D Form – Dorian Mode

2nd Degree Of The Major Scale

Key of C

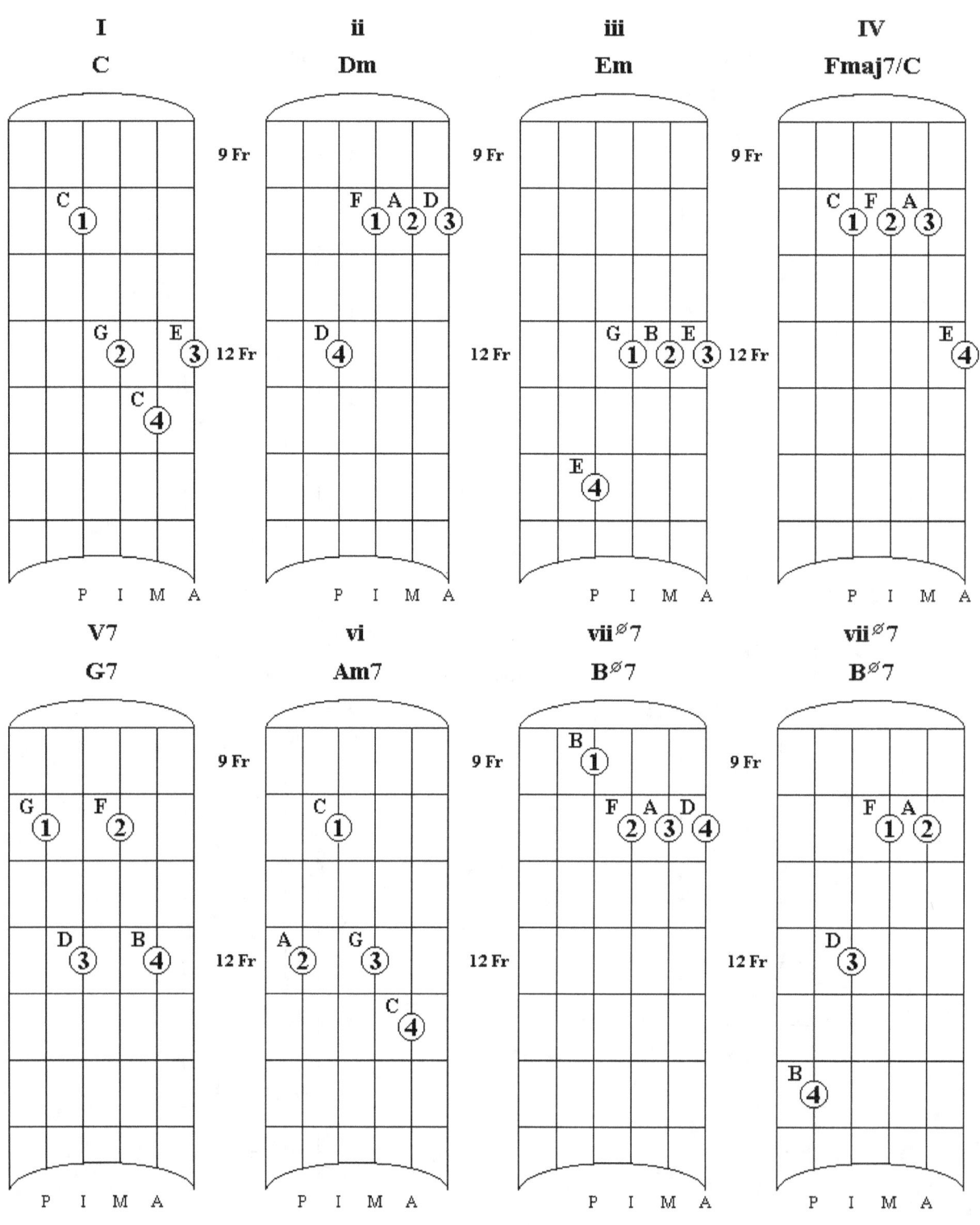

12-18

Scarborough Fair
Dorian Mode

Anonymous

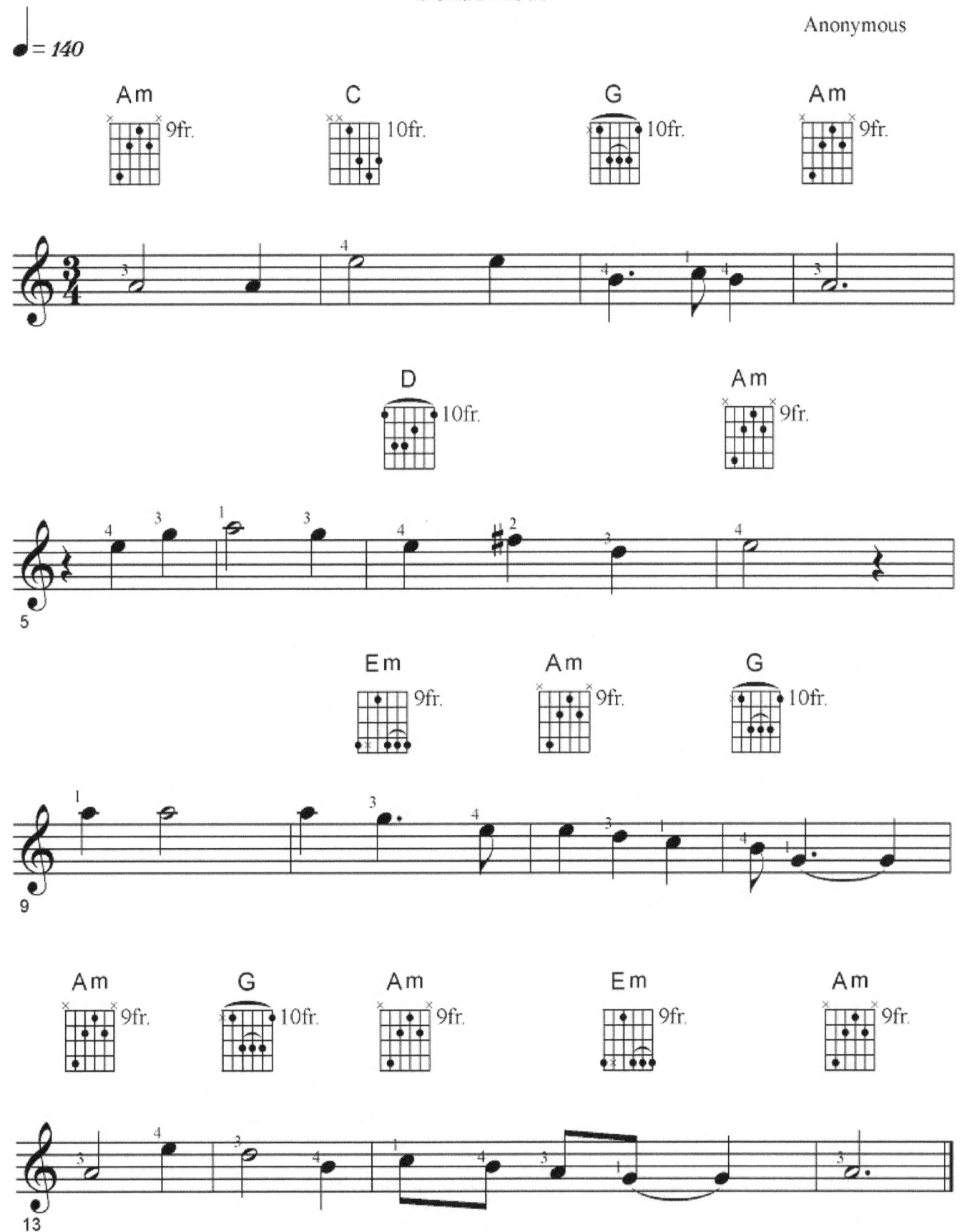

Phrygian Mode

C Form

3rd Degree Of The Major Scale

Key Of C

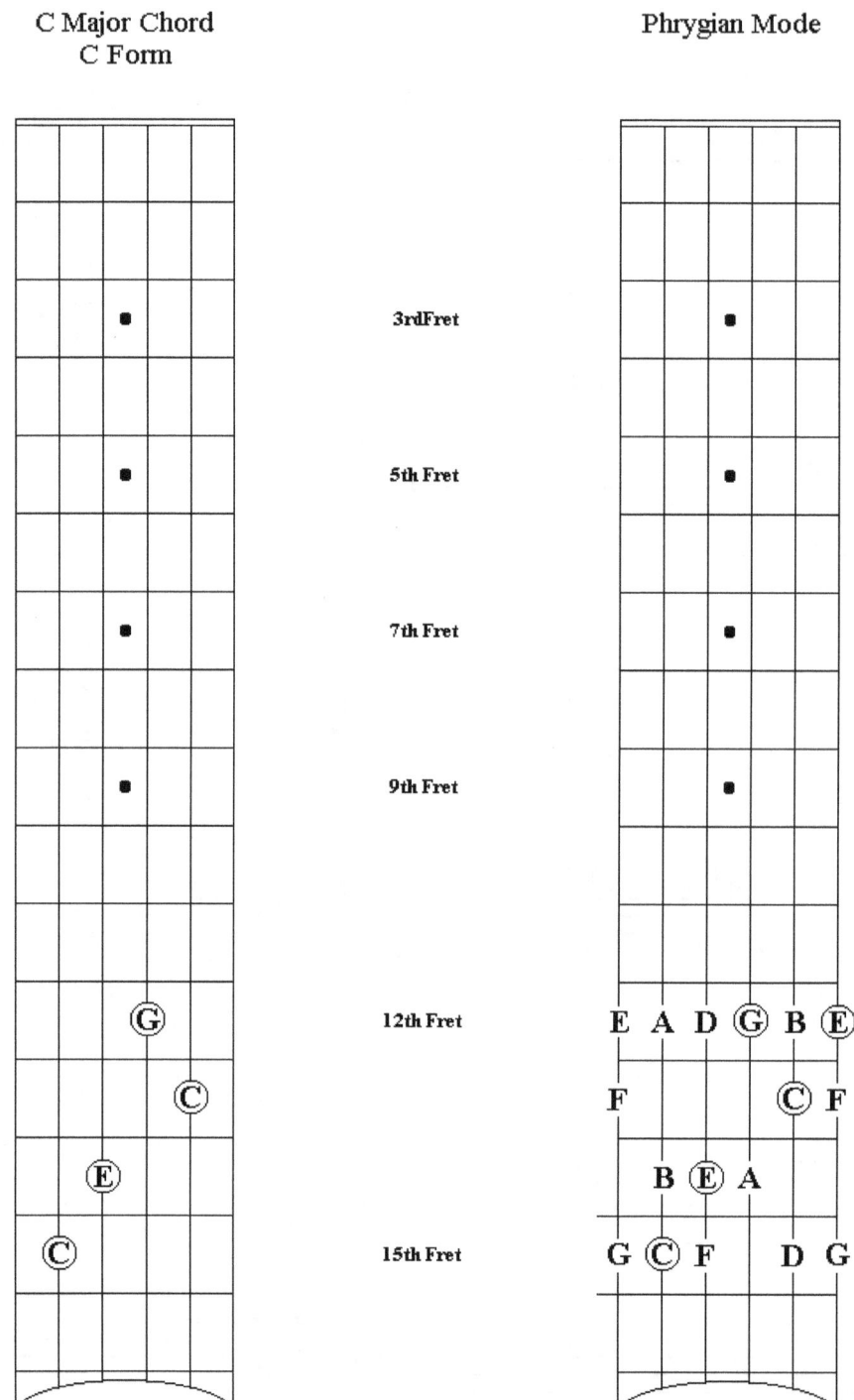

C Major Chord Scale

C Form – Phrygian Mode

3rd Degree Of The Major Scale

Key of C

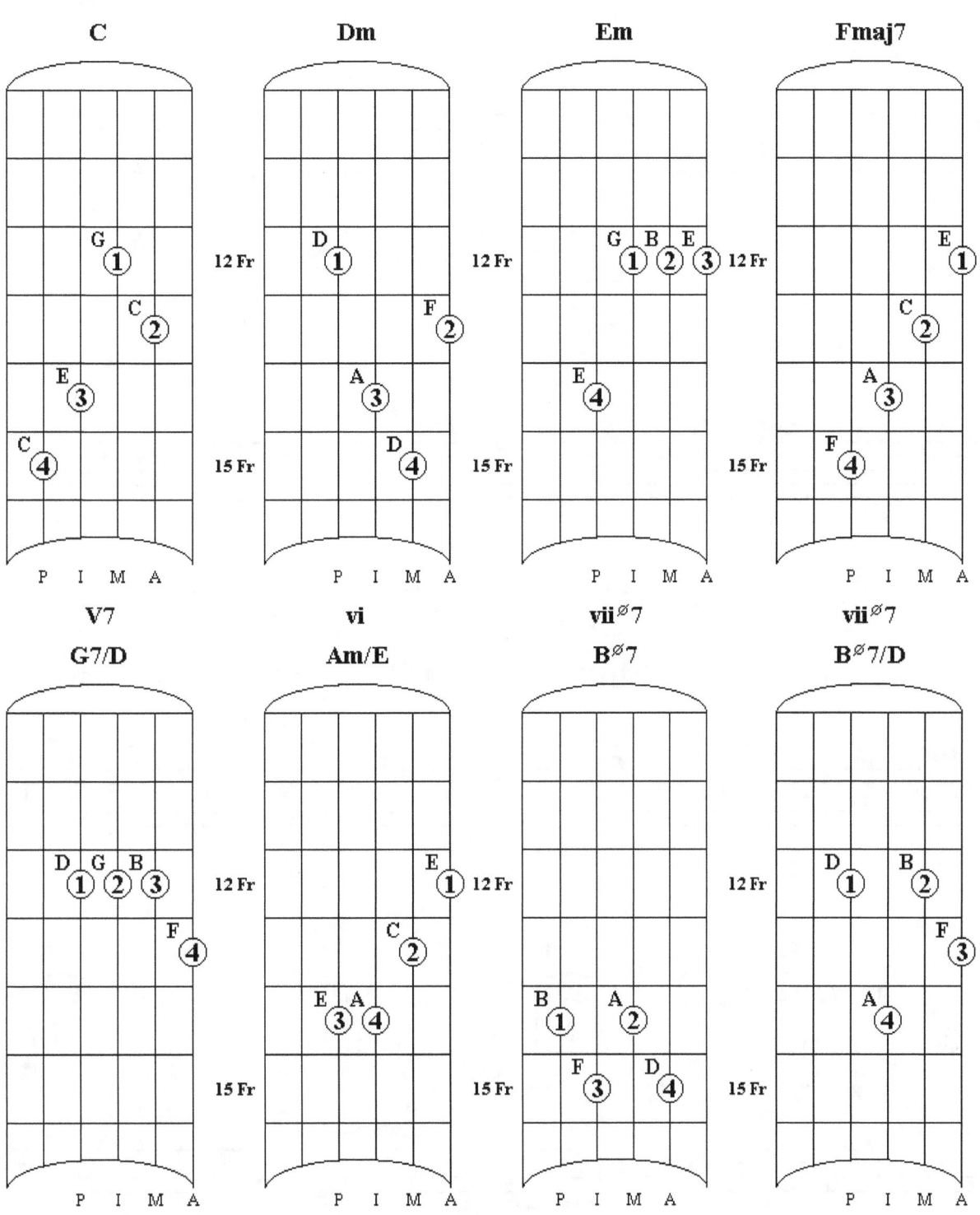

Scarborough Fair

Phrygian Mode - Octave

Anonymous

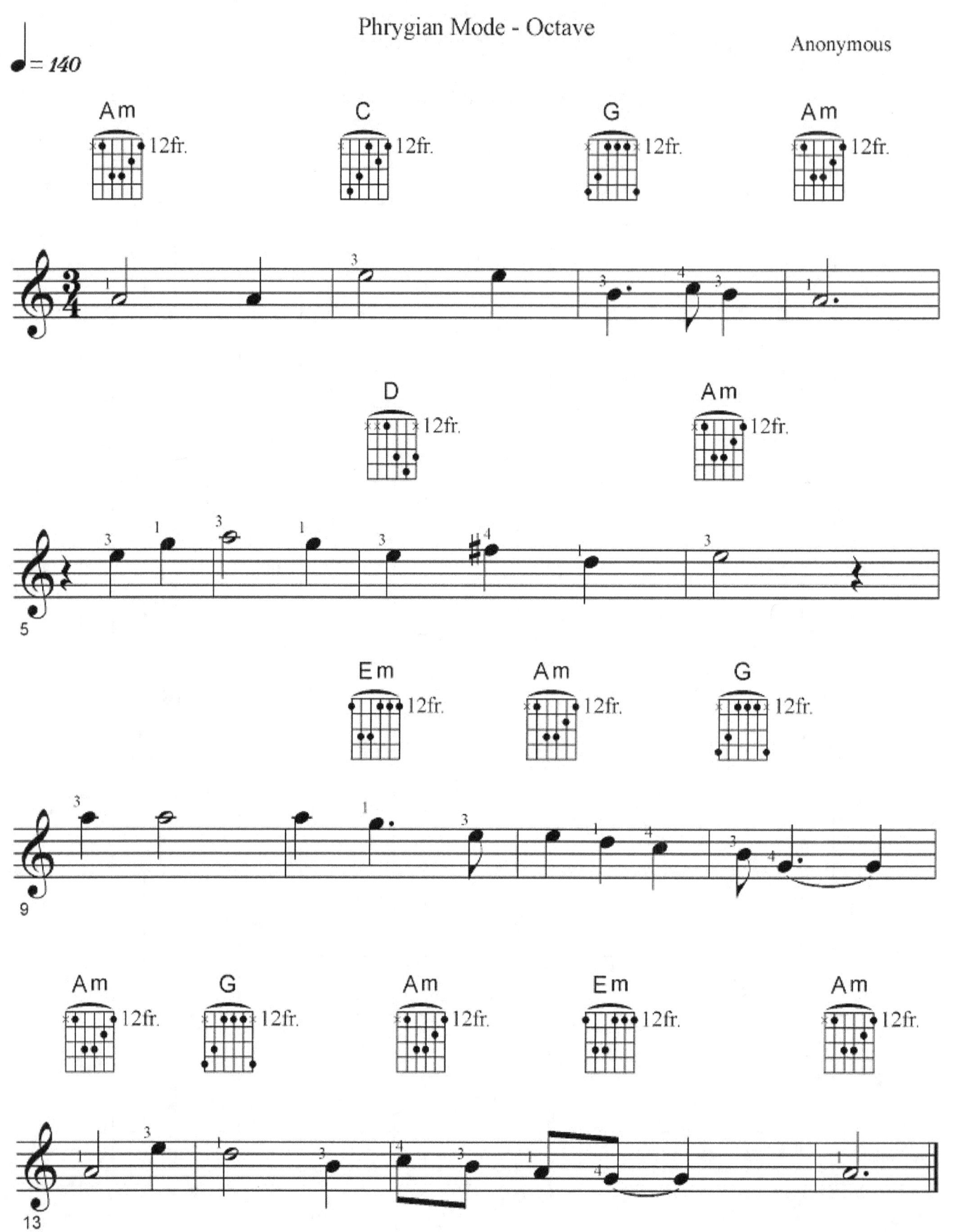

Chapter 13

The Conveyor Belt

The Conveyor Belt

Key Of E

The Ionian mode starts in the open position in the Key of E as shown below on the guitar fret board diagram. The guitar fret board is portrayed as a conveyor belt.

The imaginary conveyor belt with the modes in their defined order simply moves until it reaches the new key. The fret board hand is actually the conveyor belt as it moves to a new position to play a different key. As the fret board hand shifts to the new position of the different key the modes in their defined order shift as well.

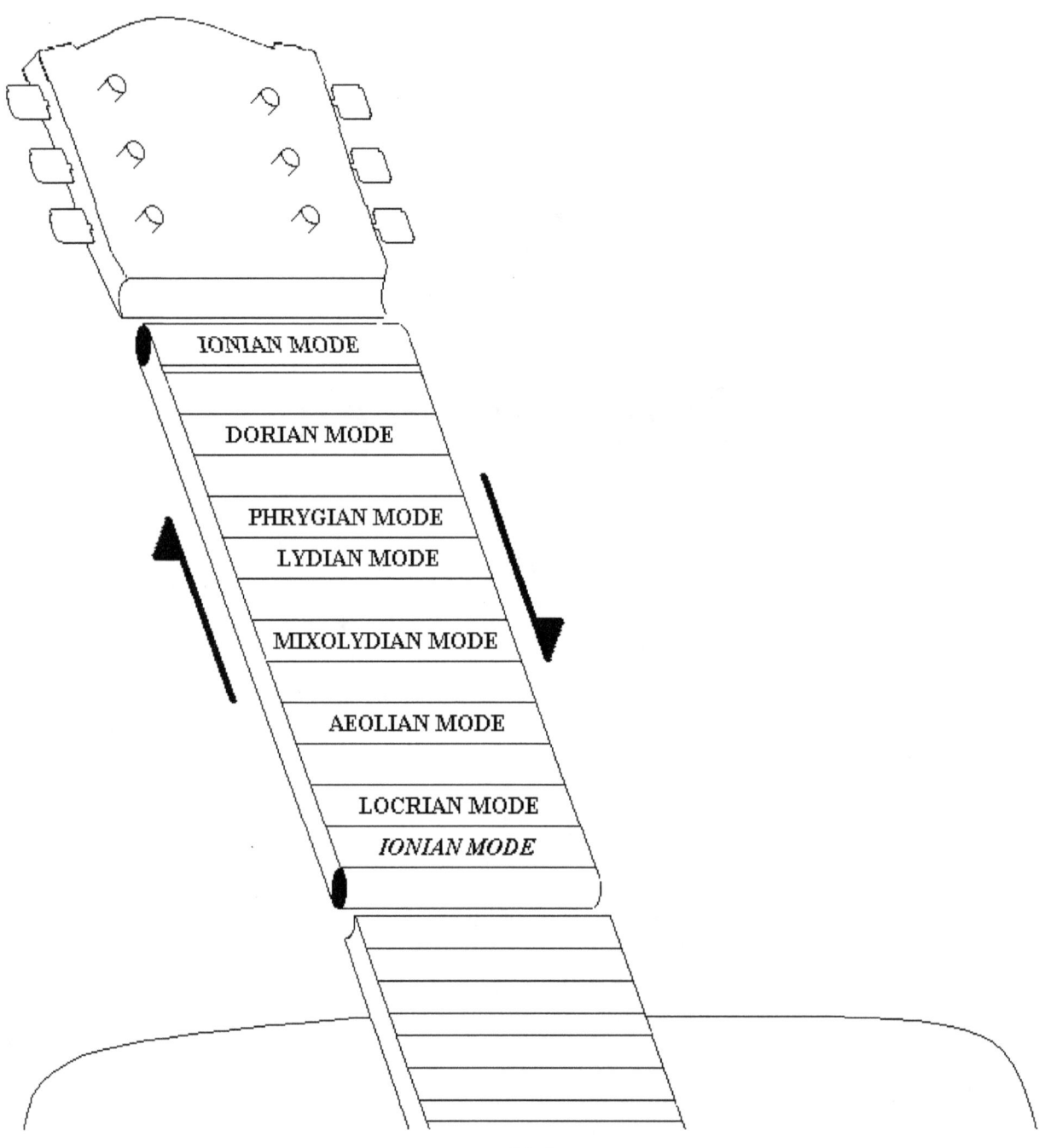

The Conveyor Belt

Key Of G

The Ionian mode starts on the third fret in the Key of G as shown below on the guitar fret board diagram. This guitar fret board is also portrayed as a conveyor belt for comparison.

It can be seen that the Ionian mode is now on the third fret as it is in the Key of G. The defined order of the modes has remained the same as they were in the Key of E. The modes in their defined order have shifted to the new Key of G following the fret board hand. What applies here applies to all twelve keys. To learn the modes in one key is to learn them in all keys.

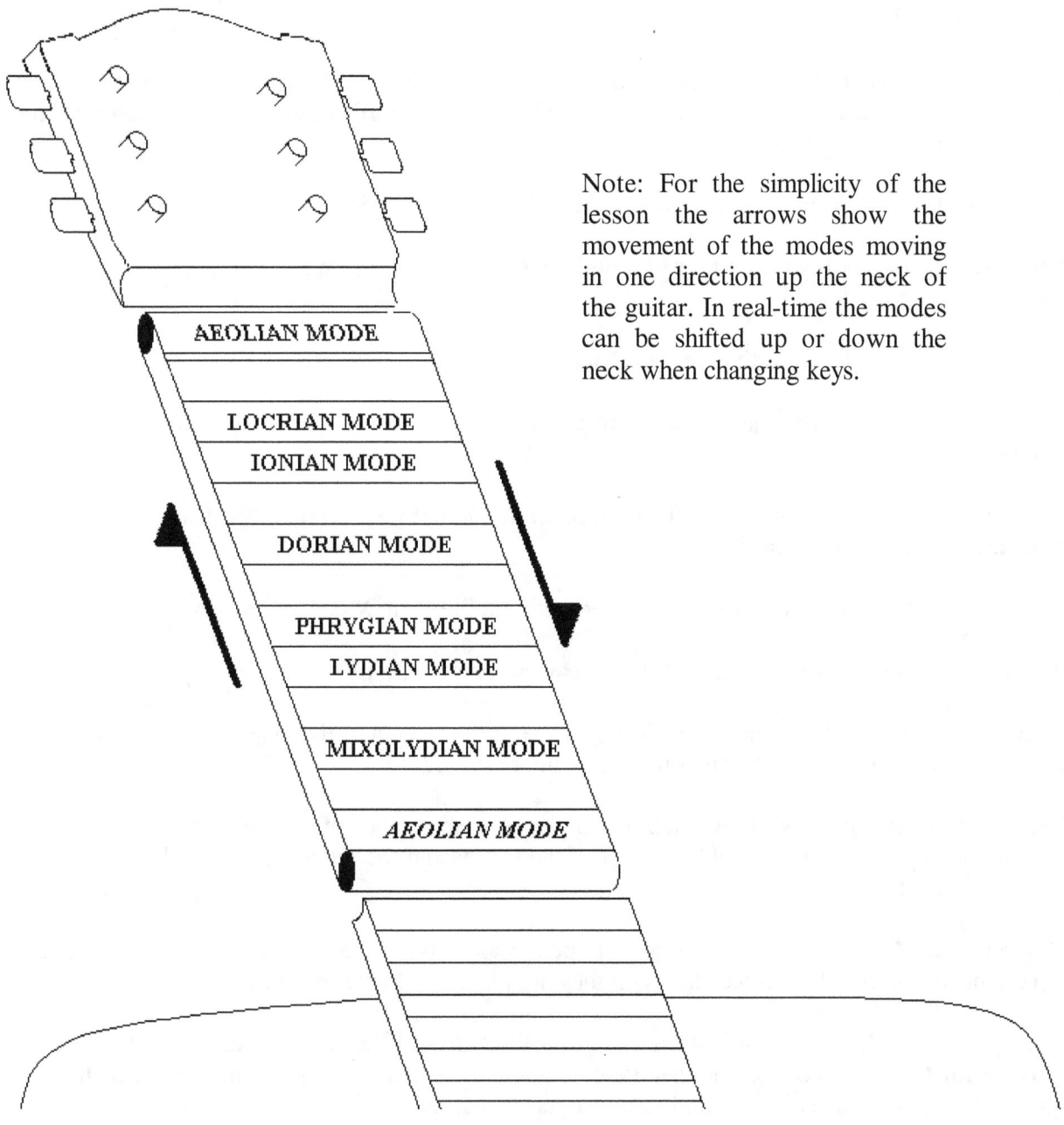

Note: For the simplicity of the lesson the arrows show the movement of the modes moving in one direction up the neck of the guitar. In real-time the modes can be shifted up or down the neck when changing keys.

Applying The Fretboard Map

The first thing you want to do is lay out the modes and chords on the guitar in the key of the song.

For example, let's say the song is in the Key of G. (Reference P. 14-7 and P. 14-8)

The easiest and fastest way is to find the sixth degree Aeolian Mode and in this case it is in the open position, beginning with the sixth string open E note.

With the modes memorized you will be able to visualize the pattern.

Next you'll want to visualize the G major chord scale.

As you become well practiced, this will become second nature.

Take a hold of the G chord, (G form, fingered 3, 2, and 4) on the third fret and then remove your third finger from the sixth string and place it on the second fret of the fourth string, remove your fourth finger and now your playing the relative miner Em chord.

Remember the G chord form is always associated with the Aeolian Mode.

Now you have all the tools you need for playing in the open position as well as an octave higher on the twelfth fret.

The second location to locate is the Phrygian Mode.

The easiest way is to find the relative minor Em chord barred on the fifth string, which in the Key of G is on the seventh fret.

Now take your fourth finger off the third string, ninth fret and place it on the fifth string, tenth fret and now you are playing the G chord in the C form.

Remember the C chord form is always associated with the Phrygian Mode.

Next you'll want to visualize the G major chord scale at the seventh fret.

Now you have all the tools you need for playing in the sixth position of the major scale as well as an octave higher on the nineteenth fret if you have a guitar with 22 frets.

Having four positions on the guitar visualized, you have an abundance of tools available at your finger tips to play with, plus it is easy to fill in the rest of the modes and their associated chord scales in between as you play.

The Phrygian and Aeolian modes are the most popular modes being that they are easy to play and they are very similar to each other, especially when they are played as Pentatonic scales.

For example, on the third and fourth strings, the four fingerings of the Aeolian Pentatonic Scale are the same as the four fingerings of the Phrygian Pentatonic Scale, only the notes are different, which makes for an easy to do and interesting call and response musical phrase.

Section Four

All Together Now

Notes

Chapter 14

Patterns For Creative Expression

Patterns For Creative Expression

The diagrams in this chapter put all the chords, modes and scales for each style of music on facing pages for ease of use.

This is the only section of the book that shows the pentatonic, hexatonic and octatonic scales.

The Key of G is chosen because of the popularity and the ease of use of the relative minor Key of Em and the altered relative minor Key of E7, both of which are derived from the parent Key of G. What is true here in the Key of G is true for all keys.

Jazz

On page 14-3 the five major chord scales are presented in the Key of G major seven. Notice that all of the chords are shown either as major seven, minor seven or dominant seven. This is the basic chord structure for Jazz. The seventh will remain but the possibilities of chord development using different intervals are vast. There are five positions - six with the octave for the chord scales giving the player more variety for expression. On page 14-4, in the four columns, the modes column and the pentatonic scales column give the smooth sound of Jazz with the pentatonic scales being lighter and more melodic. The Hexatonic scales column will give a blues sound due to the flatted fifth and the Octatonic scales column will create a sophisticated sound with the flatted third, flatted ninth and the augmented fifth / flatted thirteenth.

The Relative Minor Key

By taking the minor second (ii), minor third (iii) and the relative minor sixth (vi) chords of the major chord scale and rearranging their order as shown below into a i - iv - v chord progression the minor key is derived from the parent key. In the diagram below it is shown how the Key of Em7 is derived from the parent Key of Gmaj7.

G Major Chord Scale:	Gmaj7	Am7	Bm7	Cmaj7	D7	Em7	F#ø7	Gmaj7
Chord Scale Degrees:	I	ii	iii	IV	V	vi	vii	VIII
i - iv - v Chord Progression:	Em7			Am7	Bm7			
Chord Scale Degrees:	i			iv	v			

On page 14-5 the Em7 blues chords are presented in five positions on the neck of the guitar in their basic i7 - iv7 - v7 progressions. Also on page 14-5 in the last three columns, the pentatonic scales column plays the minor blues with the flatted third, the Hexatonic scales column plays the flatted fifth and the Octatonic scales column plays between the major and minor third, the flatted and perfect fifth and the major and minor seventh tones for a more sophisticated sound. The Octatonic scale requires thoughtful playing, as there are tones that if ended on or sustained will be dissonant. Playing these passing tones as either slides, bends or eighth notes the dissonance is too short lived for the ear to distinguish it as a dissonant note. The ear will then hear them only as interesting connecting tones.

Patterns For Creative Expression

Dominant Seven Blues

Now by taking the minor second (ii), minor third (iii) and the relative minor sixth (vi), chords of the major chord scale and changing them into dominant seventh chords, then rearrange their order as shown into a I7 - IV7 - V7 chord progression the dominant seven Blues are born. In the diagram below it shows how the Key of E7 is derived from the parent Key of G.

G Major Chord Scale:	G	Am	Bm	C	D7	Em	F#ø7	G
Chord Scale Degrees:	I	ii	iii	IV	V7	vi	vii#ø7	VIII
Changed To Dominant Seventh Chords:		(A7)	(B7)			(E7)		
I7 - IV7 - V7 Chord Progression:	E7			A7	B7			
Chord Scale Degrees:	I7			IV7	V7			

On page 14-6 the E7 Blues chords are presented in five positions on the neck of the guitar in their basic I7 - IV7 - V7 progressions.

Also on page 14-6 in the last three columns, the pentatonic scales column plays the dominant seven blues with the flatted third, the Hexatonic scales column plays the flatted fifth and the Octatonic scales column plays between the major and minor third, the flatted and perfect fifth and the major and minor seventh tones for a more sophisticated sound.

The I and IV chords can be changed into major sevenths and the ii - iii - vi - vii chords can be changed into minor sevenths for Jazz. The modes are use for Rock, Country and Jazz. The pentatonics are used for all types. The hexatonics and octatonics are used for Blues and Jazz.

Rock And Country Music

On page 14-7 all of the chords can be used in rock and country music. Rock music can also be played with a short form of the chords called five chords, more commonly referred to as power chords. These chords simply use the root and the fifth of the chord and can be played off of the sixth, fifth and fourth strings as shown below.

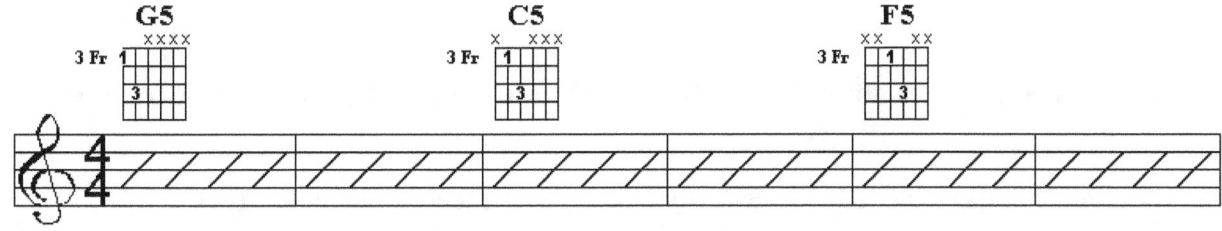

On page 14-8 the pentatonic scale will be used for rock music most of the time with occasional usage of the mode it is derived from. Country music, like Jazz can utilize all of the scales including the Chromatic scale. The Octatonic and Chromatic scales require thoughtful playing, as there are passing tones that if sustained will be dissonant as previously explained on page 14-1.

Now here's a neat trick that will allow you to immediately take your guitar comping chordal harmony into overdrive when its your turn to solo.

The example Jazz, Pop, Rock or Country song is in the Key of G and your playing the G, C and D chords in the open position.

You can play filler notes from the Aeolian Mode also in the open position.

Everything at this point is harmonious, the scale and the chords are all of the same notes.

Now it's time for your solo and you want to stand out with an interesting and exciting solo, so you raise the volume with the foot pedal, shift the Aeolian Pentatonic Scale up from the open position to the third fret position and play.

What has happened is the scale was moved up the neck of the guitar a minor third, which creates that particular sound of the Blues.

When the solo is finished you simply move back down to the Aeolian Mode in the open position and resume comping.

Here's what happened:

The Key of G is: G -A - B - C - D - E - F#.

The notes of the Aeolian Pentatonic Scale pattern played at the third fret are: G - Bb - C - D - F.

The G chord has the notes G - B - D, so the Bb of the scale flats the third of the G chord and the F flats the seventh, giving it the sound of the Blues (b3, b5, b7).

In theory, you the guitarist are playing in the relative minor Key of Gm during the solo while the rest of the band is still playing in the Key of G major.

Gm is the relative minor of the Key of Bb, which is a minor third (three half-steps) up the scale from G.

It's the specific five tone symmetry of the Pentatonic Scale that allows this magical phenomenon to occur, which means you can also use the Phrygian Pentatonic Scale as well.

You would normally be playing the third degree Phrygian Mode at the seventh fret, B note in the Key of G.

So you slide the Phrygian Pentatonic Scale pattern up the neck of the guitar a minor third to the tenth fret.

The notes of the Phrygian Pentatonic Scale pattern played at the tenth fret are: D - F - G - Bb - C.

They are the same notes only rearranged, which is why the various scale patterns on the fretboard are so powerful for providing such diverse sounds from the same notes.

This simple approach can be applied to Jazz, Rock and Country music when improvising.

Notes

Chord Scales For Jazz

Key Of G Major 7

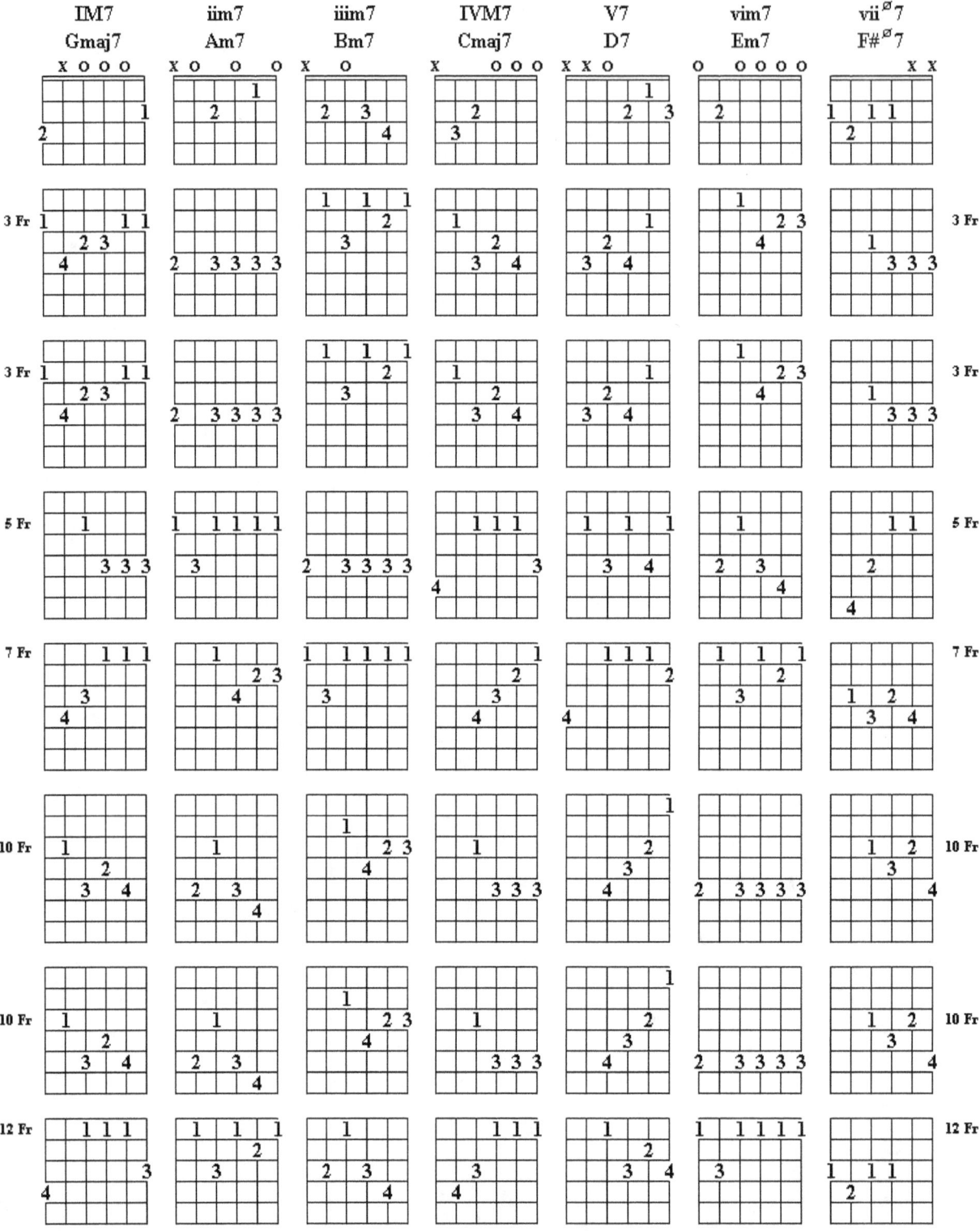

14-5

Mode And Scale Patterns For Jazz

Key Of G Major Seven

Chords And Scales For Minor 7 Blues

Key Of Em7

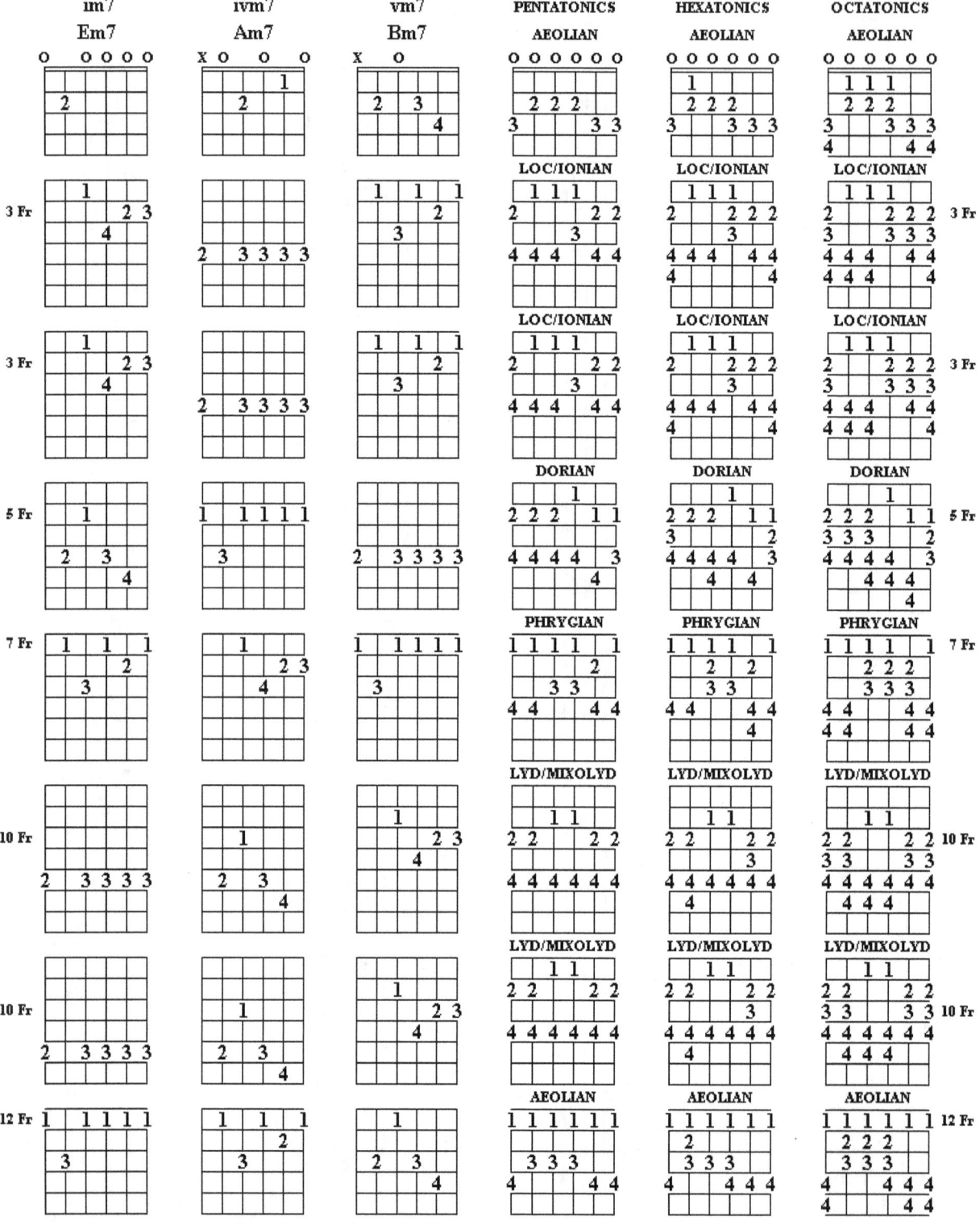

Chords And Scales For Dominant 7 Blues

Key Of E7

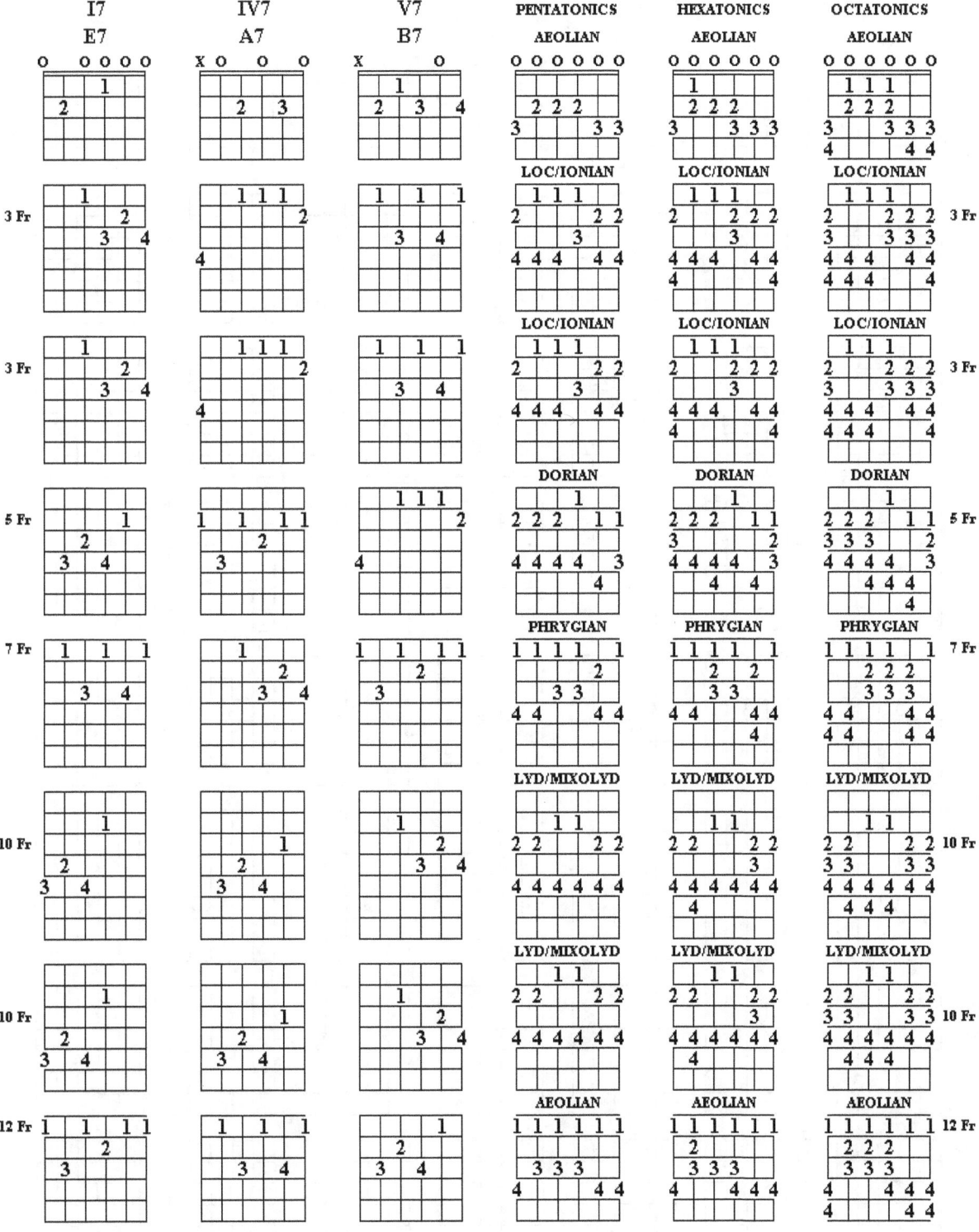

14-8

Chord Scales For Rock And Country

Key Of G

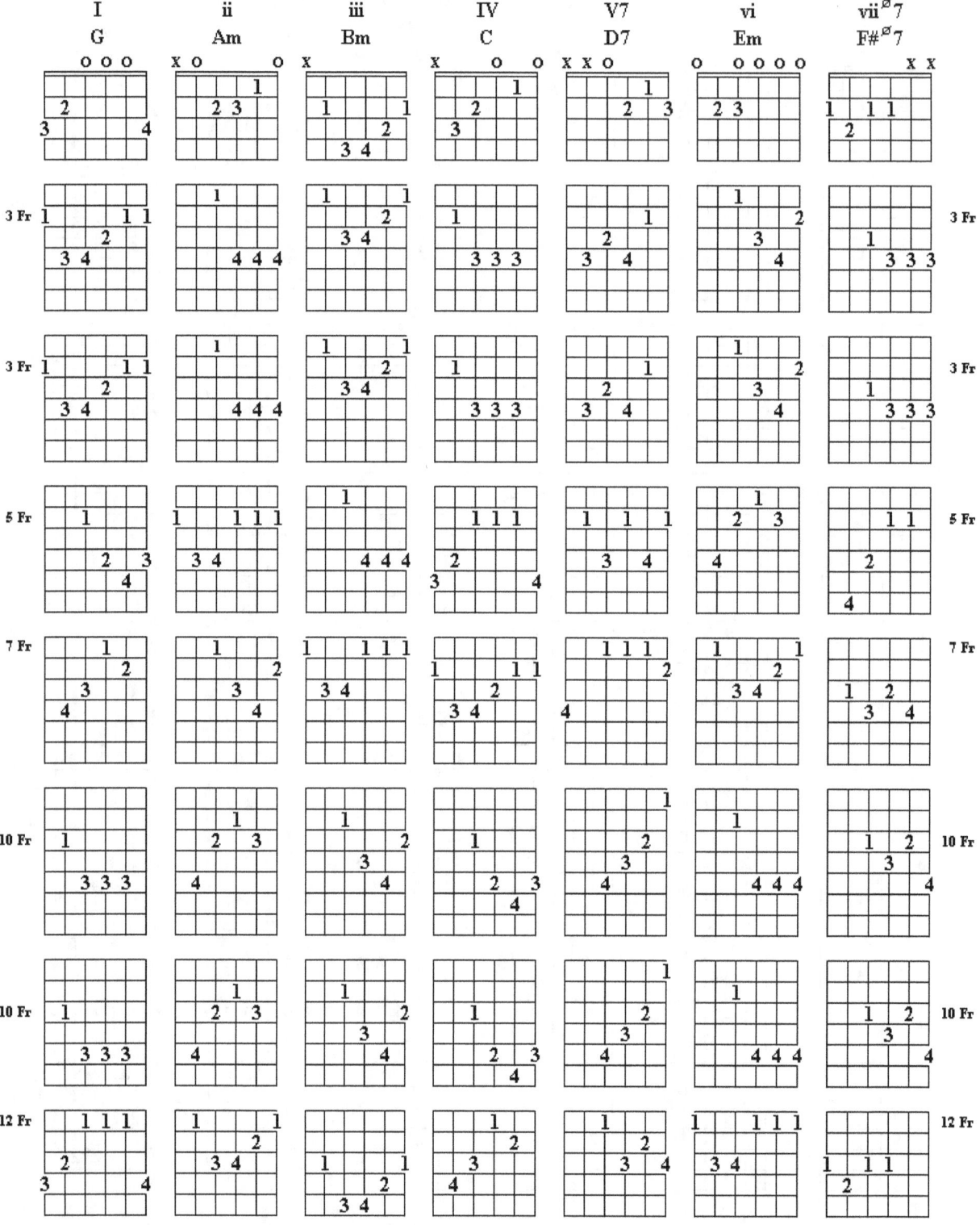

Scale Patterns For Rock And Country

Key Of G

E7 Blues Medley

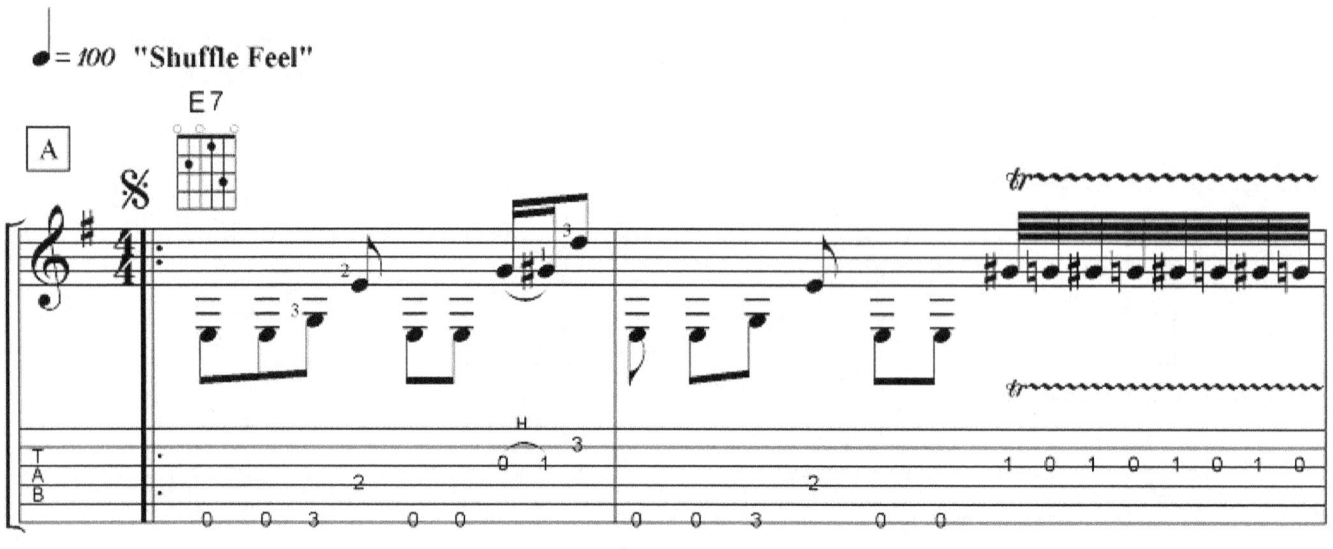
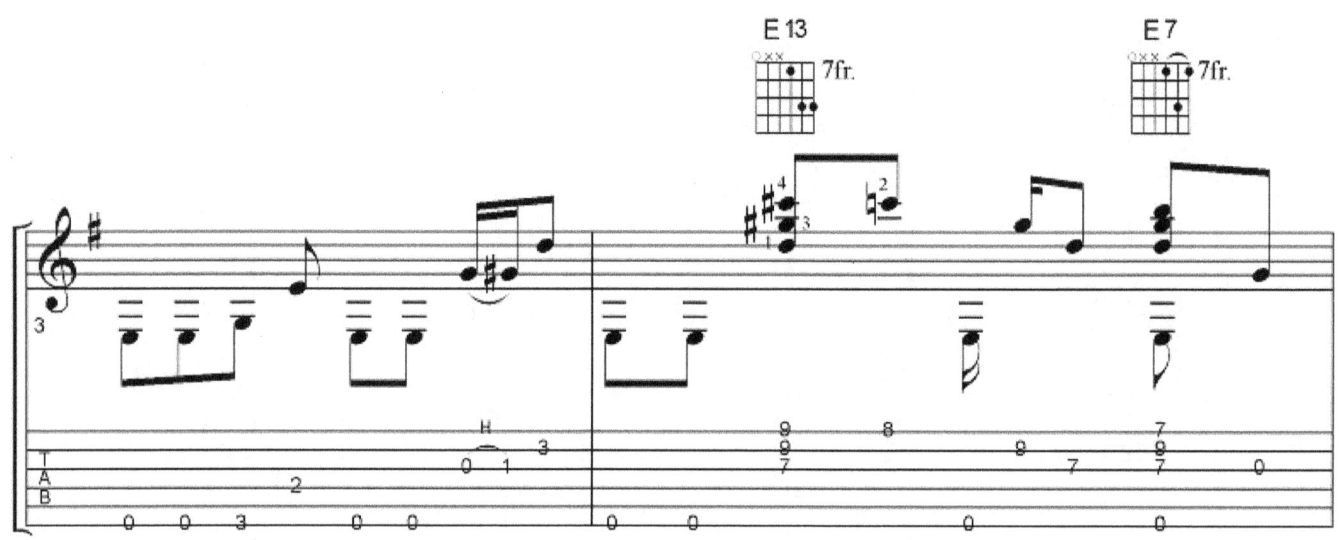

E7 Blues Medley

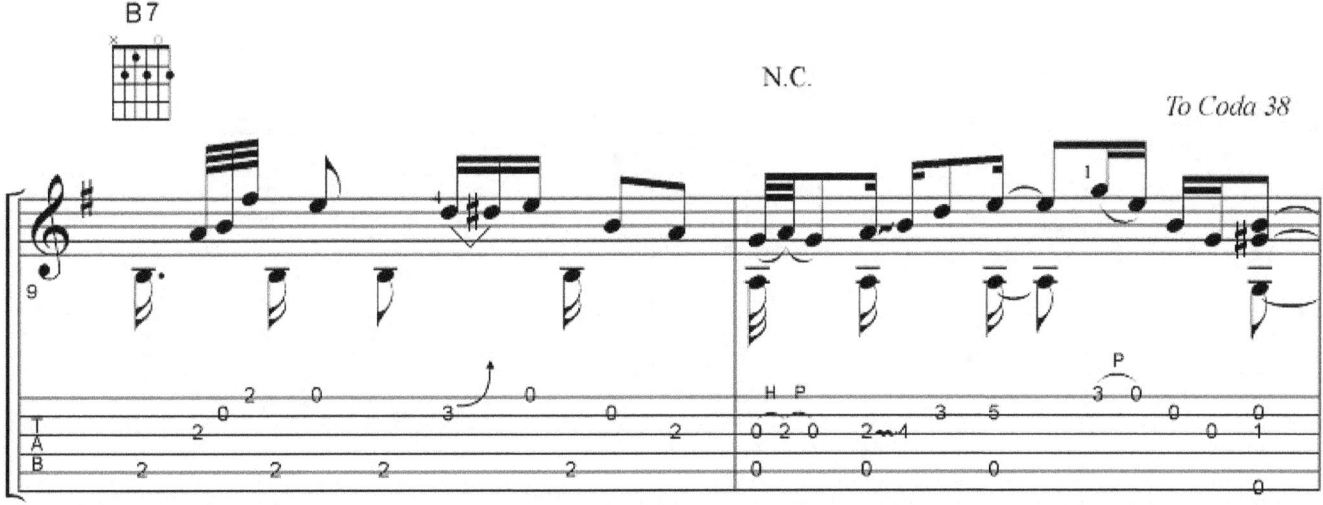

E7 Blues Medley

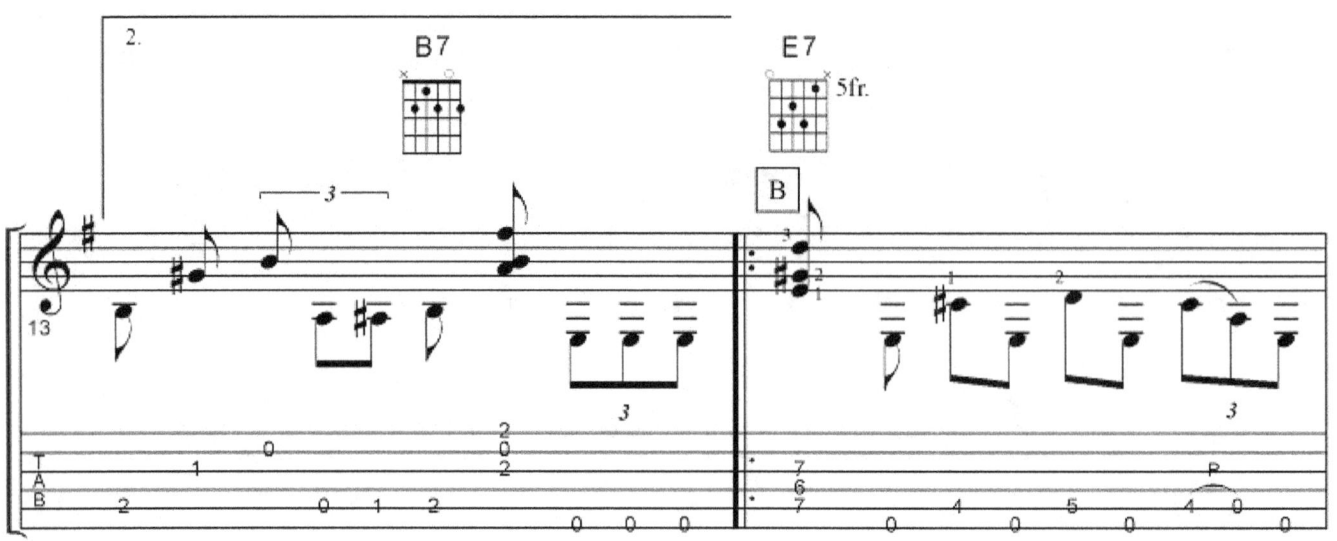
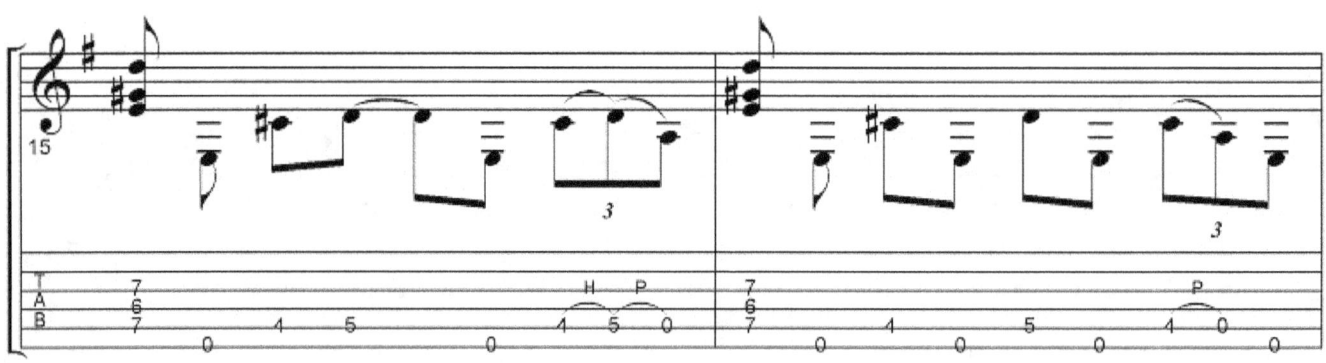
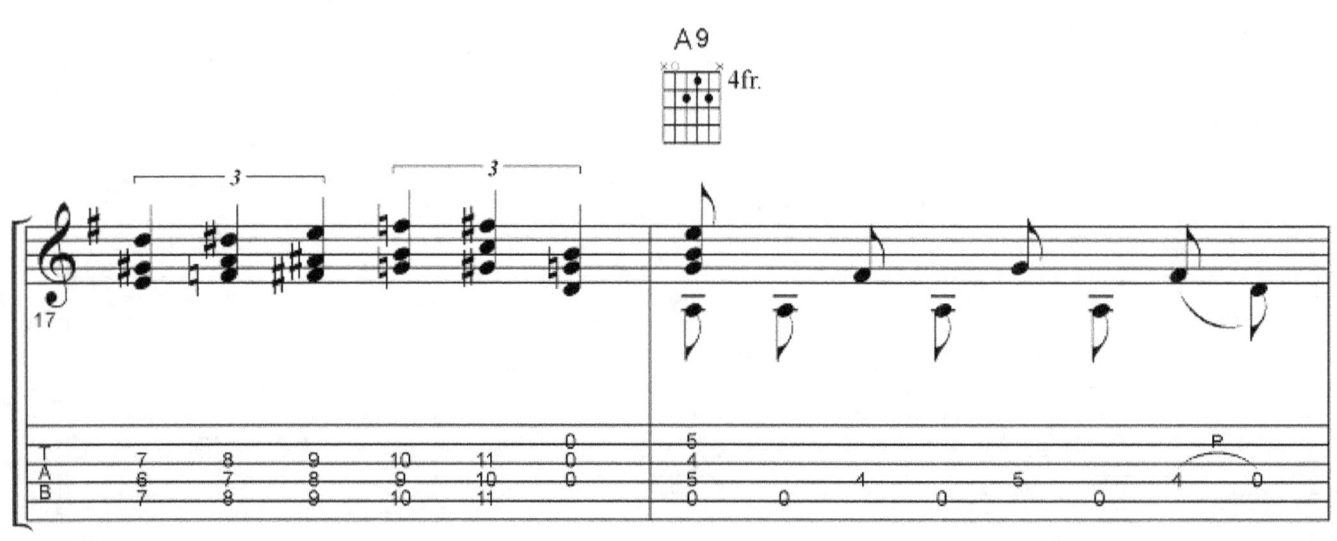

E7 Blues Medley

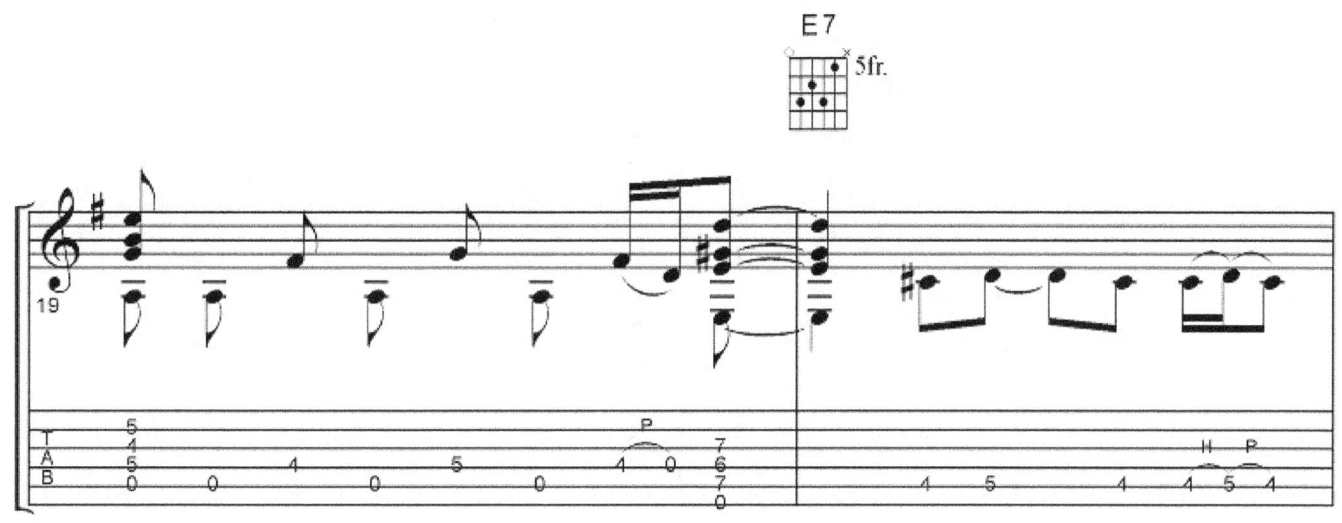

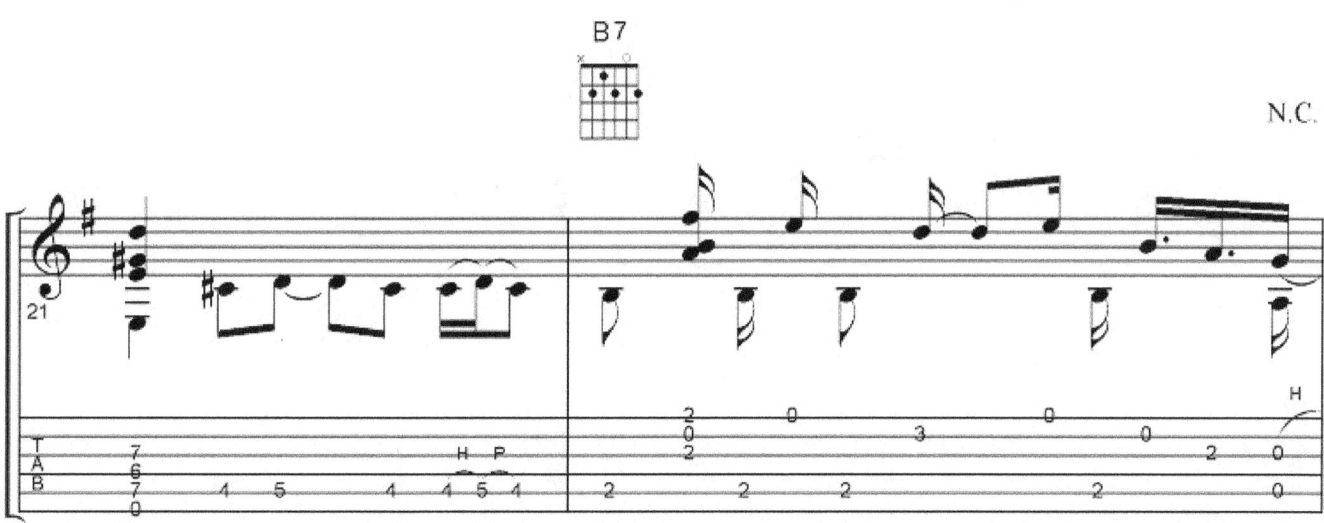

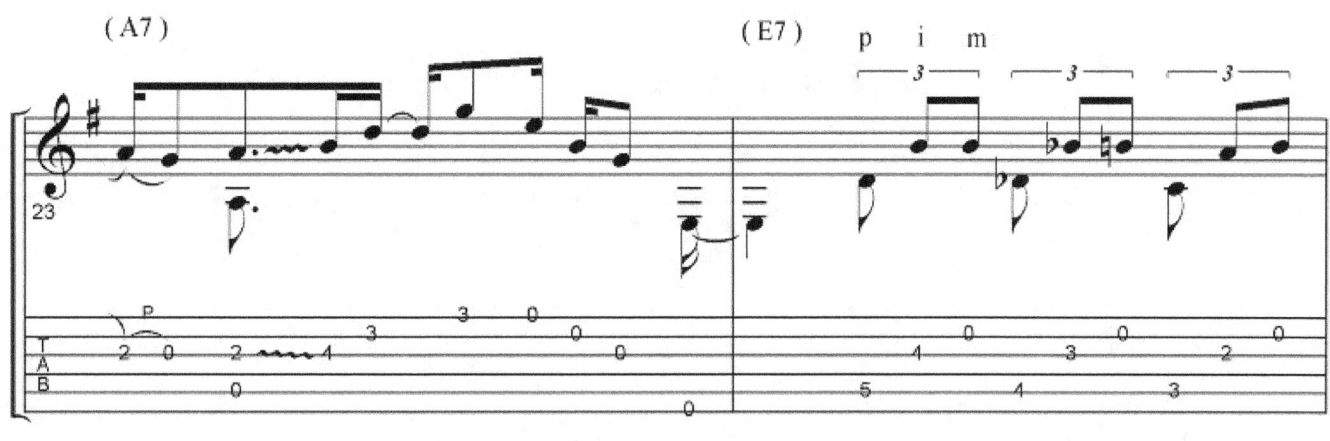

E7 Blues Medley

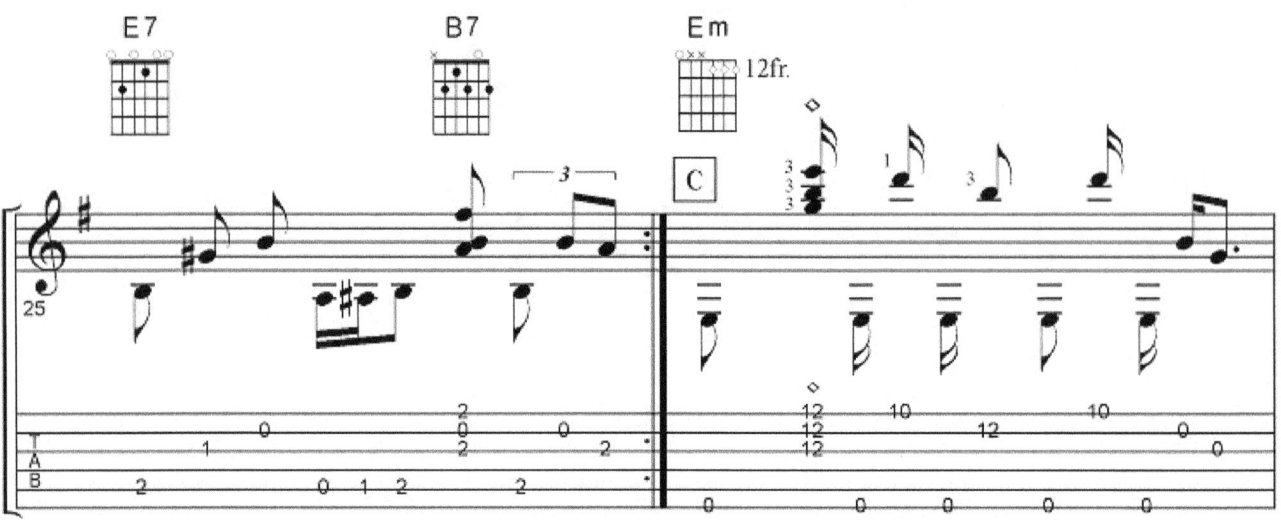
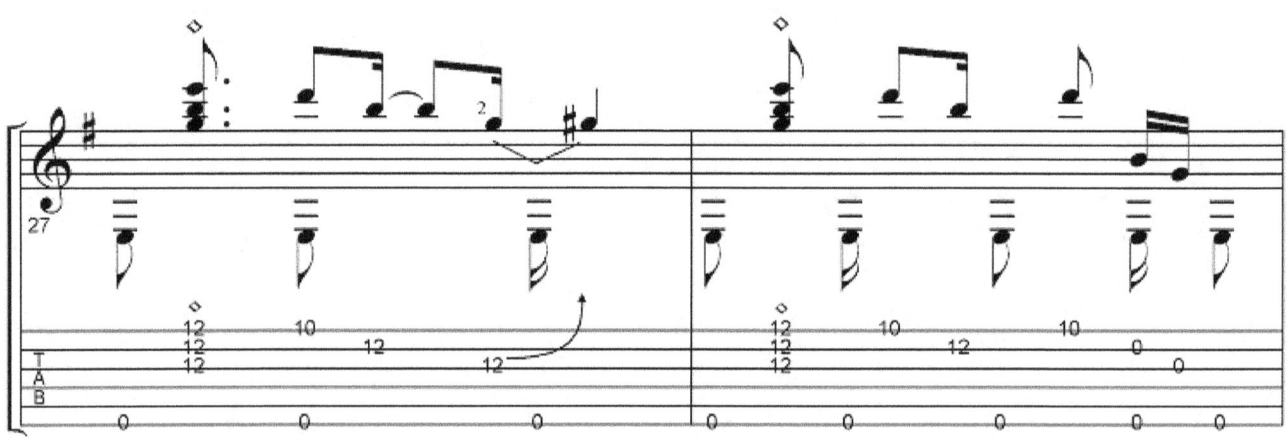
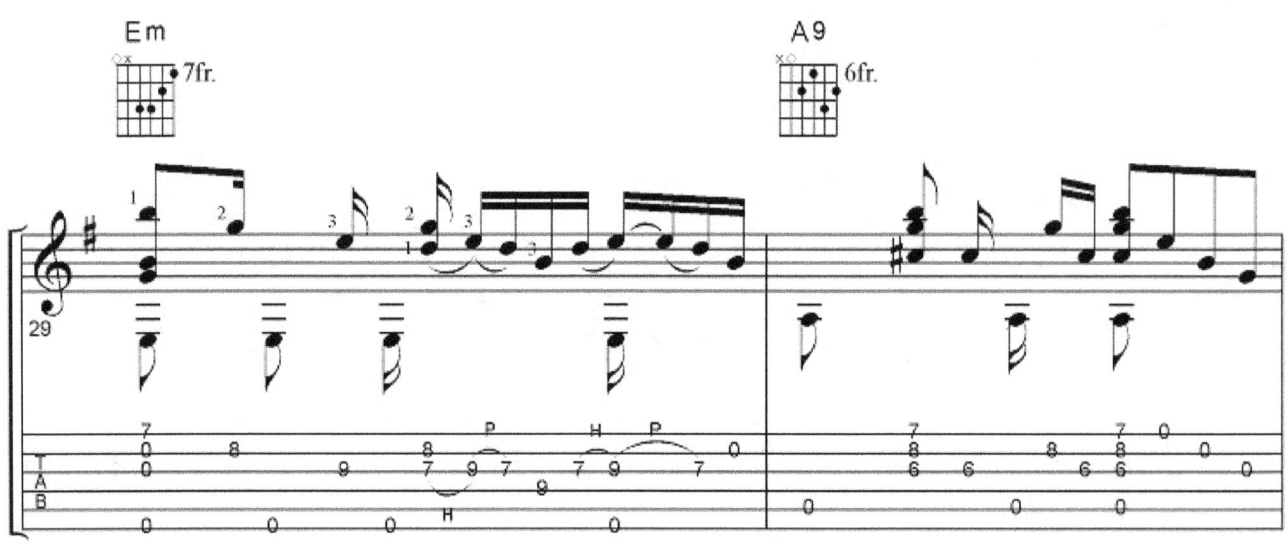

E7 Blues Medley

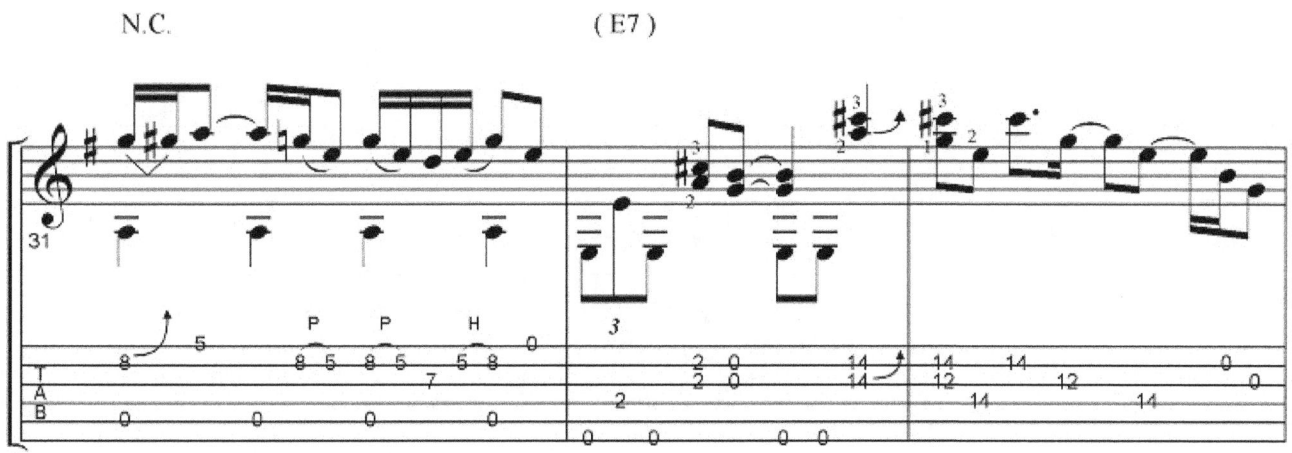

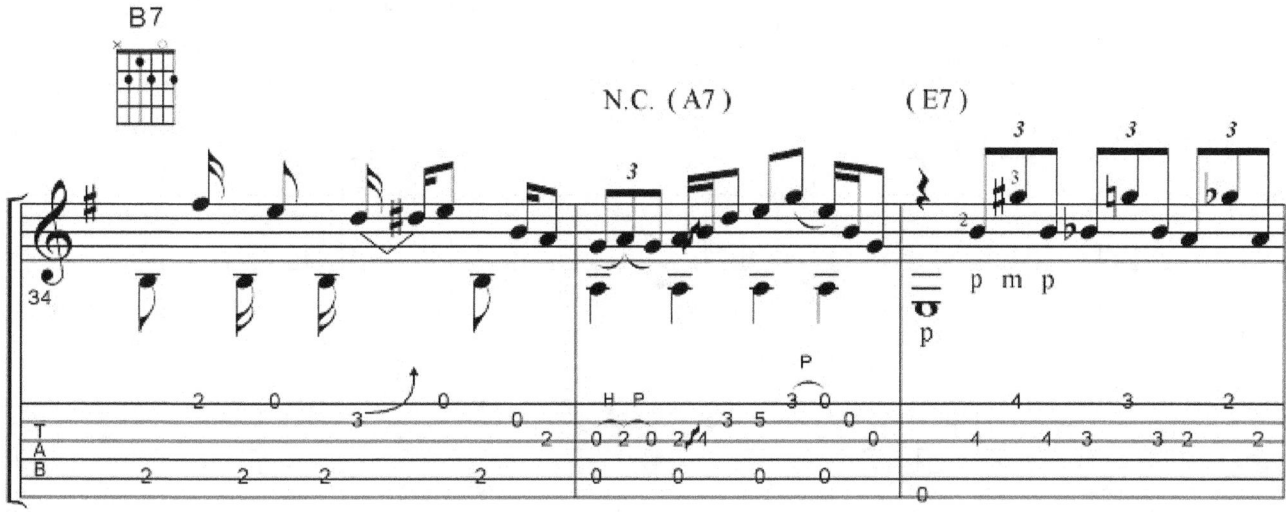

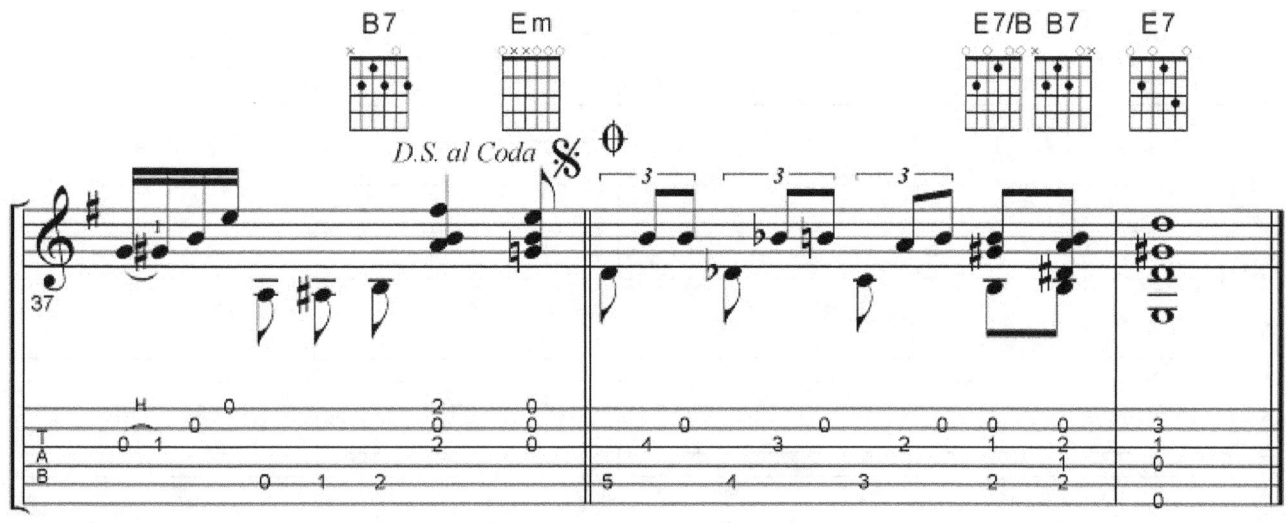

Notes

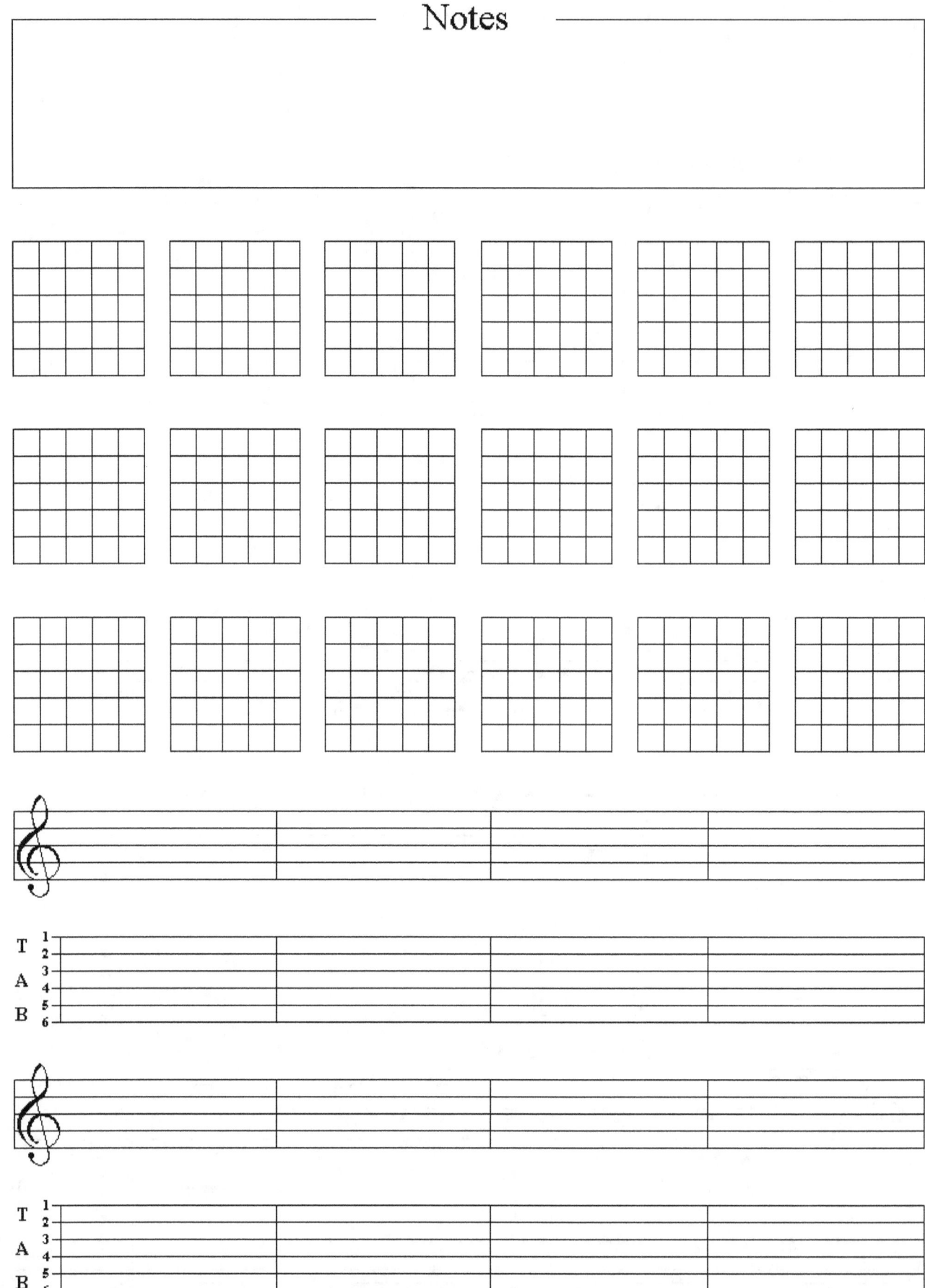

Chapter 15

The Integration Of Improvisation

The Integration Of Improvisation

The integration of improvisation into the Western musical system lies at the core foundation of this book.

Here we find that by simply changing three notes, the exciting sounds of Blues, Jazz, Country and Spanish improvised music is easily at our finger tips.

First we'll learn the theory of the major scale, then how the chord scale and relative minor key are developed from it and finally the magic of the transformation is revealed.

Degrees And Notes

The Western musical system has seven degrees, eight with the octave (1, 2, 3, 4, 5, 6, 7, 8). Each degree is assigned a letter from the English alphabet (A, B, C, D, E, F, G, A) that symbolizes or represents a notes vibration frequency (see page 3-2).

```
8 A
7 G
6 F
5 E
4 D
3 C
2 B
1 A
```

On the fret board diagram below the 5th (A) string has the notes: A, B, C, D, E, F, G and the octave A. By counting up the neck of the guitar (from left to right) it will be found that there are seven notes (eight with the octave) named after the first seven letters of the English alphabet.

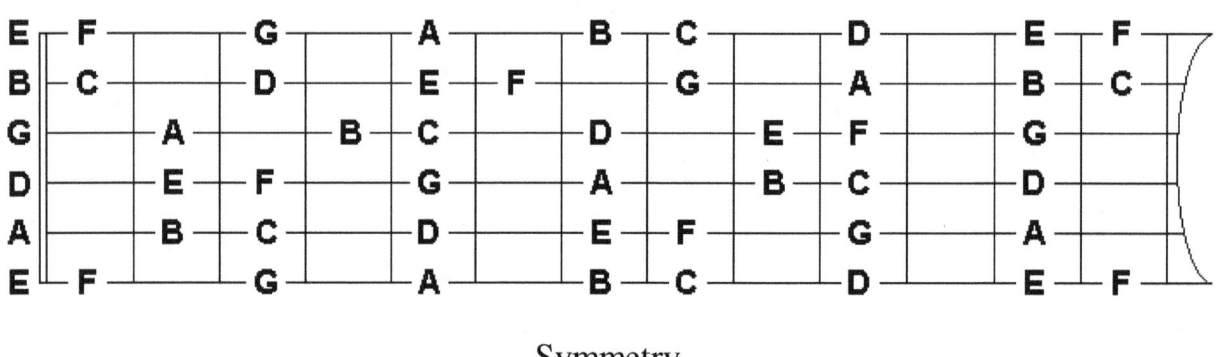

Symmetry

When Pythagoras of Greece, a mathematical genius, developed the Western musical system he did two things that created its unique sound:

1) He placed natural half steps between the 3rd, 4th and 7th, 8th degrees of the major scale.

$$\tfrac{1}{2}<\genfrac{}{}{0pt}{}{8}{7}$$
$$6$$
$$5$$
$$\tfrac{1}{2}<\genfrac{}{}{0pt}{}{4}{3}$$
$$2$$
$$1$$

2) He made E to F and B to C natural half steps. Notice they are one-half step apart, while all the other notes are a whole step apart.

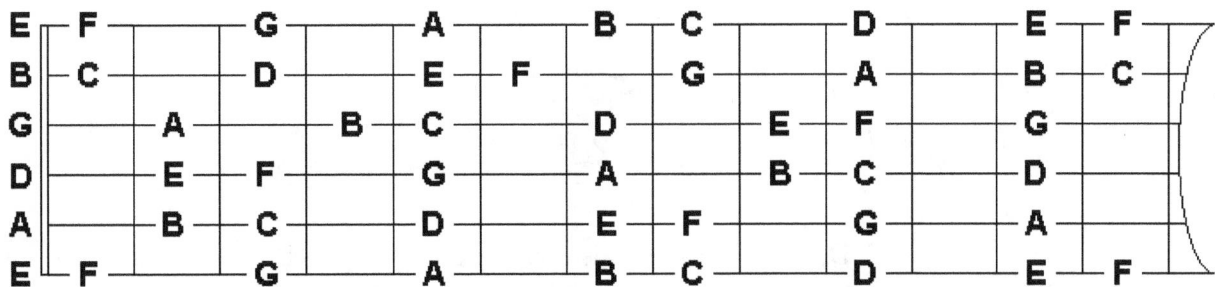

These two factors created the Do – Re – Mi – Fa – So – La – Ti – Do sound we are born into and are so familiar with. Keep in mind that this is a man made system that was created to sound a certain way.

Looking at our scale below it can be seen that the natural half steps E, F & B, C fall between the wrong degrees of the scale starting on A.

$$\tfrac{1}{2}<\genfrac{}{}{0pt}{}{8\ A}{7\ G}$$
$$6\ F$$
$$5\ E$$
$$\tfrac{1}{2}<\genfrac{}{}{0pt}{}{4\ D}{3\ C}$$
$$2\ B$$
$$1\ A$$

So the natural half steps E, F & B, C of the major scale line up with the half step degrees 3, 4 & 7, 8 of the major scale, we'll use the Key of C:

$$\tfrac{1}{2}<\genfrac{}{}{0pt}{}{8\ C}{7\ B}$$
$$6\ A$$
$$5\ G$$
$$\tfrac{1}{2}<\genfrac{}{}{0pt}{}{4\ F}{3\ E}$$
$$2\ D$$
$$1\ C$$

Now it can be seen that the natural half steps E, F & B, C of the scale are placed next to the designated half steps 3, 4 & 7, 8 of the scale degrees. This is why the Key of C is known as the natural key.

Chords

Chords are simply three notes of the major scale put together causing harmony. When you hear three singers singing in harmony they are actually singing chords. To develop chords from the major scale it is done in thirds:

$$\frac{1}{2} < \begin{matrix} 8\ C \\ 7\ B \end{matrix}$$
$$6\ A$$
$$\boxed{5\ G}$$
$$\frac{1}{2} < \begin{matrix} 4\ F \\ \boxed{3\ E} \end{matrix}$$
$$2\ D$$
$$\boxed{1\ C}$$

C to E is three steps: 1, 2, 3 – C, D, E and E to G is also three steps: 3, 4, 5 – E, F, G. So, our first chord is a C chord developed in thirds from the major scale and is made up of the notes C – E – G. The chord is named after its root, the lowest bass note.

$$5\ G$$
$$3\ E$$
$$1\ C - \text{Root}$$

Since there are seven notes in the major scale there will also be seven chords:

[seven chord diagrams showing the C major chord scale triads built on each scale degree]

The seven chords, also known as triads, are extracted from the major scale. This is known as a major chord scale and by being in the Key of C it is more specifically known as the C major chord scale:

G	A	B	C	D	E	F
E	F	G	A	B	C	D
C	D	E	F	G	A	B

When played on the guitar, the notes do not have to be in order and the notes can be duplicated to make it sound fuller. Here is what these chords look like on a guitar grid in the open position at the nut:

C Major Chord Scale

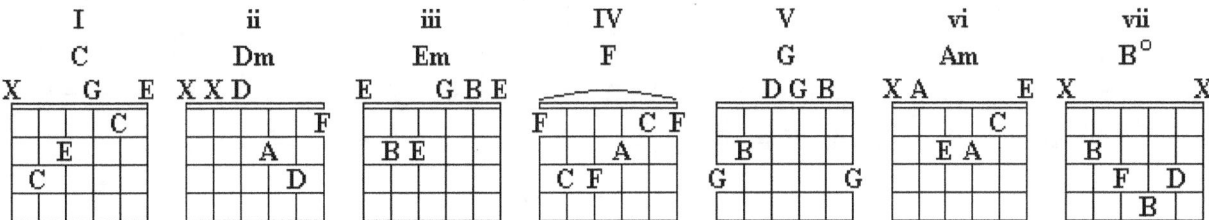

Since the chords of the major chord scale are developed from the major scale, the half steps between the 3rd, 4th & 7th, 8th degrees of the major scale affect the chords causing some to be major and some to be minor. The major scale is designated by Arabic numbers and the major chord scale is designated by upper case Roman numerals for the major chords and lower case Roman numerals for the minor chords:

	Major Scale	Major Chord Scale
$\frac{1}{2}$ <	8 C	VIII C
	7 B	vii B°
	6 A	vi Am
	5 G	V G
$\frac{1}{2}$ <	4 F	IV F
	3 E	iii Em
	2 D	ii Dm
	1 C	I C

Before we learn the details that make a chord major or minor, it must be understood what defines major and minor (Note - This is originally explained in greater detail in Chapter 7):

Two whole steps between the root and third of the chord makes the chord major and one and a half steps between the root and the third of the chord makes the chord minor.

Looking at the diagram on the next page it can be seen that between the C and D notes on the 3rd and 5th frets of the 5th string (the A string) are a whole step apart. It can also be seen that the D and E notes on the 5th and 7th frets of the 5th string are a whole step apart. So there are two whole steps between the root (C) and the 3rd (E) of the C major chord. Now let's look at the Dm chord. Once again looking at the diagram below it can be seen that between the D and E notes on the 5th and 7th frets of the 5th string are a whole step apart. It can also be seen that the E and F notes on the 7th and 8th frets of the 5th string are a half step apart. So there is a whole step and a half step between the root (D) and the 3rd (F) of the D minor chord.

The major chord is a positive, up lifting sound being that the intervals are expanded by two whole steps and the minor chord is a dark, heavy sound because the intervals are contracted to one whole step and one half step.

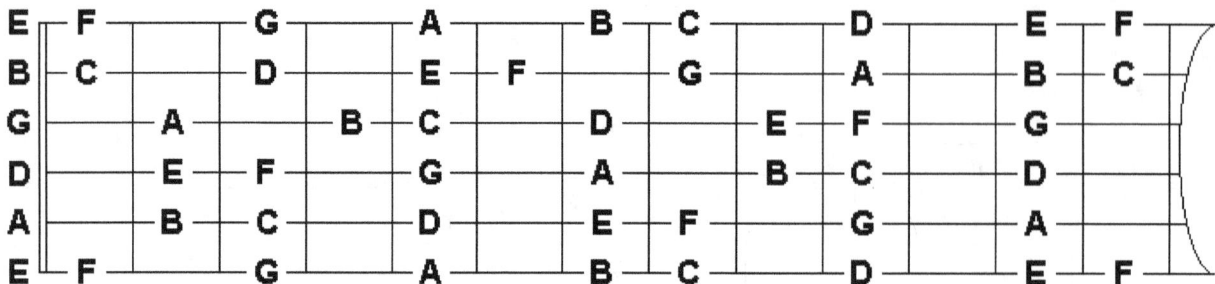

Two prominent emotions in our lives are happiness and unhappiness. The major chord represents happiness and the minor chord represents unhappiness. This also applies to health / sickness, rich / poor, etc. In real-time play the D major chord then play the D minor chord. By simply lowering the major 3rd (F#) to a minor 3rd (F) the difference can be heard:

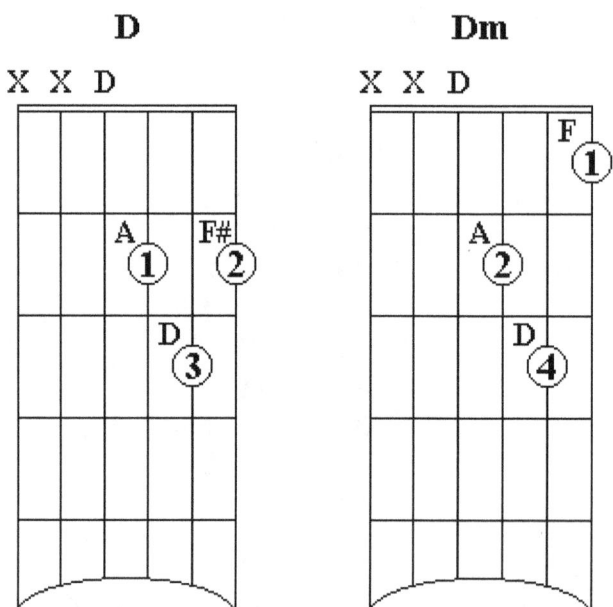

Now let's look at how the major and minor chords affect the major chord scale. In the diagram below the chords that were previously developed from the major scale are presented again only this time with the two whole steps (major) or the one and a half steps (minor) between the root and the third of the triads designated by numbers:

$$2 < \begin{matrix} G \\ E \\ C \end{matrix} \quad 1\tfrac{1}{2} < \begin{matrix} A \\ F \\ D \end{matrix} \quad 1\tfrac{1}{2} < \begin{matrix} B \\ G \\ E \end{matrix} \quad 2 < \begin{matrix} C \\ A \\ F \end{matrix} \quad 2 < \begin{matrix} D \\ B \\ G \end{matrix} \quad 1\tfrac{1}{2} < \begin{matrix} E \\ C \\ A \end{matrix} \quad 1\tfrac{1}{2} < \begin{matrix} F \\ D \\ B \end{matrix}$$

$$\quad\;\; I \qquad\quad\; ii \qquad\quad iii \qquad\quad IV \qquad\quad V \qquad\quad vi \qquad\quad vii$$

The symmetry of the half steps between the 3rd, 4th & 7th, 8th degrees of the major scale is remarkable in how it affects the major chord scale. Remember, humans created the Western musical system and we are born into it so it sounds correct to us. Chinese music, which uses a different harmonic system, was very strange to us when we first heard it.

Now you know how chords are developed and why they are major or minor.

Chord Progressions

A chord progression is simply chords being played in succession. The most popular chord progression in Western music is the I-IV-V chord progression. In the Key of C it would be C – F – G. It is a major chord progression reflecting the strong, bold way of the Western culture. However, when looking at nature it reveals that there is an opposing force that keeps everything in perfect balance. Since the Western musical system is derived from observing nature it is necessary to also have an opposing force: this is where the minor chords make their appearance.

To simplify and make the chord progressions logical we will extract the vi, ii and iii minor chords from the parent key's major chord scale and give them a key of their own. This is called the relative minor key. The 6th degree of the major chord scale is known as the relative minor.

The vi minor chord will be given the i position of the relative minor key, the ii minor chord will be given the iv position of the relative minor key and the iii minor chord will be given the v position of the relative minor key.

	Major Scale	Major Chord Scale	The Relative Minor Key of Am
$\frac{1}{2} <$	8 C	VIII C	
	7 B	vii B°	
	6 A	vi Am	
	5 G	V G	v Em
$\frac{1}{2} <$	4 F	IV F	iv Dm
	3 E	iii Em	
	2 D	ii Dm	
	1 C	I C	i Am

Now we have two progressions: a I – IV - V of the major key and a i – iv - v of the minor key.
This gives us the contrast in our music that will make the musical conversation interesting. Remember there are only seven tones of the major scale to work with! We need all the tools we can find to make things interesting. Musicians are always looking for something different so their music will stand out and be noticed but it should stay within the musical system otherwise it may not be related to by the listener. Of course there is fusion that educates the listeners ear, which combine different genres together such as what Steely Dan did with rock and jazz, the combining of different cultural music's by Carlos Santana with Latin/rock and the Beatles' George Harrison with Indian and pop music on the Rubber Soul album, to mention a few. These are examples of creative music that steps outside of the traditional sound that have been done discreetly.

Chord Substitution

You may be asking "Why do I need to extract the vi, ii & iii minor chords from the major chord scale and give them a key of their own?" Because the I – IV – V chord progression is so significant in Western music it is also carried over to the relative minor key as a i – iv – v chord progression. The interesting factor that arises from this is that the relative minor chords substitute for the parent key major chords. The diagrams on the next page show how this works.

For clarity the C major chord scale is shown with numbered degrees.

G	A	B	C	D	E	F	G
E	F	G	A	B	C	D	E
C	D	E	F	G	A	B	C
I	ii	iii	IV	V	vi	vii	VIII

In the diagram below it can be seen that the relative vi minor chord has two notes the same as the I major chord, the ii minor chord has two notes the same as the IV major chord and the iii minor chord has two notes the same as the V major chord. Although they sound similar, one is major and one is minor. The minor chords can now substitute for the major chords, fulfilling the need for contrast, making the musical conversation more interesting.

	G		A	B		C			D		E	F	G
E	E		F	G	A	A		B	B		C	D	E
C	C		D	E	F	F		G	G		A	B	C
	A					D			E				
	I		ii	iii		IV			V		vi	vii	VIII
	vi					ii			iii				

The vii-diminished chord is used in jazz as a substitute for the V major chord. Its 5th tone is the 7th tone of the V major chord. In the Key of C example below, the F of the diminished vii chord is the 7th of the G major V chord. In jazz the V major chord is always played as a V7 dominant 7th chord. This explains its usefulness as a chord substitution.

	G		A	B		C				F		E	F	G
E	E		F	G	A	A		B	D	D		C	D	E
C	C		D	E	F	F		G	B	B		A	B	C
	A					D			G	G				
	I		ii	iii		IV			E	vii		vi	vii	VIII
	vi					ii			iii					

A song will be played in a specific key (Chapter 6), so with this knowledge it is now easy to figure out the chord progression knowing each chord will be one of the seven chords in the key. It is very common for a song to fluctuate between the major key (parent key) and the relative minor key. Below is a diagram showing the substitute relationship between the parent Key of C and its relative minor Key of Am.

```
                    Major      Major        The
                    Scale      Chord      Relative
                               Scale       Minor
                                         Key of Am
           ½ ⎧ 8 C    VIII C
             ⎩ 7 B     vii B°
               6 A     vi  Am
               5 G     V   G  ←— v  Em
           ½ ⎧ 4 F     IV  F  ←— iv Dm
             ⎩ 3 E     iii Em
               2 D     ii  Dm
               1 C     I   C  ←— i  Am
```

Here is a chord progression that will clarify the lesson in real-time.

$$\text{C - Em - Dm7 - Fmaj7 - G7 - Am - Am/G - Fmaj7 - B}^{\o}\text{7 - G7sus - C}$$
$$\text{I \quad v \quad iv \quad\quad IV \quad\quad V \quad\; i \quad\;\; i \quad\quad IV \quad\quad V \quad\quad V \quad\; I}$$

So by utilizing the relative minor key we now have more tools with which to create with and by realizing the substitutions it is easy to relate to it all by thinking in terms of the I – IV – IV and i – iv – v as the foundation of chord progressions. The B half-diminished 7 chord substituting for the V chord could also be thought of as a G9/B with the root note G omitted. The A note is the ninth of G and the B note, the 3rd of G, in the root position defines it as a 1st inversion chord (see Page 7-14). Here it can be seen that chords can be called by different names depending on their application. Music has its foundation but has flexibility, which as a "living and breathing" system gives it it's unlimited creative potential.

The ii – V – I Chord Progression

Although the I – IV – V chord progression is the backbone of our musical system, it is not the only one. The ii – V – I is another popular chord progression which is used to establish the key the song is being played in or a new key during key modulations. For a complete study of the ii – V – I chord progression see Page 16-4.

The Blues Effect

Before the Blues, music was straightforward, except for Spanish, which altered one of the relative minor chords. There was the basic I – IV – V chord progression and the relative minor being played in Classical and Folk music. Improvisation was limited to the articulation of the tone and the Spanish, who played quick little note flurries between the chords that were derived from the scale. Today, the Blues are essentially drawing most people to the guitar since Jazz and Rock are derived from the Blues with its nature that has given us the phenomenal ability to play creative leads and improvisation. However, it has also created a lot of confusion theoretically as to how it actually works causing the student difficulty in understanding and learning songs by ear. This confusion can be overcome when the Blues are looked at from the perspective of the relative minor; it is here that a whole new window opens on understanding the integrated relationship of the guitar.

As The Story Goes

Pythagoras of Greece developed the Western musical system by observing the relationship of humans in nature. He chose the major sound of the I – IV – V chord progression as the basis of the musical system to represent the positive strength of Western man's culture. In Europe the Spanish had a unique culture and they decided to alter the Western musical system to represent their culture. They realized that Pythagoras had created the Western musical system to suit his culture so they realized they could do the same. They simply took the minor v chord of the relative minor key and changed it to a major V chord by raising the 3rd degree of the chord. To help clarify this when analyzing the music an sV symbol (the "s" signifies Spanish) can be used. This can be seen in the diagram on the next page.

	Major Scale	Major Chord Scale		The Relative Minor Key of Am	Spanish
½ <	8 C	VIII C			
	7 B	vii B°			
	6 A	vi Am			
	5 G	V G	v Em	sV E	
½ <	4 F	IV F	iv Dm	iv Dm	
	3 E	iii Em			
	2 D	ii Dm			
	1 C	I C	i Am	i Am	

They continued to use the same major scale of the parent key, which created the fiery sound that is associated with Spanish music by causing the G# major 3rd note of the E chord to be played against the G natural of the major scale thus creating that particular sound. The Spanish accepted this sound to represent their culture. Note: When analyzing a chord that does not belong in the key, it is necessary to refer to the chords own key as seen in the next diagram.

	Parent Key Of E	
1/2 [	8 E	
	7 D#	
	6 C#	
	5 B	E Chord
1/2 [	4 A	
	3 G#	5 B
	2 F#	3 G#
	1 E	1 E

Now when the African found himself in America as a slave he found it was necessary to define his new culture so he set forth to make some alterations of his own to the Western musical system. It must be realized that the African was educated when the English had overrun the African continent in its quest to become an empire. The African understood the Western musical system. They decided that by altering the relative minor chords to dominant seven chords (raising the third and adding the seventh) and playing the scale of the parent key it would be a sound that expressed their culture. This can be seen in the diagram below.

	Major Scale	Major Chord Scale	The Relative Minor Key of Am	Spanish	Blues
½ <	8 C	VIII C			
	7 B	vii B°			
	6 A	vi Am			
	5 G	V G	v Em	sV E	V7 E7
½ <	4 F	IV F	iv Dm	iv Dm	IV7 D7
	3 E	iii Em			
	2 D	ii Dm			
	1 C	I C	i Am	i Am	I7 A7

The rules of the Blues require a b3rd, b5th and a b7th for its unique sound. These flatted tones are a part of the chord structure as is found in the 7th tone of the dominant seven chord as well as from the tones of the parent key major scale.

What Is A Dominant Seven Chord?

```
Parent
Key Of A
    8 A
1/2[
    7 G#
    6 F#      A7
    5 E      Chord
    4 D       7 G
1/2[
    3 C#      5 E
    2 B       3 C#
    1 A       1 A
```

The dominant seventh chord is a major chord with a minor 7th. It has a major 3rd interval between its root and 3rd degree and a minor 3rd interval between its 5th and 7th degrees. For example: the A7 chord in the diagram to the left has a whole step between A & B and a whole step between B & C# creating a major 3rd interval between the root and 3rd degrees. It also has a whole step between E & F# and half step between F# & G creating a minor 3rd interval between the 5th and 7th degrees.

It is the lowered/flatted 7th that gives the chord its Blues sound. In the Key of A the 7th tone of the major scale is naturally a G#, a major 7th interval (E to F# is a whole step and F# to G# is a whole step).

Even though the dominant 7th chord is an altered chord from the relative minor key, it is always analyzed from the perspective of the parent key for the sake of clarity. For example, the A7 chord is altered from the relative minor chord Am which is originally derived from the parent Key of C. The Am7 chord would be analyzed from the perspective of the Key of C and the A7 chord would be analyzed from the perspective of the Key of A to get the notes correct with the exception of the altered flatted 7th.

The dominant 7th chord is so named to eliminate any conflict between itself and the minor 7th chord. Since the dominant V chord (see Page 7-2) in jazz is played with a minor 7th interval it makes sense to name all major chords with a minor 7th interval as dominant 7 chords.

The minor 7th chord has a minor 3rd interval between both its root & 3rd interval and its 5th & 7th interval, where as the dominant 7th chord has a major 3rd interval between its root & 3rd interval and a minor 3rd interval between its 5th & 7th interval.

```
        Parent                      Parent
       Key Of C                    Key Of A
      ½[ 8 C                      ½[ 8 A
         7 B                         7 G#
         6 A       Am7                6 F#       A7
         5 G      Chord               5 E       Chord
      ½[ 4 F     1½[ 7 G           ½[ 4 D     1½[ 7 G
         3 E         5 E              3 C#        5 E
         2 D     1½[ 3 C              2 B      2[ 3 C#
         1 C         1 A              1 A         1 A
```

15-10

The Integrated Blues

The rules of the Blues is to have a flatted 3rd, 5th and 7th. With the dominant 7 chords being altered from the relative minor key as a major chord with a minor 7th to create the Blues, we get the flatted 7th. When the Dominant 7 chords are played with the major scale from the parent key we now get the flatted 3rd.

	Major Scale	Major Chord Scale	The Relative Minor	Key of Am	Spanish	Blues	
$\frac{1}{2}<$	8 C	VIII C					
	7 B	vii B°					
	6 A	vi Am					
	5 G	V G	v Em	sV E	V7 E7		
$\frac{1}{2}<$	4 F	IV F	iv Dm	iv Dm	IV7 D7		
	3 E	iii Em					
	2 D	ii Dm					
	1 C	I C	i Am	i Am	I7 A7		

For example: The A7 chord has a C# for its 3rd and the scale plays over it with a C. The D7 chord has a F# for its 3rd and the scale plays over it with an F. The E7 chord has a G# for its 3rd and the scale plays over it with a G. In the diagram below the A7, D7 and E7 chords are presented for visual clarification:

A7 Chord	D7 Chord	E7 Chord
7 G	7 C	7 D
5 E	5 A	5 B
3 C#	3 F#	3 G#
1 A	1 D	1 E

Now that you are on the inside of this knowledge it can be seen how the uneducated musician would never be able to figure it out therefore, only being able to emulate another's creative experience.

What Key Is The Song In?

The easiest way to find the key of a song is to listen to the bass. The bass usually plays the root of the chord. Although it doesn't happen all the time since bass players also like to harmonize the chords, they do generally stay around the roots of the chords giving the song a solid bottom end that is easy to follow.

However if this is not the case or if the song begins with only a guitar or piano then the first chord will generally provide you with the key. To verify this, play the last chord of the song and if it is the same as the first chord it will most likely be the key of the song. There are some exceptions to be aware of: A) Songs can modulate (see Page 16-3) into other keys which would mean the first and last chords would be different. B) Perhaps the song might end on a suspended 2 (sus2) chord or suspended 4 (sus4) chord symbolizing that the song story is unresolved.

The sure and quickest way to find what key the song is in is to jam along with the song playing your favorite pentatonic scale (see Page 14-8) until you find where it harmonizes (see below under What Chords Are They Playing?).

Once you find the key you will need to know if the key is major or minor. This can usually be known by the first chord being played. If it is major then you have found the parent key, if it is minor then you will have most likely found the relative minor key. If it is the relative minor key then it will have come from the 6th degree of the major key. You'll need to count up the scale (alphabet) three degrees to find the parent key. For example: If the song is in the Key of Am by counting A, B then C the parent key is C. Now you can write your degree numbers with the major scale letters next to them and then develop your chords in 3rds, extract the relative minor out of the parent key and you will have a handy blueprint of the chords available in the song.

Major Scale	Major Chord Scale	The Relative Minor Key of Am
8 C	VIII C	
7 B	vii B°	
6 A	vi Am	
5 G	V G	v Em
4 F	IV F	iv Dm
3 E	iii Em	
2 D	ii Dm	
1 C	I C	i Am

(½ between 8–7 and between 4–3)

Which Chords Are They Playing?

With the key of the song known you will now know the seven chords available for the song. This narrows the guesswork making the learning of songs by ear much easier and faster. You will, over a period of time, learn from experience, the sound of the different chords. This is a natural process of ear training. For example: is it a major or minor chord. Also, the bass will generally provide you with the root of the chord making it easier to hear than a chord since sometimes chords can be; inverted (see Page 7-13), a substitution (see Page 16-6), using altered tones (see Chapter 14) or using color tones (see Page 7-1).

Okay, so your playing the Aeolian pentatonic scale beginning at the A on the 5th fret and it harmonizes with the chord progression. Since the Aeolian always plays off of the 6th degree of the major scale which, is where the relative minor comes from, this will reveal one of the following keys:

1) If the chord progression is C - F – G then the song is in the Key of C.
2) If the chord progression is Am – Dm – Em then the song is in the relative minor Key of Am, which is derived from the Key of C.
3) If the chord progression is A7 - D7 - E7 then the song is in the Blues Key of A7.
4) If the chord progression is A – D – E then the song is in the Rock or Country Key of A.

Which Modes And Scales Do I Play

The modes are simply the starting points from each of the seven degrees of the major scale that give us guitarists seven positions on the neck to play in. I refer to these modes as "playgrounds" since all our playing; whether it be chords, melody, lead or improvisation will be played within these patterns.

Now that you have the modes and pentatonic scales memorized and you have found the key the song is in, it is simply a matter of playing within any of the modes or scales in that key. When you play another song in another key, the modes and scales will remain in the same order but will shift up or down the neck of the guitar according to the key the new song is in. See the Conveyor Belt on Pages 13-1 and 13-2 to see how the order of the modes remains the same as they shift in relationship to each key.

Summary

Learning songs by ear is only one part of the whole learning process of playing the guitar. It is significantly important for ear training and also helpful to learn what other guitarists and musicians are creating thus helping to entertain ideas that will open new ideas for you. I am asked frequently, "Why is it necessary to learn the theory of music when I can just learn songs by ear?" If all you want to do is emulate others then learning songs by ear is all you need to do. However if you want to tap the Creative then you must learn how music works (theory) and you must train your fingers (technical) to go where you want, when you want them to. Being trained and educated you have now become a prepared receiver that is capable of having the Creative flow through you. Then it is those who just want to emulate others that will now be emulating you! I speak from experience – being as skilled and knowledgeable about the guitar as I have trained myself to be over the years, the creative process is now an ongoing daily process for me with no end in sight. I remember how I dreamed of being a creative guitarist when I first took it up and now what a joy it is that it has become a reality.

In its simplest terms, the song will tell you how it wants to sound and if you "listen" and have the tools (knowledge and skills) available, you will be able to compose it with satisfaction.

For the other part of the guitar: The two things we do on the guitar is to play scales and chords in their various arrangements making interesting conversation. If we learn about these scales and chords and how they interact with each other (harmony) in the different genres of music then we are playing creatively on our own terms and interactively with the music.

You have made a giant leap towards playing the guitar up to this point so let us continue forward to learn more about this intriguing instrument in the proceeding chapters.

Section Five

The Finishing Touches

Notes

Chapter 16 Chord Progressions

Chord Progressions

The most common and basic chord progression in music is the I - IV - V chord progression.

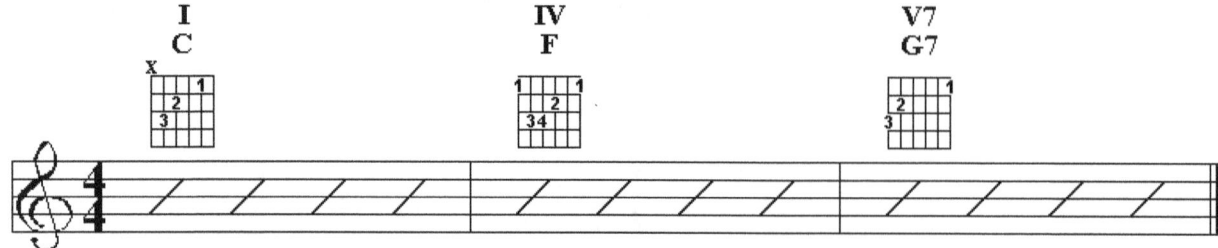

In the major chord scale the I - IV - V chords are major and the ii - iii - vi - vii chords are minor.

C - Dm - Em - F - G - Am - Bm - C
I   ii   iii   IV   V   vi   vii   VIII

The major chords are the foundation of the song and the minor chords are the variables that offer variations to the theme for more interesting music. Playing back and forth between the major and minor chords is that which gives contrast to a song. Think of the painter using light and dark shades for contrast to highlight the subject. Let's look at Row Your Boat again only this time we'll jazz it up with major seven, diminished, minor seven and dominant seven chords to make the point. The melody will be playing the major third harmony for the first two bars of this arrangement. In the last measure the Dm7 is on the fifth fret and the D69(b5) is on the fourth fret.

Row Your Boat

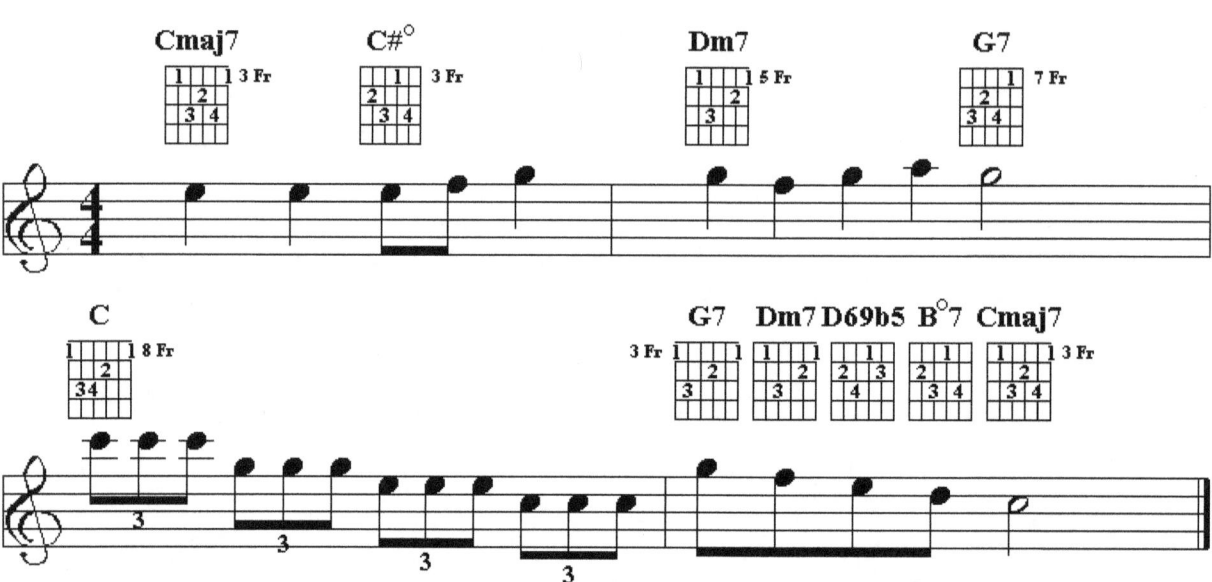

While I was working out this arrangement several different chord substitutions were available for me to use. I chose these chords because of the dreamy nature of the song and these chords expressed that best for me. The student should explore the possibilities and create their own arrangement according to their taste.

The five staves below look at some of the more common chord progressions starting with the key establishing ii - V7 - I chord progression and evolving to some more involved chord progressions. Presented here are just a few chord progressions to give the student an awareness of their function. All of the chord progressions ever played would fill a volume of their own. Over the years of playing and learning new songs, the many chord progressions will become a part of the students ever growing repertoire. Play these chord progressions in all twelve keys for fretboard mastery.

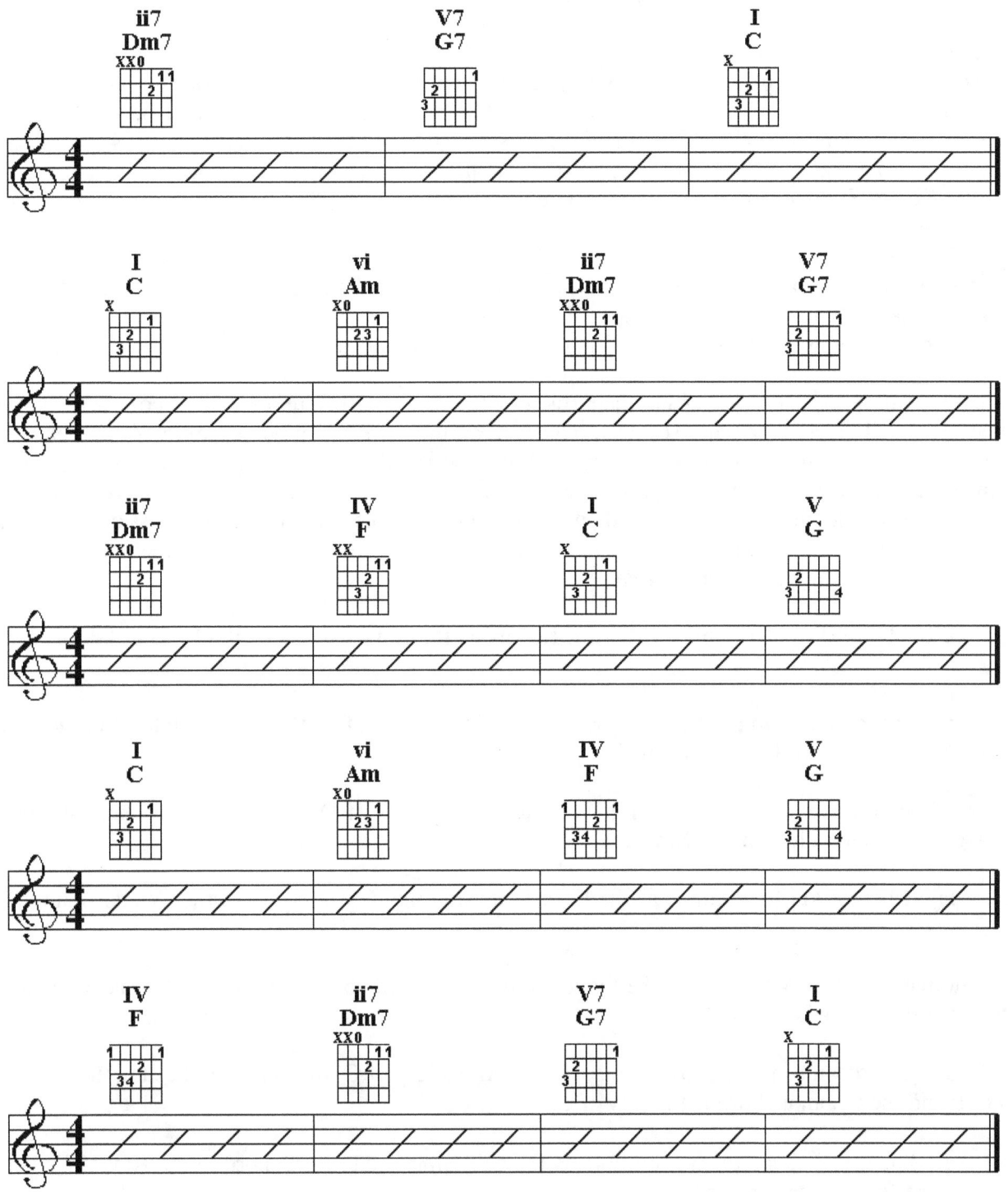

Key Modulations

Key modulations are a more complex chord progression giving the guitarist more variety to express with for a more interesting and complex musical conversation. Key modulations are a factor that confuses the untrained musician when trying to follow along with the music.

The easiest key modulations to understand are the modulations of a half step and a whole step. Simply take the song that you're playing and step it up a half step. For example if your playing in the Key of C you would modulate the song up to the Key of C# which means everything you were playing in the Key of C would slide up the neck of the guitar a half step. If you were to modulate up a whole step the process would be the same. For example, if your playing in the Key of C you would modulate the song up to the Key of D, which means everything you were playing in the Key of C, would slide up the neck of the guitar a whole step.

The second and also easy is to simply play around the circle of fifths as we did with the five basic chords in Chapter One: C - G - D - A - E. Although there are songs using this modulating chord progression, it is not as common as the first two types of key modulations.

The key modulations that move within the circle of fifths and fourths are a bit more complex. First let's look at the possibilities. In a major scale we have learned there are seven notes from which seven chords can be built. Two of these chords are major; the I and the IV, three are minor; the ii, iii and vi, one is a dominant seven; the V7 and one is a half diminished seven; the vii. Because these chords, except for the V7 and the vii half dim.7, can be found in keys other than the parent key the possibilities for key modulation is greatly increased. Presented below are the chords from the seven degrees of the C major scale and their relationship with other keys:

The C major, I chord can be found as the root I chord in the Key of C and as the IV chord in the Key of G.

The Dmi, ii chord can be found as the ii minor chord in the Key of C, the iii minor chord in the Key of Bb and the vi minor chord in the Key of F.

The Emi, iii chord can be found as the ii minor chord in the Key of D, as the iii minor chord in the Key of C and the vi minor chord in the Key of G.

The F Major, IV chord can be found as the Root I chord in the Key of F and as the IV chord in the Key of C.

The G dominant seven, V7 chord can be found as the V7 major chord in the Key of C. The V7 will only be found in the parent key.

The Ami, vi chord can be found as the ii minor chord in the Key of G, the iii minor chord in the Key of F and the vi minor chord in the Key of C.

The B half dim.7, ($B^{\emptyset}7$) chord can be found as the half diminished seven chord in the Key of C. The vii 7 will only be found in the parent key.

The ii – V7 – I Chord Progression

The ii - V7 - I chord progression is an important progression that will be found frequently throughout a standard jazz song. The ii - V7 - I chord progression establishes the key of the song. It will be found at the end of the intro section in the beginning of the song, at the end of phrases within the songs verses and at the end of the song. This repetition of the ii - V7 - I chord progression throughout the song makes a strong statement as to the key the song is in.

The repetition is also necessary because the song will modulate to different keys several times throughout its' course. The ii - V7 - I chord progression establishes the new key the song has modulated into and also re-establishes the original key when the song modulates back into it. For example: In the Key of Eb the song plays a Fm7 - Bb7 - Ebmaj7 chord progression. This is a ii - V7 - I in the Key of Eb that establishes the key. Then the song plays an Am7 - D7 - Gmaj9 chord progression. This is a ii - V7 - I that establishes the new Key of G in the song. Next the song plays an Fm7 - Bb7 - Ebmaj7 chord progression. This is a ii - V7 - I that re-establishes the song in the original Key of Eb.

Memorization of the Circle Of Fifths and the Circle Of Fourths diagrams presented below is the only way the player will be able to use this information in real-time playing.

Circle Of Fifths			Circle Of Fourths		
ii - V7 - I			ii - V7 - I		
Key Of C:	Dm7 - G7	- C	Key Of C:	Dm7 - G7	- C
Key Of G:	Am7 - D7	- G	Key Of F:	Gm7 - C7	- F
Key Of D:	Em7 - A7	- D	Key Of Bb:	Cm7 - F7	- Bb
Key Of A:	Bm7 - E7	- A	Key Of Eb:	Fm7 - Bb7	- Eb
Key Of E:	F#m7 - B7	- E	Key of Ab:	Bbm7 - Eb7	- Ab
Key Of B:	C#m7 - F#7	- B	Key Of Db:	Ebm7 - Ab7	- Db
Key Of F#:	G#m7 - C#7	- F#	Key Of Gb:	Abm7 - Db7	- Gb

Because the barred E and A forms are easiest to play, the two most popular barred ii7 - V7 chord progressions are presented below in measures one, two and three, four to get you started. To explore the three other basic chord forms and their variations used for these chord modulations, the Chord Guide in Chapter 19 will provide you with all the possibilities. Play the ii7 - V7 chord progressions in all keys using the five basic chord forms and their variations for mastery of the guitar neck. This is one more tool for the guitarist to have to create with.

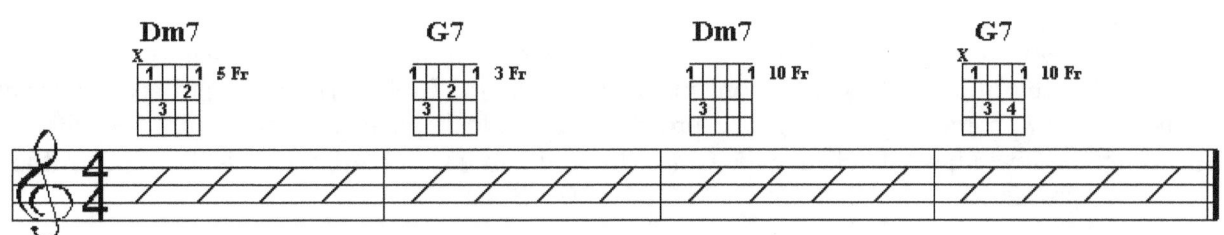

Downstep Modulation

A chord progression is a succession of chords alternating between different chord structures. Chord structure means major, minor, augmented, diminished and suspended. The major or minor third of a chord will always be present unless the chord is a sus2 or a sus4, which eliminates the third. The augmented chord gives the effect of expansion while the diminished chord compresses.

Shown below in the Key of C is a standard modulation in which the Em7 to A7 chord change is a modulation into the Key of D while the Dm7 to G7 is a return to the parent Key of C.

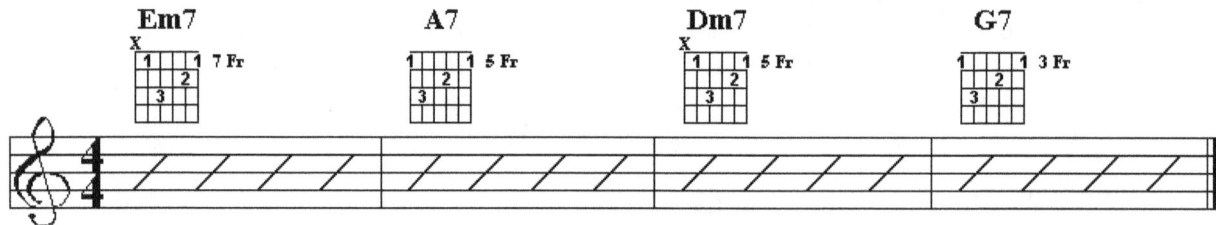

Another approach to the above downstep modulation is when the root of the chords move downward chromatically. In this downstep modulation, the Em7 slides down to an Eb7, then a Dm7 and last to the Db7. The Eb7 substitutes for the A7 and the Db7 substitutes for the G7.

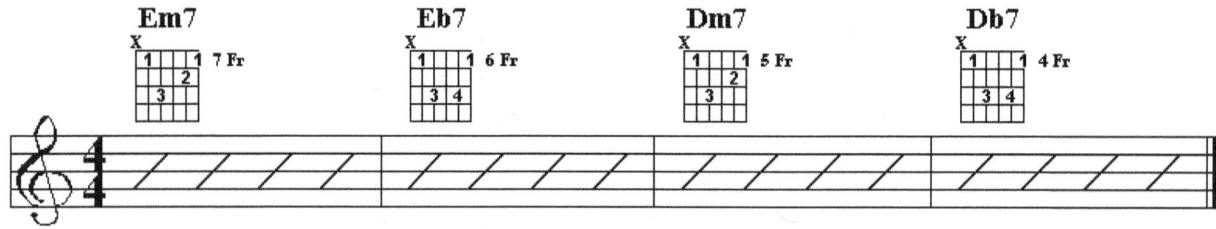

To continue this progression still from another angle it can be seen that the Em9 is sliding down to an A13/Eb, then to the Dm9 and last the G13/Db. The A13/Eb and the G13/Db chords could also be called an Eb7+9 and a Db7+9. Inverted chords sound more sophisticated and complex.

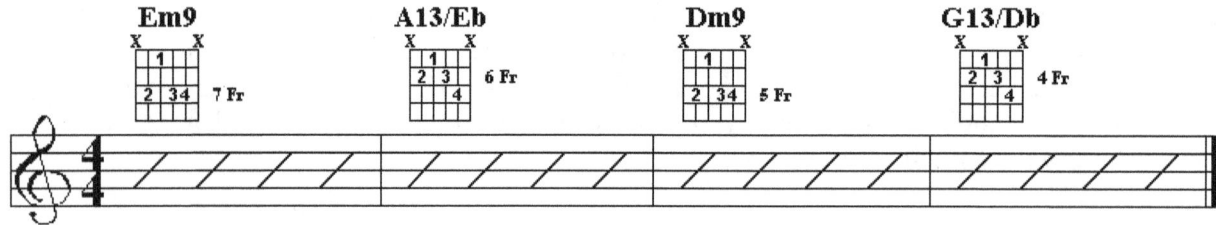

Downstep modulations not only apply to the root of the chord but also to the third and the seventh. For example, in the Key of C the Cmaj7 I chord modulates to a cm7 by lowering the third and the seventh and is now the ii7 in the Key of Bb. The progression would be: Cmaj7 - cm7 - F7 - Bbmaj7. By lowering only the seventh would change the Cmaj7 I chord into a C7 chord, which is the V7 chord in the Key of F. This progression would be: Cmaj7 - C7 - Fmaj7 - Bbmaj7.

Chord Substitutions

Chord substitutions are another way of using more tools to open other passageways to further the creative process, which in turn makes the song more interesting. Chord substitutions by their very nature give us a deeper insight into chord progressions. In Downstep Modulation we already saw the value of substituting the Eb7 and the Db7 for the A7 and G7 chords respectively. Variety is the key word here. If the same theme is going to repeat over again several times it would be in the interest of the composer to use a variety of chords to break up the monotony for the interest of the listener.

A common substitution of the dominant V7 chord is the bII7 chord. In the Key of F the V7 chord is C7 and its bII7 substitute is a Gb7. C - E - G – Bb are the notes in the C7 chord and Gb - Bb - Db - Fb are the notes in the Gb7 chord. As a chord substitute of the C7 chord, the Gb is the diminished fifth or the augmented eleventh and the Db is the flatted ninth. The Bb, the dominant seventh and Fb (E), the major third, are found in both chords. The end result is a C7b5b9 or a C7b9+11 without the root note C that would generally be played by the bass player or pianist.

Chord substitutions require certain intervals within the chord to make it interesting. The V7 chord has the dominant seven to connect it to the IV chord. The IV chord and the V7 chord both have a pull to resolve towards the root chord, as they are the three major chords in that key. The bII7 chord also has the necessary ingredients to resolve to the root chord as well. In the Key of F the b5 that is derived from the bII7 chord substitution, Gb7 wants to resolve to the root note of the root chord, which in this case is Gb to F and the b9 wants to resolve itself to the fifth of the root chord, which in this case is Db to C.

Polychords

Polychords are the combining of two related chords. For example: In the Key of C, take the Cmaj7 (I) chord and place the Dm (ii) chord on top of it and the C chord now becomes a Cmaj9(11)(13).

$$C - E - G - B + D - F - A$$

The nine, eleven and thirteen must be present in the polychord as they are the defining name of the chord. The seventh must also be present unless the chord asks for an add 9(11)(13). In this case the polychord would be written out as:

$$C - E - G + D - F - A$$

Polychords do not require the seventh of the second chord to be used, as it will only be duplicated. Generally a triad will suffice. The fifth of the base chord is also expendable unless it is a defining factor of the chord such as a Cmaj9b5(11)(13). The root note of the base chord is generally played by the bass or piano player. The trick is to play the notes that express the sound the polychord is looking for within the song and leave out the insignificant ones. Polychords are a creative tool for playing as an arpeggio in a solo or an improvisation.

Turnarounds

When we move from one section to another in a song each section comes to an end usually resolving to the root chord thus ending a phrase or a musical thought. The next new section usually starts with the same root chord. This means there are several bars at the end of each section with the same root chord. To relieve the monotony and connect the two sections together a turnaround is used. There are many variations of turnarounds in which most will begin with the root chord and end with a V7 chord or a V7 chord substitute. The example given below is a popular turnaround and ends with a flat II chord that is a commonly used V7 chord substitute.

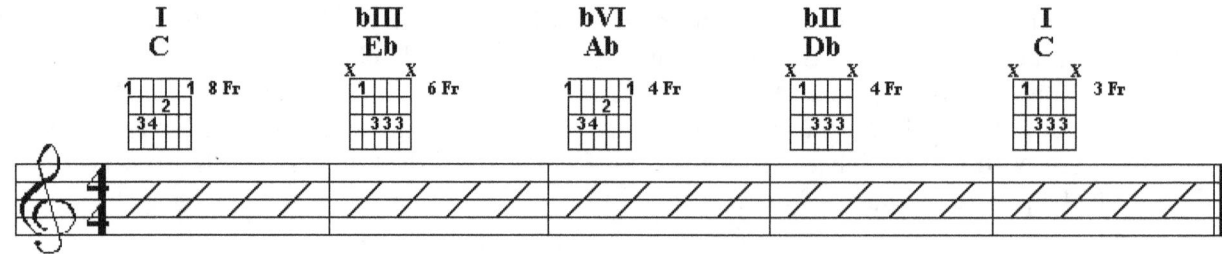

When one first looks at this turnaround it doesn't seem that it would work but when played it makes for an interesting phrase ending that gives a positive direction to the next section. Let's analyze this movement and see why it works. Take the C major scale: C - D - E - F - G - A - B - C. Let's look at the notes in the chords and their relationship to the C major scale.

CHORDS

			C	Eb	Ab	Db
SCALE	8	C				
	7	B		b7		
	6	A			b6	b6
	5	G	5	5		
	4	F				4
	3	E	3	b3	b3	
	2	D				b2
	1	C	1		1	

The Eb chord has the b3, b7 which is all blues. The Ab chord with the b6 would be thought of as a b13 an octave higher for a jazz sound. The Db chord with the b2 would be thought of as the b9 an octave higher for a blues and jazz sound and the 4th is either a suspended 4th or the 11th an octave higher giving an airy jazz sound. All of these non-diatonic tones in the Key of C give the turnaround a blues and jazz sound. Since rock and jazz are derived from the blues it becomes clear how this turnaround is harmonically feasible. The chords in the turnaround can be major, minor, major seven or dominant seven depending on the style of music being played.

These non-diatonic tones are derived from the chromatic scale giving us more creative choices.

A Classic Blues Turnaround

This chromatic, walk down in triplets, turnaround is a cornerstone sound of the blues. In the Twelve Bar Blues diagram below the turnaround begins with the E7 chord in the eleventh measure and ends with the B7 chord in measure twelve.

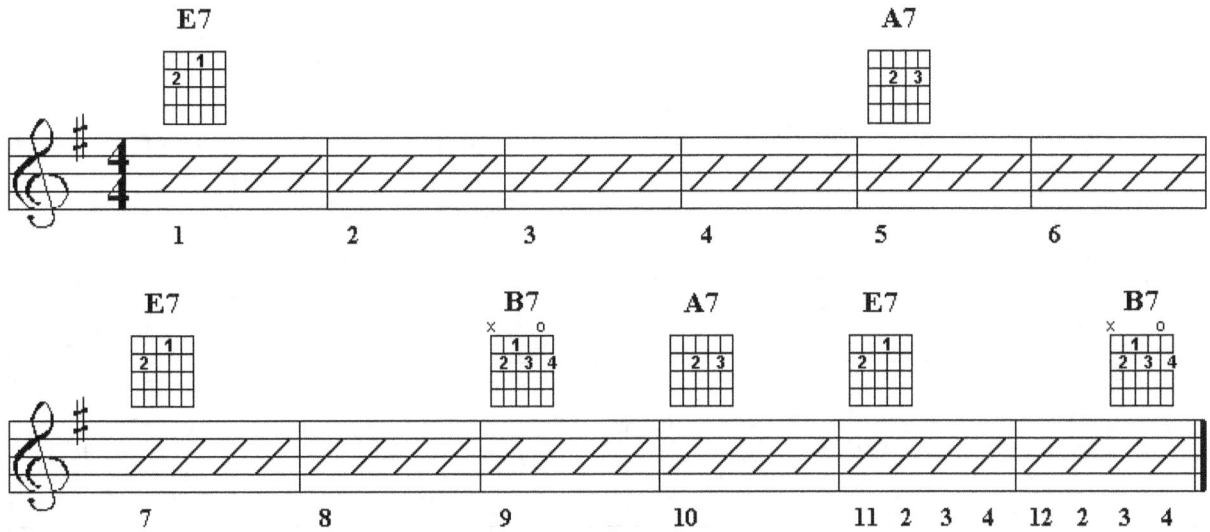

Below is measures eleven and twelve with the notated turnaround.

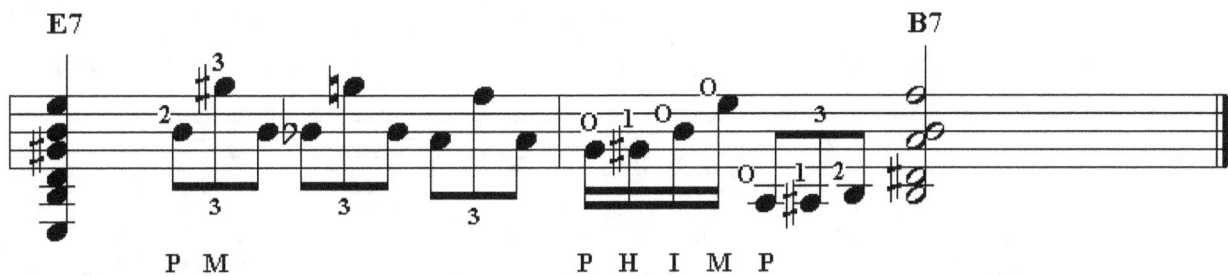

As seen below this blues turnaround is mostly chordal. Starting with the first triplet on beat two of the eleventh measure the interval of a minor third B and G# are derived from the E7 chord of the D form. The second triplet on beat three is a minor third interval Bb and G derived from the Edim7 chord of the D form. The third triplet on beat four is a minor third interval A and F# derived from the D7 chord of the D form. The first note of the sixteenth note run on beat one of the twelfth measure is a hint of an Em chord changing to an E7 chord. The chromatic walking bass on beat two of the 12th measure is a scale passage that is derived from the 6th tone of the Aeolian hexatonic scale.

A Standard Jazz Tune

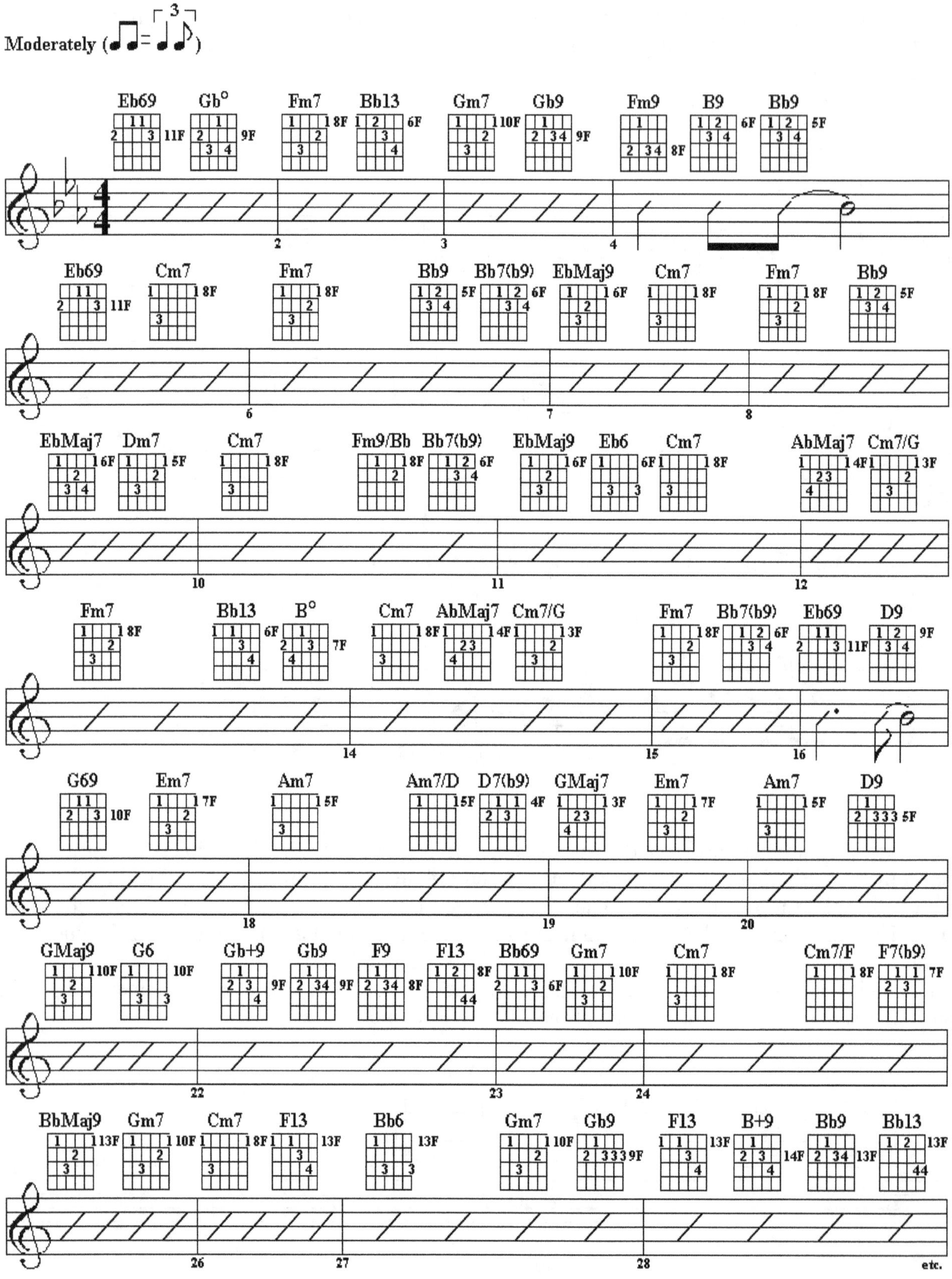

Analysis Of A Standard Jazz Tune

The information at the beginning of the song is telling us to play the song moderately around 115 beats per minute with a swing feel in 4/4 time in the Key of Eb. Below is the Eb major chord scale for reference.

$$\text{Eb - Fm - Gm - Ab - Bb7 - Cm - Dm - Eb}$$
$$\text{I} \quad \text{ii} \quad \text{iii} \quad \text{IV} \quad \text{V7} \quad \text{vi} \quad \text{vii} \quad \text{VIII}$$

Measures 1 – 4: The first four measures are the Intro of the song. The Intro introduces a general feel of what the song is about. The Eb69 to the Gbdim chords, a I - biii movement in the first measure is an interval of a minor third giving a feel of the blues from the onset. The Fm7 to the Bb13 chord change in the second measure establishes the Key of Eb with the ii7 - V7 movement. In the third and fourth measures the Gm7, Gb9 and Fm7 chord changes are a iii7 - bIII7 - ii7 downward chromatic movement that creates an interesting turnaround while re-establishing the Key of Eb with the Fm7 and Bb9 chord changes being a ii7 - V7 movement in the fourth measure. The B9 to the Bb9 chord changes are a #V7 - V7 movement also in the fourth measure adding drama, release and a finality to the introductory phrase laying down the red carpet for the Eb69, the I chord in the first verse.

Measures 5 – 8: In the first verse measure five is a I - vi movement with the Eb69 changing to the Cm7. Measure six is once again establishing the Key of Eb with the Fm7 and Bb9 chord changes, a ii7 - V7 movement. The Bb7(b9) is for variety. Measures seven and eight are repeats of measures five and six with the exceptions of the Ebma9 chord for variety and without the variation of the Bb7(b9) chord.

Measures 9 – 12: Measures nine and ten are simply moving down the Eb major chord scale from EbMaj7 to the Dm7 and then the Cm7, which is a IMaj7 - vii7 - vi7. In measure ten the familiar key establishing ii7 - V7 movement is present with the Fm9/Bb to the Bb7(b9). The Fm9 with the Bb in the bass creates a suspended effect, as the Bb is the fourth of F. This very nicely resolves to the fifth of the Bb7(b9), which is F and then finally resolving to the EbMaj9 in measure eleven. The Eb6 is a variation of the Eb chord, which moves to the Cm7, the vi7 chord that then strengthens the movement by playing the AbMaj7, the IVMaj7 chord. The AbMaj7 chord in the twelfth measure begins a chromatic bass movement downward as the Cm7/G chord with the G in its bass continues to the F of the Fm7 chord in the thirteenth measure.

Measures 13 – 16: The same ii7 - V7 and ii7 - IVMaj7 - ii7 chord progressions are being played again to the sixteenth measure when the Eb69 moves a half step down to the D9 establishing a new key. D9 is a dominant seventh chord, a fifth from G. The song has now modulated into the Key of G. This is an interesting modulation because G is the major third of Eb.

Measures 17 – 22: In measures seventeen through twenty the progression is I - vi7 - ii7 - V7 repeated twice. In measure twenty one the I chord Gma9 and G6 hold and then in measure twenty two chromatically move downwards to Gb+9 and Gb9 then F9 to F13. The F9 and F13 are dominant seventh chords that belong in the Key of Bb. Again the song has modulated into a new key. Once again this is an interesting modulation because Bb is the perfect fifth in the Key of Eb.

Measures 23 – 29: In the new Key of Bb the progression is again I - vi7 - ii7 - V7 repeated twice. In measure twenty-eight the progression changes as the I - vi7 chromatically moves downward with the Gb9, a bVI7 chord, to the F13 in measure twenty-nine. The B+9 releasing downward to the Bb9 and Bb13 gives a feeling of finality to the phrase and signals that the song is modulating again. Bb13 is the dominant seventh chord of the songs original Key of Eb. The song has now modulated back to the Key of Eb to play a couple of more verses before ending.

Notes

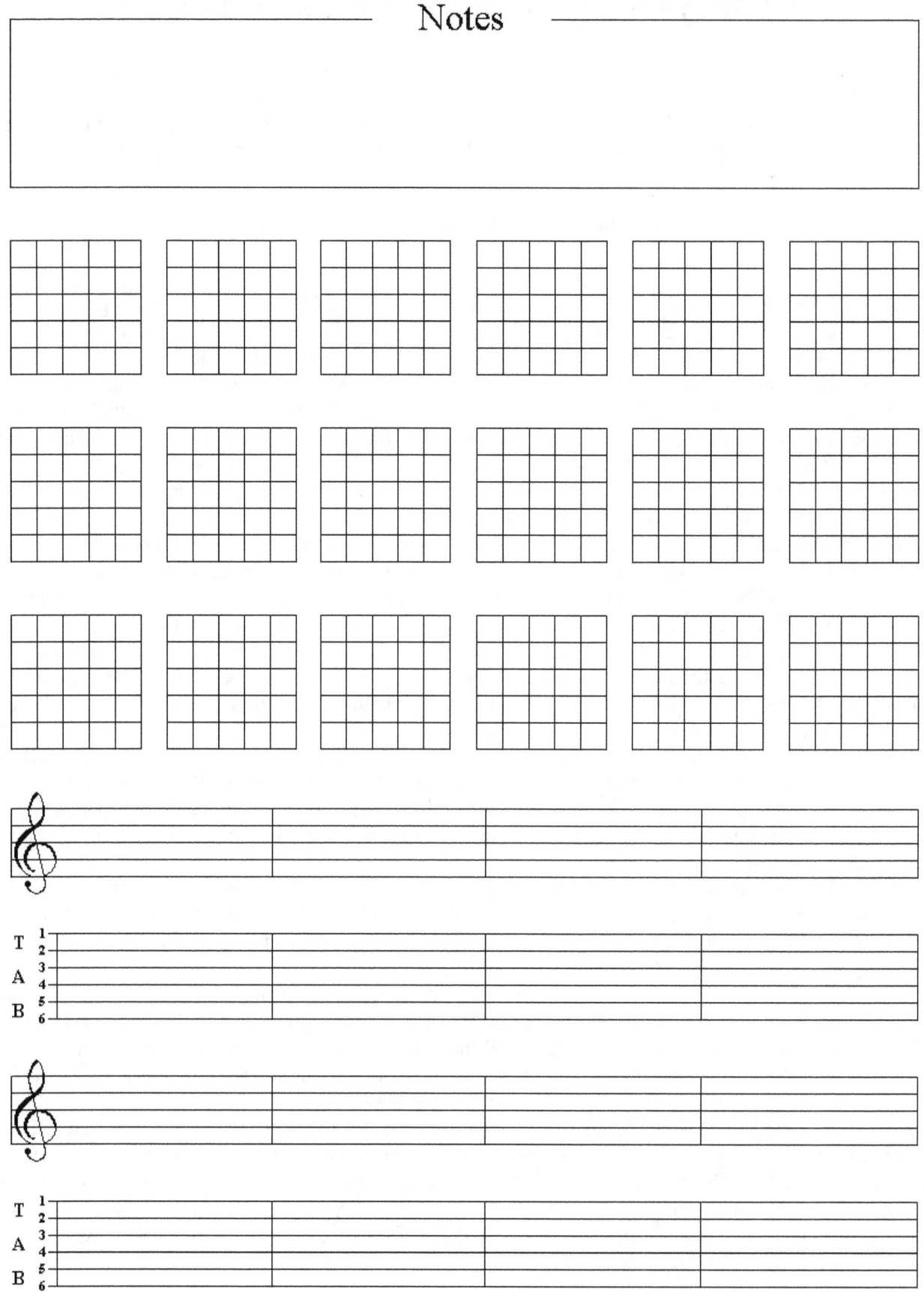

Chapter 17

Specialty Scales

Specialty Scales

Because the major scale has its modes and chords that are derived from it, specific scales must be used to play with altered chords that do not belong to that specific key. It is necessary to know which chords are to be played in a song. The lead player must know those chords so the correct scale or chord can be chosen to make the improvisation interesting. Lead sheets or scores are important since they let the musicians know what's being played when. Since there is a scale for almost every altered chord, which would require a volume of its own, only the five most commonly used specialty scales are shown in this chapter.

The **Diminished Scale** is symmetrical and is not related to any key. Thus to identify the scale, the interval steps of a whole, half, whole, half, whole, half, whole, half must be present. 1) The diminished scale inverts and will produce four diminished scales and four diminished chords from the 1 - b3 - b5 - bb7 degrees of the scale, all of which are interchangeable. They all are made up of the same notes; only the scales and the chords roots start on different scale degree notes. 2) There are in sound only three diminished scales and three diminished chords: C, Db and D. These three diminished scales and chords will each produce four diminished scales and chords, which encompass the twelve tones of the musical system. The three staves shown below reveal the different pitches present in each of the three different diminished scales and the three, two octave diminished scale patterns shown to the left are presented for visual clarity and ease of memorization. Notice only the position changes, the pattern remains the same.

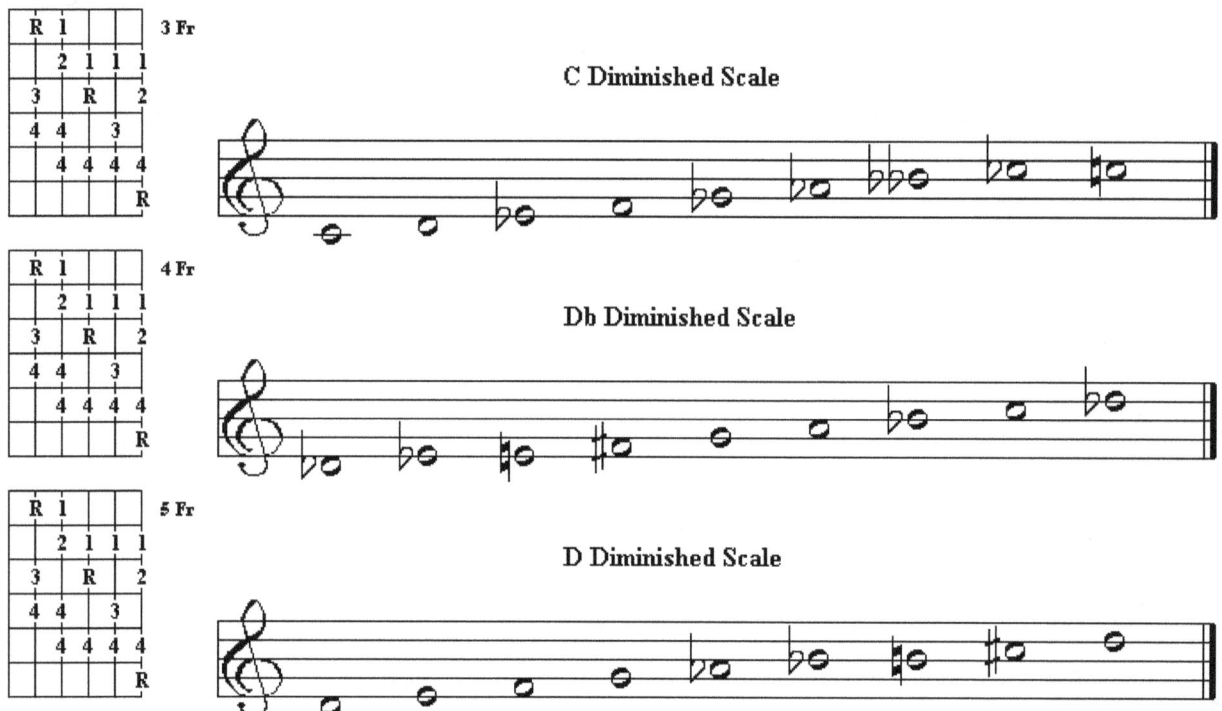

Because of the number of half steps, the diminished scale has nine notes. There are other diminished scale pattern possibilities and these should be explored by the student. The diminished scale is played with diminished chords and can also be used with the V7, dominant seven chord in jazz by starting the scale a half step up from the root of the dominant seventh chord, which adds the b9, #9, #11 and 13th color tones to the chord.

The symmetry of the **Diminished Chords** is equally as interesting as the diminished scales. It can be seen that each of the chord names could be placed on any one of the other chords since the notes are the same only arranged differently which would be an inversion. An example of one form is presented in these four chord diagrams:

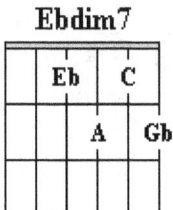
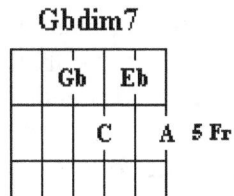
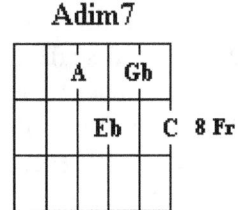
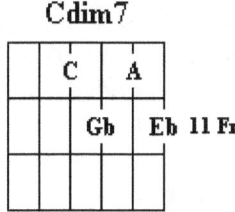

Here are three popular diminished chord forms that are used frequently:

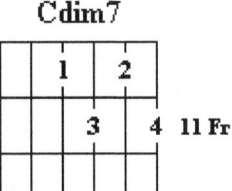
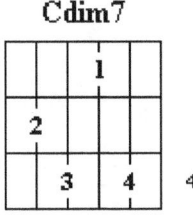
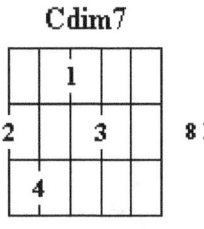

These three spreading forms can be played as arpeggios or as chords on the latter two:

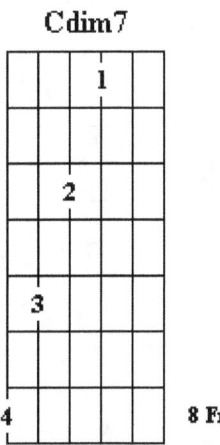
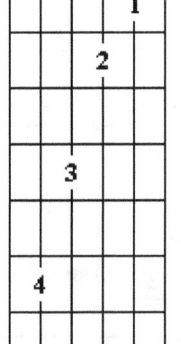
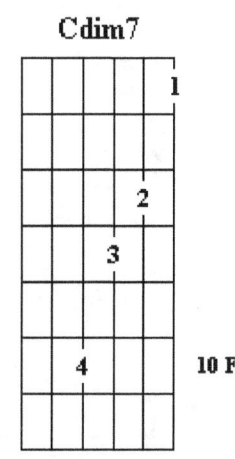

Next is a commonly used progression with an ascending walking bass from the Ima7 chord to the ii7 chord. The A#dim7 chord in this IM7 - ii7 - V7 movement offers a smooth transition.

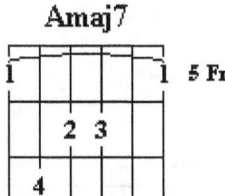
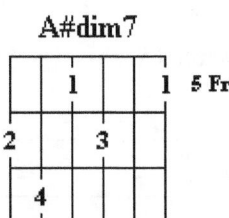
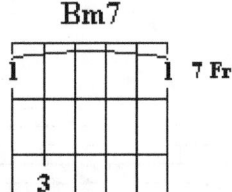
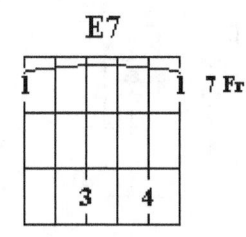

The diminished scales and chords provide interesting airy and floating qualities that want to be resolved. The resolution is the creativeness the musician brings to the performance. The diminished seven chords also share their forms with some of the inverted ninth chords.

The **Augmented Scale** is also symmetrical and is not related to any key. Thus to identify the scale, the interval steps of one and a half, half, one and a half, half, one and a half, half must be present. The augmented scale will produce three symmetrical augmented scales and chords from the 1 - 3 - #5 degrees of the scale, all of which are interchangeable. Although the notes are in different arrangements, they all are made up of the same notes; only the scales and the chords roots start on different scale degree notes. The augmented scale will also produce two different augmented chords each of which will be present in one of the other augmented scales. There are in sound only four augmented scales and four augmented chords: C, C#, D and D#. These four augmented scales and chords will each produce three diminished scales and chords that encompass the twelve tones of the musical system. The four staves shown below reveal the different pitches present in each of the four different augmented scales and the four, two octave augmented scale patterns shown in the fret board diagrams to the left of the staves are presented for their visual clarity for ease of memorization. Although the scale can be played as written on the staff it usually begins a half step below the root as shown in the diagram. Notice, only the scale position changes, the pattern remains the same.

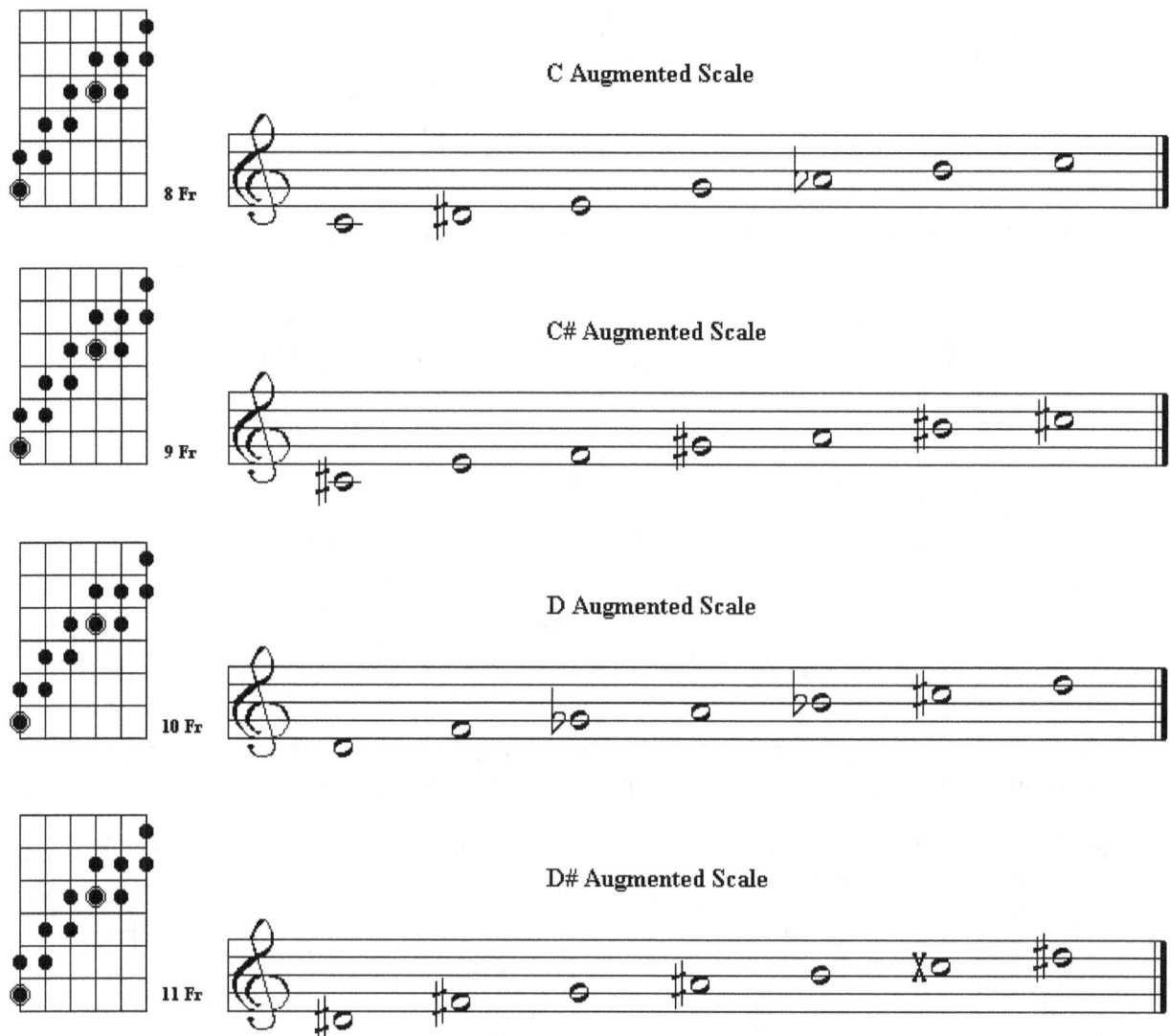

Because the augmented scale has the distance of the augmented second intervals, there are only seven notes in the scale rather than the usual eight.

The symmetry of the **Augmented Chords** are also interesting and it can be seen that each of the chord names could be placed on any one of the chords which would then be considered an inversion. An example of one form is presented in these three chord diagrams:

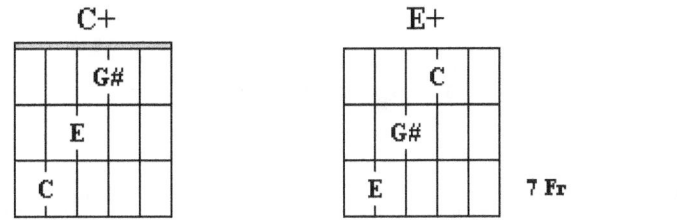

Here are three popular augmented chord forms:

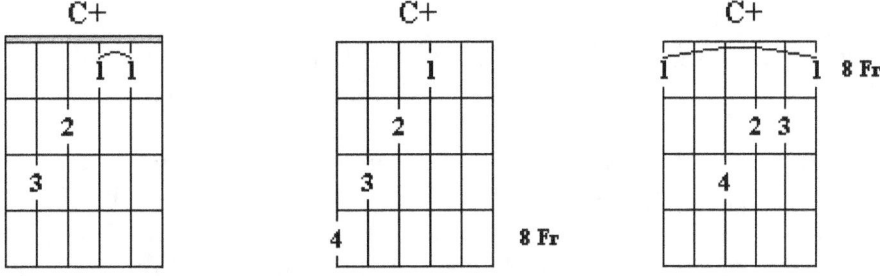

An interesting chord progression using an augmented chord is shown in measures 12, 20, 22 and 24 in the Emi Shuffle song on page 17-6. Three of the B7#5 chords in measures 12, 22 and 24 resolve to the root chord Em7. In measure 20 the B7#5 resolves to the B7, V7 chord before moving to the Am9, iv9 chord in measure 21 giving a suspended feeling allowing the B7#5 chord to resolve twice in measures 22, 23 and 24, before leading to the finality of the im7, Em7 chord.

The **Whole Tone Scale** has no relationship to any key. The name of the scale is derived from the interval of a whole-step between each note. Because of the distance of the whole-step intervals, the whole tone scale has seven notes. The whole tone scale produces six whole tone scales in which all have the same notes with each scales starting pitch setting it apart from the other scales.

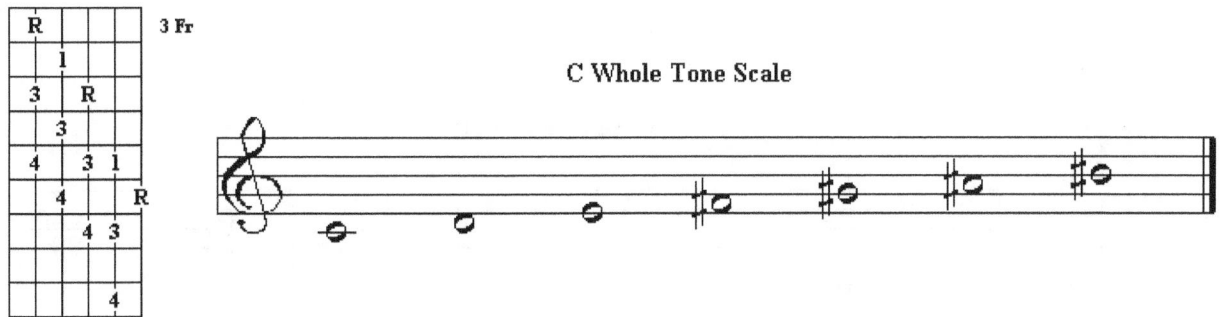

By extracting the 1 - 3 - #5 degrees from the whole tone scale the C+ chord is formed. By extracting the 1 - 3 - #5 - #6 degrees the C+7 chord is formed. The correct spelling for the seventh tone of the augmented seven chord is flatted since the seventh is dominant. For example, the C+7 chord is spelled C - E - G# - Bb.

17-4

The **Lydian Augmented Scale** is derived from the Lydian mode of the major scale with the 5th degree raised.

It is a useful scale for the dominant seventh chord by playing the altered b5 and #11 tones. For example: in the Key of G, play the Lydian augmented scale which would begin with the note C from the fourth degree of the G major scale with the V7, D7b5 chord. From the 1 - 3 - #5 - 7 degrees of the scale the seventh, ninth, flat five or augmented eleventh and thirteenth notes of the D7b5 chord are played.

The Lydian augmented scale is also useful by starting on a dominant seventh chords third degree for playing the b5 or #11, #5, 7, b9 and #9 notes of that chord. Once again in the Key of G, so the scale pitch remains the same, let's use the IIb7, Ab7 chord that is a commonly used V7 chord substitute. By starting on the third degree of the Ab7 chord, C, the C Lydian augmented scale will play the #11, #5, 7, b9 and #9 notes of that chord from the scale tones.

A good example of a progression for the Lydian augmented scale to be used with is the V7b5 - Imaj7 - IIb7 - Imaj9 turnaround.

The **Harmonic Minor Scale** is an exotic sounding scale and is derived from the Natural minor scale, which is also known as the Aeolian mode. The Harmonic minor scale begins on the sixth degree of the major scale like the Aeolian mode but has its seventh degree raised a half-step which makes things interesting when played with minor chords by adding a flatted fifth to the ii7 chord, a major third to the iii7 chord and a major seventh to the vi7 chord. In the Key of Eb for example, these chords would now be written as: Fm7b5, G7 and CmMa7. With the iii7 chord being altered to a III7 chord, the Harmonic minor scale also works well with a III7+5 chord. Staying with the same example, the chord would be written as: G7+5.

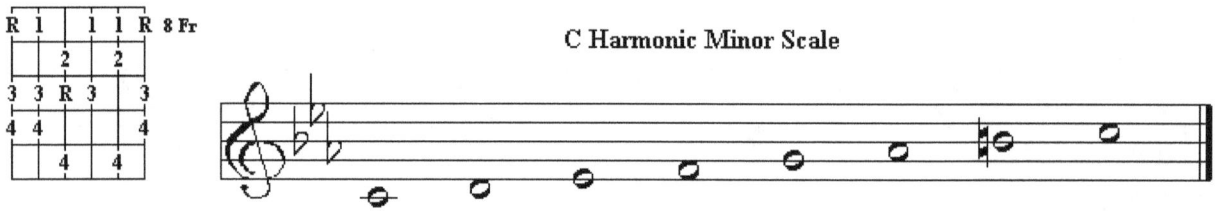

The Harmonic minor scale is an important scale to the classical musician as it was in use during the Baroque period. In jazz the Harmonic minor scale raises the opportunity to alter more chords thus creating more interesting improvisational possibilities.

E Minor 7 Blues Shuffle

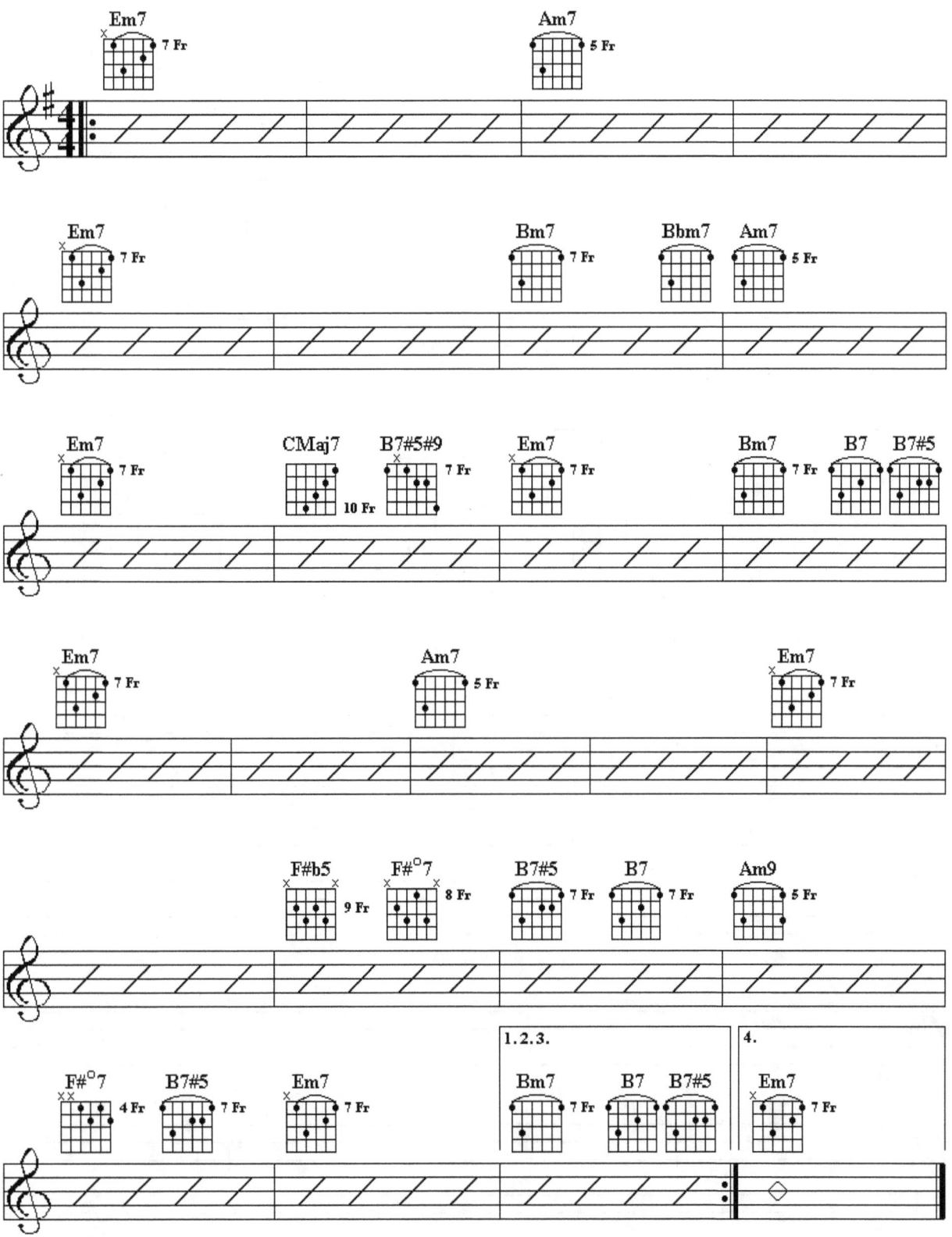

Notes

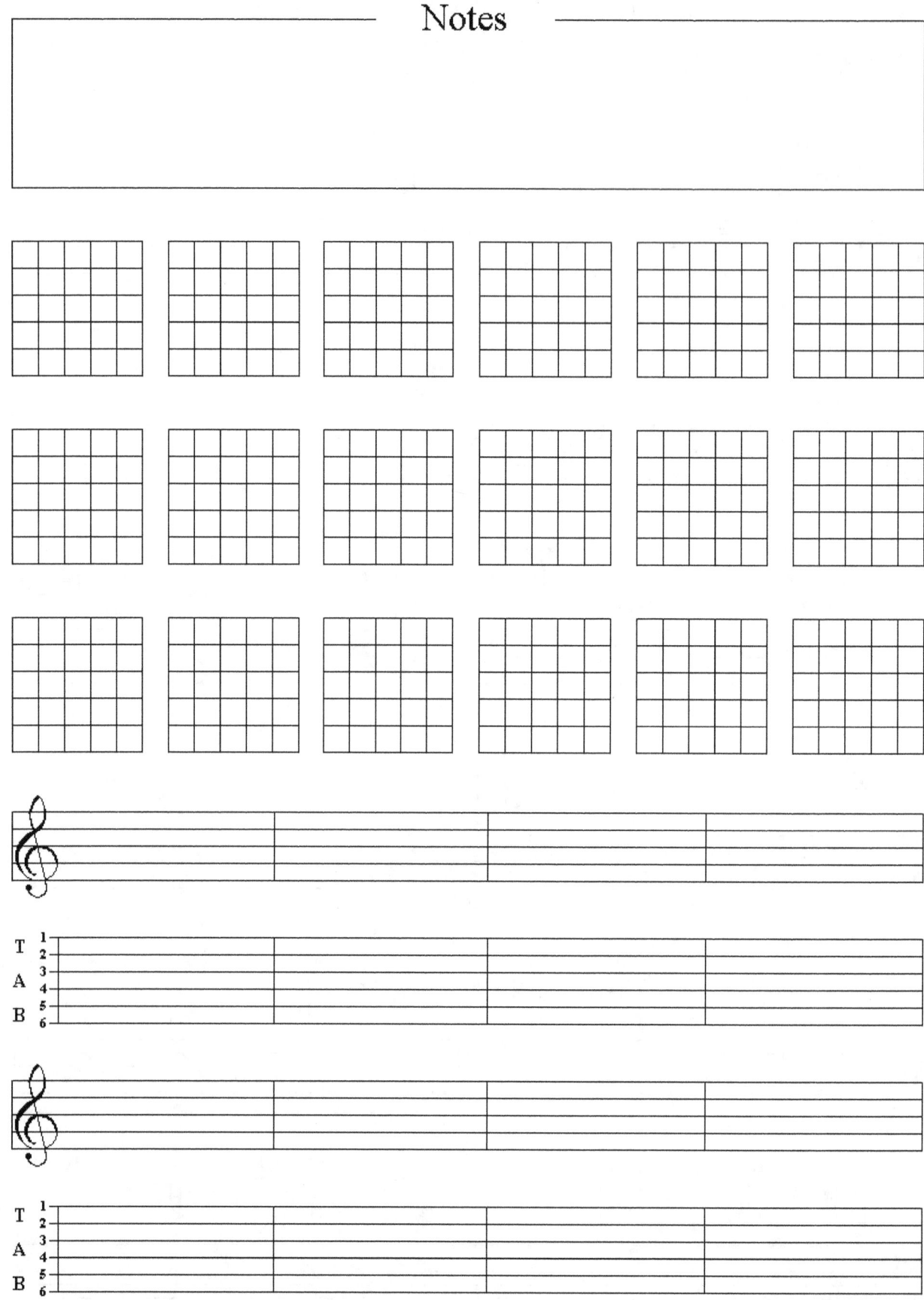

Chapter 18 Linear Chord Scales

The Linear Chord Scale

The linear chord scale is another interesting aspect of the chordal possibilities of the guitar. In this section we are taking the same major chord scale progressions: Major - minor - minor - Major - Major - minor - minor - Major, as played in the lateral movement sections and applying them to a linear movement up and down the neck of the guitar for more creative possibilities.

From the lateral movement perspective, everything is in a position or a block with a lateral back and forth movement across the neck and moving up and down the neck by leaving one position for another. With linear chord scales, a smooth connection between positions can be accomplished by moving linearly up or down the chord scale to each position. Since the chords of the linear chord scale are found in the lateral position chord scales, as we intersect each position, with practice we can find our place in that position and play within the lateral mode and chord scale found there.

Connecting different modes together by scale runs and/or chord arpeggios is one of the secrets to great melodies, solos and exciting improvisation.

The linear chord scales presented in this chapter all start from the open position and end one octave higher and once again follow the circle of fifths around the five basic chords for ease of memorization. Of course these linear chord scales can start on any fret in all keys. The more tools we have at our finger tips directly equates to the more possibilities our creative capabilities will have a chance to be expressed.

PRACTICE

Practice the linear chord scales as arpeggios, one note after another in staccato, removing each finger as the next finger is being played in each chord, ascending and descending the linear chord scale from octave to octave.

The picking hand plays only four strings in a straight forward P - I - M - A pattern for each chord in the chord scale.

With a metronome, drum machine or computer program playing at a slow steady beat, practice moving from one chord to the next in a smooth even movement without any hesitation between the chord changes.

Remember we are practicing the chords that will be used in our everyday playing. Not only are we learning the chord patterns we'll be playing but we are also strengthening our fingers and developing finger technique all at the same time.

When you are comfortable playing the linear chord scales in this section, start intersecting each of the linear chord scales chords with the corresponding mode and chord scale in each of the seven positions in their respective keys. At first the going will be slow but as you become more familiar with the patterns it becomes apparent the possibilities are endless. Creativity knows no boundaries

C Linear Chord Scale

Key Of C

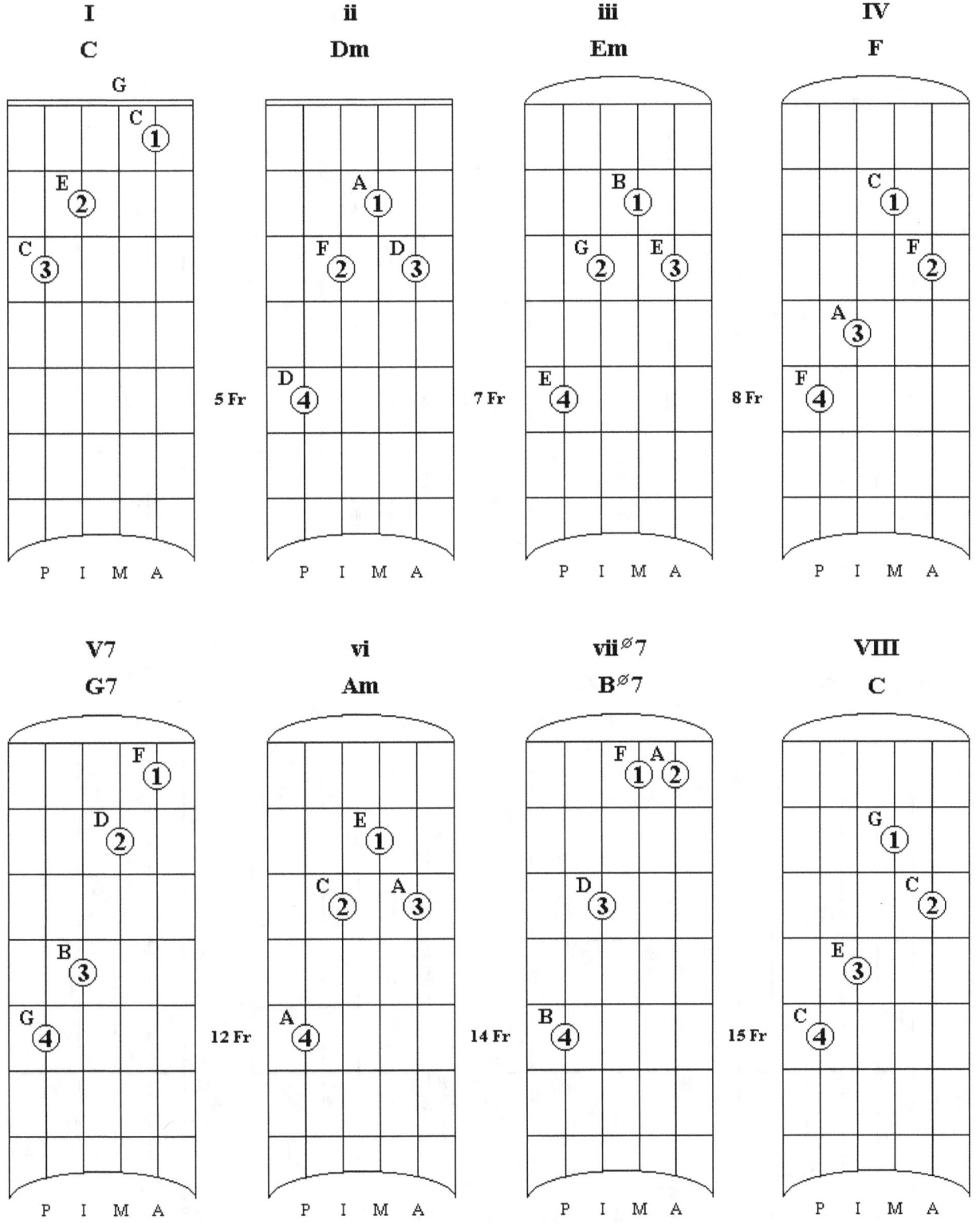

18-2

G Linear Chord Scale

Key Of G

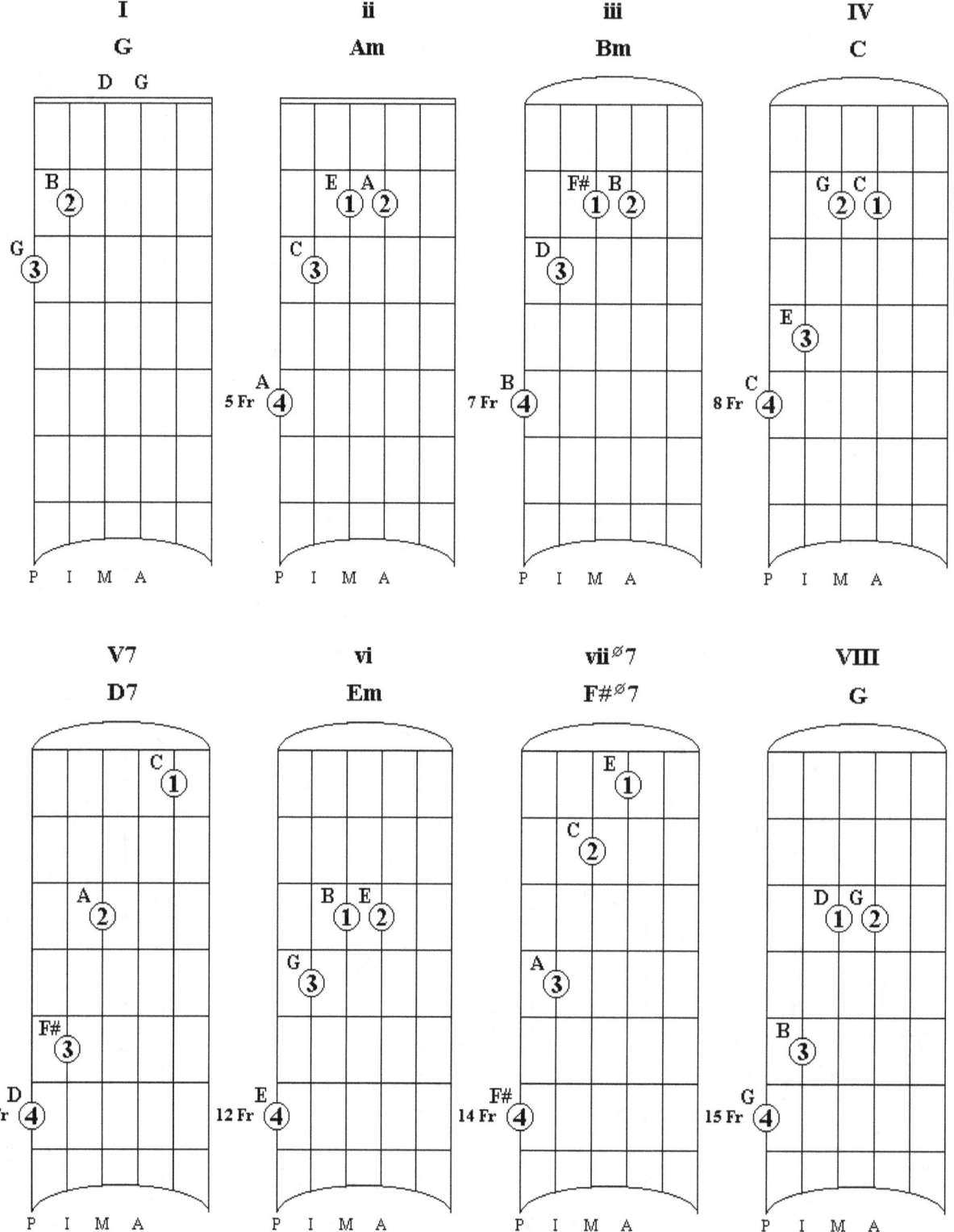

D Linear Chord Scale

Key Of D

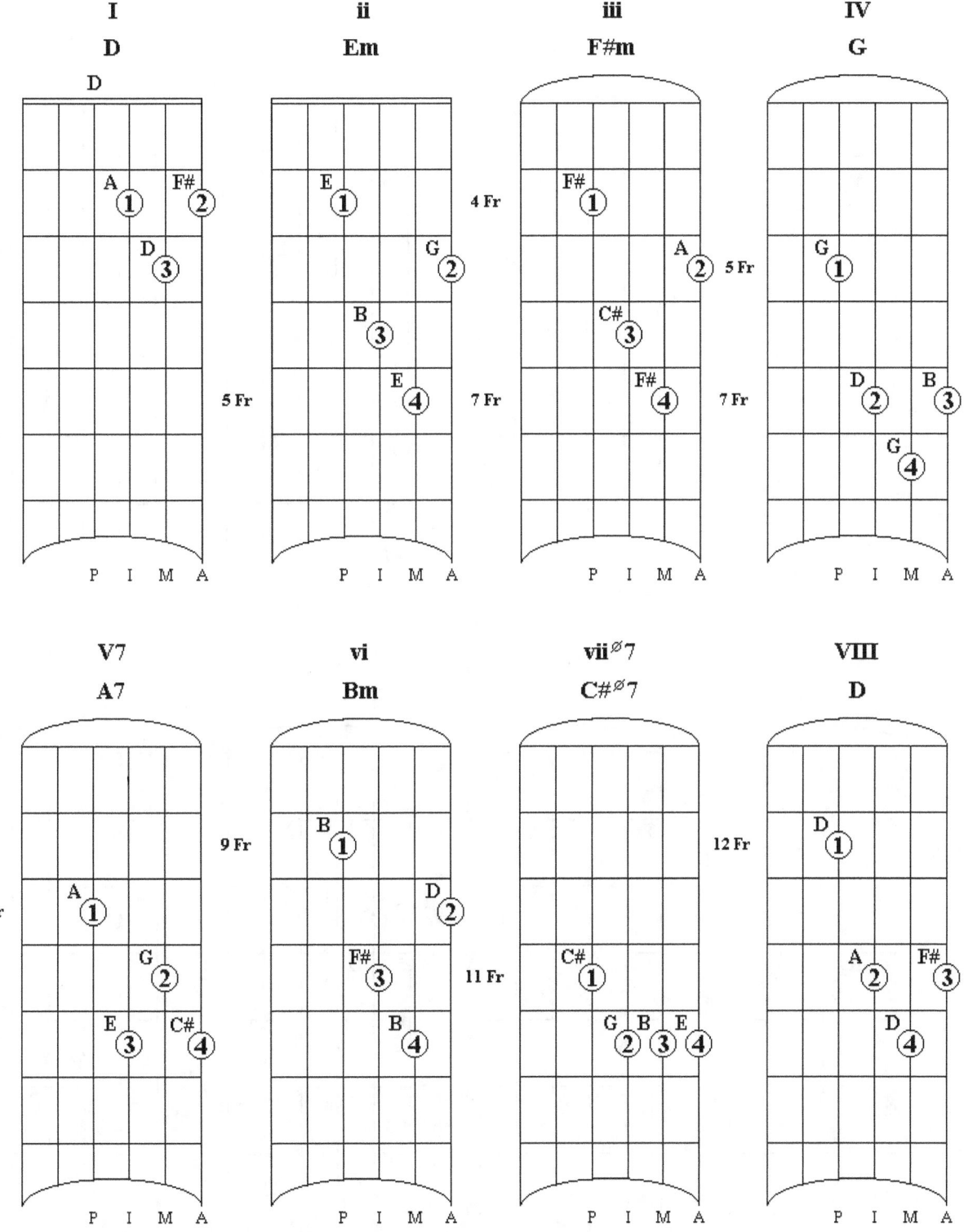

A Linear Chord Scale

Key Of A

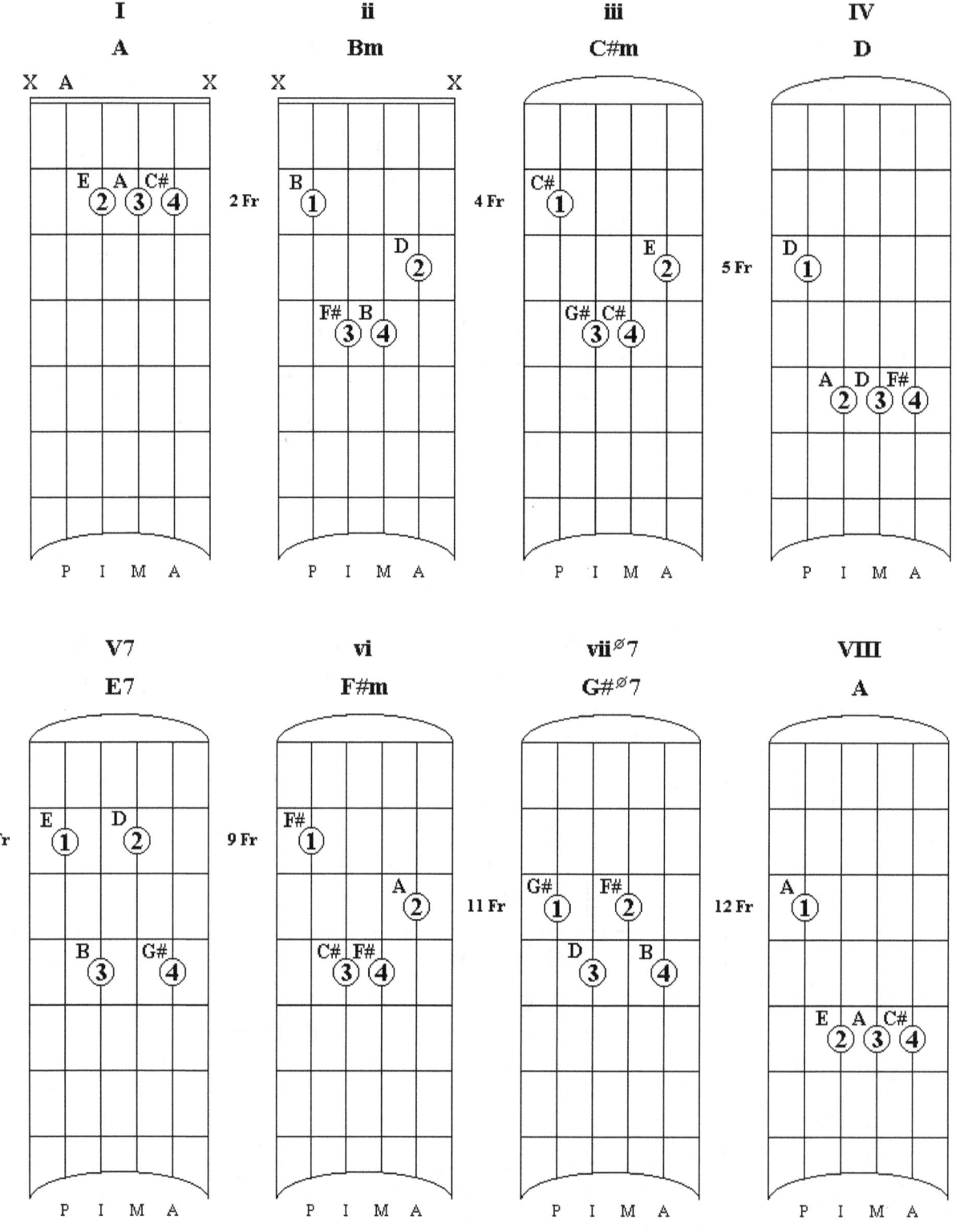

E Linear Chord Scale

Key Of E

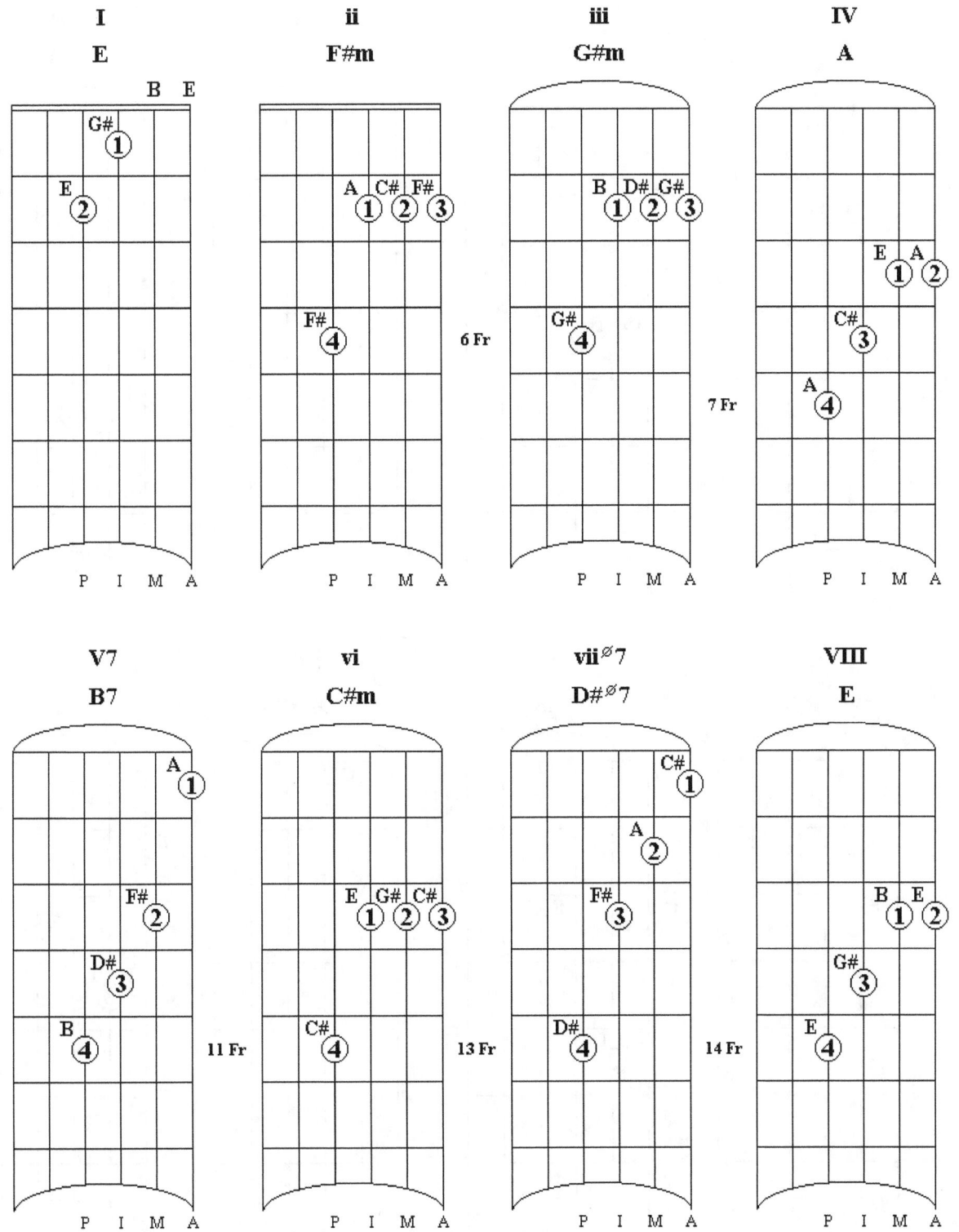

18-6

E Linear Chord Scale

Alternative Lower Octave - Key Of E

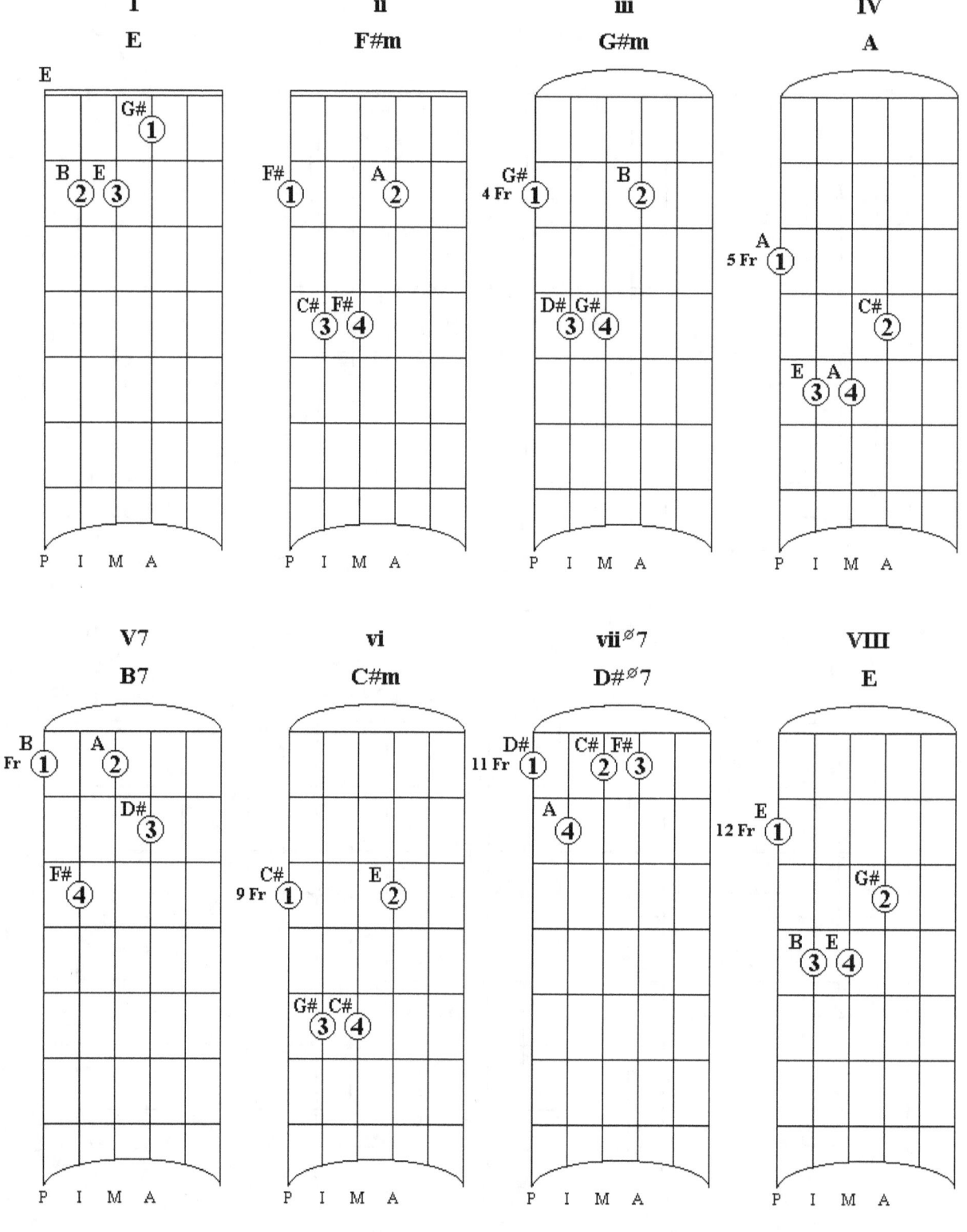

Section Six

Chords For Everyone

Chapter

19

The Chord Guide

The Chord Guide

The chords in this chapter are categorized according to the root chord form they are derived from. The root note is shaded in black. In each of the five basic chord forms of C-G-D-A-E there are twenty seven to twenty eight chord forms. These chord forms are variations of the basic chord form. This takes the identification of chords to the simplest level. Each of the chord forms can be played in all twelve keys. Learn the chord form in the open position then look it up on the opposing page in the moveable position and play it up and down the neck of the guitar in all twelve keys.

The chords are based on the root note without inversions, substitutions or polychords as these infinite possibilities are left for the creative enjoyment of the player to indulge in. The third degree of the chord will always be present to establish whether the chord is major or minor. The fifth degree is present unless it is omitted as necessary to make room for the seventh and the color tones; the ninth, eleventh and thirteenth degrees. The fifth degree will be present if it is giving the chord its name such as b5, #5 or (+) augmented. Likewise, the degree tones that give each chord its unique name are also present. The seventh is present with the color tones unless the chord is an add9, add11 or add13, which is telling us the seventh, is omitted. The chords progress in order as they are developed from the root up to the thirteenth of the major scale they are derived from.

The practical usage of this section is for the selection of chord voicings with finger arrangements that best fit the song. The timbre or sound of a chord within a phrase is important to the outcome of the arrangement. Since there are five basic chord forms there will be five choices of each chord name to choose from. For example: The chord is G9. There will be five (9) chords to choose from, because there are five different forms of that chord; the C form, G form, D form, A form and E form. The C form works off of the fifth string, the G form works off the sixth string, the D form works off of the fourth string, the A form works off of the fifth string and the E form works off of the sixth string. Try each form until the one that feels right, sounds right and flows smoothly within the arrangement is found. One of the forms will work best. Remember these chords are all in their root position so by inverting the chords the possibilities become even greater. Experimentation and listening to other guitarist's arrangements is the key here.

An arrangement of a song is how the chord voicings in the song are played. Because there are so many possibilities each arranger can have a unique arrangement of a song. This is why there are so many arrangements of the same song recorded. Each arranger likes the song and feels different about how it should sound. It is not necessarily true that one is better than the other, they are just different. There will be audience members that like one arrangement while others like another. Usually the original arrangement will be the most popular but there will always be many fans of other arrangements of the same song.

The Standard Jazz Chord Voicings on Page 19-12 is a presentation of standard jazz chords found in standard jazz songs. Using these chord voicings will automatically give you the sound of most other jazz guitarists. There are also standard jazz chord voicings in the other chord presentations that have not been presented on Page 19-12 for the sake of repetition. There are chord grids left blank so the student can add to the collection with any other chord voicings they find.

Variations Of The C Form
Open Position

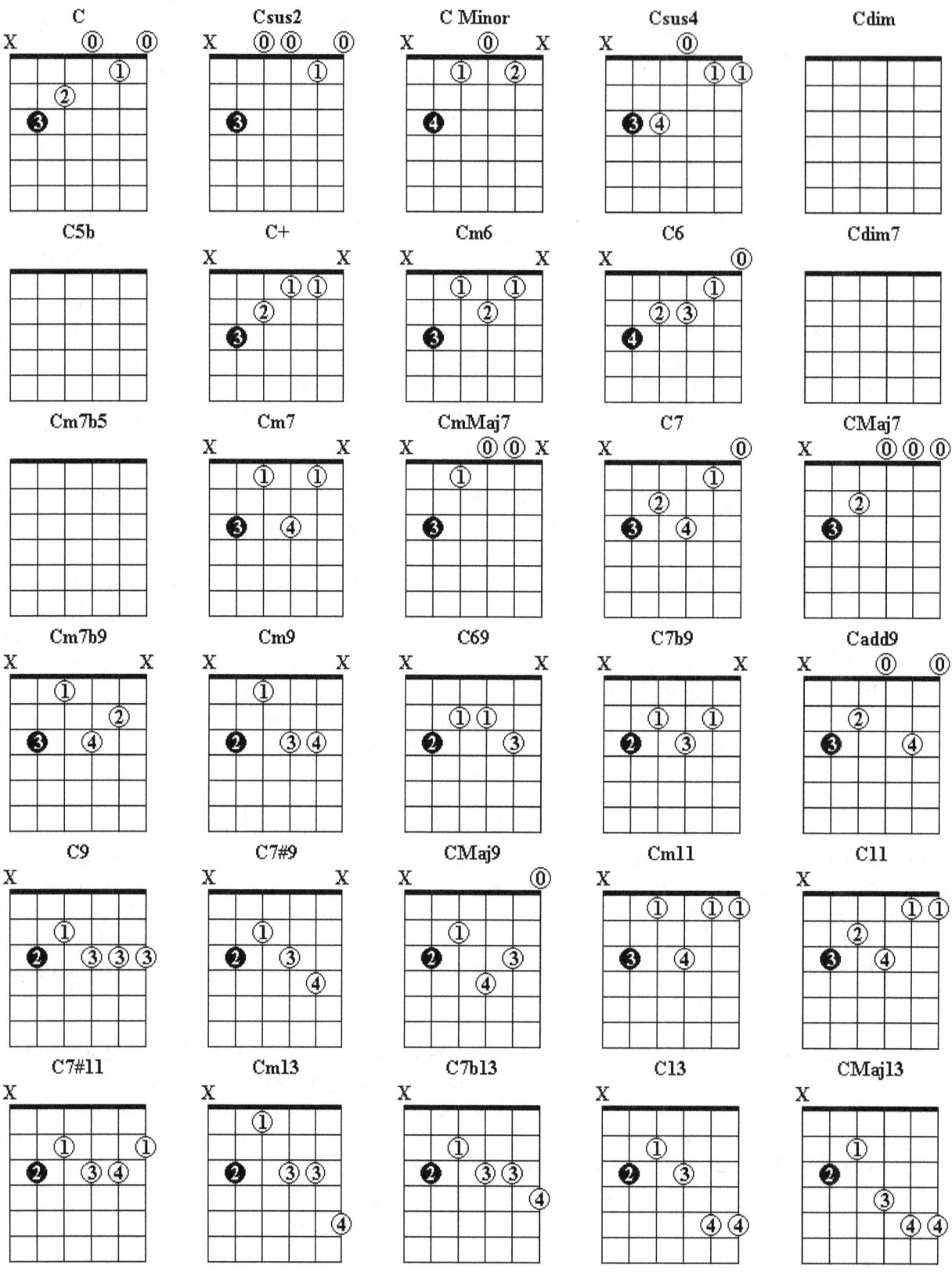

19-2

Variations Of The C Form
Moveable Position

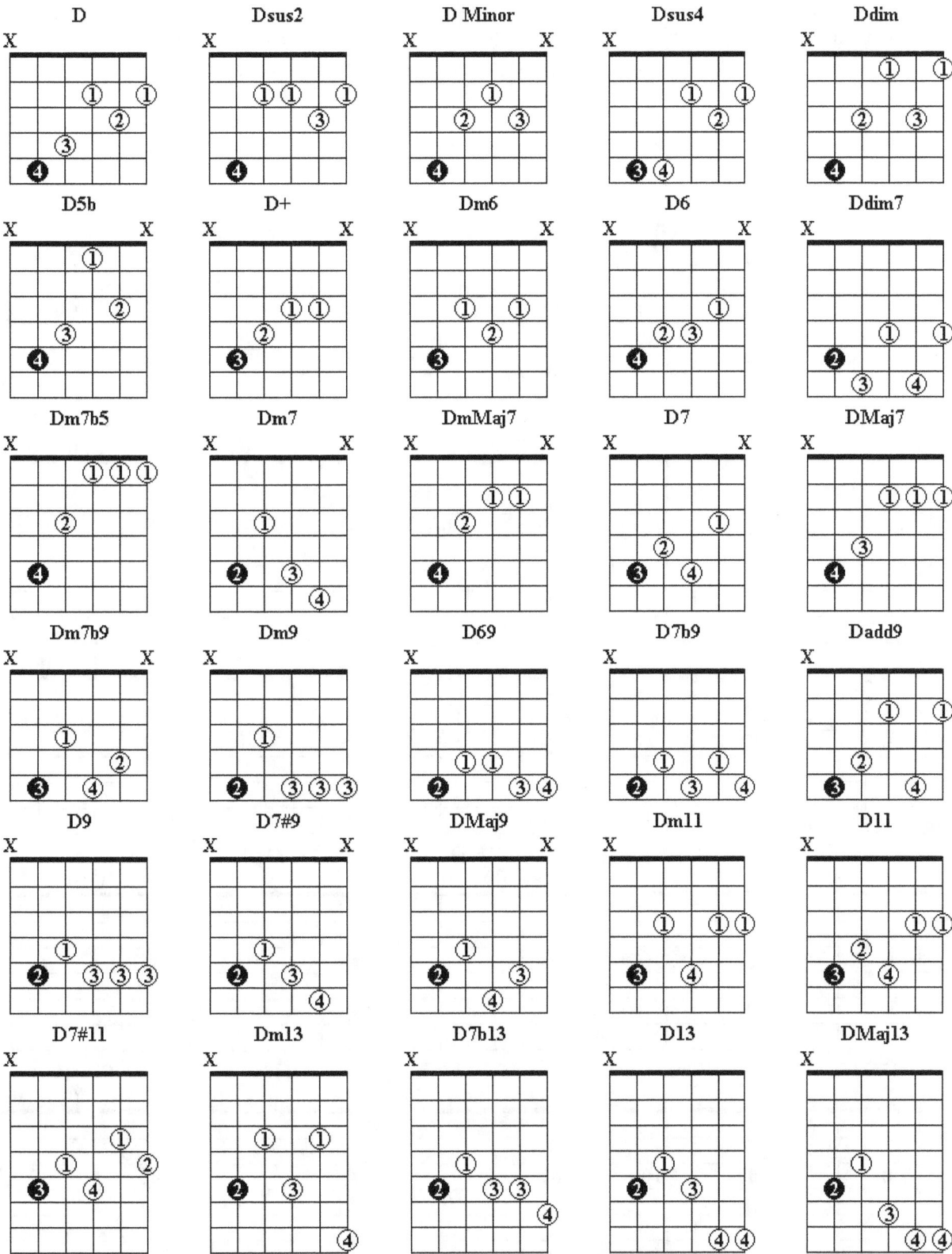

19-3

Variations Of The G Form
Open Position

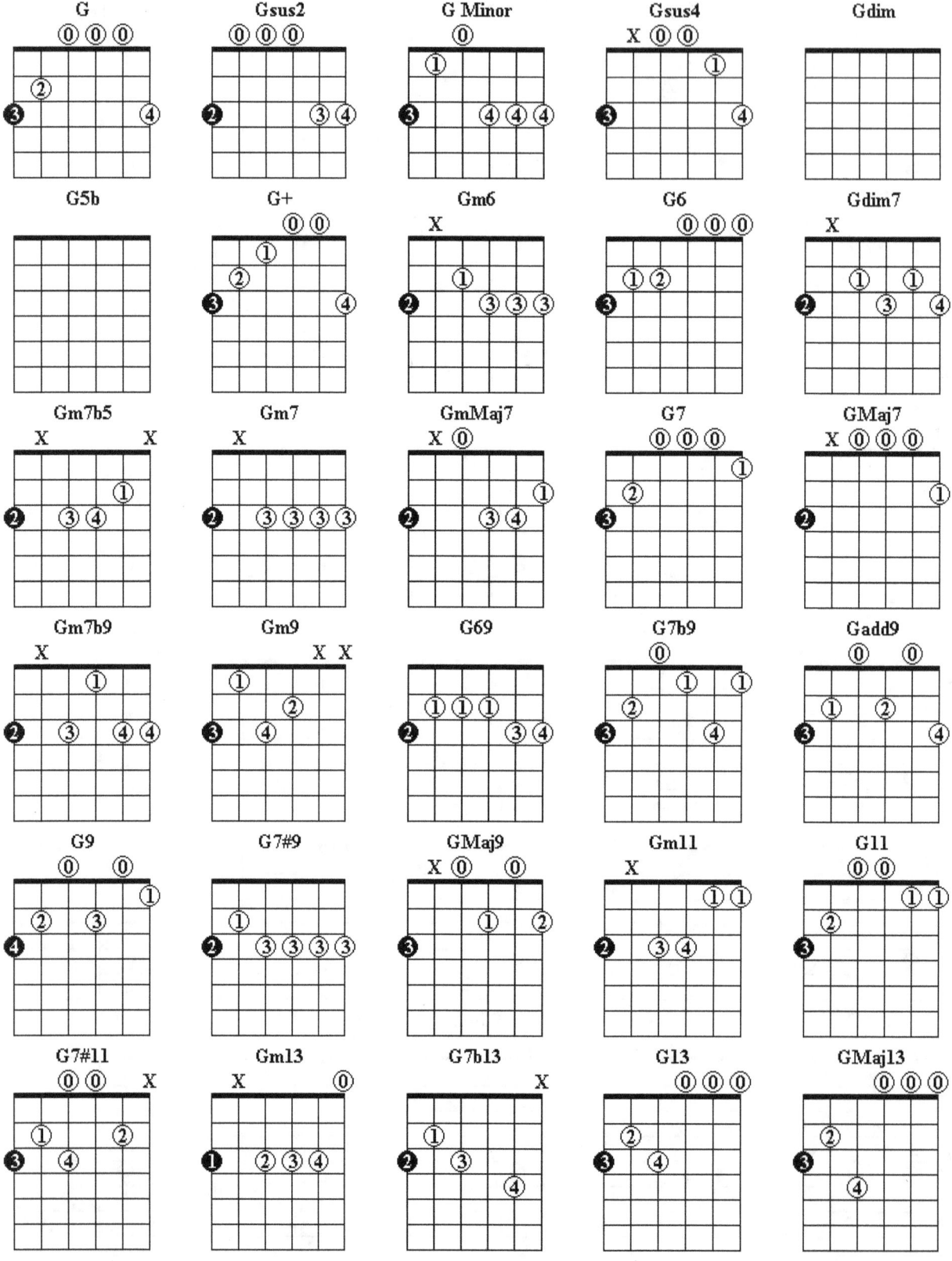

19-4

Variations Of The G Form
Moveable Position

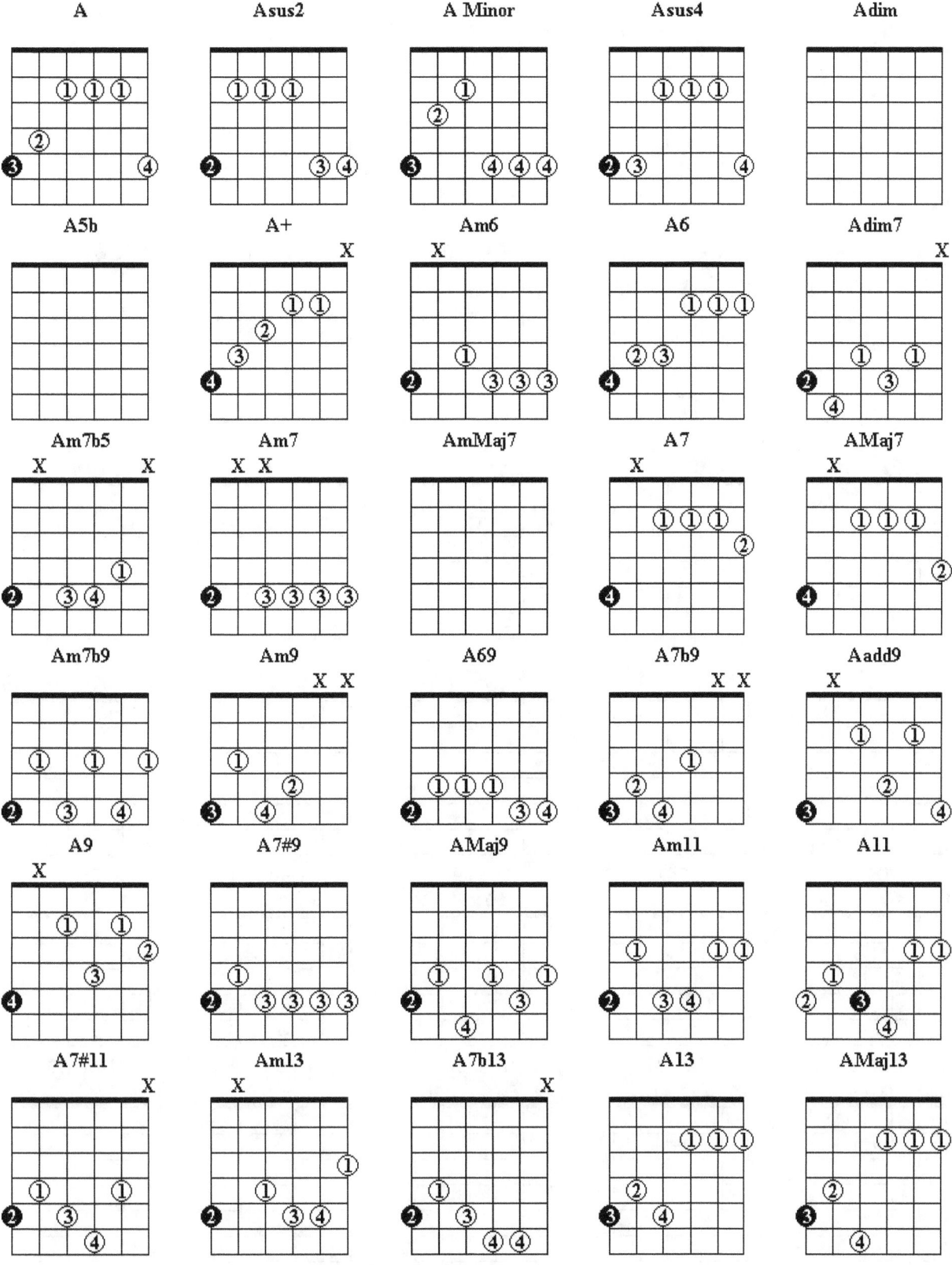

Variations Of The D Form
Open Position

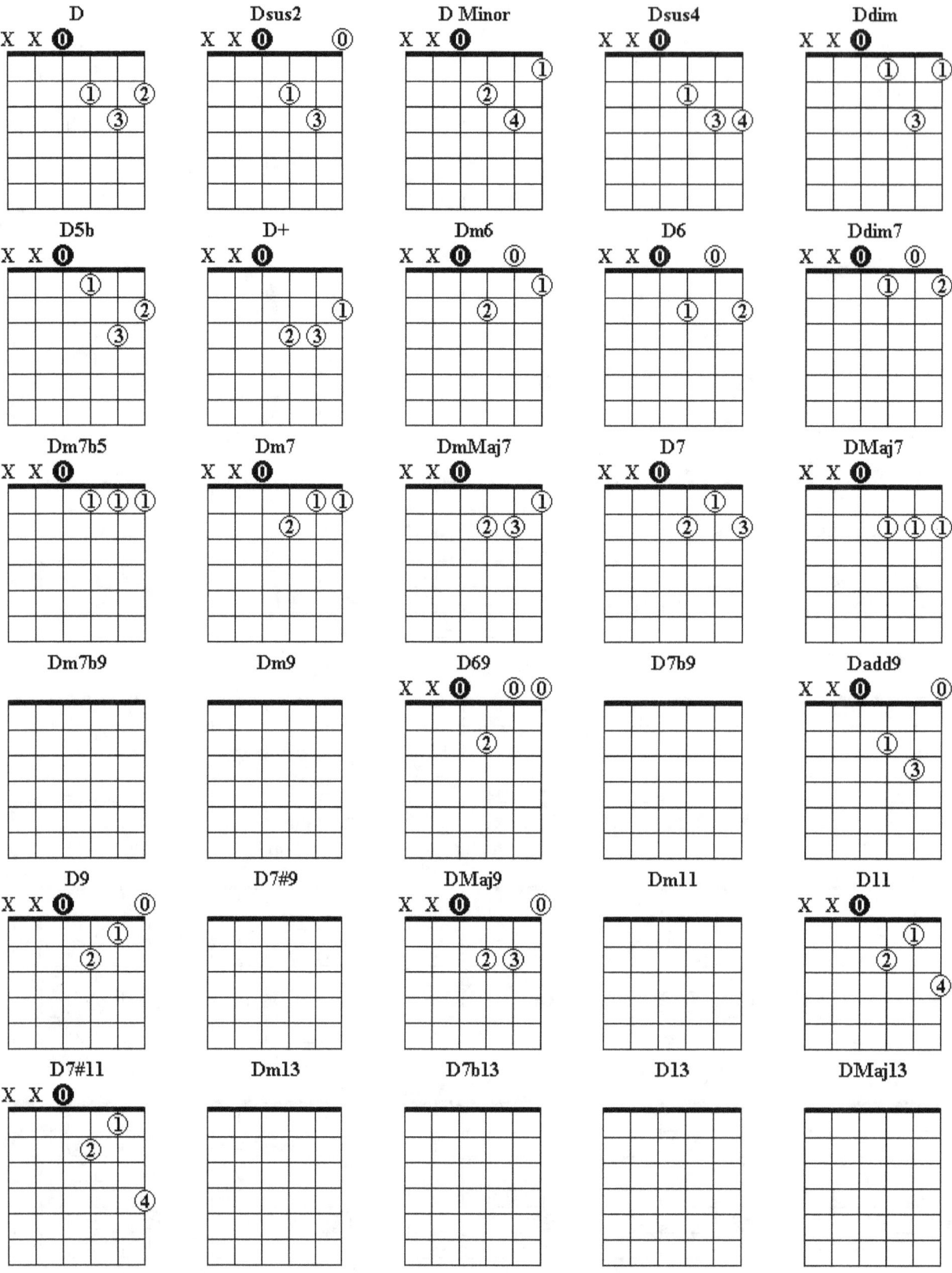

Variations Of The D Form
Moveable Position

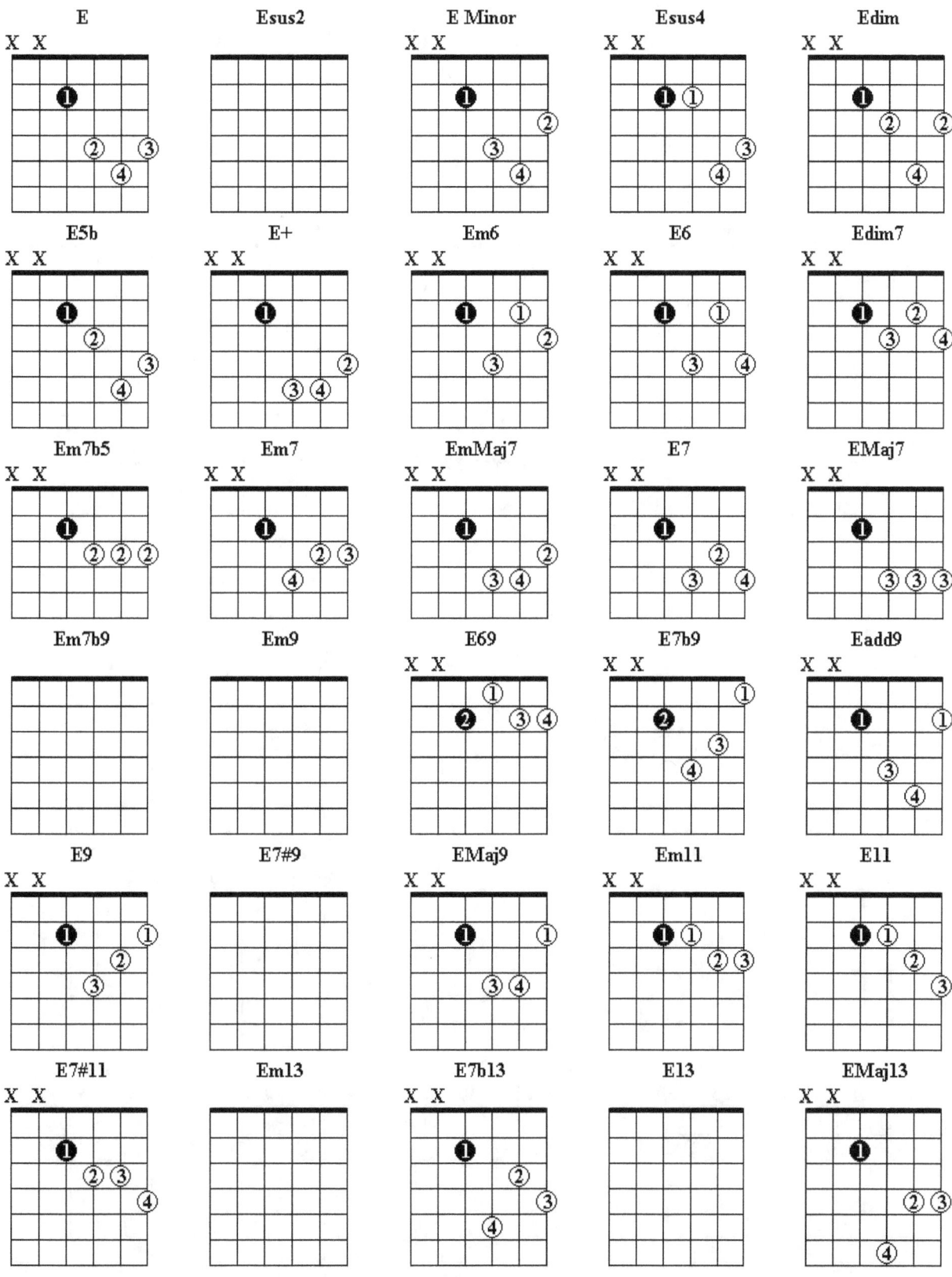

Variations Of The A Form
Open Position

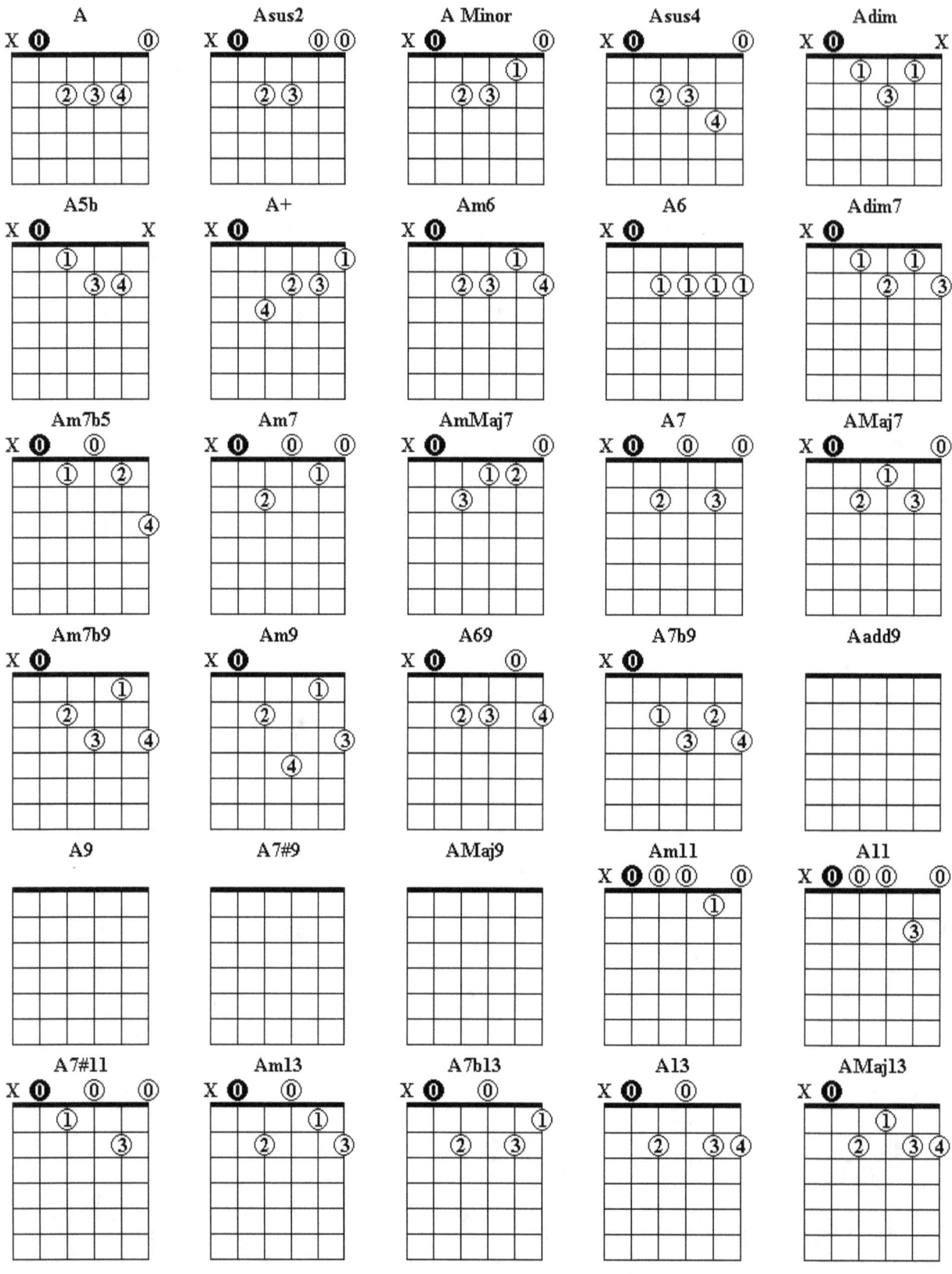

19-8

Variations Of The A Form
Moveable Position

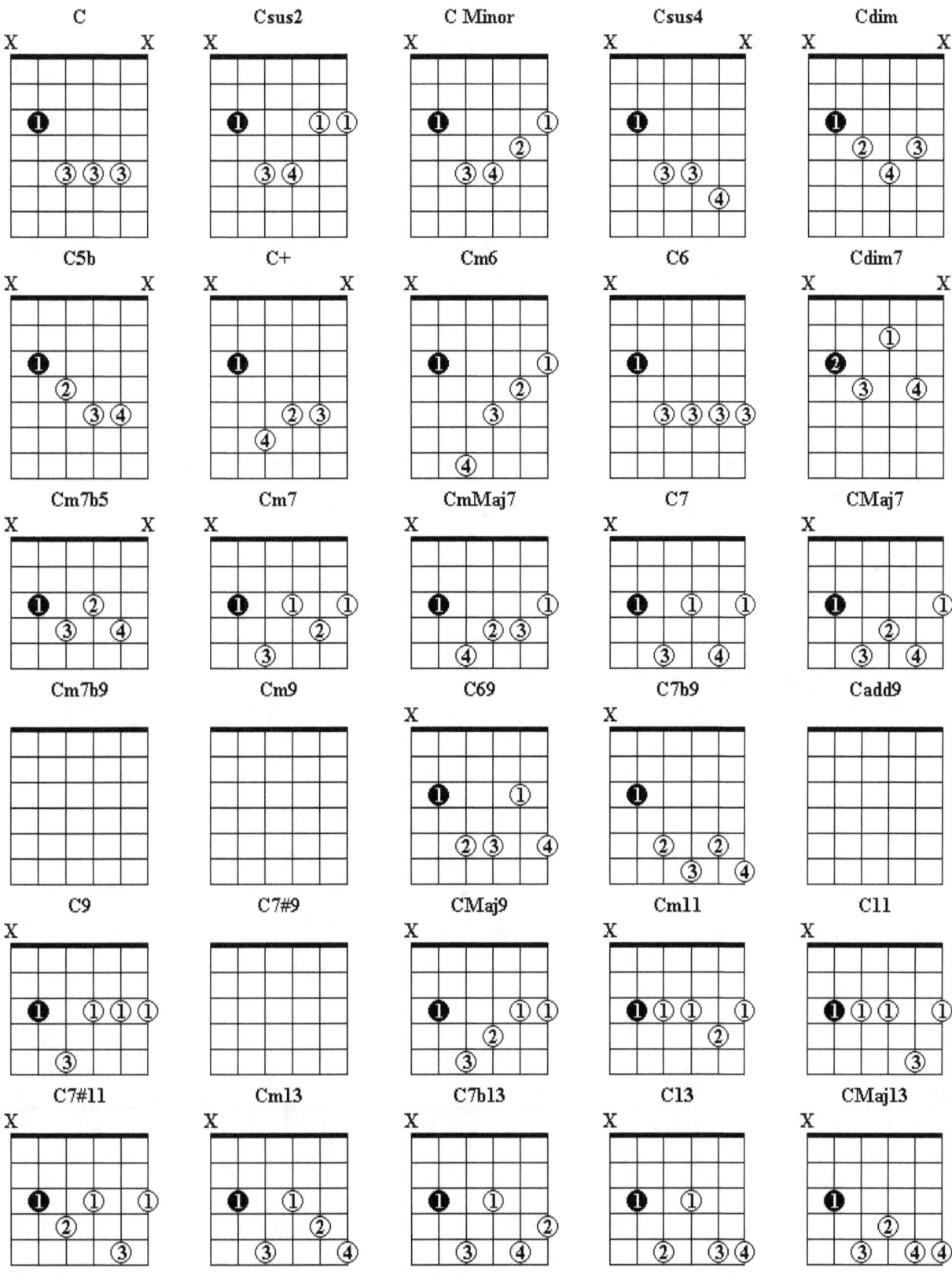

Variations Of The E Form

Open Position

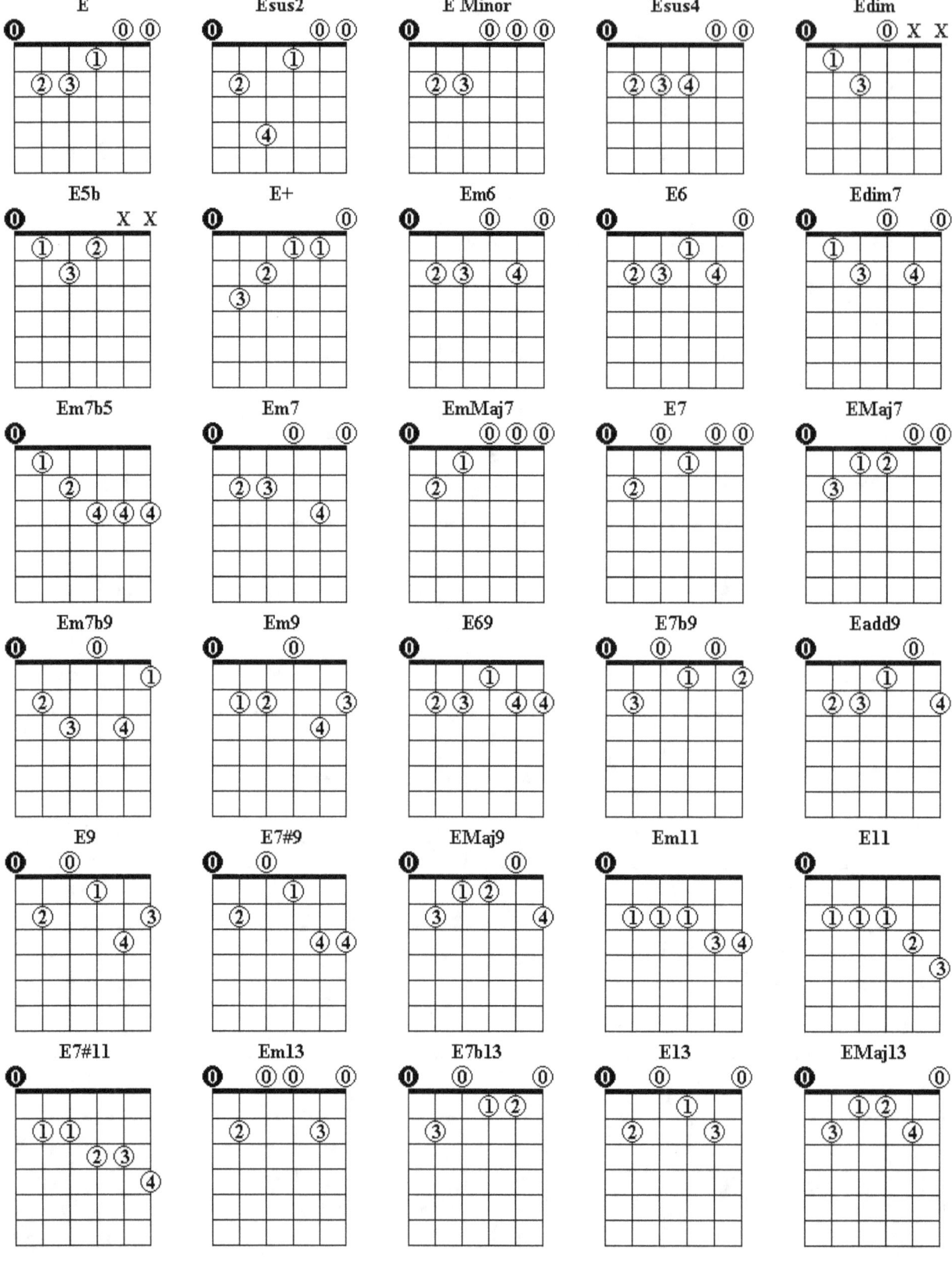

Variations Of The E Form
Moveable Position

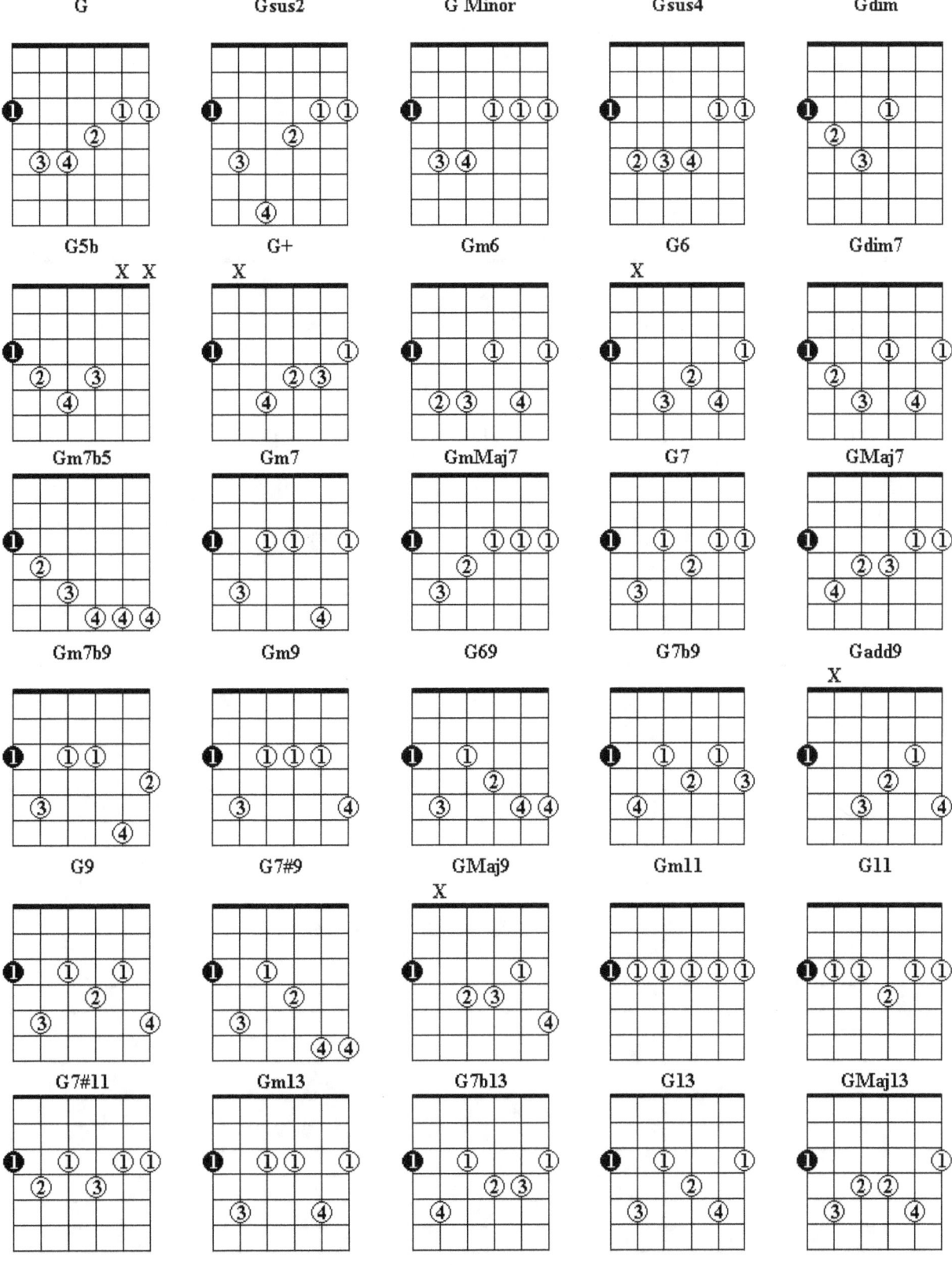

Standard Jazz Chords
Moveable Position

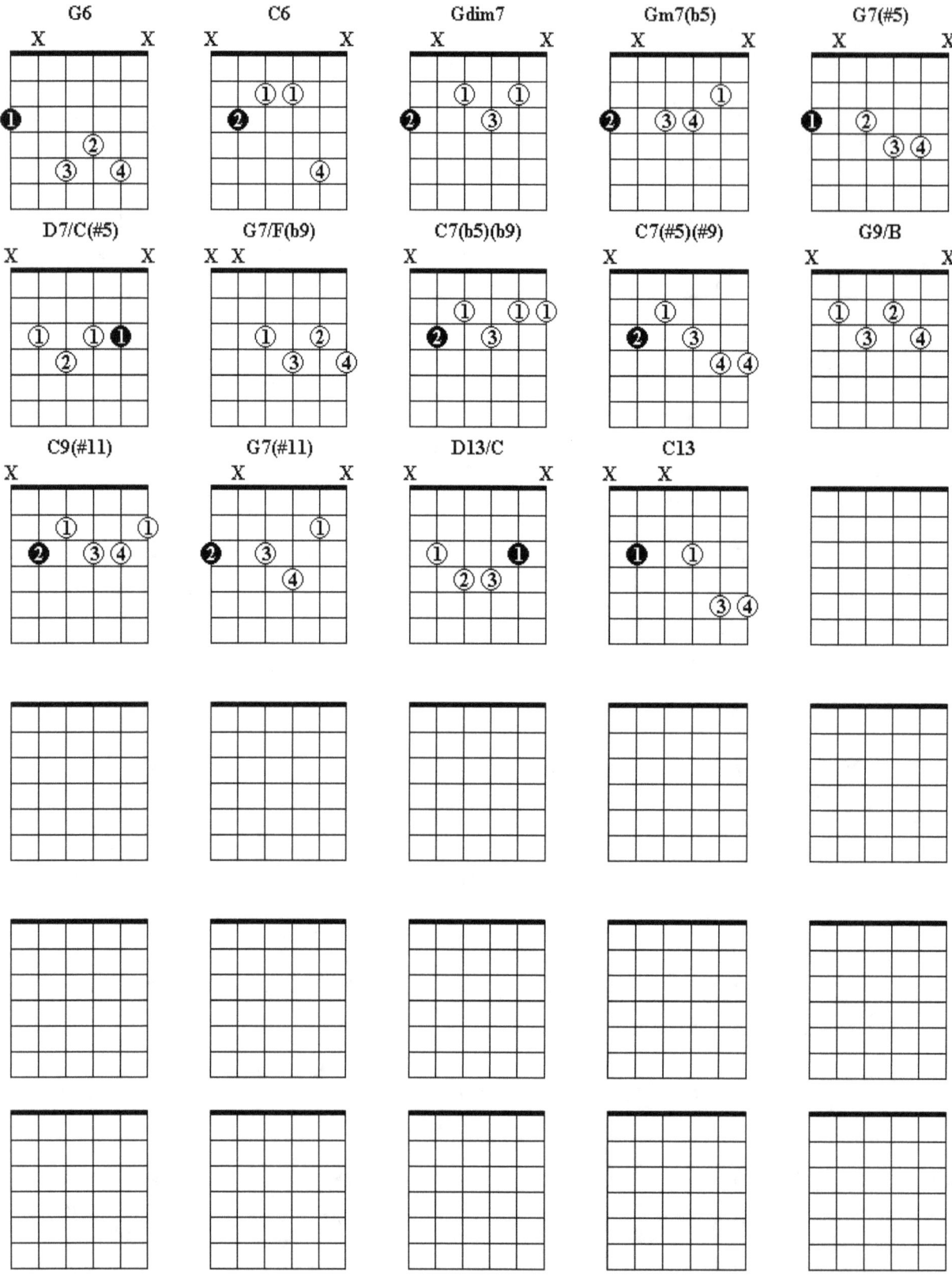

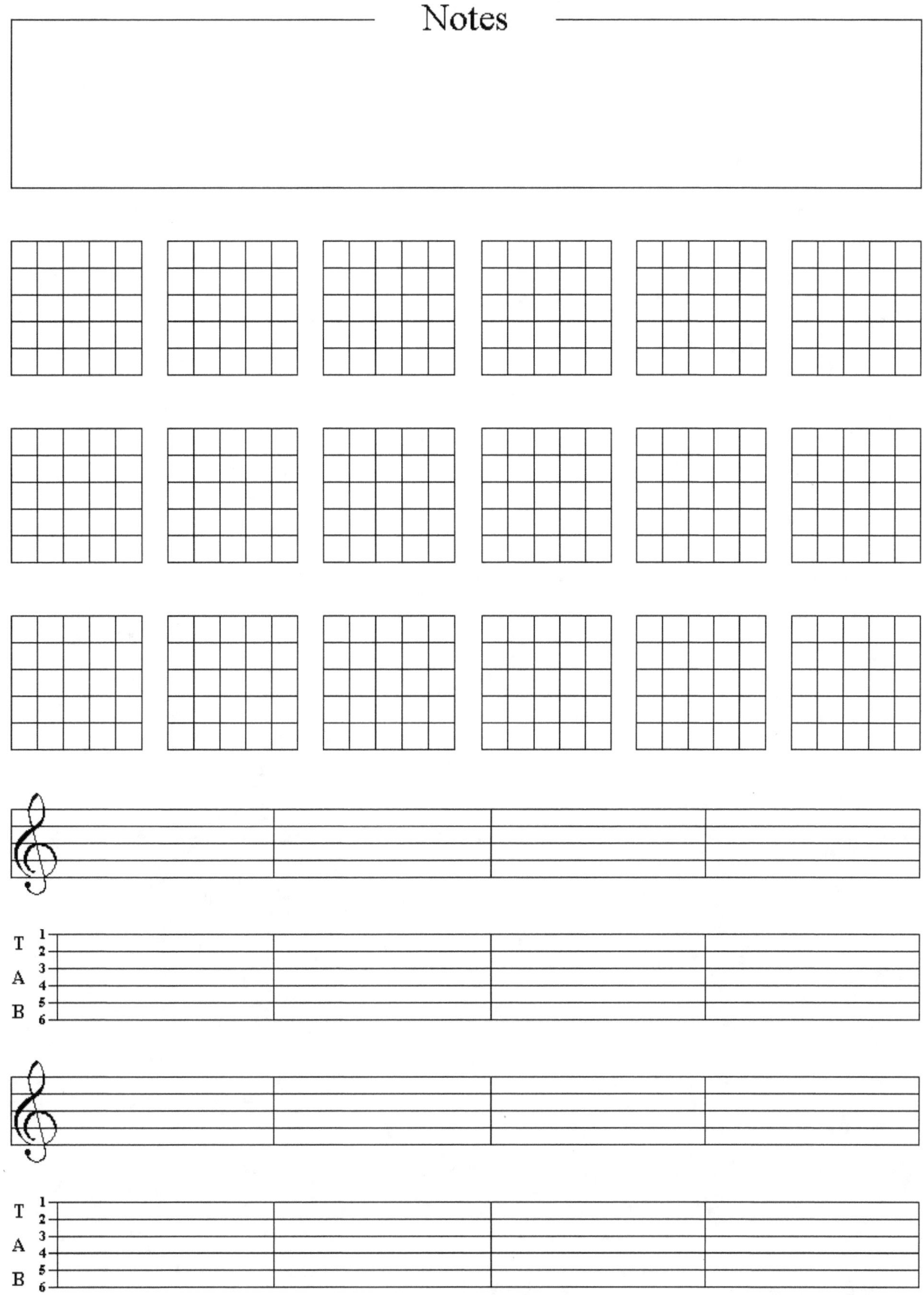

www.ingramcontent.com/pod-product-compliance
Lightning Source LLC
Chambersburg PA
CBHW081354290426
44110CB00018B/2373